WCNN'95-WASHINGTON, D.C.

WORLD CONGRESS ON NEURAL NETWORKS

**1995 International
Neural Network Society
Annual Meeting**

 Routledge
Taylor & Francis Group

LONDON AND NEW YORK

Volume III

Sponsored by the International Neural Network Society

First published 1995 by Lawrence Erlbaum Associates and INNS Press

Published 2018 by Routledge
2 Park Square, Milton Park, Abingdon, Oxon OX14 4RN
52 Vanderbilt Avenue, New York, NY 10017

First issued in hardback 2018

Routledge is an imprint of the Taylor & Francis Group, an informa business

ISBN 13: 978-1-138-87658-3 (hbk)
ISBN 13: 978-0-8058-2203-8 (pbk)

MIX
Paper from
responsible sources
FSC™ C013985
www.fsc.org

Printed in the United Kingdom
by Henry Ling Limited

PREFACE

This volume for WCNN'95, the Novel Results Session (Volume 3), provides a collection of papers which otherwise may not have been available to participants. The motivation for this volume included the desire to present the work of researchers who may have missed the earlier call for papers as well as to encourage more widespread participation in the only major neural network conference to be held in the United States during 1995. The local availability of willing, dedicated student volunteers to create, edit, and publish this volume made the idea cost effective.

This volume grew out of a suggestion by the Local Organizing Committee for WCNN'95 to the Organizing Committee of WCNN'95, information having been shared with the Governing Board of INNS. Upon approval, a call for papers was issued electronically. The announcement was widely distributed by the Connectionist Bulletin Board, Neurodigest, Wavelet Digest, and the World Wide Web. More than 60 papers were received in response to the annoucement. Any paper specifically endorsed by an INNS Governor or Special Interest Group Chairperson was accepted. All other received papers were reviewed by the SIGINN DC chapter.

The broad range of papers presented here is indicative of the diverse backgrounds of researchers in the neural networks field. The papers encompass areas such as live cellular oscillators, learning in biological neural networks, fractal associative memory, statistical theory of neural networks, parallel hardware architecture, Gabor and wavelet representations, chaotic and fuzzy function approximation. Applications include communications, tracking, flight control, color correction, and manufacturing. The Local Organizing Committee believes the papers provide a useful addition to their oral and poster presentations at the conference to the benefit of the readers and the neural network community.

> Harold Szu
> Local Organizing Committee Chair

Creating this volume required the time, effort, and perseverance of many people, several of whom deserve special thanks: Dr. Harold Szu who initiated the idea, and pursued it to reality; Mary O'Connor of Tally Management for coordination with the hotel and other matters; Ray O'Connell of L.E.A. for his help on the cover; and John Taylor, Bob Pap, Charles Hsu, Joe Landa, and Kim Scheff for help ranging from reviewing papers, to printing the volume. Finally, this volume would not exist without the financial support from the INNS editorial board and INNS program committee.

The success of this tome belongs to the individual contributors. Any weaknesses in editing and publishing are the responsibility of the undersigned.

> Joe DeWitte
> Jeff Willey
> Associate Editors

WCNN'95 ORGANIZING COMMITTEE

GENERAL CHAIR:

John G. Taylor, *King's College London*
Walter Freeman, *University of California, Berkeley*
Harold Szu, *Naval Surface Warfare Center DD*
Rolf Eckmiller, *University of Bonn*
Shun-ichi Amari, *University of Tokyo*
David Casasent, *Carnegie Mellon University*

WCNN'95 COOPERATING SOCIETIES/INSTITUTIONS

American Association for Artificial Intelligence
American Institute of Chemical Engineers
American Physical Society
Asian Pacific Neural Network Association
Center for Devices and Radiological Health, US Food and Drug Administration
Cognitive Science Society
European Neural Network Society
IEEE - Systems, Man and Cybernetics Society
International Fuzzy Systems Association
Japanese Neural Network Society
US National Institute of Allergy and Infectious Diseases
US Office of Naval Research
Society of Manufacturing Engineers
SPIE - The International Society for Optical Engineering
Division of Cancer Treatment, US National Cancer Institute

WCNN'95 CONFERENCE SPONSOR

The International Neural Network Society (INNS) is the sponsor of WCNN'95

PRESIDENT	**Walter J. Freeman,** *University of California*
PRESIDENT-ELECT	**John G. Taylor,** *King's College London*
PAST PRESIDENT	**Harold Szu,** *Naval Surface Warfare Center DD*
SECRETARY	**Gail Carpenter,** *Boston University*
TREASURER	**Judith Dayhoff,** *University of Maryland*
EXECUTIVE DIRECTOR	**Robert K. Talley,** *Talley Management Group, Inc.*

BOARD OF GOVERNORS:

Shun-ichi Amari, *University of Tokyo*
James A. Anderson, *Brown University*
Andrew Barto, *University of Massachusetts*
David Casasent, *Carnegie Mellon University*
Leon Cooper, *Brown University*
Rolf Eckmiller, *University of Bonn*
Kunihiko Fukushima, *Osaka University*
Stephen Grossberg, *Boston University*
Mitsuo Kawato, *Advanced Telecommunications Research Institute*
Christof Koch, *California Institute of Technology*
Teuvo Kohonen, *Helsinki University of Technology*
Bart Kosko, *University of Southern California*
Christoph von der Malsburg, *Ruhr-Universitat Bochum*
Alianna Maren, *Accurate Automation Corporation*
Paul Werbos, *National Science Foundation*
Bernard Widrow, *Stanford University*
Lotfi A. Zadeh, *University of California*

WCNN'95 PROGRAM COMMITTEE

Daniel I. Alkon, *National Institutes of Health*
Shun-ichi Amari, *University of Tokyo*
James A. Anderson, *Brown University*
Kaveh Ashenayi, *University of Tulsa*
Etienne Barnard, *Oregon Graduate Institute*
Andrew R. Barron, *Yale University*
Andrew Barto, *University of Massachusetts*
Gianfranco Basti, *University of Rome*
Theodore Berger, *University of Southern California*
Horacio Bouzas, *Geoquest*
Artie Briggs, *Pan Canadian Petroleum, Ltd.*
David G. Brown, *Center for Devices and Radiological Health, FDA*
Gail Carpenter, *Boston University*
David Casasent, *Carnegie Mellon University*
Ralph H. Castain, *Los Alamos National Laboratory*
Ting Chen, *Argonne National Laboratory*
Vladimir S. Cherkassky, *University of Minnesota*
Huisheng Chi, *Peking University*
Cihan H. Dagli, *University of Missouri*
Judith Dayhoff, *University of Maryland*
Nicholas DeClaris, *University of Maryland Medical School*
Julie A. Dickerson, *Iowa State University*
Rolf Eckmiller, *University of Bonn*
Jeff Elman, *University of California*
Terrence L. Fine, *Cornell University*
Gary Fleming, *SFA Inc.*
Francoise Fogelman-Soulie, *SLIGOS*
Walter J. Freeman, *University of California*
Kunihiko Fukushima, *Osaka University*
Patric Gallinari, *University of Paris*
Apostolos Georgopoulos, *Virginia Medical Center*
Stephen Grossberg, *Boston University*
John B. Hampshire II, *California Institute of Technology*
Michael Hasselmo, *Harvard University*
Robert Hecht-Nielsen, *HNC, Inc.*
Vasant Honavar, *Iowa State University*
Akira Iwata, *Nagoya Institute of Technology*
Jari Kangas, *Helsinki University of Technology*
Bert Kappen, *SNN*
Teuvo Kohonen, *Helsinki University of Technology*
Bart Kosko, *University of Southern California*
Kenneth Kreutz-Delgado, *University of California*

WCNN'95 PROGRAM COMMITTEE

Clifford Lau, *U.S. Office of Naval Research*
Soo-Young Lee, *Korea Advanced Institute of Science and Technology*
George Lendaris, *Portland State University*
Sam Leven, *For a New Social Science*
Daniel S. Levine, *University of Texas-Arlington*
William B. Levy, *University of Virginia*
S. C. Ben Lo, *Georgetown University Medical Center*
Christoph von der Malsburg, *Ruhr-Universitat Bochum*
Alianna Maren, *Accurate Automation Corporation*
Lina Massone, *Northwestern University*
Larry Medsker, *American University*
Lance Optican, *National Eye Institute*
Robert Pap, *Accurate Automation Corporation*
Andras J. Pellionisz, *Silicon Valley Neurocomputing Institute*
Antonio L. Perrone, *University of Rome*
Richard Peterson, *Motorola, Inc*
Alex Pouget, *Salk Institute*
Paul Refenes, *London Business School*
Brian D. Ripley, *University of Oxford*
Mohammed Sayeh, *Southern Illinois University*
Dejan J. Sobajic, *Electric Power Research Institute*
Jeffrey Sutton, *Massachusetts General Hospital*
Harold Szu, *Naval Surface Warfare Center DD*
John G. Taylor, *King's College London*
Hideyuki Takagi, *Kyushu Insitute of Design*
Brian Telfer, *Naval Surface Warfare Center DD*
Shiro Usui, *Toyhohashi University of Technology*
DeLiang Wang, *The Ohio State University*
Andreas Weigend, *University of Colorado*
John N. Weinstein, *National Cancer Institute, US National Institutes of Health*
Paul Werbos, *U. S. National Science Foundation*
Hal White, *University of California*
Bernard Widrow, *Stanford University*
Daniel Wolpert, *MIT*
Ronald Yager, *Iona College*
Takeshi Yamakawa, *Kyushu Institute of Technology*
Kenji Yamanishi, *NEC Research Institute*
Mona E. Zaghloul, *George Washington University*
Lotfi A. Zadeh, *University of California*

WCNN'95 SPECIAL SESSION CHAIRS

NEURAL NETWORK APPLICATIONS IN THE ELECTRICAL UTILITY INDUSTRY
Dejan J. Sobajic, *Electric Power Research Institute*
Bernard Widrow, *Stanford University*

BIOMEDICAL APPLICATIONS AND IMAGING/COMPUTER AIDED DIAGNOSIS IN MEDICAL IMAGING
David G. Brown, *Center for Devices and Radiological Health, FDA*
John N. Weinstein, *National Cancer Institute, US National Institutes of Health*
S. C. Ben Lo, *Department of Radiology, Georgetown University Medical Center*
Nicholas DeClaris, *University of Maryland Medical School*

STATISTICS AND NEURAL NETWORKS
Vladimir S. Cherkassky, *University of Minnesota*

DYNAMICAL SYSTEMS IN FINANCIAL ENGINEERING
Paul Refenes, *London Business School*

MIND, BRAIN AND CONSCIOUSNESS
John G. Taylor, *King's College London*

PHYSICS AND NEURAL NETWORKS
Antonio L. Perrone, *University of Rome*
Gianfranco Basti, *University of Rome*

BIOLOGICAL NEURAL NETWORKS I
Stephen Grossberg, *Boston University*

BIOLOGICAL NEURAL NETWORKS II
Judith Dayhoff, *University of Maryland*

NEURAL FUZZY SYSTEMS I
Ronald Yager, *Iona College*
Lotfi A. Zadeh, *University of California*

NEURAL FUZZY SYSTEMS II
Bart Kosko, *University of Southern California*
Julie A. Dickerson, *Iowa State University*

MONDAY, JULY 17, 1995
Industrial Enterprise Day - Grand Ballroom South

Panel on Entrepreneurship (8:00 AM - 12:00 PM)
Chair: R. Hecht-Nielsen

9:45 AM -10:00 AM   Break

The Practical Applications of Neural/Fuzzy Systems to the Automobile (1:00 PM - 5:00 PM)
Chair: T. Yamakawa

1:30 PM - 2:15 PM — Application of Fuzzy, Neural and Hybrid Methods to an Autonomously Driven Vehicle
S. Halgamuge, M. Glesner

2:15 PM - 3:00 PM — Anti-Slip System for Four Wheel Driven Vehicles
K. Kansala

3:00 PM - 3:45 PM — Emulation of Car-Following Behavior: Use of Neuro-Fuzzy Systems
P. Chakroborty, S. Kikuchi

3:45 PM - 4:30 PM — A Direct Adaptive Fuzzy Controller and Its Application for Active Suspension
V. Gorrini, H. Bersini, S. Boverie, A. Titli

4:30 PM - 5:00 PM — Fuzzy Reasoning Method with Learning Function for Rear-end Collision Avoidance System (Video Demonstration without Talk)
T. Ito, Y. Hiroshima, K. Nishioka

Clean Cars (5:00 PM - 6:30 PM)
Chair: P. Werbos
Panelists: R. Chapman, L. Feldkamp, and B. McCormick

Government Panel (6:30 PM - 8:00 PM)
Chair: S.-I. Amari, H. Szu, J. Taylor
Panelists: H. Chi, Y.T. Chien, D. Collins, R. Eckmiller, H. Hawkins, Z.Y. He, H. Meleis, T. McKenna, R. Nakamura, Z. Sha, P. Werbos, Y. Wu, Y. X. Zhong, S. Zornetzer

THURSDAY, JULY 20, 1995
Novel Results Session - Conference Room 9
Session Chair: Magdy Bayoumi and Dean Collins

Biological Neural Networks (8:30 AM - 10:30 AM)

8:00 AM - 8:30 AM	**Invited Talk:** The Functional Role of the Hippocampus in the Organization of Memory *J. Taylor, L. Michalis*
8:30 AM - 8:45 AM	**Invited Talk:** Neural Circuitry and Behavior; Synaptodenritic Microprocesses and Conscious Experience: Data and Theory *K. H. Pribram*
8:45 AM - 9:00 AM	An Evaluation of Stability in Live Cellular Oscillators *S. Wolpert, Andrew J. Laffely*
9:00 AM - 9:15 AM	Temporal Pattern Detection and Recognition using the Temporal Noisy Leaky Integrator neuron model with the Postsynaptic Delays trained using Hebbian Learning *C. Christodoulou, T. Clarkson, J. Taylor*
9:15 AM - 9:30 AM	A MIMD Environment for Multi-Level Neural Modeling *J. Fellous*
9:30 AM - 9:45 AM	Delayed Random Walk Models of Neural Information Processing *T. Ohira*
9:45 AM - 10:15 AM	**Invited Talk:** The Creative Process (Especially in Technology): A Knowledge Level Cognitive Model and its Implications *S. Dasgupta*
10:15 AM - 10:30 AM	Oral Summaries of Posters
10:30 AM - 10:45 AM	Break

Neural Network Applications (10:45 AM -12:30 PM)

10:45 AM - 11:00 AM	Neurocontrol Technology for the LoFLYTE Testbed Aircraft *R. Saeks, C. Lewis, R. Pap, K. Priddy, and C. Cox*
11:00 AM - 11:15 AM	Ultra-High-Speed Relay Fault Detection Using Dynamic Models and Neural Network Classifiers *M. Carley, B. Parker, M. Szabo*
11:15 AM - 11:30 AM	Finite Alphabets Least Relative Entropy Algorithm for Channel Equalization *N. Li, T. Adali, X. Liu*
11:30 AM - 11:45 AM	Fuzzy Logic Oriented to Active Rule Selector and Membership Function Generator for High Speed Digital Fuzzy μ-Processor *F. Boschetti, A. Gabrielli, E. Gandolfi, and M. Masetti*
11:45 AM - 12:00 AM	GENET and Tabu Search for Combinatorial Optimization Problems *J. Boyce, C. Dimitropoulos, G. vom Scheidt, J. Taylor*
12:00 AM - 12:15 AM	Motion Estimation Using A Compounded Self Organizing Map Multi Layer Perceptron Network *B. Michaelis, O. Schnelting, U. Seiffert, R. Meck*
12:15 AM - 12:30 PM	Device-Independent Color Correction for Multimedia Applications Using Neural Networks and Abductive Modeling Approaches *V. Shastri, E. Onyejekwe, L. Rabel*
12:30 PM - 12:45 PM	Neural Networks for Optimal Data Association in Detection of Hot Plate *J. Kim, H. Jeong*
12:45 PM - 1:00 PM	Oral Summaries of Posters
1:00 PM - 1:30 PM	Break

Theory and Architecture (1:30 PM- 3:30 PM)

1:30 PM - 1:45 PM	A Comparative Study of Gabor and Pixel Representations in Original and PC Spaces *L. Shams, J. Fellous, C. von der Malsburg*
1:45 PM - 2:00 PM	Long-term Dependencies in NARX Networks *T. Lin, B. Horne, P. Tino, C. Giles*
2:00 PM - 2:15 PM	SONNET 2: A New Unsupervised Neural Network for Segmentation *A. Nigrin*

SCHEDULE continued

2:15 PM - 2:30 PM	Toward a Model of Consolidation: The Retention and Transfer of Neural Net Task Knowledge *D. Silver, R. Mercer*
2:30 PM - 2:45 PM	Derivation of a Convex Hull Energy Function *J. Willey, M. Zaghloul, and H. Szu*
2:45 PM - 3:00 PM	Time-Pulse Neural Network of the Autowave Type *Y. Balkarey, A. Cohen, M. Elinson, M. Evitkhov, Y. Orlov*
3:00 PM - 3:15 PM	Some Statistical Results for Winner-Take-All Networks with Sparse Random Innervation and Coactivity-based Learning *P. Shoemaker*
3:15 PM - 3:30 PM	**Invited Talk.** A Scalable Hybrid Neural Accelerator *B. Alhalabi, M. Bayoumi*
3:30 PM - 3:45 PM	Oral Summaries of Posters
3:45 PM - 4:00 PM	Break

Function Approximation (4:00 PM - 5:45 PM)

4:00 PM - 4:15 PM	Novel Results on Stochastic Modelling Hints for Neural Network Prediction *R. Drossu, Z. Obradovic*
4:15 PM - 4:30 PM	Function Learning with Stochastic Spike Train Input: Weight compensation by Learning Rate Adjustment *Y. Guan, X. Meng, T. Clarkson, J. Taylor*
4:30 PM - 4:45 PM	Neural Learning of Chaotic Symbolic Sequences: A Dynamical Information Loss Analysis *C. Schittenkopf, G. Deco*
4:45 PM - 5:00 PM	Comparing RBF and Fuzzy Inference Systems on Theoretical and Practical Basis *H. Bersini, G. Bontempi, C. Decaestecker*
5:00 PM - 5:15 PM	Generalization Capability of MLP-GBF and RBF Neural Networks *B. Verma*
5:15 PM - 5:30 PM	Error-Driven Placement of Neural Resources to Learn Trajectories *N. Goerke, R. Eckmiller*
5:30 PM - 5:45 PM	Oral Summaries of Posters

TABLE OF CONTENTS

Industrial Enterprise Day (Monday, July 17, 1995)

The Practical Applications of Neural/Fuzzy Systems to the Automobile

Novel Results Session (Thursday, July 20, 1995)

Biological Neural Networks

Neural Network Applications

Theory and Architecture

Function Approximation

Industrial Enterprise Day

The Practical Applications of Neural/Fuzzy Systems

to the Automobile

Application of Fuzzy, Neural and Hybrid Methods to an Autonomously Driven Vehicle

Saman K. Halgamuge and Manfred Glesner
Darmstadt University of Technology
Department of Computer Engineering
Institute of Microelectronic Systems
Karlstr. 15, D-64283 Darmstadt, Germany
Tel.: ++49 6151 16-4337   Fax.: ++49 6151 16-4936
Email: saman@microelectronic.e-technik.th-darmstadt.de

Abstract

After a brief description of author's previous research on fuzzy and neural techniques in mechatronic systems, the novel results obtained with a model truck application are presented. The truck driven with a long trailer is able to avoid critical situations in reverse driving with the help of a fuzzy expert system in the semi-autonomous mode. The fully autonomous driving of the model truck with an ultrasonic sensor mounted is presented with reinforcement type neural networks and fuzzy systems generated with the help of neural networks or evolutionary algorithms. All the developed methods compared for assessment are implemented in a digital signal processing board (DSP) mounted in truck to allow real-time operation.

1   Introduction

A mechatronic system is the final product in combining information technology with mechanical and electrical engineering considering the economical and production relevant aspects [9]. Typically such a systems contains at least three major functions that can be described as perception, cognition and action. In most cases they have only limited interaction with the operator, and the reliability of the systems must be very high due to the requirements leading to embedded solutions.

Two applications are reported from the special research area on Mechatronics at Darmstadt University of Technology. The overall purpose of the first research project is to create an *intelligent* or *self-supervising* friction clutch for automobiles. It is to control the engagement phase by selecting a proper temporal torque level limiting the heating up of the clutch and the impact of the torque. In [9] several solutions including a conventional and a fuzzy solution are compared with real-time implementations.

The application of fuzzy-neural system FuNe I [3] for identification of road surface using sensor information is the second application project under the same special project area. A hall sensor embedded in a tire of a vehicle supplies data containing information on the pressure patterns preprocessed in order to extract input features for feeding the real-time implementation of the extracted fuzzy system of FuNe I, which identifies the road surface as dry, wet, icy or sand. Identification of the road surface helps in calculating the critical values of slip for Anti-Block-Systems (ABS) [5].

Several experiments are performed with a model truck, the third and the major application of this paper, in a semi-autonomous (no sensors are included) and in fully autonomous (a sensor is mounted and no driver is present).

- fuzzy controlled reverse driving support for trucks with long trailers in semi-autonomous mode

- autonomous truck driving with a fuzzy expert system

Driving a vehicle with a trailer in the reverse direction is a difficult task for a beginner. Even experienced drivers have to undertake a "trial and error" approach, i.e. if the trailer comes to a position where the angle between the longitudinal axes of the vehicle and the trailer can not be

Figure 1: Truck and trailer

increased even by maximum angel of the steering wheel in reverse driving, then the driver has to change the gear and drive forward in order to avoid further bending (critical angle). Since this is a nonlinear problem, a support system can be designed using Fuzzy Control in an efficient manner to overcome this situation. The "expert knowledge" of continuous reverse driving (i.e. without changing the gear) in such situations can be formulated using fuzzy rules. The realtime implementation of a hierarchically organized crisp-fuzzy hybrid controller to handle this problem of a model truck (52.2 cm long, 18 cm width and 23.5 cm height) and trailer (67.8 cm long, 18.7 cm width and 20 cm height) is described in [7] (see also Fig. 1).

The fully autonomous truck driving without the trailer is discussed in the next sections.

2 Autonomous Driving with Collision Avoidance

Autonomous driving of the truck is tested with following real time systems using prototype boards containing Digital Signal Processor (DSP):

- fuzzy expert system designed manually
- reinforcement neural network
- fuzzy expert system generated automatically
  - using a neural network
  - using a genetic algorithm

A single rotating sensor mounted to the truck delivers the input vector to the real-time system. The mechatronic system can be described as:

- perception: a rotating ultrasonic sensor reading the distances to the objects in the environment
- cognition: real-time system decides upon the speed and direction of moving
- action: driving with appropriate speed without collision

The inputs of the autonomous forward driving system are the distances of the vehicle to the obstacles in its world (walls, other vehicles etc.), which are measured by an ultrasonic distance sensor rotated with a servo motor (see Fig. 2). Due to the low operation speed of the sensor the ultrasonic sensor is stepped to only 7 discrete directions at the angles $-60°$, $-40°$, $-20°$, $0°$, $20°$, $40°$, and $60°$.

The hardware based on TMS 320C30 DSP from Texas Instruments provides a flexible platform in which the fuzzy system software developed in C language can be converted into the assembler code using the commercially available compiler, which can be down-loaded to the DSP using a serial interface of a Personal Computer.

Figure 2: Autonomous model truck with the sensor

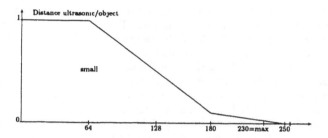

Figure 3: The membership function for the distance in the autonomous truck

In the manual design of the fuzzy expert system described in [8], the rule base and the membership functions (Fig. 3) are designed with a trial and error method. It mainly consists of seven rules (one for each sensing direction) of the form IF *distance in this direction* IS *small* THEN *turn to other direction*. The collision avoidance directions (lg = left great, ls = left small, s = straight, ls= left small, rg = right great) are used for the respective 7 sensor positions. The fuzzy set "small" is a monotonously decreasing function in the distance, which for reasons of geometry is defined as shown in Fig. 3. If an obstacle is nearer than 64 distance units, a collison is hardly avoidable, while obstacles at a distance of >180 units need only little consideration.

3 Neural Network Optimization With External Reinforcement

Having in mind that an autonomous truck with a certain structured knowledge based system (e.g. fuzzy controller or a neural network) moving in a dynamically changing environment, one can imagine that the most valuable and realistic information to get is a record of input/output data (or situation-action pairs) with an evaluation of quality. The input can be taken as the distance measures obtained from different sensors, and the output is the moving direction and the speed. Depending on the external reinforcement signal which can be a function of the inputs, the internal knowledge base can be constructed.

A selection of situation-action pairs depending on their "Quality" should be considered for further optimization of the existing system. Since the storing capabilities of real-time systems are limited, an effective method of data compression must be achieved.

- availability of a limited storage of data can be used to update/generate/delete membership functions and rules in case of fuzzy systems

- situation-action pairs can be used to update weights of a neural or fuzzy-neural network considering the connecting weights as storage elements

The reinforcement learning can be used to update weights in neural networks considering the situation-action pairs. The external reinforcement signal obtained from the environment asses the quality of the action. Based on Q-learning [13] several algorithms are proposed in literature. A combination of Q-learning with Temporal-Difference-Learning [12] is proposed in [10]. This algorithm is not suitable for on-line training since all situation-action pairs must be stored.

A modified connectionist Q-Learning (MCQ-L) is proposed in [11] allowing on-line training, and therfore suitable for application in truck in the autonomous mode. Nevertheless a software parcour is selected, since the batteries in the model truck will not last long in case of on-line training, and the parcours can be constructed easily in computers rather than in real environments ! The software simulation of the model truck is similar to the real one described in the last section.

Three identical networks with sensor values as inputs are created for three possible actions:

- turn to the left
- drive straight
- turn to the right

Similar to the work described in [11], the inputs are coded in the first stage. The network weights are initialised between -0.25 and 0.25 at the beginning. The reinforcement signal is generated using sensor values in 3 different directions ($-15^0, 0, 15^0$ to the longitudinal axis of the truck). An action resulting a reduction in sensor reading (i.e. reduction in distance to the objects of collision) on the driving direction is weighted with "-1". Otherwise the action is weighted with "1".

Since the Boltzmann-distribution with decreasing "temperature" (increasing the confidence in the reinforcement information) is used, actions are selected randomly at the beginning and the ones with the highest quality value are selected at the end of training.

The simulated model truck is started from predefined positions in circular paths and if it come close to an obstacle or the wall by 5 simulation steps, a new trail is started from that position.

Fig. 4 (a) shows a typical driving characteristic at the beginning of training and Fig. 4 (c) shows the trained truck driving almost without a collision. Similar to the experience reported in [11], authors also found the ideal value for "discount factor" or γ, as 0.9. In case of $\gamma = 0$ the algorithm will be of purely gradient descent nature with the character of forgetting whatever learned in the past.

After about 500 new starts (or 499 collisions), the network could be considerd as well trained and maintained a collision free driving. Before testing the trained network in real-time, authors tested in software using a new parcour shown in Fig. 4 (e). The trained network could manage new situations such as the crossing point found in the middle of the new parcour and not known in the ones used for training.

The neural network down-loaded to the DSP card could sucessfully drive the autonomous truck in real environments in real-time as recorded by a video camera. This neural network can be extended as a fuzzy neural network generating fuzzy rules and the training could be in real-time if the technical problem of batteries are solved.

4 Automatic Generation of Fuzzy Systems

If the truck is driven in a known environment by an experienced driver capable of avoiding obstacles then the input/output data can be stored using a prototype board based on a DSP and enough memory capacity. The stored data can be used to generate a fuzzy expert system using fuzzy neural systems [3, 4, 6]. A fuzzy system generated with FuNe I [3] is compared with the manually designed simple fuzzy expert system. The automatically generated controller is more flexible in facing bends and the ability of avoiding deadlocks (for an example trapping into a corner). Depending on data a better fuzzy system can be generated using a fuzzy-neural system.

But this is not appropriate if no representative data exist. A dynamic genetic algorithm is used to evolve a fuzzy system in such cases simulated with parcours used in the last section, and the resulting fuzzy system is tested in real-time on autonomous truck. In using Genetic algorithms fuzzy rules and membership functions are coded as bit strings that are updated using crossover and mutation operators guided by the optimization function. The known problem of remaining in a local minima or *Premature Convergence* ([1, 2]) is solved using a dynamic adjustment of mutation rate and crossover rate.

Fig. 4 (b) shows the performance at the beginning and Fig. 4 (d) at the end of optimization. The test with a new parcour is shown in Fig. 4 (f). In contrast to the reinforcement neural network the software truck is taken back to a new position after a collision. The straight lines shown in Fig. 4 (b) indicates this step. Authors used 30-50 Individuals per generation to get this results.

5 Conclusion

It is shown in this paper that neural networks or genetic algorithms can be used to generate fuzzy systems for driving an autonomous model truck. A generalised solution found in software simulations considering the restrictions in real truck is sufficient to be implemented in real-truck driving in real unknown environments. However, an attractive solution would be to start with the simple expert knowledge available (e.g. the manual fuzzy systems described), and the tuning and adding automatically generated knowledge in on-line to improve the system. Authors work on this line of research considering in addition a direction of a goal to reach.

References

[1] Th. Bäck and H.-P. Schwefel. An overview of evolutionary algorithms for parameter optimization. *Evolutionary Computation*, 1(1):1–23, 1993.

[2] D. Beasley, D. R. Bull, and R. R. Martin. An Overview of Genetic Algorithms: Part 1, Fundamentals. *University Computing*, 15(2):58–69, 1993.

[3] S. K. Halgamuge and M. Glesner. Neural Networks in Designing Fuzzy Systems for Real World Applications. *International Journal for Fuzzy Sets and Systems*, 65(1):1–12, 1994. North Holland.

[4] S. K. Halgamuge and M. Glesner. Fuzzy Neural Networks: Between Functional Equivalence and Applicability. *IEE International Journal on Neural Systems*, June, 1995. World Scientific Publishing.

[5] S. K. Halgamuge, H.-J. Herpel, and M. Glesner. An Automotive Application With Neural Network Based Knowledge Extraction. In *Mechatronical Computer Systems for Perception and Action' 93*, pages 295–299, Halmstadt University, Sweden, June 1993. Center of Computer Studies. ISBN 91-630-1847-0.

[6] S. K. Halgamuge, W. Pöchmüller, and M. Glesner. An Alternative Approach for Generation of Membership Functions and Fuzzy Rules Based on Radial and Cubic Basis Function Networks. *International Journal of Approximate Reasoning (in press)*, 1995. Elsevier.

[7] S. K. Halgamuge, T. A. Runkler, and M. Glesner. A Hierarchical Hybrid Fuzzy Controller for Realtime Reverse Driving Support of Vehicles with Long Trailers. In *IEEE International Conference on Fuzzy Systems' 94*, Orlando, USA, June 1994.

[8] S. K. Halgamuge, T. A. Runkler, and M. Glesner. Autonomous Truck Driving Based on On-line Fuzzy Control. In *International Symposium on Automotive Technology and Automation*, Aachen, Germany, 1994. ISBN: 094771-968-7.

[9] H.-J. Herpel, S. K. Halgamuge, M. Glesner, J. Stöcker, and S. Ernesti. Fuzzy Logic Applied to Control and Data Analysis Problems in Automotive Applications. In *International Symposium on Automotive Technology and Automation*, Aachen, Germany, 1994. ISBN: 094771-968-7.

[10] L. Lin. Self-improving reactive agents based on reinforcement learning, planning and teaching. *Machine Learning*, (8), 1992.

[11] G. A. Rummery and M. Niranjan. On-Line Q-Learning using connectionist systems. *Machine Learning*, (3), 1994.

[12] R. S. Sutton. Learning to predict by the methods of temporal differences. *Machine Learning*, (3), 1989.

[13] C. J. C. H. Watkins and P. Dayan. Technical Note: Q-Learning. *Reinforcement Learning (Editor: R. S. Sutton)*, 16(3/4), 1992.

Reinforcement Neural Networks   Automatically Generated Fuzzy Systems

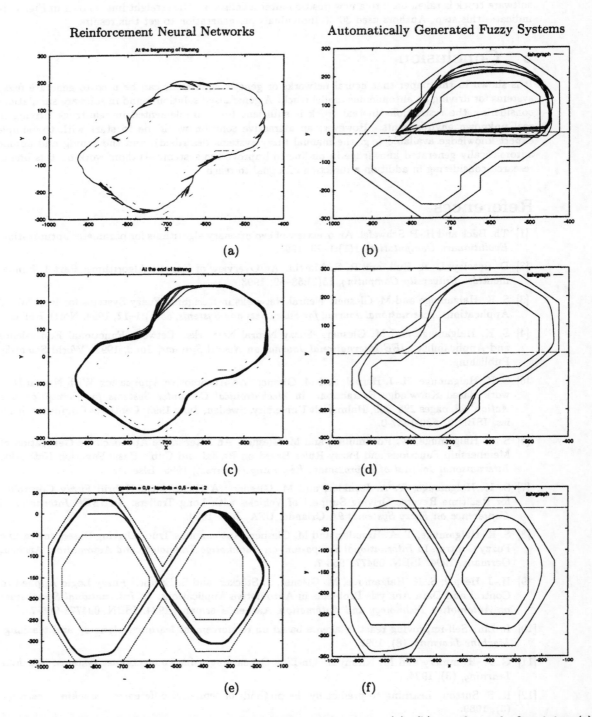

(a)   (b)

(c)   (d)

(e)   (f)

Figure 4: Comparison of performance at the beginning of training (a), (b); at the end of training (c), (d), and with a new parcour (e), (f)

Anti-Slip System for Four Wheel Driven Vehicles

Klaus Känsälä

Technical Research Centre of Finland

Abstract -When a four wheel driven vehicle moves on flat surface and surface friction is big enough there is no need for anti-slip. This is a typical situation when driving on a highway on summer conditions. The situation changes when the surface of the road gets wet or icy. When driving off road it may happen that one of the wheels is temporarily loses contact to the surface. In these circumstances a proper anti-slip system is very valuable. Typically this is a mechanical differential lock in the rear axle of the vehicle. In some cases this has been replaced with a viscous-clutch or with a Torsen-type differential lock. All these are rather expensive and they increase the size and weight of the power transmission system. They are also fully operational only when the vehicle moves straight forward.

Introduction

This paper describes a distributed mechatronic anti slip system for vehicles with hydrostatic power transmission. The same principles can be applied to vehicles using ABS braking system because the anti-slip function is based on active usage of wheel brakes. The hardware is deliberately designed to be distributed, redundant, and fault tolerant. A Controller Area Network (CAN) interconnects the controllers and enables exchange of sensor data and control information. The control part is based on sophisticated data pre-processing for speed, acceleration, and turning angle calculations. Two fuzzy controllers have been implemented and provide best performance under normal operation and systemic redundancy when faced to partial system breakdowns.

All methods presented here have been tested in real working conditions using a full scale working prototype. The fuzzy controller has proven to be both robust and reliable and has given a significant improvement compared to the old anti-slip control method.

Theoretical approach

In contrast to other approaches [1], [2],[5] we did try to work out how anti-slip function could be implemented to an existing vehicle with minimum hardware changes.

When the contact between the surface and the wheel is lost the rotation speed of this wheel starts to increase until all other wheels are stationary and the vehicle stops. This could be avoided by active control of the wheel brake.

The idea behind this is to maximise traction force by adjusting brake forces individually for each wheel. The equations (1) and (2) express this.

$$T_i = T_{wheel\_1} = T_{wheel\_2} = ... = T_{wheel\_n} \quad (1)$$

$$T_{wheel\_n} = T_{surf} + T_b \quad (2)$$

In equation (1) each wheel torque should be equal, whereas (2) the torque on each wheel is determined by the surface friction coefficient torque T_{surf} and the brake torque T_b. The changes in surface friction must be balanced by adjusting brake pressure to yield highest traction. This would prevent the vehicle to stop if a wheel starts to slip. What is then slip and what normal behaviour of wheel depends on the friction coefficient between surface and wheel.

Unfortunately, surface friction is unpredictable, non-linear and changes rapidly. Thus, we needed a controller that is able to give fast response in non-linear environment without computable model. Eventually, we decided to use a simple fuzzy controller [3], [4], [6].

Fuzzy control

In the test case we decided to use three different indicators for wheel slip. Two of them; speed and acceleration of the wheel were quite obvious. The last indicator was the speed difference between the wheels. The usage of wheel speed and acceleration is visualised in Fig. 1. When the slip starts there is a rapid chance in wheel speed. This can be used as a direct indicator of starting point of slip. Acceleration gives a classification information about the size of the speed difference. It is useful when the amount of brake power is estimated. These indicators are satisfactory when the slip is 'fast'. We noticed that there was also other type of slip that we called slow slip. In the latter case the slip increased gradually and was harder to detect. For this kind of slip we used the third indicator; the speed difference between the wheels.

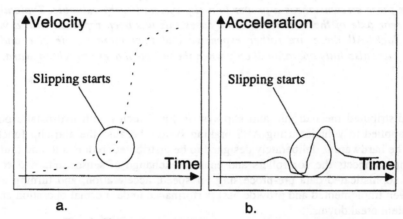

Fig. 1. Slip estimation; wheel speed and acceleration

This indicator was calculated from the global speed data of the vehicle. The calculation was based on estimates of individual wheel speeds and an estimate of driving status. Driving status was defined in terms of driving speed and turning angle of the wheels. Both of these variables were obtained from the wheel speed information. If the vehicle was driving a curve the inner wheels should have lower speed than the outer wheels. This speed difference was calculated and used to correct the global speed information. The result was more exact slip detection and reliable anti-slip control also when the vehicle was making a curve. The fuzzy controller had always two inputs and one output which was used to operate the wheel brake.
We tried two control methods for the wheel brake. The first very straightforward way was to set the brake directly according to the output of the controller. This is what we call class A controller. Class B controller gave an increment to the last brake value used.

> *Direct brake control : indicator of slippage* → *brake value*   Class A   (3)

> *Incremental brake control : indicator of slippage* → Δ *brake value*   Class B   (4)

The advantages and disadvantages are the following: Class A controllers react with direct brake settings whereas Class B controllers react by incrementally setting or releasing brakes. This causes Class B controllers to be more precise but slower in reaction, since they have to 'find' the appropriate brake force to stop slippage, whereas Class A controllers have to 'guess' the appropriate brake force. This is of course faster, but although more imprecise and less adaptive to changing brake behaviour due to wear, ageing or different temperatures. Experimental results showed an excellent control behaviour of Class B controller compared to Class A controller as to be expected from theoretical analysis of the two controller types.
We tried all combinations of global/local slip detection and class A/B controller. In the following we depict the membership functions used within our implementations and the test runs carried out under real working conditions. Fig. 2 shows the four basic controller types implemented and tested.

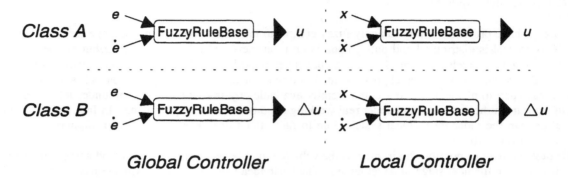

Fig. 2. The Fuzzy Controllers developed and tested. $x, \dot{x}$ denote the wheel velocity and acceleration, whereas $e, \dot{e}$ denote the velocity error (wheel velocity-vehicle velocity), local wheel acceleration.

The fuzzy controllers were designed using Togai InfraLogics TIL Shell [TOG92a,b] to define the membership functions of the in- and output variables. The inference mechanism chosen is min-max and the defuzzification method is the centroid method.

Since the global fuzzy controller performs much better due to the far better slippage indicator this is the controller used in normal operation whereas the local one is used in case of failure to provide basic operability to the system.

Robustness and fail-safe action

The system hardware was designed according to military specifications. The system was distributed to four CPU-units. Each one of these was controlling one wheel. The CAN-bus was used to combine the units together. In a case of malfunction or failure the other CPU-units could take the tasks of the broken CPU-unit. There was also a constant procedure of checking the network status. In a case of network breakdown the local control was selected (Fig 3.).

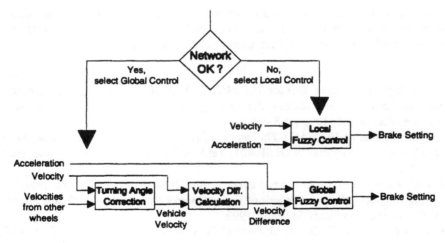

Figure 3. Local and Global Fuzzy Controller

Results & Further development

In this paper we have presented a way to apply fuzzy control to the task of controlling slippage for heavy duty industrial vehicles. This control is distributed and puts emphasis on robustness and reliability by distributing the control task and also by providing two levels of control. The global level provides the best performance under normal equipment operating conditions and the kernel level provides the basic functionality under equipment partial fault conditions.

The system has been implemented into a commercially available city tractor and has been under test for over one year. The results both from the test track and under real working conditions are very promising. In fact, the system has shown to be superior than the older mechanical system, due to far better force development under slippery conditions and its excellent curve driving abilities.

Due to the huge number of possible environments the vehicle might be used, we decided to add some capabilities to adapt to the environment in the next stage of development. The basic idea behind this is to evaluate past reactions by how long it took to get the wheel back into a normal (i.e. not slipping) state. This is done by gradually changing the membership functions for the brake force depending on the degree of success of the last actions. Hence, the control system adapts to different environmental conditions by shortening the control cycle times in average, e.g. with faster, stronger responses (ice, snow), or slower, weaker responses' profiles (forest) without any operator interactions.

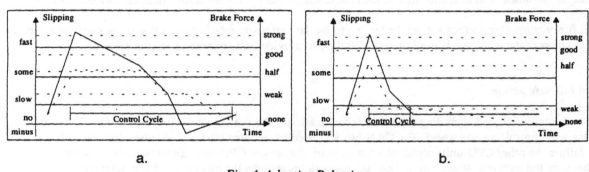

a.   b.

Fig. 4. Adaptive Behaviour

Figure 4 depicts the (idealised) behaviour of the anti slip control system before (a) and after (b) adapting the membership functions for brake force. Further attention has to be paid on minimising braking activities to avoid brake damage through overheating. Right now, this problem is tackled by using special heat resisting brake materials.

[1]   Friman Edward, Asplund Christer, Erikson Ulf, Mohr Erik. *Evaluation of a Single Circuit All Hydrostatic Transmission with variable Wheel Motors,* 27p., Sveriges Lantbruksuniversitet, Institutionen för skogsteknik, Uppsatser och Resultat nr 229, 1992 (in Swedish)

[2]   Göhring E., et al. (Mercedes-Benz AG). *The Impact of Different ABS-Philosophies on the Directional Behaviour of Commercial Vehicles,* SAE SP-801, Vehicle Dynamics: Related to Braking and Steering. Paper 892500, 12p, 1989

[3]   Pedrycz, Witold. *Fuzzy Control and Fuzzy Systems,* 260p., John Wiley & Sons Inc. New York, 1989

[4]   Pok, Yang-Ming. Jian-Xin Xu. An Analysis of Fuzzy Control Systems Using Vector Space, IEEE Second International Conference On Fuzzy Systems, 1993.

[5]   Shiraishi S., et al. (Honda R&D CO., Ltd), *Control Concept for Traction Control System (TCS) and Its Preformance,* 12th International Conference on Experimental Safety Vehicles, Gothenburg, Sweden, 1989, pages 846-853

[6]   Wang Li-Xin, Mendel Jerry M. *Generating Fuzzy Rules by Learning from Example,* 13p., IEEE Transactions on Systems, Man, and Cybernetics, Vol. 22, No. 6, 1992

[7]   Hasemann Jörg-Michael, Känsälä Klaus. *Avoiding Slippage with Fuzzy Logic,* Industrial Horizons, VTT Publications, Helsinki, 1994

Emulation of Car-Following Behavior: Use of Fuzzy-Neural Systems

Partha Chakroborty
Assistant Professor
Department of Civil Engineering
Indian Institute of Technology, Kanpur
Kanpur- India

Shinya Kikuchi
Professor
Department of Civil Engineering
University of Delaware
Newark - U.S.A.

INTRODUCTION

A model of driver behavior in close headway situations (car-following) is presented. The model represents how the driver of the following vehicle, FV, reacts to the actions of the vehicle ahead (the Lead Vehicle, LV) in order to maintain a safe headway as well as match the speed of the LV. Models of Car-following behavior is important to the study of traffic flow as well as the development of self-adjusting speed controllers for *intelligent vehicles*. This paper presents a fuzzy inference based car-following model.

PROBLEM STATEMENT: DESCRIPTION OF THE CAR-FOLLOWING PHENOMENON

Car-following phenomenon is a complex human control behavior where the controlled states are dynamic and affected by the actions of the driver of the FV. The actions of the driver are based on his/her perception of certain driving conditions (or state variables) such as speed of FV, distance headway between LV and FV, relative speed, etc. As observed the car-following phenomenon has the following important properties:

1. Human control system: A driver perceives a certain set of stimulus, reasons as to the appropriate action and reponds accordingly. Neither perception, nor reasoning, nor response is precise or deterministic; they are approximate.

2. Behavioral differences: The process of car-following varies from one person to another in terms of reaction to stimulus, comfortable headway, and acceleration/deceleration rate; for example, an aggressive driver may feel comfortable at a much closer distance headway than a conservative driver.

3. Asymmetric response: Driver's response are more sensitive to reduction in distance headway than to increase in distance headway.

4. Local stability (Temporal Stability): Perturbations introduced by the LV die down with time; that is, the FV achieves stability after a certain period of time from the introduction of the perturbations by the LV.

5. Asymptotic Stability (Spatial Stability): Perturbations introduced by the LV do not affect a vehicle sufficiently upstream in the platoon. That is, the perturbations die down as it proceeds upstream.

6. Stable conditions: Stable condition is determined by a zero relative speed and safe distance headway for the given speed. The concept of safe distance headway is dynamic and varies with the speed of travel. This peculiarity of car-following behavior makes it a difficult system to model.

In the following section, a fuzzy inference based model of the car-following behavior together with a neural network representation of the model are presented.

THE MODEL

The first subsection describes the fuzzy inference based model of car-following. The second subsection describes the neural network representation of the fuzzy inference based model. This representation allows self-adjustment of the inference model.

Fuzzy Inference Model

The fuzzy inference model of car-following is motivated by the fact that car-following behavior is a human control system; where the response is based on imprecise perceptions of stimuli and approximate reasoning using vaguely defined rules.

The inference based model functions with three stimuli and a rule-base of 396 rules. The stimuli which form the premise variables of each of the rules are:

- Distance headway between the LV and the FV; the perceptions of the distance headway vary with the speed at which the FV is traveling. The same distance headway, for example 100 feet, may be perceived as **large** if FV is traveling at 30 ft/s or it may be perceived as **small** if FV is traveling at 70 ft/s.

- Relative Speed between LV and FV.

- Acceleration and deceleration rate of the LV.

The consequence of the rules are in terms of Acceleration/Deceleration of the FV.

The rules in the rule-base may be thought of as rules-of-thumb specific to each driver and developed from commonsense knowledge and driving experience. A typical rule in the rule-base is of the following form:

Example Rule: IF   Distance headway is **adequate** AND
                              Relative speed is **near zero** AND
                              Acceleration of LV is **mild**
          THEN   FV accelerate **mildly**

Given a set of conditions many of such rules are activated; the level of activation is determined by the minimum of the truth values of each of the antecedents. The response under a given condition is determined by the weighted average of the consequences of the different rules which fired.

A detailed description of the fuzzy inference based car-following model may be found in Kikuchi and Chakroborty [1], and Chakroborty [2]. Some results from the car-following model are provided in the next section.

Presently, the authors are working on a more efficient model of car-following based on only two premise variables, namely the distance headway and relative speed. This model contains only 36 rules. Some result from this model are also presented in the next section.

The Neural Network Representation

One of the features lacking in the previous model is that the membership functions in the rules are incapable of adjusting themselves to suit the driving behavior of different individuals. This feature is important since it allows the model to capture and therefore closely emulate various types of drivers and not just an average driver. This capability is important as it will enhance the usefulness of the model as the backbone of traffic flow modeling as well as speed control systems of automobiles.

In order to introduce the capability of self-adjustment the fuzzy inference model is represented as a neural network. The representation used was motivated by Horikawa et al. [3]. The essence of the representation lies in the parallel, distributed nature of neural networks, and the similarity between membership functions of fuzzy sets and the activation function of neural networks. (According to Williams, activation functions of the form $f(x) \rightarrow [0, 1]$ perform the task of deriving the "degree of confidence that a preferred feature is present;" [4] the degree of confidence is a "measure of truth in some unit-interval-valued logic, such as fuzzy logic" [4]. It should be noted that the membership function of a fuzzy set does exactly the same task.) A detailed description of the neural network representation may be found in Chakroborty [2].

The backpropagation algorithm and the Delta rule are used for the modification of the membership functions. Chakroborty has shown that the delta rule implements a logical modification procedure for the inference system [2].

RESULTS

In this section some of the results obtained from the fuzzy inference based car-following model and its neural network representation are presented.

Figure 1, shows the process in which an LV-FV pair reached stability after the LV performed some actions through acceleration and deceleration. In this figure, the LV accelerated or decelerated from a speed of 50 ft/s to the value shown in the figure. Three different acceleration and deceleration patterns were used for each of the final speeds. As can be seen from the figure, in every situation stability was achieved. Further, the stable condition is sensitive only to the final speed and insensitive to the initial conditions and acceleration/deceleration patterns of the LV. This result was obtained from the 396 rule version of the car-following model.

Figure 2, shows a result obtained from the 36 rule version of the car-following model. In this figure the a platoon of 11 vehicles were simulated. The LV decelerated from 70 ft/s to 58.5 ft/s in 5 seconds, remained at 58.5 ft/s for five seconds and then accelerated back to 70 ft/s in 5 seconds. The distance headway variation for each of the vehicles following the LV are shown. As can be seen, each vehicle pair eventually attained stability, further the perturbation reduces monotonically as it travels upstream through the platoon.

Figure 3 (a) and (b) show the observed response and the predicted response before and after calibration of the inference system, respectively. As can be seen, the predicted responses match the observations substantially better after calibration.

CONCLUSIONS

The fuzzy inference based model and its neural network representation are found to be a realistic model of the car-following behavior. The model can adjust itself to the driving behavior of different drivers. This feature makes the model particularly useful for the development of controllers for automobiles. Such controllers would drive the vehicle as the driver would. Further, the model of car-following will be useful for developing a realistic simulation of traffic flow for traffic flow management.

REFERENCES

1. S. Kikuchi and P. Chakroborty. "Car-Following Model Based on Fuzzy Inference System." *Transportation Research Record 1365*, Transportation Research Board, 1992, pp. 82-91.

2. P. Chakroborty. *A Model of Car-Following: A Fuzzy-Inference-Based System*, University of Delaware, 1993.

3. S. Horikawa, T. Furuhashi, Y. Uchikawa, and T. Tagawa. "A Study of Fuzzy Modelling using Fuzzy Neural Network." *Proc. of the International Fuzzy Engg. Symp.*, 1991, pp. 562-573.

4. R.J. Williams. "The Logic of Activation Functions." *Parallel Distributed Processing: Explorations in the Microstructure of Cognition*, Volume 1, The MIT Press, Cambridge, Mass., 1986, pp. 423-443.

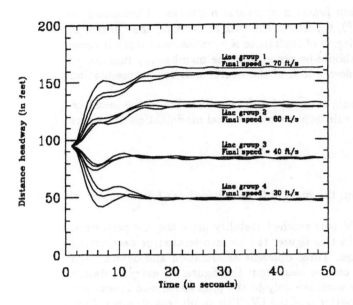

Figure 1.: Local Stability under different perturbations and final speed.

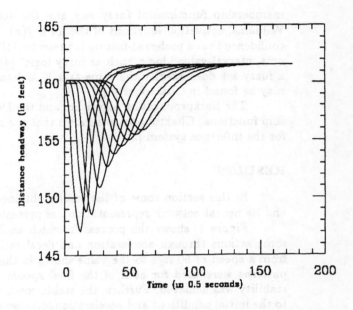

Figure 2.: Asymptotic Stability (platoon size = 11 vehicles)

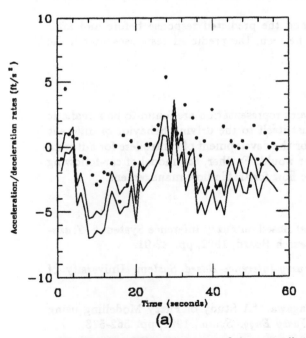

(a)

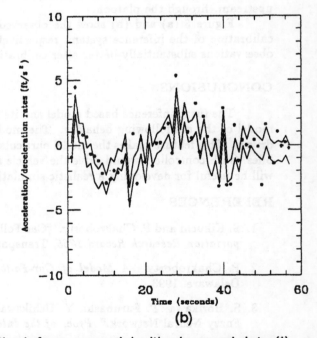

(b)

Figure 3.: Comparison of the prediction from the Inference model with observed data (*) before (a) and after (b) calibration.

A DIRECT ADAPTIVE FUZZY CONTROLLER AND ITS APPLICATION FOR ACTIVE SUSPENSION

Vittorio GORRINI[b,c] , Hugues BERSINI[c] , Serge BOVERIE[b] and André TITLI[a,b]

[a]INSA. LAAS/CNRS, 7, Av. du Colonel Roche 31077 Toulouse Cedex - France

[b]MIRGAS Laboratory, SIEMENS AUTOMOTIVE SA, Av. du Mirail, BP 1149, 31036 Toulouse Cedex - France

[c]IRIDIA, Université Libre de Bruxelles, CP 194/6, 50 Av. Franklin Roosevelt, 1050 Bruxelles - Belgium

Abstract. Once a fuzzy controller is supplied with a gradient method for the automatic tuning of its input and output membership functions, it is very easy, besides the easy human interfacing that they allow, to import methods and ideas that have emerged in the neural net community for adaptive control applications. We have developed a direct adaptive fuzzy controller largely inspired from previous works based on neural networks and tested it on various applications among which, active suspension. Active and semi-active suspensions are among the most developed electronic functions on modern cars. It is possible to design such automatic systems using mathematical model, but here the approach to be presented is completely grounded in the merging of fuzzy controllers with optimization methods. Simulation results illustrate the efficiency of the approach.

Keywords: Fuzzy control, adaptive fuzzy control, optimization techniques, active and semi-active suspensions.

1. Introduction

A classical model (corresponding to a quarter car model with 2 D.O.F) often used for the design of active and semi-active suspension is given in Fig. 1.

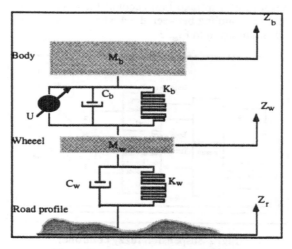

Fig. 1 Quarter car model (2 D.O.F).

This simplification of the real world gives us (applying the fundamental laws of the mechanics) a linear model which can be used for the design of optimal controllers, adaptive controller, variable structure controller (see [5]). But these approaches based on a linear model do not take into account some constraints like:
a) non linearities of physical phenomena (dry friction for example).
b) saturation on actuators.
c) discrete values of the control forces delivered by the actuators.
d) need for robustness of the closed loop system.
e) noise on measurements.
f) approximate measurements.

The first aim was to develop a robust non linear controller exploiting the expertise of automotive engineers and avoiding the use of a process mathematical model sometimes difficult to obtain or with limited validity. For this, we used fuzzy inference systems to design a preliminary fuzzy controller coming out the interfacing with human experts and a sufficient amount of trial-and-errors. The four internal variables of the process to supervise and regulate are $x_1 = z_b - z_c$ "the suspension deflection", $x_2 = dz_b/dt$ "the body speed", $x_3 = z_w - z_r$ "the tire deflection" and $x_4 = dz_w/dt$ "the wheel speed". There is only one control parameter for adjusting the body suspension designated by F.

It is easy to see by the open loop dynamical analysis that the physical system has two different dynamics, one corresponding to the wheel hop (the fast part of the system) the other one corresponding to the car body (the slow part of the system) and we try to take profit of this dynamical property to design two parallel fuzzy controllers: one limited to x_1 and x_2 and a second one limited to x_3 and x_4. Finally both controllers are coordinated by a fuzzy supervisor.

2. Basic Fuzzy Controller

On the whole the fuzzy controller is based on linguistic rules originating from human expertise like: IF *the suspension deflection is Negative Big* THEN *the controller action is Positive Big*. Standard set of rules can be written using some analogies with sliding model control.

Here we have taken profit of the system dynamical properties to design two parallel fuzzy controllers coordinated by a fuzzy supervisor:

- The first controller is dedicated to comfort. It calculates a control force F_c. It uses as inputs the suspension deflection and the body vertical speed: Fc(x_1 and x_2).
- The second controller is dedicated to safety. It calculates a control force F_s. It uses as inputs the tire deflection and the wheel absolute vertical velocity: Fs(x_3 and x_4).
- The global controller action F is calculated as a combination of these two forces: F(x_1, x_2, x_3, x_4)=αF_c (x_1, x_2) +(1-α)F_s, (x_3, x_4) where α is a weighting parameter (0≤α≤1). The determination of this weighting parameter is done by the fuzzy supervisor using as input the following global vehicle information:
- vehicle speed V.
- vehicle acceleration or deceleration A.
- braking pressure F.
- steering angle .
- body height H.

The design of the fuzzy supervisor allows to take into account the overall dynamic of the vehicle without global mathematical model and consequently the coupling between the 4 wheels. The general structure of the controller is given in Fig. 2. Details of the fuzzy supervisor are given in Fig. 3.

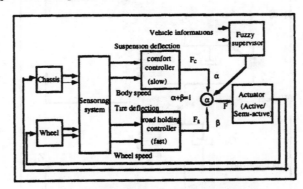

Fig. 2 Suspension fuzzy controller.

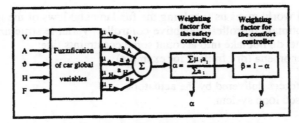

Fig.3 Suspension fuzzy supervisor.

Each controller is defined by rules such:

IF $x_1(t)$ is A_1^k AND $x_2(t)$ is A_2^h THEN $F(t)$ is γ^m (1)

Where A_j^k represents the membership function coding the linguistic term k associated to the variable j and γ^m represents the crisp output of linguistic term m. According to [1] [2] we assimilate such an output to a crisp value. For instance, the third linguistic term for the output i.e. $m=3$ (*negative small* for instance) is given by: $\gamma^3 = -2$.

In our approach, fuzzy controllers are realized by using isosceles triangles for membership functions, and Sugeno method for inference and defuzzification; therefore fuzzy output is a derivable function with respect to each input and each parameter.

The parameters shaping the triangle A_j^k are the center α_j^k, the base β_j^k. Membership values, i-th rule strength, and fuzzy output (force) are respectively computed as follows:

$$A_j^k(x_j) = max\left(1 - \frac{2|x_j - \alpha_j^k|}{\beta_j^k}, 0\right) \qquad (2)$$

$$\mu_i = \prod_j A_j^k(x_j) \qquad (3)$$

$$F = \begin{cases} \dfrac{\sum_i \mu_i \gamma_i}{\sum_i \mu_i} & \text{if } \sum_i \mu_i \neq 0 \\[4mm] 0 & \text{if } \sum_i \mu_i = 0 \end{cases} \qquad (4)$$

Where x_j represents generic variable and γ_i the output of the rule i.

3. Optimization of the fuzzy local controllers

There are basically two reasons for grafting an optimization method on fuzzy controllers: first to automatically discover them so as to possibly support the human interfacing and the manual trial-and-error procedure, thus to improve them on-line like in a classical closed-loop adaptive control scheme. In this paper we show that fuzzy inference systems, provided a gradient descent for the automatic tuning of their membership functions, can benefit from ideas and methods appeared these last years when unsing neural nets for adaptive control.. In our approach due to the controllers separation, the two controllers membership functions will be automatically tuned in an independent way. Since the optimization process is the same for each controller and, for sake of clarity, we will restrict the following developments to the comfort controller.

We perform optimization with respect to discrete time with period T.

Let ω_C be a generic parameter (α_j^k, β_j^k or γ^k) of comfort controller and η the iteration parameter. The optimization rule will be

$$(\omega_C)_{T+1} = (\omega_C)_T - \eta\left(\frac{\partial E_C}{\partial \omega_C}\right)_T \qquad (5)$$

Once defined the comfort controller square error at time T given by:

$$E_C(T) = \tfrac{1}{2}\left(x_1^2(T) + x_2^2(T)\right) \qquad (6)$$

its derivative with respect to generic ω_C is:

$$\frac{\partial E_C}{\partial \omega_C} = \left(\frac{\partial E_C}{\partial x_1}\frac{\partial x_1}{\partial F} + \frac{\partial E_C}{\partial x_2}\frac{\partial x_2}{\partial F}\right)\frac{\partial F}{\partial \omega_C} \qquad (7)$$

What is unknown in the absence of an analytical model of the process is the Jacobian $\partial x_j/\partial F$. When using a gradient-based technique, a perfect knowledge of the Jacobian is not required: since substituting $\partial x_j/\partial F$ by its sign ± 1 just alters the amplitude of the variation but not its direction, the gradient method can still give an adequate value of the control parameters [4]. Reducing to such a minimum the knowledge of the process required for its control makes the resulting control nearly direct. The process can remain somewhat "black-box" with just few holes allowing to observe qualitatively the way it reacts to increases and decreases of its inputs. This type of knowledge is quite common and certainly the first shallow type of knowledge a user or observer of the process is aware of and able to communicate.

Since parameters ω_C do not depend on F_S we may write:

$$\frac{\partial F}{\partial \omega_C} = \alpha \frac{\partial F_C}{\partial \omega_C} \qquad (8)$$

When deriving expression (4) we finally found the expression of derivatives for centers and bases of membership functions and crisp outputs given respectively by:

$$\frac{\partial F_C}{\partial \alpha_j^k} = \frac{1}{\sum_i \mu_i} \left(\sum_{i \in I_j^k} \mu_i \gamma_i - F_C \sum_{i \in I_j^k} \mu_i \right) \frac{2\, sgn\left(x_j - \alpha_j^k\right)}{A_j^k(x_j)\beta_j^k} \quad (9)$$

$$\frac{\partial F_C}{\partial \beta_j^k} = \frac{1}{\sum_i \mu_i} \left(\sum_{i \in I_j^k} \mu_i \gamma_i - F_C \sum_{i \in I_j^k} \mu_i \right) \frac{1 - A_j^k(x_j)}{A_j^k(x_j)\beta_j^k} \quad (10)$$

$$\frac{\partial F_C}{\partial \gamma^k} = \frac{1}{\sum_i \mu_i} \sum_{i \in I^k} \mu_i \qquad (11)$$

where I^k represents the set of rules in which γ^k appears and I_j^k the set of rules in which α_j^k and β_j^k appear.

These set of derivatives, very similar to the one presented in [3], have been discussed in [1], [2]. Their originality resides in the fact that just the linguistic terms are optimized and not all the parameters appearing in the rules (this justifies the presence of I^k and I_j^k).

4. Simulation results - Comments

Our controllers have been tested using the simulation tool EASY5/X from Boeing on a HP workstation. We integrate the system using the variable step Runge-Kutta method. Each input variable is associated to a linguistic term taken among seven possibilities, so each fuzzy controller is defined by up to 49 rules. In our simulations we use all rules and thus the whole controller is composed of 98 rules. Crisp output are also defined by seven crisp values. The gradient descent is applied to each parameter every 0.002 seconds. Simulation results show the ability of our controller to improve the suspension response when applying a single step in input (the road profile).

Figures 4 to 7 show the system course (the body position B and the wheel position W) when applying a 5 cm. step during one second. We may observe the improved behavior of the optimized systems. It is important to remark that when using a passive suspension the oscillations of state variables are 30 % wider and the period 5 times longer.

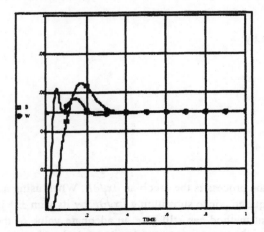

Fig. 4 No optimization.

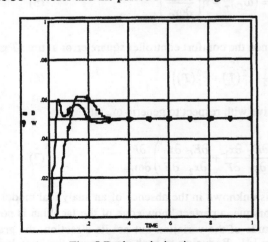

Fig. 5 Both optimizations.

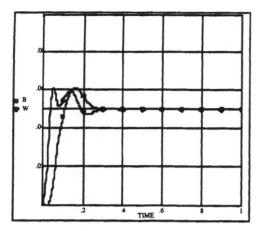

Fig. 6 Only comfort optimization.

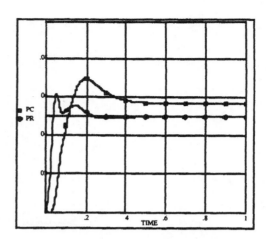

Fig. 7 Only safety optimization.

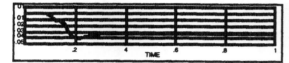

Fig. 8 Optimization of center for fuzzy set ZERO.

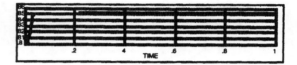

Fig. 9 Optimization of crisp output Negative Small.

Figures 8 and 9 show the behavior of some parameters defining the fuzzy controller (the center position corresponding to the fuzzy set *Zero* and the and the value of the crisp output *Positive Small*) during the adaptation process.

We performed several simulations with different values of α, changing the mass and adapting only one controller at time. Results have shown a reasonable improvement and a good robustness when optimizing at least the comfort controller. The best results were obtained by optimizing only the comfort controller but a lot of extra works remain to be done in order to understand better and validate the whole approach.

5. Conclusions

Without using any mathematical model of the process, but taking profit of the physical characteristics of the system to be controlled, we have designed a fuzzy controller resulting from the additive composition of 2 fuzzy sub-controllers (one oriented toward a security goal, the second toward a comfort goal), supervised by a simple fuzzy system using global information on the car.

Robustness and adaptability have been introduced by using an optimization technique to tune the local fuzzy controllers.

Satisfactory results have been obtained on simulations.

References

1. H. Bersini and V. Gorrini,, "FUNNY (FUzzY or Neural Net) Methods for Adaptive Process Control". *Proceedings of the first European Congress on Fuzzy and Intelligent Technologies*, pp. 55-61, 1993.
2. H. Bersini, J.P. Nordvik and A. Bonarini,, "A Simple Direct Adaptive Fuzzy Controller Derived from its Neural Equivalent". *Proceedings of the Second IEEE International Conference on Fuzzy Systems*, pp. 345- 350, 1993.
3. H. Nomura, I. Hayashi and N. Wakami, "A learning method of fuzzy inference rules by descent method". *Proceedings of the First IEEE International Conference on Fuzzy Systems*, pp. 203-210, 1992.
4. Renders J.-M., Bersini H. & Saerens M., "Adaptive neurocontrol: How Simple and Black-box can it be ?". *Proceedings of the tenth International Workshop on Machine Learning*, Amherst, pp. 260-267, 1993.
5. S. Roukieh," Contribution des commandes optimale, à structure variable et par logique loue à la synthèse de suspensions automobile". PhD Thesis LAAS - INSA Toulouse, 1993.

Fig. 7. Only safety optimization.

Fig. 6. Only comfort optimization.

Fig. 8 Optimization of center for fuzzy set ZERO.

Fig. 9 Optimization of center output Negative Small

Figures 8 and 9 show the behavior of some parameters defining the fuzzy controller (the center positions corresponding to the fuzzy set Zero and the and the map output "fuzzy SetA") during the optimization process.

We performed several simulations with different values b.c.t. changing the mass and adapting only one controller at time. Results have shown a reasonable improvement and a good robustness when optimizing at last one controller. The best results were obtained by obtaining only one control controller but a lot of extra work remain to be done in order to understand better and validate the whole approach.

5. Conclusions:

Without using any mathematical model of the process but taking profit of the physical understanding of the system to be controlled we have designed a fuzzy controller resulting from the additive composition of 2 fuzzy sub-controllers (one oriented toward a security goal, the second toward a control goal), supervised by a simple fuzzy system using global information on the car.

Robustness and adaptability have been introduced by using an optimization technique to tune the local fuzzy controllers.

Satisfactory results have been obtained on simulations.

References

1. B. Bersini and V.Gorrini, "FUN'N'FUzzY et Neural Net Methods for Adaptive Process Control", Proceedings of the first European Congress on Fuzzy and Intelligent Technologies, pp. 55 CI, 1993.

2. H. Bersini, I.P. Nordvik and A. Bolarini, "A Simple Direct Adaptive Fuzzy Controller Derived from its Neural Equivalent", Proceeding of the Second IEEE International Conference on Fuzzy Systems, pp. 345-350, 1993.

3. H. Nomura, I. Hayashi and N. Watam, "A learning method of fuzzy inference rules by descent method", Proceedings of the First IEEE International Conference on Fuzzy Systems, pp. 203-210, 1992.

4. Renders J.-M., Bersini H. & Saerens M., "Adaptive neurocontrol: how blackbox and blackbox can it be?", Proceedings of the tenth International Workshop on Machine Learning, Amherst, pp. 560-567, 1993.

5. S. Boudaid, "Contribution des commandes optimale à structure variable et par logique floue à la synthèse de asservissement automobile", PhD Thesis LAAS-CNRS Toulouse 1992.

Novel Results Session

Biological Neural Networks

The Functional Role of the Hippocampus in the Organization of Memory

J. G. Taylor and L. Michalis

Department of Mathematics
King's College, London
London WC2R 2LS, U.K.

Abstract

Highly specific in each task. the behavioural correlate of single cell activity in the hippocampus changes across tasks [Otto and Eichenbaum. 1992]. Selective to particular configurations of cues in simultaneous discrimination. single cells demonstrate a selectivity to sequences of cues in simultaneous discrimination. and to "the outcome of the comparison between cues across trials" in a cDNM task [Otto and Eichenbaum. 1992]. Changing across tasks. single cell selectivity reflects in each task the properties. or relations that are critical to reinforcement [Otto and Eichenbaum. 1992]. A model of the hippocampus is presented in which critical features. or relations are extracted as invariant across trials properties of. or relations between single. or configural stimuli. This process depends upon the the comparison of current to stored sensory experiences. There is no explicit transfer of information from the hippocampus onto the neocortex. Instead. cortical and hippocampal codes are simultaneously updated in a declarative memory organization that reflects the relevant. or critical relations between individual sensory events.

1. Introduction

Specific in each task the behavioural correlate of unit cell firing in CA3-CA1 changes across tasks reflecting the "nature" and conditions of each task [Otto and Eichenbaum. 1992]. Single CA1 cells which in a "sequential discrimination" task [Otto and Eichenbaum. 1992] are activated by specific sequences of cues. they respond. in the "continuous Delayed Non-match to Sample" task. to the "outcome of the comparison between cues on successive trials independentently of the perceptual qualities of the cues" [Otto and Eichenbaum. 1992]. Highly specific in each task. and changing across tasks the behavioural correlate of single cell activity demonstrates an invariant across tasks form of processing aimed at extracting and encoding in each task the relations that are critical for performance in the task.

2. The enoding of 'critical' features from across trial correlations

Correlations between individual features are extracted from the interaction between stored (from earlier trials) and current patterns of neocortical coactivations. Changes involve active properties of the current pattern. or reactivated properties of stored patterns and are recorded by the LTM trace of their adaptive projections. Both types of projections are updated: associative between coactive representations in CA3 of neocortical activations. and "vertical" from neocortical activations onto CA3 (Figure 1).

Excitatory between positively correlated features and inhibitory between negatively correlated features. signals along the recurrent collaterals of CA3 demonstrate by their polarity opposite biases in the projections between positively and negatively correlated features. Manifested by opposite effects these biases are recorded in the relative strengths of projections which for excitatory projections are relatively greater between positively correlated features and smaller between negatively correlated features. Inhibitory projections are weighted in the opposite manner.

Cooperative between positively correlated features and competitive between negatively correlated features. the coupling organization of CA3 is adaptively calibrated in each task to the relevant correlations between individual features. From an initially random. or uncalibrated organization. individual features of single. or configural stimuli may be combined by recurrent signals into a coupling configuration whose form - competitive or cooperative - dependes upon the sign of the correlation between features. Positive correlations give rise to a cooperative coupling and reciprocal excitatory signals that tend to enhance the activity of positively correlated features. Negative correlations instead. give rise to a competitive form of coupling and reciprocal inhibitory signals that tend to suppress the activity of negatively correlated features. The limit pattern of activity is the initial pattern of activity transformed by the two types of interaction.

Dependent upon the correlations that are relevant in each task. coupling interactions demonstrate a distinct organization in each task. There is no fixed gradient of connections. Instead the coupling organization of CA3 is adaptively recalibrated in each task to the correlations between individual features binding positively correlated features into a synchronized activity pattern and inhibiting the activity of negatively correlated features. Bound by synchronized activity. active features across CA3 are then combined by convergent projections into a unitary code in CA1 (Figure 1).

3. The relational organization of memory

Projections from CA1 onto the cortex function so as to recall in the cortex a sequence of stored episodes. Episodes and sequences of episodes are seperately represented at two distinct levels of abstraction in a hierarchical memory organization. Knowledge from each level of the hierarchy is combined into progressively more abstract themes at progressively higher levels of the hierarchy. knowledge structures are combined from each level to the next by means of a "vertical" associative memory scheme. Individual episodes. encoded by distinct cells in a field of cells FC_1 are combined by vertical associative interactions into the representation of a sequence in FC_2. Reciprocal connections from FC_2 to FC_1 function to selectively activate episodes of a sequence in FC_2.

The context of individual episodes depends upon the task. or the context in which they are recalled. They may represent a sequence of odor stimuli in a successive odor discrimination task. or words from word pairs in a paired associate task. Compared against episodes of the current sequence. episodes of a recalled sequence function to generate a response which may be an expectation of reward. or nonreward in an odor discrimination task. or the second word of a word pair cued by its first word in a paired associate task.

The comparison of a stored sequence against episodes of a current sequence corresponds to the "evaluation phase" of the "generative retrieval process" [Conway. 1990]. In that phase accessed. or recalled memories are evaluated in terms of the original context i.e. task demands. etc. The aim of the evaluation phase is to determine whether or not the retrieval process can be terminated and a response be executed [Conway. 1990].

Individual episodes of a sequence are successively activated and compared to current episodes. CA1 signals act to start the performance of a sequence by activating its initial element. Each of the subsequent elements is activated by its preceding event in the sequence if that is matched by a current event and the sequential performance is interrupted if some episode of a stored sequence is mismatched against a current episode.

The sequential activation of episodes from a stored sequence is performed by reciprocal thalamo-cortical interactions: both direct excitatory and indirect inhibitory/disinhibitory by cortical projections through the basal ganglia (Figure 2a). The two forms of projections have opposite effects. Reciprocal excitatory interactions function so as to preserve by reverberating activity the representation of an individual episode in STM. Interactions through the inhibitory layers of the basal ganglia function to suppress the reverberation of an active episode. and activate the next stage/episode of the sequence.

Sequential performance arises from the interaction of the two processes: The reciprocal excitatory action between cortical and thalamic cells and the selective inhibitory/disinhibitory action of cortical on thalamic cells by means of the inhibitory layers of the striatum and the globus pallibus (Figure 2a). The two processes are related to the two needs associated with sequential performance: the need to sustain an active memory representation of the current episode. and the need to suppress the reverberation of the current episode and activate the next episode/stage of the sequence.

The two processes impose an asymmetrical function on cortical and thalamic cells. Cortical cells by means of a selective inhibitory/disinhibitory action on thalamic cells act to inhibit the reverberation in STM of the current episode and disinhibit. or facilitate the performance of the next episode. Thalamic cells function to activate. or build up the activity of the next episode.

Build up by reciprocal excitatory signals. the activity of each cortical cell $v_{fc.i}$ acts to inhibit itself and disinhibit the activity of the next cell $v_{fc.i+1}$. Both actions are initiated by an excitatory signal from $v_{fc.i}$ onto $v_{str.i}$. Lateral inhibitory interactions across the striatum inhibit other active cells and so inhibit the activity of $v_{str.i-1}$. The inhibition of $v_{str.i-1}$ disinhibits $v_{gp.i-1}$ which in turn inhibits $v_{th.i-1}$ switching off the reverberation between $v_{th.i-1}$ and $v_{fc.i}$.

At the same time that lateral inhibitory interactions ihibit other active cells across the striatum. an inhibitory signal from $v_{str.i}$ onto $v_{gp.i}$ acts to disinhibit the activation of $v_{th.i}$. The release of an excitatory signal from $v_{th.i}$ and of a reciprocal excitatory signal from $v_{fc.i+1}$ act to start the reverberation of the next episode in STM (Figure 2a).

Individual episodes of a sequence in FC_2 as they become successively active function to activate the representation of that sequence in FC_2. In an organization of FC_2 as a 'masking field' [Grossberg. 1978]. longer sequences have a competitive advantage over shorter sequences. Sequentially activated. individual episodes in FC_1 may be combined into multiple groupings. Of all the potential groupings the one is selected that is appropriate to the sequence of preceding episodes as well as to the current episode (Figure 2b).

4. References

Cohen N. and Eichenbaum H. (1993) Memory. Amnesia and the Hippocampal System. MIT Press

Conway M (1990) A Structural Model of Autobiographical Memory in Theoritical Perspectives on Autobiographical Memory. Conway M.. Rubin D.. Spinnler. and Wagenaar eds

Eichenbaum H. and Otto T. (1992) Neuronal Activity in the Hippocampus During Delayed Non-Match to Sample Performance in Rats: Evidence for Hippocampal Processing in Recognition Memory. Hippocampus. Vol. 2. No. 3: 323 - 334

Eichenbaum H. and Otto T. (1992) Toward a Comprehensive Account of Hippocampal Function: Studies of Olfactory Learning Permit an Integration of Data across Multiple Levels of Neurological Analysis. in Neuropsychology of Memory. L. Squire and N. Butters eds.

Gray J. (1990) The Neuropsychology of Anxiety. Oxford:Clarendon Press

Grossberg S. and Somers D. (1992) Synchronized Oscillations for Binding Spatially Distributed Feature Codes into Coherent Spatial Patterns. in Pattern Recognition. S. Grossberg and G. Carpenter eds.

Grossberg S. (1976) Adaptive Pattern Classification and Universal Recoding. II: Feedback. Expectation. Olfaction. Illusions. in Pattern Recognition by Self-Organizing Neural Networks. S. Grossberg and G. Carpenter eds.

Wickelgren W. (1979) Chunking and Consolidation: ATheoritical Synthesis of Semantic Networks. Configuring in Conditioning. S-R versus Cognitive Learning. Normal Forgetting. the Amnesic Syndrome. and the Hippocampal Arousal System. Psychological Review. Vol. 86. No. 1: 44 - 60

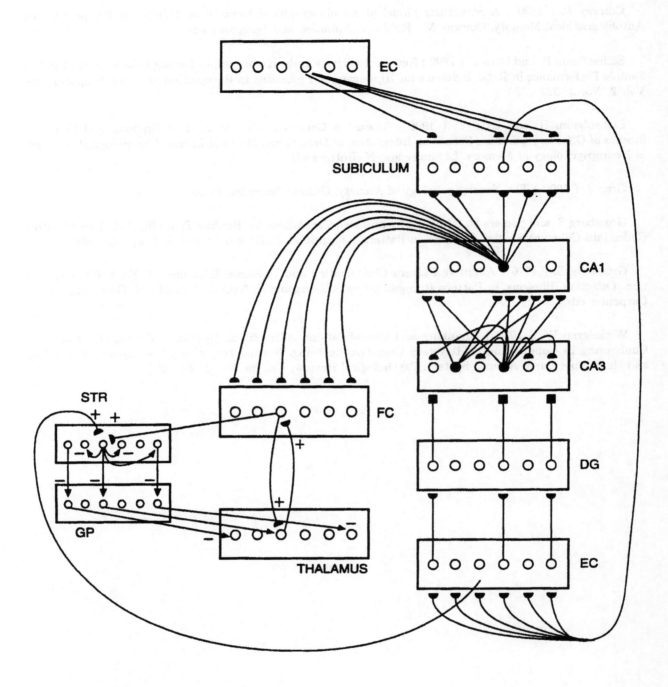

Figure 1: Critical features, or relations are extracted as invariant across trials properties of, or relatioins between single, or configural stimuli. This process depend upon the comparison of current to stored sensory experiences. There is no explicit transfer of information from the hippocampus onto the neo-cortex. Instead, cortical and hippocampal codes are simultaneoulsy updated in a declarative memory organisation that reflects the relevant, or critical relations between individual sensory events.

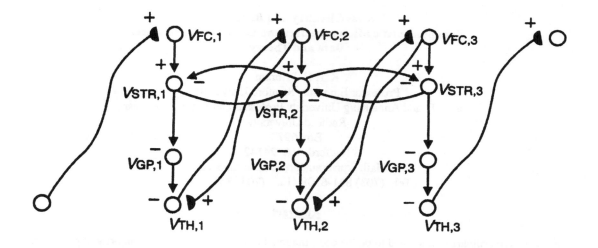

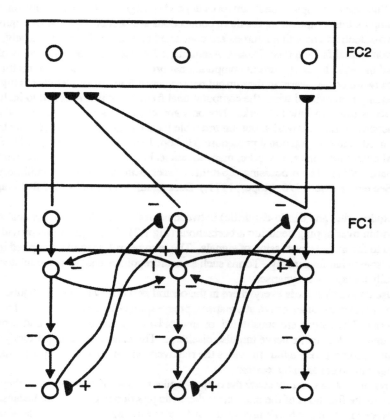

Figure 2: a. Sequential performance arises from the interaction of two processes: the reciprocal excitatory action between cortical and thalamic cells and the selective inhibitory/disinhibitory action of cortical on thalamic cells by means of the inhibitory layers of the striatum. **b.** Individual episodes of a sequence as they become successively active function to activate the representation of that sequence in FC2

Neural Circuitry and Behavior;
Synaptodendritic Microprocesses and Conscious Experience:
Data and Theory

Karl H. Pribram
Professor Emeritus, Stanford University
James P. and Anna King University Professor and Eminent Scholar
Radford University
Box 6977
Radford, VA 24142
E-Mail: kpribram@ruacad.ac.runet.edu
Tel: (703) 831-6108 / Fax: (703) 831-6113

Abstract

Neurons are ordinarily conceived to be the computational units of the brain. The majority of processing theories since the seminal contribution of McCulloch and Pitts (1943) have taken the axonal discharge of the neuron, the nerve impulse, as the currency of computation. However, this framework for computational theory has led to considerable misunderstanding between neuroscientist and those interested in computational processing. Successful computational networks depend on highly--often randomly--interconnected elements. The more complex the computation, the more connections are needed: the law of requisite variety (Ashby, 1960). Neuro-scientists know that neurons are connected nonrandomly, often sparsely, and always in a specifically configured fashion (see Crick & Asanuma, 1986, for a neuroscience view of connectionist computational theory). In short, current computational processing emphasizes a minimum of constraints in the processing wetware or hardware; in the current neuroscience framework wetware is highly constrained. Misunderstanding is alleviated when the computational framework is broadened to include the microprocessing that takes place within dendritic networks. Not only are axonal-dendritic synapses that connect neurons subject to local influences in these networks, but innumerable local circuit operations provide the unconstrained high connectivity needed in computational procedure (Bishop, 1956; Pribram, 1960, 1971; Schmitt, Dev, & Smith, 1976). Local circuit neurons are found in many locations in the sensory and central nervous system (see Table, p. 9, in Shepard, 1981). The processing capability of such neurons (primarily inhibitory) is often dendro-dendritic. (See e.g., Rakic, 1976; Sloper, 1971.) Data manifolds are presented that map these dendritic fields.

Junctions (axodendritic and dendo-dendritic) between neurons in the form of chemical synapses and electrical gap junctions occur within overlapping dendritic arborizations (Fig 1.2). These junctions provide the possibility for processing as opposed to the mere transmission of signals. The term neurotransmitters applied to chemicals acting at junctions is, therefore, somewhat misleading. Terms such as neuroregulator and neuromodulator convey more of the meaning of what actually transpires at synapses.

Nerve impulse conduction leads everywhere in the central nervous system to such junctional dendritic microprocessing. When nerve impulses arrive at synapses, presynaptic polarizations result. These are never solitary but constitute arrival patterns. The patters are constituted of sinusoidally fluctuating hyper- and depolarizations which are insufficiently large to immediately incite nerve impulse discharge The delay affords opportunity for computational complexity. The dendritic microprocess thus provides the relatively unconstrained computational power of the brain, especially when arranged in layers as in the cortex.

The neurophysiologist can readily study the output--spike trains-- of neurons when they act as channels but he has only limited access to the functions of the interactive dendritic junctional architecture because of the small scale at which the processes proceed. A major breakthrough toward understanding was achieved, however, when Kuffler (1953) noted that he could *map* the functional dendritic field of a retinal ganglion cell by recording impulses from the ganglion cell's axon located in the optic nerve. This was accomplished by moving a spot of light in front of a paralyzed eye and recording the locations of the spot that produced a response in the axon. The locations mapped the extent of the responding dendritic field of that axon's parent neuron. The direction of response, inhibitory or excitatory, at each location indicated whether the dendrites at that location were hyperpolarizing of depolarizing.

The current study explores the relations among local field potentials by mapping receptive field organization using the Kuffler technique. The specific questions posed and answered in the affirmative are 1) whether this technique can map the spectral properties of synaptodendritic receptive field potentials, and 2) whether such maps of receptive fields in the somatosensory cortex show properties of patch (quantum) holography (that is, of Gabor elementary functions) similar to those recorded from the visual cortex.

In our experiments, sensory input is generated by the spacings of the grooves on the cylinders and the speed with which the cylinders are rotated. The results provide maps of the number of bursts or spikes generated at each spectral location as determined by the spatial and temporal parameters of the sensory input. (Figure 1). The activity above or below baseline which resulted from whisker stimulation is plotted as a manifold describing total number of bursts (or spikes) per 100 secs. of stimulation. Spatial frequencies are scaled in terms of grooves per revolution, while temporal frequencies are scaled in terms of revolutions per second. Thus, the density of stimulation of a whisker (or set of whiskers) is a function of both the spacings of the cylinder grooves and the speed with which the cylinder rotates. It is this density *per se* which composes the spectral domain.

According to signal processing theory, the general shape of a field potential manifold is the same for each combination of spatial and temporal frequencies. However, a central peak, reflecting the density of response for that spectral location in the manifold, will be shifted within the field according to the particular spatial and temporal stimulation values.

In order to discern whether, indeed, our data fit the requirements of signal processing theory, a simulation of the procedure was executed. The first stage of the simulation was to construct a putative truncated field potential manifold. Any extent of manifold is best described formally by a truncated spectral function such as a constrained Fourier representation. Gabor (1946 p.431) defined such a function as follows: "Let us now tentatively adopt the view that both time and frequency are legitimate references for describing a signal and illustrate this . . . by taking them as orthogonal coordinates. Its frequency is exactly defined [only] while its epoch is entirely undefined. A sudden surge or 'delta function' (also called a 'unit impulse function') has a sharply defined epoch, but its energy is distributed over the whole frequency spectrum" Daugman (1990), McLennon (1993) and Pribram and Carlton (1986), have extended this illustration to include, in addition to the time parameter, two spatial dimensions.

In our simulations each plot is a manifold of a spectral density function of a rectangular windowed continuous two-dimensional sinusoidal signal. When, in other experiments, only a single frequency of stimulation is used, a spatiotemporal "connection" matrix can be constructed from recordings made with multiple electrode arrays to represent the data (Barcala, Nicolelis and Chapin 1993). Our version of such a matrix represents the variety of spatially and temporally constrained spectral data gathered in our experiments as a sinc function, centered at the frequency of each stimulation pair, i.e.

$$F(\omega_1, \omega_2) = A \operatorname{sinc}(\omega_1 - \omega_{01}) \operatorname{sinc}(\omega_2 - \omega_{02})$$

where A is a scaling constant, ω_1 and ω_2 are spatial and temporal frequencies of the spectrum, and ω_{01} and ω_{02} are the spatial and temporal frequencies of the stimulation. The function $\operatorname{sinc}(\omega)$ is defined as :

$$\operatorname{sinc}(\omega) = \frac{\sin(\omega)}{\omega}$$

The second stage of the simulation uses as a probe, a Gaussian (exponential) function. When this probe represents a single neuron it is limited by the spatial extent of the local field potentials fluctuating among that neuron's dendrites. When a burst manifold is modelled, the spatial constraint is assumed to portray a greater reach and is limited by the barrel (columnar) arrangement of the somatosensory cortex. Sampling is performed by the generative activity of the axon hillock, which, due to the upper and lower temporal limits of spike generation, functions as a bandpass filter which is the response of the sensory system. This filter is multiplied with the sinc function to yield a display of the manifold. Figure 2 depicts manifolds and contours derived from these simulations. Note the close fit to the experimentally derived manifolds and contours shown in Figure 1. A total of 48 manifolds were experimentally generated. Of those, three were essentially flat. Of the remaining 45, we simulated six; all but two of the remaining 39 have a shape that can be seen to be successfully simulatable with the technique described.

The similarity of these manifolds obtained from recordings made from the somatosensory cortex to the receptive field characteristics demonstrated in the primary visual cortex (DeValois and DeValois, 1988; Pollen, and Taylor, 1974; Pribram and Carlton, 1986; Daugman, 1990) suggests that this processing medium is ubiquitous in the cortical synaptodendritic network.

The manifolds derived from our data are constructed of two orthogonal dimensions: one dimension reflects the spatial frequency of the stimulus and the other its temporal frequency. Because spatial and temporal variables constrain the spectral density response, a Gabor-like rather than a simple Fourier representation describes our results. Thus the results of our experiments can be interpreted in terms of an information field composed of Gabor-like elementary functions, that is, of truncated two-dimensional sinusoids.

References

Ashby, W.R. (1960). *Design for a brain: The origin of adaptive behaviour.* (2nd Ed.). New York: Wiley.

Barcala, L.A., Nicolelis, M.A.L., and Chapin, J.K. (1993) Quantifying the connectivity properties underlying the dynamics of the rodent trigeminal network (Abstract), *Society For Neuroscience Abstracts: 23rd Annual Meeting, Vol. 19, Part 1.*

Bishop, G. (1956). Natural history of the nerve impulse. *Physiological Review, 36,* 376-399.

Crick, F.H.C., & Asanuma, C. (1986). Certain aspects of the anatomy and physiology of the cerebral cortex. In J.L. McClelland & D.E. Rumelhart (Eds.), *Parallel distributed processing: Explorations in the microstructure of cognition, Vol. II: Psychological and biological models.* Cambridge, MA: MIT Press.

Daugman, J.G. (1990). An information-theoretic view of analog representation in strate cortex. In E. Schwartz (Ed.), *Computational neuroscience.* Cambridge, MA: MIT Press.

DeValois, R.L., DeValois, K.K. (1988). *Spatial vision* Oxford psychology series No. 14). New York: Oxford University Press.

Gabor, D. (1946). Theory of communication. *Journal of the Institute of Electrical Engineers, 93,* 429-441.

Kuffler, S.W. (1953). Discharge patterns and functional organization of mammalian retina. *Journal of Neurophysiology, 16,* 37-69.

MacLennon, B. (1993). Information Processing in the Dendritic Net. In Pribram (Ed.) *Rethinking Neural Networks: Quantum Fields and Biological Data. INNS Publications* New Jersey: Lawrence Erlbaum Associates.

McCullough, W.S. & Pitts, W. (1943). Logical calculus of the ideas immanent in nervous activity. *Bulletin of Mathematical Biophysics, 5,* 115-133.

Pollen, D.A. & Taylor, J.H. (1974). The striate cortex and the spatial analysis of visual space. In F.O. Schmitt & F.G. Worden (Eds.), *The Neurosciences Third Study Program* (pp. 239-247). Cambridge, MA: The MIT Press.

Pribram, K.H. (1960). The intrinsic systems of the forebrain. In J. Field, H.W. Magoun, & V.E. Hall (Eds.), *Handbook on physiology, neurophysiology II* (pp. 1323-1344). Washington, DC: American Physiological Society.

Pribram, K.H. (1971). *Languages of the brain: Experimental paradoxes and principles in neuropsychology.* Englewood Cliffs, NJ: Prentice-Hall.

Pribram, K.H., & Carlton, E.H. (1986) Holonomic brain theory in imaging and object perception. *Acta Psycholgica, 63,* 175-210.

Rakic, P. (1976). *Local circuit neurons.* Cambridge, MA: MIT Press.

Schmitt, F.O., Dev, P., & Smith, B.H. (1976). Electronic processing of information by brain cells. *Science,* 193, 114-120.

Shepard, R.N. (1981). Psychophysical complementarity. In M. Kubovy & J. Pomerantz (Eds.), *Perceptual organization* (pp. 279-341). Hillsdale, NJ: Lawrence Erlbaum Associates.

Sloper, J.J. (1971). Dendro-dendritic synapses in the primate motor cortex. *Brain Research, 34,* 186-192.

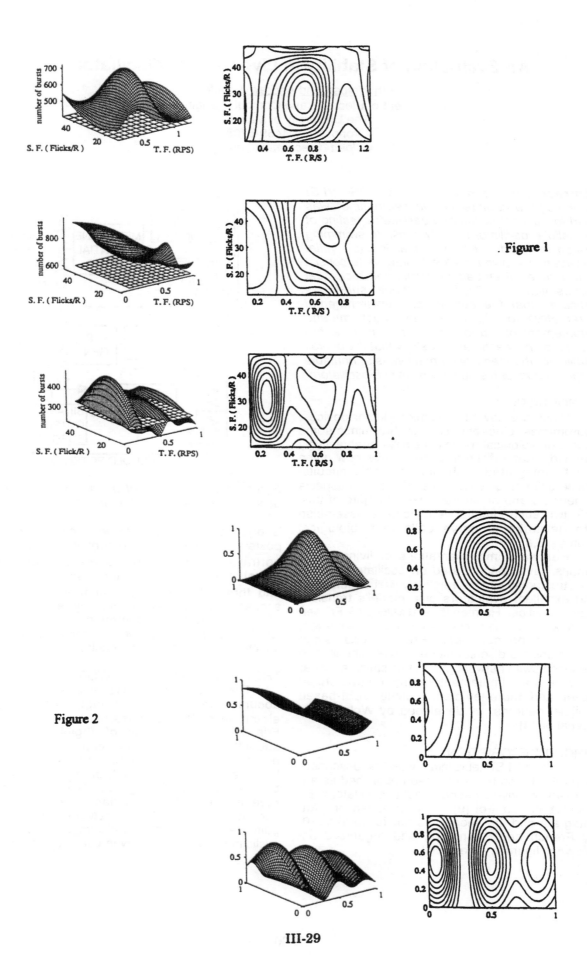

Figure 1

Figure 2

An Evaluation of Stability in Live Cellular Oscillators

Seth Wolpert and Andrew J. Laffely
Department of Electrical and Computer Engineering,
The University of Maine,
Orono, ME, 04469-5708
wolpert@eece.maine.edu

abstractUsing conventional CMOS VLSI technology, a comprehensive neuromime was used for reconstruction and parametric testing of the cellular oscillator that gives rise to swimming motion in hirudo, the medicinal leech. Initial observation showed the leech network to consist of a number of embedded cyclic and reciprocal sub-oscillators. Tests on these sub-types indicated that the cellular and environmental parameters to which they are most immune complement one another. Tests on an entire subunit of the leech network show that the overall stability of the leech swim network is attributable to the product of the stability of its sub-oscillators.

INTRODUCTION

Since the advent of semiconductor devices, neuromimes, electronic circuits that mimic some aspect of biological nerve cells have been actively pursued. Early discrete circuits have now given rise to integrated [1-4] neuromorphic circuits, whose ultimate goal was to study various aspects of neurons and nerve networks. In spite of this, only two such circuits were actually assembled into newtorks of nerve cells from biological sources [5,6].

Hardware implementations of living nerve circuits have concentrated on oscillators, which are structurally simple, relatively well understood, and excellent evaluators of a model's transient characteristics. Harmon [5] and Mitchell & Friesen [6] describe cyclic oscillator models in two, three, and four phases, and Friesen has since implemented a discrete model of one subunit from the leech swim network [7]. In this study, a similar network was implemented and characterized faster and more efficiently using VLSI-based artificial neurons, as developed by Wolpert and Tzanakou [4].

CIRCUIT DESCRIPTION

The VLSI neuromime was first described in 1986 [4], and has since been published as an element for investigating cellular oscillators [8] and robotic control [9]. It was based on an 'integrate and fire' model, as published in 1970 by French and Stein [10], and organized as shown in figure 1. The circuit

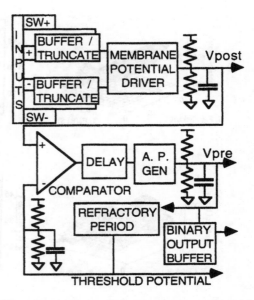

Figure 2-Organization of the VLSI neuromime used to recreate the leech swim network.

is organized around three circuit nodes, postsynaptic membrane potential, V_{POST}, which portrays dendritic and somatic membrane potential, V_{PRE}, which portrays axonal potential, and threshold potential. All three nodes are accessed and biased off-chip by RC networks, affording continuous control over their resting levels and time constants. Transients may be affected from either on or off-chip.

THE LEECH SWIM OSCILLATOR

The leech swim oscillator circuit has been documented in years of morphological and electrophysiological observation by W. Otto Friesen of the University of Virginia [11]. One subunit of that oscillator consists of eleven neurons, plus several motor neurons, which have been shown not to contribute to oscillatory behavior, as shown in figure 2. Visual inspection reveals surprising redundacny, with 34 sub-oscillators embedded in the network: six reciprocal pairs, seven three-celled cyclic rings, 14 five-celled cyclic rings, and seven seven-celled cyclic rings.

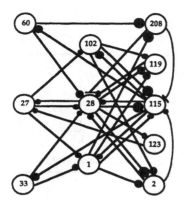

Figure 2-One subunit of the swim oscillator network of hirudo, as reported by Friesen in [11].

THE IMPLEMENTATION

Electrical design of neuromime circuits was done on an ULTRIX DEC station 2100 using SPICE 3C.1, and physical design conducted on the same platform using MAGIC6, following two micron CMOS double level metal design rules. Each neuromime's active circuitry occupies under 0.5 mm^2 of die area, and eight I/O pins plus V_{DD} and V_{SS} terminals. Neuromimes are packaged three to a chip in 40-pin 600-mil ceramic DIP packages and assembled, with tunable biasing components into the oscillatory subunit on a single 11 by 14 inch circuit board. Circuit tests were conducted usingconventional bench instruments.

All cells and synapses were tuned to the self-excitatory frequency and coupling weight of their biological counterparts, as given by Friesen. The circuit was then assembled and retuned. Not only did the network exhibit stable oscillation at a realistic frequency, but each cell was found to operate within 40° of its biological counterpart. One example is shown in figure 3, where waveforms from cells 1 and 115 of the *hirudo* swim network are shown alongside digitally sampled extracts from their counterparts in the silicon model. Similar data from the remainder of the network will be presented in the results section. Note that connections from cell 115 to cells 33 and 60 have been proposed by Friesen, but never confirmed in laboratory tests. It is expected that the electronic model will serve well as a sound platform to confirm or disprove such synapses.

RESULTS

Although the subunit consists of only 11 cells, it contains 34 distinct oscillators in four different configurations. Characterizing such a complex system warranted a methodical approach. In initial stages, each sub-oscillator type would undergo an analysis of its sensitivity to a number of cellular

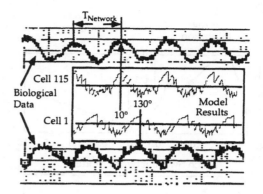

Figure 3-Comparison of activity in cells 1 and 115 in the hirudo swim network with their counterparts in the electronic model

and environmental parameters, as they affect resting and transient response of membrane potential, threshold potential, and synaptic weight. These factors would then be correlated with similar measurements taken on the overall network. The flexible design of the neuromime allows all adjustments to be made by simple variation of discrete off-chip component values.

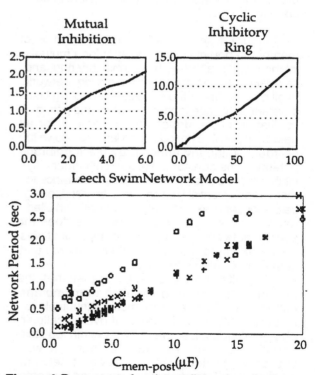

Figure 4-Response of reciprocally and cyclically inhibited subnetworks and the overall swim network to variation in membrane potential time constant.

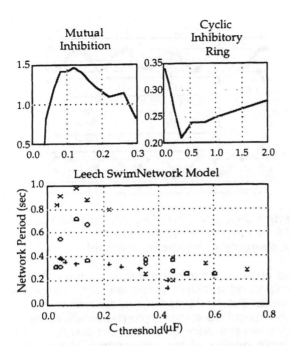

Figure 5-*Response of reciprocally and cyclically inhibited subnetworks and the overall swim network to variation in threshold potential time constant.*

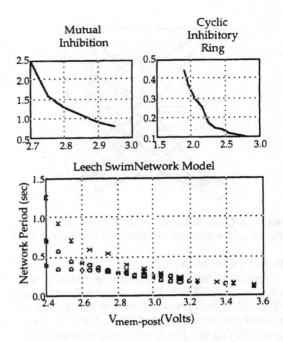

Figure 6-*Response of reciprocally and cyclically inhibited subnetworks and the overall swim network to variation in tresting membrane potential*

Figure 4 shows the results of variation of membrane potential time constant for a mutually inhibitory pair, a three-phase inhibitory ring, and several variations of the compete swim network. In all plots, value of the capacitor controlling time constant is the independent variable, and period of oscillation is the dependent variable. For all network types, the period of oscillation is shown to be roughly linearly affected by the membrane potential time constant. Reciprocally (mutually) inhibitory pairs show the most limited tolerance to membrane potential time constant, only supporting oscillation for a six-fold range. Cyclically inhibited rings show a much wider range, as does the overall network. In all tests, no upper limit was ever found in for membrane time constant that caused oscillations to cease.

Results from this test suggest that the network's tolerance to variation in membrane potential time constant is primarily attributable to its cyclic networks. In terms of overall cellular phase relationships, the network exhibited little variation from its nominal settings. It was interesting to note that two different network periods were interchangably observed for some values of capacitance. This was attributed to contention by the various embedded sub-networks for control of overall rhythm.

Figure 5 shows similar network behavior for variation in threshold time constant, also known

as refractory period. Note that refractory period duration has a roughly linear effect on the cyclic sub-oscillators, yet little coherent effect on the mutual network. The overall network shows two distinct operating regions. For capacitor values between 0.025 and 0.22 uF, the network acts as if it was paced primarily by mutually inhibitory forces. For capacitor values above this range, cyclic rhythms appear to predominate.

Figure 6 also shows influences of both oscillator types. Note that small variations in membrane potential cause drastic changes in the mutually inhibitory pair frequency. Once again, the left portion of the swim network graph seems to be oriented toward mutually inhibited control. In this case, the swim network remains stable beyond the range of both sub-network types. This is most likely a result of the overlap of the various sub-networks in the swim oscillator.

The facility for synaptic fatigue was needed for connections within mutually inhibitory pairs, but not in cyclic rings. Figure 7 shows that the time constant of synaptic fatigue exerts roughly linear influences on the period of mutually inhibitory pairs. For the overall network however, this influence was observed in some portion of the operating region, absent in other ranges. Under different biasing conditions, it was absent altogether.

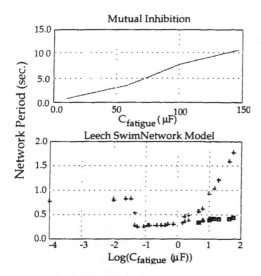

Figure 7-*Response of reciprocally inhibited subnetwork and the overall swim network to variation in synaptic fatigue time constant.*

DISCUSSION

In this study, a well-documented cellular oscillator was reconstructed in silicon, using a comprehensive VLSI-based neuromime. At its nominal settings, the network showed excellent correlation with its biological counterpart. In a series of parametric tests, it was observed that the network relies on the stability of its constituent sub-networks interchangably. These observations will be key to understanding the network's "design" for stability and reliability.

Although 34 sub-oscillators are identifiable in the structure of the network, few correlate well with its operating phases. Two of the six mutual oscillators showed phase differences within 10% of 180°. Four of the seven three-celled cyclic rings showed a similar correlation to network behavior. None of the five or seven-cell rings correlated, even to a levelof 50%. It is apparent that the network's rhythm is dominated by only a few of its embedded sub-networks. The role of the remaining connections will be assessed in subsequent tests, which will examine inputs from contralateral subunits, intersegmental connections, trigger inputs, and steering inputs.

The methodology of recreating live nerve circuits on a cell-by-cell, synapse-by-synapse basis was designed to be transferrable to other network types with application to motion, learning, computation, categorization, image processing, and nonlinear prediction. Not only will such networks serve as platforms for investigating the structure, connectivity, and management of neural networks, but the also offer a method for evaluating the duality of the relationship between the hardware and software of nerve circuitry.

Although electronic models of nerve cells have been available for over thirty years, only recently has broad access to VLSI technology afforded circuit comprehensiveness, reliability, economy, power efficiency, and noise immunity to enable investigating nerve circuits from living organisms in comprehensive detail.

ACKNOWLEDGEMENTS

Development of VLSI-based Neuromimes and oscillators has been supported by NSF grants MIP-9210945 and EID-9200039. The authors also wish to thank Dr. Friesen, who generously gave of his time and insights into the *hirudo* swim network.

REFERENCES

[1] Mahowald M, Douglas R *Silicon Neuron*, Nature, 354:6354-6356,1991.

[2] DeYong M R, Findley R L, and Fields C, *The Design, Fabrication, and Test of a New VLSI Hybrid Analog-Digital Neural Processing Element*   , IEEE Trans. on Neural Networks, 3: 3, 1992.

[3] Linares-Barranco B, Sanchez-Sinencio E, Rodriguez-Vazquez A., Huertas JL, *A CMOS Implementation of the FitzHugh-Nagurno Model*   , IEEE J. Solid-state Circuits, 26: 7,1991.

[4] Wolpert S, Tzanakou E, *An Integrated Circuit Realization of a Neuronal Model*. Proc. IEEE 12th NE Bioeng. Conf., Yale Univ., New Haven, CT, March 13-14, 1986.

[5] Mitchell C E, Friesen W O, *A Neuromime System for Neural Circuit Analysis*, Biol. Cybern. 40: 127-137, 1981.

[6] Harmon L D, *Studies with Artificial Neurons I: Properties and Functions of an Artificial Neuron*, Kybernetik, 1: 3, 1991.

[7] Friesen, W O, personal consultation,10/93.

[8] Wolpert S, *Modeling Neural Oscillations using VLSI-Based Neuromimes* , Proc. MIND Conf. on Oscillation in Neural Systems, The Univ. of Texas, Arlington, TX, May 5-7, 1994.

[9] Wolpert S, Laffely A. J, and Hilton J,   *Control of Prosthetic Motion using Neuron-Like Elements*, in *Case Studies in Medical Instrument Design*, H T Nagle and W J Tompkins, eds, IEEE Press, pp 139-148, 1991.

[10] French A S, Stein R B, *A Flexible Neuronal Analog Using Integrated Circuits*. IEEE Trans. on Biomed. Eng. 17: 248-253,1970.

[11] Friesen W O *Neuronal Control of Leech Swimming Movements* in J W Jacklet (ed) *Neuronal and Cellular Oscillators* Marcel-Dekker inc., pp 269-288, 1989.

Temporal Pattern Detection and Recognition using the Temporal Noisy Leaky Integrator neuron model with the Postsynaptic Delays trained using Hebbian learning

*Chris Christodoulou, Trevor G. Clarkson and John G. Taylor**

Department of Electronic and Electrical Engineering
*Deparment of Mathematics
King's College London
Strand, London WC2R 2LS
England, UK

ABSTRACT

In this paper we are presenting how a simple Hebbian-based learning rule can be used to train postsynaptic delays in the Temporal Noisy-Leaky Integrator (TNLI) neuron model, for temporal pattern detection and recognition. The TNLI is a biologically inspired, hardware realisable neuron model, which incorporates *time* at the neuron level. More specifically, it models the temporal summation of dendritic postsynaptic response currents, which have controlled delay and duration and the decay of the somatic potential due to its membrane leak. The structure and the theory of the model is described first and then the Hebbian-based learning approach is explained and some preliminary results are given. The results show that the TNLI can be trained to detect a temporal pattern, which can represent motion, a phoneme, a temporal sequence or any other dynamic pattern.

1. Introduction

It is quite important for artificial neuron models to be able to detect and recognise patterns with temporal context. Such an ability is important for tasks like motion detection, phoneme and subsequently speech recognition and certainly for many other dynamic time-dependent tasks. The Temporal Noisy-Leaky Integrator (TNLI) neuron model [2-4], exhibits temporal behaviour since it incorporates in its sructure temporal real neuron features. In addition, the TNLI models the stochastic neurotransmitter release by real neuron synapses, by using probabilistic RAMs (pRAMs) [5], [6] at each input. This close modelling of biological neuronal features makes the TNLI suitable for reproducing real neuron behaviour and for investigating real neuron responses [3], [4].

As shown elsewhere [2], the TNLI has been successfully used in a motion and velocity detection system. In that application no learning was applied to the system. In this paper we show a learning techique that enables the TNLI to be successfully trained to detect any arbitrary temporal pattern.

2. Architecture and Features of the TNLI neuron model

An analogue hardware outline of the TNLI using a pRAM at each input and a Hodgkin and Huxley equivalent circuit [8] for a leaky cell membrane, is shown in Fig. 1. In the TNLI, the pRAMs model the stochastic and spontaneous neurotransmitter release by the synapses of real neurons. They therefore enable generation of noise in the synaptic level of the TNLI which complies with the biological neuron, as opposed to other models in which noise is generated at the threshold level.

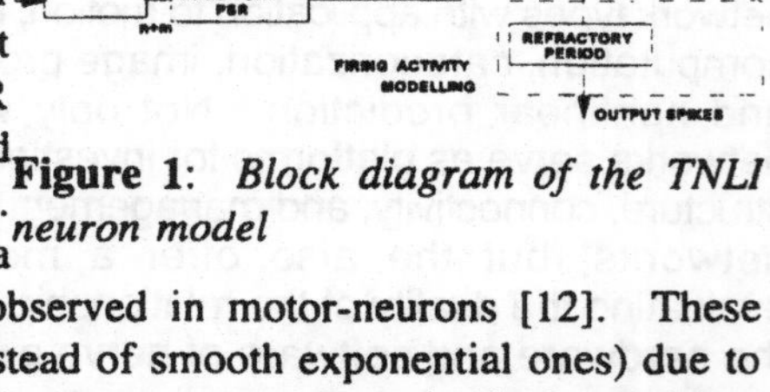

The postsynaptic response (PSR) generators shown in the diagram of Fig. 1, model the dendritic propagation of the postsynaptic current responses. For every spike generated by the pRAMs, the PSR generators produce postsynaptic current responses ($PSR_i(t)$) of controlled shapes, shown in Fig. 2, which can either be excitatory or inhibitory. Therefore, in the TNLI we have included the temporal function as a property of the spike propagation in the postsynaptic dendrite as observed in motor-neurons [12]. These particular ramp shapes were chosen for the postsynaptic responses (instead of smooth exponential ones) due to the fact that they can easily be implemented and because their defined parameters can be trained. In addition,

Figure 1: *Block diagram of the TNLI neuron model*

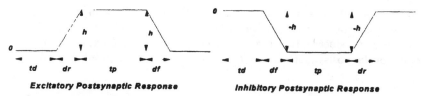

Figure 2: *Postsynaptic Response shapes used in the TNLI*

these shapes result in smoother responses after passing through the leaky integrator circuit, if long rise and fall times (d_r and d_f) are selected, compared to responses produced by rectangular shapes commonly used as inputs to neurons. This enables us to reproduce the smooth postsynaptic potentials produced in distal dendrites of real neurons [14] as seen at the soma. In other words, spatial effects can be incorporated in the TNLI by having either long or short responses corresponding to distal and proximal sites on the dendritic tree respectively. The postsynaptic current responses are then summed spatio-temporally and the total postsynaptic current response is fed into the RC circuit (Fig. 1). The capacitance C and the resistance R represent the soma and the leaky membrane of real neurons respectively and therefore this circuit models the decay that occurs in the somatic potential of the biological neuron due to its membrane leak. The capacitance C and the resistance R are fixed at a suitable value to give the leaky membrane time constant ($\tau = RC$). This intrinsic leakage of R is used to give additional temporality of biologically realistic form. If the potential of the capacitor exceeds a constant threshold (V_{th}), then the TNLI neuron fires. The potential of the capacitor can be either reset whenever the neuron fires (as in some other leaky integrator models, see for example [1], [9] and [11]), or not reset at all, while the accumulated current due to the temporal summation of the PSRs on each input is not reset (as in [13]). For the simulations described in this paper the potential of the capacitor is not reset. The TNLI neuron then waits for a refractory period (t_R) and fires again if the potential is above the threshold. Therefore, the maximum firing rate of the TNLI is given by $1/t_R$.

Further details about the digital hardware structure and the theoretical ananysis of the TNLI can be found elsewhere [2-4].

3. Hebbian Learning for training the Postsynaptic Delays

In order to see how the TNLI (Fig. 1) can be trained to detect and recognise a temporal pattern, a simple Hebbian-based learning rule was incorporated [7]. The rule aims in detecting the overlap between two postsynaptic response currents (PSRs, see Fig. 2) formed by any pair of spikes and increase or decrease that overlap by modifying the postsynaptic delays according to the relative difference between the maximum membrane potential at time t ($V_{out}(t)$) and the maximum membrane potential at time $t-1$ ($V_{out}(t-1)$) which is basically directly related to the neuron's output. In order for the temporal pattern to be detected, the TNLI neuron should fire at any point in time when the pattern passes in front of the neuron inputs. In other words, the maximum membrane potential should go above the threshold potential in order to enable the desired detection. If different neurons are trained to respond to patterns with different temporal configuration then a dynamic pattern recognition system can be formed.

Whenever two postsynaptic response currents produced by any two spikes of a temporal pattern overlap and the maximum membrane potential produced is below the threshold then we can strengthen the synapses by modifying the postsynaptic delays to increase the PSR overlap time and consequently increase the membrane potential. For simplicity and for avoiding multiparameter training, we train only on the postsynaptic delays (t_d) of each input and we keep the area under the PSRs constant. Using a simple Hebbian-based learning for any two spikes coming at inputs m and n with the first spike arriving at input m followed by a spike at input n with certain delay T_d we have:

$$t_{d(m)}(t+1) = t_{d(m)}(t) + \Delta t_{d(m)}(t) \tag{1}$$

and

$$t_{d(n)}(t+1) = t_{d(n)}(t) - \Delta t_{d(n)}(t) \tag{2}$$

where $t_{d(m)}(t)$ and $t_{d(n)}(t)$ are the values of the postsynaptic delays at inputs m and n respectively at time t. The terms $\Delta t_{d(m)}(t)$ and $\Delta t_{d(n)}(t)$ denote the adjustment applied to the postsynaptic delays at inputs m and n respectively at time t. These are given by:

$$\Delta t_{d(m)}(t) = \eta \times [V_{out}(t) - V_{out}(t-1)] \times in_m(t) - \alpha \times t_{d(m)}(t) \tag{3}$$

and

$$\Delta t_{d(n)}(t) = \eta' \times [V_{out}(t) - V_{out}(t-1)] \times in_n(t) - \alpha' \times t_{d(n)}(t) \tag{4}$$

where η and η' denote the learning rates with $\eta > \eta'$, α and α' are positive constants with $\alpha > \alpha'$, and $in_m(t)$ and $in_n(t)$ are the input frequencies of the spikes arriving at inputs m and n respectively at time t. The second factor of the equations (3) and (4) is introduced [10] so as to impose a limit in the exponential growth or reduction and subsequent saturation of the postsynaptic delay (t_d), which would be produced if the first term is used on its own.

In other words, the PSR overlap time is increased by increasing the postsynaptic delay of the spike arriving first at input m (eqn. 1) and decreasing the postsynaptic delay of the spike arriving second at input n (eqn. 2). If there is no overlap between the postsynaptic response currents, then no learning is performed.

For testing the above learning rule the TNLI was trained to detect and recognise a temporal pattern consisting of three spikes separated by a certain delay, each arriving at a different input. For this task only excitatory postsynaptic responses were used. Three inputs only were utilised $(I_0 - I_2)$ and the parameters chosen for the postsynaptic responses (Fig. 2) are:

$(PSR)_0$: $d_{r(0)}$ (rise time) = 5ms, $t_{p(0)}$ (peak period time) = 10ms, $h_{(0)}$ (postsynaptic peak current) = 60pA, $d_{f(0)}$ (fall time) = 20ms,

$(PSR)_1$: $d_{r(1)}$ = 5ms, $t_{p(1)}$ = 10ms, $h_{(1)}$ = 60pA, $d_{f(0)}$ = 15ms and

$(PSR)_2$: $d_{r(2)}$ = 5ms, $t_{p(2)}$ = 10ms, $h_{(2)}$ = 60pA, $d_{f(2)}$ = 10ms.

The values chosen for the postsynaptic peak current of each postsynaptic response ensure that one or two responses together cannot generate an output, but allow all three responses with the correct timings to do so. The three spikes were separated by a delay of 30ms. The postsynaptic delay times which are the trainable parameters, were initially chosen to be: $t_{d(0)}$ = 20ms, $t_{d(1)}$ = 10ms and $t_{d(2)}$ = 5 ms. The rest of the TNLI parameters are: t_R = 5ms, C (Membrane Capacitance) = 60pF, R (Membrane Leakage Resistance) = 166MΩ ($\tau = RC$ = 10ms) and V_{th} = 15mV. The simulation time step is 1ms and the pattern is presented to the neuron every 500ms. The input spikes were unaffected by the 1-pRAM action since the pRAM memory contents were set to `1' for an input spike and `0' for no spike and thus they fired for each input spike.

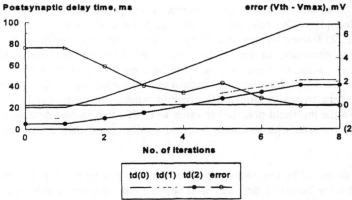

Figure 3: *Postsynaptic delay modification and error adjustment during training. Learning rates:* η = 0.3 & η' = 0.009

The learning rates chosen are η = 0.3 and η' = 0.009 and the constants: α = 0.008 and α' = 0.004. Figure 3 shows how the postsynaptic delays for the three input spikes are modified during training and the variation of the difference between the threshold potential and the maximum membrane potential expressed as: *error* = V_{th} - V_{max}. The neuron fires and in other words detects the pattern, when the *error* becomes negative. As it can be seen from the example of Fig. 3, the neuron learns to detect the pattern after the seventh iteration. Certainly, the number of iterations required for the neuron to learn to detect a temporal pattern, depends on the learning rates. This can be seen from Figure 4 which shows the same results as above with higher learning rates of η = 0.5 and η' = 0.08. The detection of the temporal pattern is now achieved at the fourth iteration.

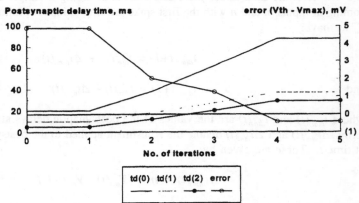

Figure 4: : *Postsynaptic delay modification and error adjustment during training. Learning rates:* η = 0.3 & η' = 0.009

Conclusion

In this paper we demonstrated that a Hebbian-based learning rule can be used to train the postsynaptic delays of the TNLI neuron so that a temporal pattern can be detected and recognised. The main target of the training is to achieve coincidence detection of the postsynaptic response currents so that the membrane potential is increased at a level above the threshold and enable thus the neuron to fire. Further work is   carried out in training a network of TNLI neurons in such a way that each neuron detects a different temporal pattern and therefore build for example a phoneme detector and a flexible motion and velocity detector. Results of this work will be presented at the conference.

ACKNOWLEDGMENT
This work is supported by a grant (Ref. Number F. 40Z) awarded by The Leverhulme Trust to King's College London (University of London).

REFERENCES
[1]   G. Bugmann, "Summation and multiplication: two distinct operation domains of leaky integrate-and-fire neurons," *Network-Computation in Neural Systems*, vol. 2, no. 4, pp. 489-509, 1991.
[2]   C. Christodoulou, G. Bugmann, J. G. Taylor and T. G. Clarkson, "An extension of the Temporal Noisy-Leaky Integrator neuron and its potential applications," *Proc. of the Int. Joint Conf. on Neural Networks*, Beijing, China, vol. III, pp. 165-170, Nov. 1992.
[3]   C. Christodoulou, G. Bugmann, T. G. Clarkson and J. G. Taylor J. G., "The Temporal Noisy-Leaky Integrator neuron with additional inhibitory inputs," *New Trends in Neural Computation*, Lecture Notes in Computer Science, ed. by J. Mira, J. Cabestany and A. Prieto, Berlin, Germany, Springer-Verlag, vol. 686, pp. 465-470, 1993.
[4]   C. Christodoulou, T. G. Clarkson, G. Bugmann and J. G. Taylor, "The stochastic firing behaviour of real neurons modelled by the Temporal Noisy-Leaky Integrator neuron model with partial reset," Submitted in the *IEEE Trans. on Biomedical Engineering*, June 1994.
[5]   T. G. Clarkson, C. K. Ng, D. Gorse and J. G. Taylor, J. G., "Learning Probabilistic RAM Nets using VLSI structures," *IEEE Trans. on Computers*, vol. 41, no. 12, pp. 1552-1561, Dec. 1992.
[6]   T. G. Clarkson, C. K. Ng and Y. Guan, "The pRAM: An adaptive VLSI chip," *IEEE Trans. on Neural Networks*, vol. 4, no. 3, pp. 408-412, May 1993.
[7]   D. Hebb, *Organisation of behaviour*. New York: John Wiley and Sons, 1949.
[8]   A. L. Hodgkin and A. F. Huxley, "A quantitative description of membrane current and its application to conduction and excitation in a nerve," *J. of Physiol.* (London), vol. 117, pp. 500-544, 1952.
[9]   B. W. Knight, "Dynamics of Encoding in a Population of Neurons," *J. of Gen. Physiol.*, vol. 59, pp. 734-766 1972.
[10]   T. Kohonen, *Self-Organisation and Associative Memory*, 2nd ed. Springer-Verlag, 1988.
[11]   L. Lapique, "Reserches quantatives sur l' excitation électrique des nerfs traitée comme une polarization," *J. Physiol. Pathol. Gen.*, vol. 9, pp. 620-635, 1907.
[12]   S. Redman, "Monosynaptic Transmission in the spinal cord," *News in Physiol. Sci.* vol 1, pp. 171-174, 1986.
[13]   J. P. Rospars and P. Lánský, "Stochastic model neuron without resetting of dendritic potential: application to the olfactory system," *Biol. Cybern.*, vol. 69, pp. 283-294, 1993.
[14]   G. M. Shepherd & C. Koch, "Appendix: Dendritic Electrotonus and Synaptic Integration," *The Synaptic Organisation of the Brain*, (3rd ed.), ed. G. M. Shepherd, Oxford Uni. Press, 1990, pp. 439-473.

A MIMD Environment for Multi-Level Neural Modeling

Jean-Marc Fellous

Center for Neural Engineering
University of Southern California
Los Angeles, CA 90089-2520
fellous@selforg.usc.edu

Abstract

This work describes a computer simulation environment (PARSIM) designed to make use of parallelism and asynchronicity to implement neural models which require the use of different coexisting levels of description. Neural pool, compartmental (single cell), multi-channels (membrane) and sub-cellular (cytoplasmic) levels are available. Each of the levels of description run independently from the others, at a their appropriate time scale, communicating with the other levels whenever necessary. As an example, we show models of levels of descriptions such as McCulloch-Pitts (leaky integrator), sets of interconnected cables (compartments), Hodgkin-Huxley dynamics (multi-channels) and levels relying on the modeling of intracellular calcium dynamics. Instances of these models can be arranged and interconnected to represent neurons at different levels of descriptions, depending on the nature of the data available and the modeling goals. This environment has been implemented on a 23 nodes transputer machine.

Introduction

Not all brain structures have been equally well studied experimentally. Data available for a particular system are often sparse and incomplete. Incomplete because of the specificity of the experimental conditions and sparse because, due to of the width of the spectrum of experimental research in neuroscience, ranging from the study of molecules (neurochemistry) to the study of brain function (cognitive neuroscience), it is rare to find results that cover that spectrum longitudinally. These aspects are reflected in modeling studies, to the extent that they are tightly coupled with experimental data. Some authors have proposed a classification of modeling studies into 2 categories depending on whether they emphasize the descriptions of the phenomena (mathematical modeling) of their overall function (computational modeling) (Dayan 1994). Such a classification will become less clear as neuroscientists gain more understanding of how structural and functional aspects of the brain will relate to each other. We will here base our differentiation of the levels of modeling on their time scale (which is not necessarily related to their spatial scale (Chauvet 1993b)), and their functional scope.

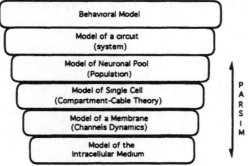

Figure 1: Model Hierarchy

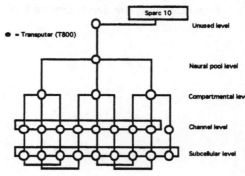

Figure 2: MIMD Topology

Most of the modeling literature addresses a problem at a given level of description (Fig 1). At the highest level, one finds behaviorally based models, which generally incorporate all the elements of the action-perception cycle. Such models rely usually on artificial intelligence techniques bearing more or less of neural analogies (see (Reeke and Sporns 1993) for a review). When restricted to the brain, large neural circuits or systems (Selverston 1993) are often modeled by abstract neurons which individually bear little resemblance to real neurons, but which together help highlight some computational properties which might be neural-like (connectionism). For obvious efficiency and robustness reasons, brain cells do not encode individually for a specific function. They are organized in more or less homogeneous populations (or pools). Neural pools (or average neurons) are modeled by McCulloch-Pitts neurons (leaky integrator). Cells of known morphological structures are modeled by compartments (cable equation). When membrane currents are known, researchers are inclined to use Hodgkin-Huxley models of channel dynamics. Finally when detailed information on intracellular phenomena are available researchers use ad-hoc models of chemical reactions or of the specific mechanisms at hand (ion pumping or buffering for example). If there is a substantial amount of models within each such levels of description, little has been attempted in terms of modeling across levels.

One can envision the need for the modeling of a circuit of cells for which partial information is available or for which not all information available is required to exhibit the desired phenomena.

Any of the level of modeling presented above brings about interesting results about the phenomena studied. However, much can be gained from the integration of such modeling studies. It is difficult to build a single model which simultaneously and gracefully addresses such a heterogeneous set of phenomena. Part of the difficulty resides in the fact that each of these levels of description require an analysis of variables at different time scales. It is of course possible to design a software that would handle such an heterogeneous model. One could possibly use a given level of description to model another, via some assumptions and simplifications. For example, (Zador & Koch 1994) have proposed a model of intracellular calcium diffusion, extrusion and buffering that uses the dynamics and terminology of cable equations. In general, it is likely however that, in order to be faithful to the data, a fair amount of randomness and artificial computational mechanisms would have to be introduced, rendering the implementation extremely model-dependent and difficult to develop, maintain and communicate to other modelers.

The work presented below is an attempt to use the inherent asynchronicity and parallelism of a multi-processor hardware to facilitate such an implementation. In this environment, each of the 4 lowest levels of the modeling hierarchy described above (Neural pools to intracellular) can be represented independently from each other and run on a separate processor, interrupted only by asynchronous events used to implement communication with the other levels, in a uniform fashion.

Method

The environment (named PARSIM) presented in this work uses a 23 nodes T800 Transputer parallel machine (MIMD), hosted by a Sparc 10 workstation, under the control of the Trollius operating system (Burns et al 1990). Nodes are arranged in a tree structure (Fig 2). Each communicate with their neighboring nodes using 4 independent 20 megabits per seconds links. The topology of the network is fixed but should ideally be model dependent, and should be chosen to minimize communication time between nodes running the same level of description (i.e. nodes modeling phenomena occurring at compatible time scales). We chose to run models of phenomena occurring at small time scales on nodes which present a high interconnectivity (bottom of the tree), while models requiring larger time scales are run on higher levels of the tree. Each node of the network can run several processes. However, at the present stage of this work, only one process per processor was allowed to run.

The design methodology required to implement a model in this environment is in many ways similar to the object oriented methodology. The environment consists in a set of independent executable (sub-models), able to run by themselves on any node of the system and of a host program interface controlling the system (X windows, menu oriented). Each sub-model can receive a certain number of messages that are buffered and processed sequentially, as they arrive. Messages are divided into 2 categories: System and Model messages. Each message is characterized by an identifier and parameters.

All submodels are able to process System messages such as parameter inspection or initialization. Model messages depend on the nature of the sub-model. For example, a leaky-integrator (LI) sub-model may send a FIRING_RATE message to a Hodgkin-Huxley (HH) sub-model in order to request for the current average firing rate of the cell it is modeling. At the reception of such a message, the HH sub-model would compute its average firing rate, and send a reply message to the LI sub-model.

Depending on the nature of the model, sub-models have to be chosen or designed. PARSIM provides 4 sub-models, each representing a different level of neural description. We will present them as separate sub-models. In practice, researchers have often blended two (rarely three) such levels in an ad hoc fashion, depending on the problem at hand.

Neural-Pool level

This level of description allows for the representation of a group of cells by a model of their average membrane potential at the axon hillock m(t) (measured in milli-volts) and firing rate F(t) (measured in spikes per seconds) (Arbib 1989). Their dynamics can be represented by the equations:

$$\tau \frac{dm(t)}{dt} = -m(t) + \sum_i W_i F_i(t) + h \quad \text{with} \quad F(t) = \sigma(m(t))$$

where τ and h are parameters representing the time constant and resting membrane potential of the pool, and where $\sigma()$ is a sigmoid function of chosen parameters. The F_i's represent the eventual inputs coming from other neurons, weighted by some constant factors (the W_i's). The F's are solely dependent on the membrane potential of the presynaptic neurons.

This modeling approach was offered in a variety of simulation tools such as NSL (Weitzenfeld & Arbib 1994). One can also interpret these quantities as average membrane potential and firing rate of a single neuron across a hypothetical sequence of identical simulations. This approach can be considered equivalent to the former one, via assumptions about the statistical independence of the neurons constituting the neural pool and of the sequence of the hypothetical simulations. This model is also known as the McCulloch-Pitts or leaky-integrator model. Typically, the time scale accounted for by such such models vary from several seconds to several minutes or hours. Models within this level are implemented as objects accepting the F_i's as input variables and outputting m, the membrane potential at the soma.

Single Neuron level

There are many cases for which a leaky integrator model is not sufficient. One may need to study the influence of the morphology of the cell on its physiological behavior. Therefore accounts for the morphology of the cell become necessary. This level of modeling is often referred to as compartmental modeling and relies on cable theory. The cell is decomposed into several cylindrical sections (compartments), each of given electrical properties. A compartment j laying between compartments j-1 and j+1 can then be modeled by the equation:

$$C_j \frac{dV_j}{dt} + Iion_j + Isyn = (V_{j-1} - V_j)G_{j-1,j} - (V_j - V_{j+1})G_{j,j+1}$$

where Iion, C and G are parameters representing the current leak, capacitance and intercompartment conductances of compartment j respectively. V_j is the membrane potential of the compartment. Isyn is the eventual current generated by a synaptic input onto compartment j. At this level of modeling, synaptic inputs are often represented as the product of a conductance and the current voltage (relative a constant voltage source Esyn). In contrast to the previous level, it is now made dependent on some presynaptic properties (Gsyn and Esyn) as well as on postsynaptic properties (V_j).

$$I_{syn} = G_{syn}(V_j - E_{syn})$$

This modeling approach has been used by a number of neural simulators such as SPICE (Segev et al 1989) or NEURON (Hines 1989). In principle, neurons can be modeled by any number of such compartments, depending on the nature of the phenomenon studied.

Models within this level are implemented as objects accepting V_i (i=/j) as inputs, and outputting V_j.

Dendritic (and axonic) potential changes are therefore decomposed into as many voltages as there are compartments. In essence, this level of description allows for a more detailed analysis of the nature of the inputs (outputs) on a neuron, by accounting for the locus of the inputs (outputs), which was not possible with the leaky integrator formulation. Typically, modeling studies use such models to study phenomena that present compartmental time scales which range from several hundreds of milliseconds to seconds.

Links with the previous level of modeling can then be derived. F can be computed on the basis of the potential at the soma with:

$$F = \sigma(m) \quad \text{with} \quad \tau \frac{dm}{dt} = -m(t) + \sum_b V_{soma}^b + \sum_i W_i F_i + h$$

where b indexes the compartmental dendritic branches of the neuron.

Membrane Level

Again, there are circumstances when the description of a compartment as an electrical cable becomes insufficient for the purpose of the modeling study. One might need to address issues related to simple channel dynamics such as the generation and propagation of an action potential for example. In such cases, models of the Na, K and Cl channels become necessary and require that attention be directed towards the currents traversing the membrane, rather than its mere overall potential.

Such models have been proposed on the basis of the seminal Hodgkin-Huxley studies of the squid giant axon. Compartment voltage is now made dependent on the flow of ions across the membrane, each modeled as an electrical current. For a given ion species M, the flow of ion is represented by the equations:

$$I_M = \overline{G}_M A_M^a H_M^i (V - E_M) \qquad \text{with} \qquad A_M = f(V,t) \text{ and } H_M = g(V,t)$$

where A and H are models of the activation and inactivation variables of the channel and E and G are parameters representing respectively the Nernst reversal potential of M and the peak conductance of the channel. a and i are constant integers.

The link with the upper level of modeling can be obtained through the computation of V (membrane potential of the compartment) using the currents with:

$$C\frac{dV}{dt} = -\sum_M I_M - Isyn \qquad \text{with} \qquad Isyn = \alpha(t)(V - E_{syn})$$

where Isyn is again the eventual current generated by a synaptic input onto the compartment. It is usually modeled as the product of the current voltage (relative to a reversal potential Esyn) and a time dependent conductance which follows a regular time course (alpha function) starting at the onset of the synaptic input. Simulators such as GENESIS (Bower & Beeman 1994) would provide an adequate framework for implementation at such a level. Typically, models using this formalism allow for the description of phenomena lasting few milliseconds. Models within this level accept the membrane potential and output the current IM of a specific ion species.

Sub-cellular level

Finally, one might need to relate channel dynamics to general cytoplasmic dynamics. Nernst potentials, for example, are known to depend on internal and external cellular concentrations, which for certain phenomena cannot be considered constant during the time of the simulation. It becomes necessary therefore to relate certain quantities used as parameters at the previous levels of modeling to more elementary sub-cellular quantities such as cytoplasmic ion concentration or chemical reactions for example. This level of modeling can take many forms depending on the problem at hand. We will simply illustrate it by taking the example of calcium dynamics.

So far, synaptic input has been modeled as a weighted sum of firing rate (neural-pool level), a current evolving proportionally to the membrane potential (compartmental level) or as a current evolving with the presynaptic membrane potential according to a predefined time dependent conductance (alpha function). It is known however that synaptic phenomena are tightly related to the flux of calcium in and out the cell. Calcium entry provokes the fusion of neurotransmitter filled vesicles onto the presynaptic membrane which then release their neurotransmitter content into the synaptic cleft. Ultimately, neurotransmitters will bind to postsynaptic site receptors and the later will finally initiate the post synaptic membrane changes (post-synaptic potentials, PSP) through ion fluxes (Isyn). It has been shown that in many simple cases, PSP can be related to the presynaptic flux of calcium by an equation of the type:

$$I_{syn} = C I_{Ca}^n$$

Where C and n are constants (Augustine et al 1985) (Yamada & Zucker 1992). This formulation requires the computation of the calcium current ICa.

Calcium dynamics involve many sub-cellular phenomena, not all well understood. Depending on the nature of the modeling problem at hand, mechanisms such as intracellular diffusion, buffering or pumping should be accounted for. In this work, and for illustration purposes, we simply modeled calcium dynamics by pumping (time constant τ) and constant intracellular diffusion and buffering expressed as a percentage (C) of the concentration of calcium entering the cell.

$$\frac{dCa_{in}}{dt} = -\frac{I_{Ca}}{2FVol} \qquad \text{and} \qquad \frac{dCa_{out}}{dt} = \frac{(Ca_{equil} - Ca_i)}{\tau} \qquad \text{with}$$

$$\frac{dCa_i}{dt} = \frac{dCa_{in}}{dt} + \frac{dCa_{out}}{dt} - C\frac{dCa_{in}}{dt}$$

where Cain and Caout are respectively the amount of calcium flowing in and out the cell. Cai is the internal concentration of calcium. Vol is the volume of the compartment, F is the Faraday constant (Yamada et al 1989).

Finally, Assuming that the external concentration of calcium Cao remains constant we have the Nernst potential and calcium current using:

$$E_{Ca} = const.Log(\frac{Ca_o}{Ca_i})$$

and we can compute the current with $\qquad I_{Ca} = \overline{G}_{Ca}A_{Ca}^a I_{Ca}^i (V - E_{Ca})$

These 2 variables can then be used by the upper level of modeling (membrane level). Typically, time scales for calcium dynamics range from hundreds of microseconds to milliseconds. Models within this level of description accept as inputs the concentrations of different ion species (inside and outside the cell) and output the contribution to the current of the ionic flux under consideration.

Results and Conclusion

We implemented the 4 levels (Fig 1) as separate executables, each able to run independently on any node of the Transputer system. We developed a X window interface able to access the transputer system (through Trollius calls) in a user friendly fashion (pop-up menus and mouse clicking). Commands such as tuning, probing, stimulating, lesioning, connecting are available through this interface.

Each level requires the integration of some variables. Due to the wide range of time scales, the precision of the integration algorithm should be carefully chosen. Each level can be modeled using any of the 4 following method of integration: Euler, Runge-Kutta 4th order, Runge-Kutta 5th order and Runge-Kutta 5th order with adaptive time step. All computations are done in double precision.

The higher order the method, the more time is spent in calculations, the further away is simulation time from real time. For example, it is often sufficient to use the Euler method at the neural-pool level. This allows for sub real time computations (1ms simulation time is equivalent to .3ms real time). Potentially, should only this level be used, and by running several (3-4) sub-models onto a single transputer, up to 70 neurons could be simulated real time. However, should Runge-Kutta 4th order be used, computations will become slower.

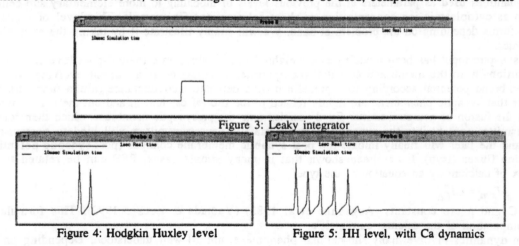

Figure 3: Leaky integrator

Figure 4: Hodgkin Huxley level   Figure 5: HH level, with Ca dynamics

Fig 3 shows the membrane potential of a leaky integrator neuron undergoing a 60msec stimulation (Euler method of integration), Fig 4 shows the membrane potential of a Hodgkin-Huxley neuron (Na, K and Cl channels) undergoing the same stimulation (Runge-Kutta 4th order integration), while Fig 5 shows the response of a Hodgkin-Huxley neuron with Calcium dynamics undergoing the same stimulation (using Runge-Kutta 5th order with adaptive time step). These 3 models have run simultaneously on 3 processors at their appropriate level (Fig 2), the stimulation occurring at approximately the same local (processor) time. One can note the difference of behavior of these 3 models, undergoing the same stimulation (same amplitude and duration). In this study we did not attempt to optimize the algorithms, nor the transputer topology. Significant improvements are expected, should such care be taken.

The work presented here is an attempt to provide an environment for the implementation of multi-level models. We have proposed a set of levels, following different dynamics. We have illustrated this implementation by showing an instance of modeling work which, depending on the level chosen, may yield different qualitative and quantitative results. The use of such an environment allows for a better understanding of the phenomena modeled, and a better choice of the level of modeling required. Other works have focused on theoretical aspects of multi-level modeling and provided mathematical frameworks (Chauvet 1993b) which root certain phenomena into their inherent multi-level nature. In particular, for a given system, integration across levels have been shown to highlight certain of its properties, such as non-locality (Chauvet 1993). It would be desirable, as future work, to bridge theory and implementation and find other modeling frameworks in which such an environment can be used.

Acknowledgments

We would like to thank Dr. C von der Malsburg for allowing us to use of Transputer System, and Dr. J. Liaw for numerous discussions.

References

(Arbib 1989)	Michael A. Arbib. The Metaphorical Brain 2. John Wiley & Sons Publishers.
(Augustine et al 1985)	George J. Augustine, Milton P. Charlton and Stephen J. Smith. Calcium entry and transmitter release at voltage-clamped nerve terminals of squid. J. Physiology 369:163-181.
(Bower & Beeman 1994)	James M. Bower and David Beeman. The book of GENESIS: Exploring Realistic neural models with the General Neural Simulation System. TELOS pubs.
(Burns et al 1990)	G.D. Burns, V.S. Dixit, R.B. Daoud and R.K. Machiraju. All about Trollius. OCCAM Users Group Newsletter, August 1990.
(Chauvet 1993)	Gilbert Chauvet. Non-locality in biological systems results from hierarchy: Application to the nervous system. Journal of Mathematical Biology, 31:475-486.
(Chauvet 1993b)	Gilbert Chauvet. Hierarchical functional organization of formal biological systems: A dynamical approach. III: The concept of non-locality leads to a field theory describing the dynamics at each level of organization of the (D-FBS) subsystem. Philosophical transactions of the Royal society of London, 339:463-481.
(Dayan 1994)	Peter Dayan. Computational Modeling. Current opinion in neurobiology, 4:212-217.
(Hines 1989)	Michael Hines. Neuron. International Journal of Biomedical computation, 24:55-68.
(Reeke & Sporns 1993)	George N. Reeke and Olaf Sporns. Behaviorally based modeling and computational approaches to neuroscience. Annual review of Neuroscience, 16:597-623.
(Segev et al 1989)	I Segev, J.W. Fleshman and R.E. Burke. Compartmental Models of Complex neurons. In Method in neural modeling. C. Koch and I Segev (Eds), pp 63-96 The MIT Press.
(Selverston 1993)	A.I. Selverston. Modeling of Neural Circuits: What have we learned? Annual Review of Neuroscience, 16:531-546.
(Weitzenfeld & Arbib 1994)	Alfredo Weitzenfeld, Michael A. Arbib. NSL: Neural Simulation Language. In Neural Networks Simulation Environments, J. Skrzypek (Ed), Kluwer Academic Press.
(Yamada et al 1989)	Yamada, Koch and Adams. Multiple channels and Calcium Dynamics. In Method in neural modeling. . C. Koch and I. Segev (Eds), pp 97-133 The MIT Press.
(Yamada & Zucker 1992)	W. Yamada and R.S. Zucker. Time course of transmitter release calculated from simulations of a calcium diffusion model. Biophysical Journal, 61(3):671-682.
(Zador & Koch 1994)	A. Zador and C. Koch. Linearized models of calcium dynamics: Formal equivalence to the cable equation. The journal of Neuroscience, 14(8):4705-4715.

Delayed Random Walk Models of Neural Information Processing

Toru Ohira

Sony Computer Science Laboratory
3-14-13 Higashi-gotanda,
Tokyo 141, Japan
ohira@csl.sony.co.jp
http://www.csl.sony.co.jp/person/ohira.html

Abstract

We present and compare two delayed random walk models of neural information processing. A delayed random walk is a random walk in which the transition probability depends on the position of the walker at a time τ in the past. The first model is of human neuro-muscular control for postural sway. The other model is for a stochastic single neuron which has a delayed self–exciting feedback. We study each model using computer simulation to examine its time–dependent and asymptotic stochastic behaviors. The similarities and differences between the two models are discussed as well as how they relate to empirical data.

1 Introduction

In biological neural information processing, fluctuations and time delays are commonly observed factors. Each factor is examined in theoretical studies of neural activities. For example, extensive applications of statistical physics have dealt with neural models with fluctuations (see, e.g., Hertz *et al.* 1991). For delays, there is a series of work using delay differential equations (see, e.g., Milton *et al.* 1989). Investigations considering these two factors at the same time, however, are rather limited (Longtin *et al.* 1990; Mackey and Nechaeva 1995).

The concept of a delayed random walk was recently proposed as a possible framework for theoretically studying dynamical systems with both fluctuations and delay (Ohira and Milton 1995; Ohira 1995). A delayed random walk is a random walk in which the transition probability depends on the position of the walker at some time in the past. In the above studies, delayed random walks are used to construct models of neural information processing. The first model is a delayed random walk with a single stochastically stable position for human posture control (Collins and De Luca 1993; Chow and Collins 1995) and give a good qualitative description of the two–point correlation function of experimental posture data. The other is a model stochastic single neuron with delayed self–exciting feedback using a delayed random walk with bistable positions. This model can be viewed as an extension with the delay from a different angle than that used in the previous study of a stochastic single neuron with self–exciting loop employing Langevin and Fokker–Planck equations (Ohira and Cowan 1995). The switching behavior of the model produced a histogram of multimodal peaks with exponentially decreasing height similar to those obtained from some interspike interval histograms of biological neurons (see, e.g., Siegel 1990).

We confine ourselves here to the numerical simulations and focus on comparing the statistical behavior of the root mean square positions of the walkers. The similarities and differences of the two models with respect to the above are discussed.

2 Delayed Random Walk Models

In this section, we give the formal definition of the two delayed random walk models.

Model with a Single Stochastically Stable Point

First, we formulate a delayed random walk with a single stochastically stable point. The position of the walker at time t is $X(t)$. Identify the origin of a one–dimensional random walk with the stable point ($X(0) = 0$)

when there is no delay and no noise and let the random walker take a step of unit length in unit time. The probability, $P(t)$, for the walker to take a step at time t to the right (positive direction) is given by

$$
\begin{aligned}
P(t) &= p && (X(t-\tau) > 0) \\
&= 0.5 && (X(t-\tau) = 0) \\
&= 1-p && (X(t-\tau) < 0)
\end{aligned}
\tag{1}
$$

where $0 < p < 1$. The origin is attractive without delay when $p < 0.5$.

Model with Two Stochastically Stable Points

We construct the model with two stochastically stable points by first defining the transition probability of the walker in such a way that movements in the direction of two stable points are more probable without delay, and then by extending the definition to incorporate the delay. We define the position of the walker at time t as $X(t)$ as before and the two stochastically stable points as being at $-a$ and a. We let the random walker start from the origin and take a step of unit length in unit time. The probability. $P(t)$, for the walker to take a step at time t to the right (positive direction) is given by

$$
\begin{aligned}
P(t) &= p && (X(t-\tau) > a) \\
&= 0.5 && (X(t-\tau) = a) \\
&= 1-p && (0 < X(t-\tau) < a) \\
&= 0.5 && (X(t-\tau) = 0) \\
&= p && (0 > X(t-\tau) > -a) \\
&= 0.5 && (X(t-\tau) = -a) \\
&= 1-p && (X(t-\tau) < -a)
\end{aligned}
\tag{2}
$$

where p is a constant $0 < p < 0.5$ making the two points $-a$ and a attractive when there is no delay ($\tau = 0$). We note that $p = 0.5$ corresponds to the case of an ordinary homogeneous random walk.

3   Statistical Behavior of the Model

In studying the statistical behavior of the delayed random walk model, we focus on the root mean square positions, σ.

Figures 1 and 2 show examples of the dynamics of the root mean square position as we increase the delay. Simulations are performed with a random walker starting from the origin. This is repeated 10,000 times for each set of parameters to compute the root mean square position.

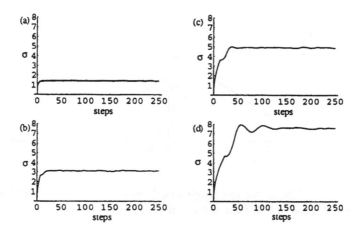

Figure 1: Dynamics of σ as we increase the delay for the single stable model. The value of parameters are $p = 0.25$, and (a)$\tau = 0$, (b)$\tau = 6$, (c)$\tau = 12$, and (d)$\tau = 21$.

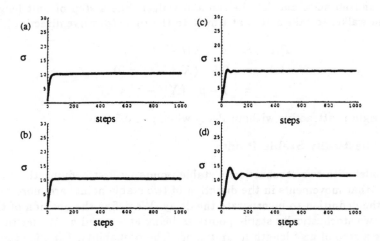

Figure 2: Dynamics of σ as we increase the delay for the bistable model. The value of parameters are $p = 0.3$, $a = 10$, and (a)$\tau = 0$, (b)$\tau = 5$, (c)$\tau = 10$, and (d)$\tau = 20$.

As the figures show, we have observed the damped oscillation for the dynamics of σ as it approaches a limiting value as we increased the delay. These oscillatory and non–oscillatory approaches to the limiting value are also seen for the two–point correlation functions for the model with a single stable point. Qualitatively similar dynamics are seen with respect to the center–of–pressure trajectories of human postural controls, and comparisons have been made (Ohira and Milton 1995).

A point of interest of the second model, which we briefly mention here, is its switching behavior between the regions around two stable points. We look at the time interval between two crossings of the origin from negative to positive direction, and construct a histogram of frequency of crossings against the time intervals. The histogram shows multimodal peaks at suitably chosen parameters (Ohira 1995). This type of interspike interval histogram with exponentially decreasing peak height is observed in activities of biological neurons with oscillating inputs. The model proposed previously (Longtin et al. 1991) successfully produced this type of histogram with an explicit oscillating input. The result from our model indicates that self–exciting feedback with delay can generate a rhythmic firing activity on its own. Investigations of this behavior of the model in relation to rythmic neural activities are left for the future.

Next, we have seen how the limiting values of σ, denoted by σ_s, depend on the delay, and obtained the results shown in Figures 3 and 4. The model with the single stable point shows an approximately linear increase of σ_s with increasing τ. For the model with two stable points, however, the relationship is different. For small delay, the σ_s increases slowly in approximately a linear function of τ from the stable point value of a. With sufficiently large delay, there is a kink on the plots and σ_s increases more quickly but again linearly.

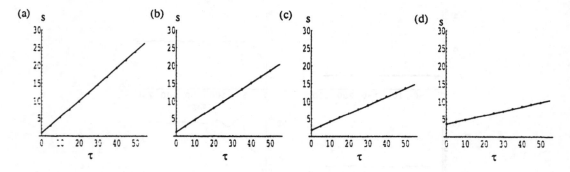

Figure 3: Plot of σ_s as a function of delay for the single stable model. The solid line is a fitted line to the data. Parameter values are (a)$p = 0.1$, (b)$p = 0.2$, (c)$p = 0.3$, and (d)$p = 0.4$.

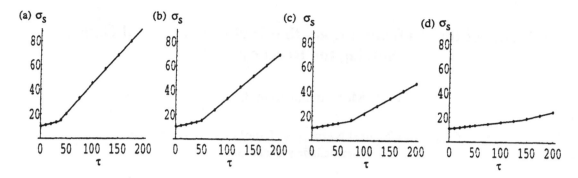

Figure 4: Plot of σ_s as a function of delay for the bistable model. The solid lines are two fitted lines to the data. Parameter values are $a = 10$, and (a)$p = 0.1$, (b)$p = 0.2$, (c)$p = 0.3$, and (d)$p = 0.4$.

4 Discussion

The qualitative behaviors of the two models show both similarities and differences. Both models have shown a damped oscillation in the dynamics of σ, and the longer delay increases the width of the peaks of the probability distribution around the stable points. The linear increase of σ_s with respect to τ is common to both, but, in the case of the bistable model the increase is approximately piecewise linear. For the single stable point model we have obtained analytical results for small τ. Analytical study of the bistable model, particularly with respect to the piecewise linear properties shown in Figure 3, is currently under investigation.

Together with the issue of better analytical understanding of these models, further comparison with experimental data needs to be explored. Whether the delayed random walk model here or its refinement can be a useful analytical tool for experimental results is yet to be determined.

Acknowledgments

I would like to thank professors J.D. Cowan and J.G. Milton for their helpful comments.

References

Chow, C. C. and Collins, J. J. 1995. to appear in *Phys. Rev. E*

Collins, J. J. and DeLuca, C. J. 1993. *Exp. Brain Res.*, **95**, pp.308.

Hertz, J., Krogh, A., and Palmer, R. G. 1991. *Introduction to the Theory of Neural Computation*. Addison-Wesley, Redwood City, CA.

Longtin, A., Milton, J. G., Bos, J., and Mackey, M. C. 1990. *Phys. Rev. E*, **41**, pp. 6992.

Longtin, A., Bulsara, A., and Moss, F. 1991. *Phys. Rev. Lett.*, **67**, pp. 656.

Mackey, M. C., and Nechaeva, I. C. 1995. *J. Dynam. Diff. Eqns.* **6**, pp. 395.

Milton, J. G., Longtin, A.. Beuter, A., Mackey, M. C., and Glass, L. 1989. *J. theor. Biol.*, **138**. pp. 129.

Ohira, T. and Cowan. J. D. 1995. *Neural Computation*, **7**, pp. 518. Also Available as Sony Computer Science Laboratoy Technical Report TR-94-27.

Ohira. T. and Milton, J. G. 1995 (to appear in *Phys. Rev. E*). Also Available as Sony Computer Science Laboratoy Technical Report TR-94-026.

Ohira, T. 1995 (submitted). Also Available as Sony Computer Science Laboratoy Technical Report TR-95-009.

Siegel, R. M. 1990. *Physica*, **42D**, pp. 385.

A Model of the Prefrontal Loop that Includes the Basal Ganglia in Solving the Recency Task.

Oury Monchi and John. G. Taylor

Centre for Neural Networks, King's College London
omonchi@mth.kcl.ac.uk

Abstract

This paper presents a recurrent neural network model which solves the recency task. To the best of our knowledge, it is the first time that this type of model is developed from a neuroanatomical perspective. The results of various types of degredations of transmission lead to a variety of deficits in performance similar to those observed in patients of various ages and suffering from a range of frontal lobe diseases and loss. This gives support to the model and generates a basis for more detailed correlation of neural degradations with symptoms. In addition, the model provides a starting point for further neuroanatomical specificity and some physiological criteria.

Introduction

The recency task is a frontal attentional task that has been devised to analyse some of the temporal deficits of frontal patients since the 1970's and that has been more recently reviewed in [1]. Typically a subject is shown a number of cards each containing 2 images (or words) followed by a card containing 2 images previously seen together with a question mark. The subject has to report which of the 2 images on the testing was last seen. This task involves what has been termed in [2] "the internal representation of context". In order to solve the task the context in question has to be retained for a period of time of the order of 10 seconds. This has been associated with a type of memory named "active memory" in [3] which is to be distinguished from short-term-memory which involves retention of the order of 2 seconds [4]. Neurons have been reported in the frontal lobe (FL) as being involved in active memory (see for instances [3], [5]). Parts of the basal ganglia (BG) and the thalamus (TH) are also playing a role in the building of active memory [3], [4].

The anatomical areas associated with the recency task are one of the frontal or basal ganglia loops reported for instance in [6]. They typically involve two pathways from the FL via the striatum to internal globus pallidus resulting in inhibition and an inhibitory connection from the latter to the TH resulting in disinhibition. Among the transmitters involved from the FL to the TH via the BG are glutamate, GABA and dopamine. There are reciprocal excitatory connections between TH and FL involving glutamate. There are cortico-cortical projections within the FL which involve glutamate. The loops we are interested in are the prefrontal loop which contains the dorsolateral prefrontal cortex involved in divided attention, temporal and cognitive tasks and the limbic loop containing the orbifrontal cortex possibly involved in autobiographic memory; both loops including the mediodorsal thalamus and the BG.

1. The model

1.1 Architecture and learning

In order to investigate how the recency task is achieved, more neuranatomical constraints were added to the model developed in [7]. The new network has an input layer consisting of 8 neurons coding for the images in a card together with 1 neuron indicating whether a card is a testing one or not. These specific type neurons are supposed to be found somewhere in posterior association cortex. The next layer is a lateral inhibitory, self excitatory layer which is meant to lie in the striatum and that will be denoted by Str. It contains 18 neurons and receives all to all connections from the input layer and outputs to another lateral inhibitory, self excitatory layer containing 18 neurons referred to as Gpi that represents part of the internal globus pallidus. The connections from Str to Gpi are one to one, fixed and inhibitory. The Gpi projects to a hidden layer containing 18 neurons denoted Th which is representing neurons in the thalamus. Each neuron in this layer inhibits its closest neighbour from each side. The connections from Gpi to Th are also one to one, fixed and inhibitory. The network contains 3 context layers denoted respectively FL1, FL2, FL3 each containing 18 neurons. All to all connections occur from FL1 to Th, FL2 to Th, FL3 to Th. Finally there is an output layer consisting of 8 neurons that are meant to be the homologues of the input layer image coding neurons in the frontal lobe. The output layer is denoted Flout and receives all to all connections from Th and outputs back to Str via all to all connections. Back propagation learning occurs from the input layer to Str, from FL1 to Th, FL2 to Th, FL3 to Th, Th to Flout and from Flout to Str. Upon the presentation of each input the output of FL2 is copied onto FL3, the output of FL1 onto FL2, and the output of Th onto FL1.

1.2 Training and testing.

Each input consisted of two image neurons set to 1 and the test neuron set to 0 if the card represented was not a testing card and was set to 1 if it was. The network was trained to fire 1 in the 2 neurons in FLout corresponding to the 2 images of the card being presented and 0 on all the other output neurons if the input card was not a testing one. Upon the presentation of a testing card the network was trained to output 1 only on the neuron in FLout corresponding to the image of the testing card that was last presented in the preceding non testing card and fire 0 on all other Flout neurons. In order to investigate the temporal capabilities of the model, it was tested on what has been defined in [7] as a hard task. Let us assume that the images in the cards are presented vertically, so we can refer to respectively the bottom image and the top image of a card. A hard task consists of a set of 2 sequences containing the same testing card. The first input of the first sequence has the same bottom image as the testing card and the second card of the first sequence has the same top image as the testing card, this is followed by a number of cards not containing any of the 2 images of the test card so that the target output after the presentation of the sequence and upon the presentation of the test card is 1 for the neuron corresponding to the top image of the test card in Flout. The second sequence is the same as the first except that the first and second cards are inverted. The expected output of the testing card after the presentation of the second sequence is therefore 1 for the neuron coding for the bottom image in Flout. One is interested in the maximum length of the sequences for which the network can learn that task. A size n hard task means that each of the 2 sequences contains n-1 non test cards and that each is followed by the testing card. The network was able to learn perfectly up to a size 12 hard task; it could not do so from a size 13 onwards hard task.

The network was then trained on the set of 10 size 8 sequences used in [7]. 2 of the sequences of this set corresponds to a size 8 hard task and only 5 test cards were used in order to insure that the output of test cards depended on the sequence preceding it. However this training set proved too long for this architecture; the network could not learn it since it was overloaded. The longest training set that could be learned perfectly by this network was a set of 5 size 8 sequences with 2 test cards. 2 of the sequences corresponded to a size 8 hard task with each of the 2 sequences being followed by the first test card. The other 3 sequences were each followed by the remaining test card and each contained exactly one card having the bottom image of the test card and exactly one card having the top image of the test card. In all of those 3 sequences "the most recent image seen previously upon testing" occurred after the second input of the sequence. In 2 of those 3 sequences the card containing the bottom image of the test card appeared before the card containing the top image of the test card and in the remaining sequence the reverse occurred. The parameters used were as follows. The self-excitatory weight for each neuron of both the Str and Gpi was set to 0.1. Each neuron of the Str and the Gpi inhibited the 10 nearest neurons on each side if they actually existed (the maximum distance between 2 neurons within each of these 2 layers being 17). All lateral inhibitory weights were set to -1. The fixed one to one inhibitory weights between the Str and Gpi and between the Gpi and Th were all set to -5. The lateral inhibitory weights occurring between each of the neurons of the Th and their nearest neighbour from each side were set to -1.

2. Neurobiological and psychological interpretation of the model.
2.1 Neurobiological considerations.

The neurons in Flout are meant to represent modality specific neurons of the frontal lobe that are thought to be of lower order in the cognitive sense (see[8]) than the ones represented by FL1, FL2,

FL3. The latter are thought to be situated in the dorsolateral prefrontal and the orbitofrontal cortex and are assumed to be used in all context dependent tasks such as the Wisconsin Card Sorting Task, the self ordering task, and not just the recency task. We suggest that they might be dealing with the overall strategy needed to solve those tasks.

The long range lateral inhibition occurring in Str and Gpi in the model could represent the overall effects of the principal spiny neurons and their long range actions reported in the neostriatum and the globus pallidus in [9]. The self-excitatory connections occurring in these 2 layers of the model could account for some of the temporal properties of those principal neurons.

The inhibitory connections occurring in the model between Str and Gpi and between Gpi and Th are there to represent the overall dishinibitory effect of the direct pathway of the basal ganglia. This occurs from the GABA and substance P connections from the striatum to the internal globus pallidus and the GABA connections from the latter to the thalamus.

The nearest neighbour inhibitory connections occurring in the Th layer of the model could represent the effect of the short range interneurons reported in [10] to be present in mediodorsal thalamus.

Interestingly when the weights between FL1 and Th, FL2 and Th, FL3 and Th, Th and Flout, Flout and Str were randomised between 0 and 1 before learning the network had better chance of converging when using the 5 size 8 sequences training set than when randomising them between -1 and 1. This would be consistent with the fact that these weights are situated on wires representing excitatory glutamate connections. However the network was not able to learn the task without letting a significant proportion of those weights becoming negative during and after learning. It is possible that some amount of inhibition actually occurs between these anatomical areas of the brain.

The fact that this model became overloaded when presented with the 10 sequence training set that the model in [7], which did not contain the Str and Gpi layers, could learn is possibly an indication that the basal ganglia has some control over the amount of information that can reach the mediodorsal thalamus from posterior associative cortex.

2.2 Lesioning and interpretations.

The evaluation of the lesioning results was based mainly on the response of the network upon the presentation of the testing cards.

No degradation in performance occurred when the self-excitatory weights in Str were augmented during testing only. As the self-excitatory weights of the Gpi are augmented from a value of 5 to a value of 10 this gives rise to a perseveration type of strategy that is often observed in frontal patients. This pattern of behaviour gets more pronounced as the values of these weights augments.

When the value of the self-excitatory weights of both the Str and Gpi reach 2.5 and over during testing only, then the network tends to output similar values for both images in the testing cards and also, sometimes, fires strongly on the images of the wrong testing card. This is reminiscent of the lack of inhibitory control that frontal patients have over past irrelevant input or responses and their resulting undecidability.

When the lateral inhibition distance of the Gpi is reduced towards inhibiting just each neuron's neighbour on each side during testing only, then the network tends to fire towards a high value for the wrong image of the test card and a low value for the right image on the testing card. The same type of behaviour occurs as the lateral inhibition distance of both the Str and the Gpi is reduced towards 1 on both side of each neuron during testing only. This could be similar to the cognitive deficits observed in Huntingdon's disease as the loss of striatal neurons occurs.

When the inhibitory value of weights between Str and Gpi is reduced to -1 during testing only, the network always fire on both images of the testing card corresponding to the hard task irrespective of the testing card being presented. This perseveration behaviour could also result from striatal degradation.

When the inhibitory value of weights between Gpi and Th is reduced to -1 during testing only the network starts to fire on images that are not present of either of the testing cards as well as firing on the wrong image of the testing card being presented. This type of behaviour also occurs when the value of the weights between from Str to Gpi and from Gpi to Th is reduced to -1. This is reminiscent of the hyperreflexive orienting of attention or lack of latent inhibition reported in schizophrenics and Parkinson's disease patients. This latter effect is thought to arise from a basal ganglia deficit.

Following the method of [2] the gain of neurons in various layers was reduced in order to model transmitter deregulation.

Reducing the gain of the neurons in Str during testing did not affect performance up until values below 0.1. The network could learn the 5 sequence task with gain as low as 0.25 in the Str; below that value the network did not converge anymore.

As the gain of the neurons in Gpi was reduced below 0.3 during testing only, all of the neurons in Flout fired towards 0. The same pattern of behaviour occurred when the gain of the neurons of both Str and Gpi was reduced below 0.45. This is reminiscent of the perseveration and undecidability syndrome of frontal lobe patients.

As the gain of the neurons in the Gpi was set below 0.8 during training the network did not converge anymore.

As the gain of the neurons in Th were reduced below 0.4 during testing only, all the neurons in Flout tended to fire towards 0. If however, following this test, the network carries on learning with the gain in Th remaining changed, the network will converge again for the reduced value of the gain. That is, upon testing, it will perform perfectly for the reduced value of the gains in Th, but if the gain is set back to 1 again the performance upon testing breaks down. This phenomenon occurs for gains reduced as low as 0.2 in the neurons of the Th. This could account for some cases of recovery, especially in young patients where the neurons plasticity might be great enough to cope with a possible deregulation of neurotransmitters.

Similarly to the result found in [7], changing the gain to any value in the neurons of FL1, FL2, FL3 separately or together, during testing only, does not affect performance. However adding sufficient noise to the output of the neurons of each of them or to one of them during testing does brake down performance.

Conclusion:

The recurrent neural network presented here is suggested as bringing models of such type for the first time closer to neuroanatomical reality. The results of various types of degradations of transmission lead to a variety of deficits in performance similar to those observed in patients of various ages and suffering from a range of frontal lobe diseases and loss. This gives support to the extended model, at the same time providing a test-bed for more detailed correlation of neural degradations with symptoms. Even more, the models gives an initial version which requires further extension.

One amplification of the model may be achieved by inclusion of more detail of the neuroanatomy. Thus only the main nuclei of the basal ganglia have been included; further addition of related nuclei (the sub-talamic nucleus, the substantia nigra pars compacta, etc.) and more detailed specifications of wiring diagrams is possible. This could also be done for the dorso-lateral prefrontal cortex and the orbital frontal cortex where we suggested neurons responsible for the overall strategy of context-dependent delayed memory and attentional tasks are situated.

A further source of extension is that of learning laws and neuronal action. The use of back-propagation is only to achieve the required functionality. Degradation of trained networks may lead, using Hebbian or reinforcement learning to different deficits than if back-propagation learning were used. Moreover, spiky effects of neuronal activity may lead to some modification of the above results. These and other features will be explored elsewhere.

References

[1] Milner, B., McAndrews, M. P., Leonard G. (1990), Cold Spring Harbor Symposia on Quantitative Biology, vol. LV, pp: 987-994.

[2] Cohen, J. D. and Servan-Schreiber, D. (1992), Psychological Review, vol. 99, No.1, pp: 45-77.

[3] Fuster, J. M. (1993), Current Opinion in Neurobiology, vol. 3, pp:160-165.

[4] Bappi, R., Bugmann, G., Levine, D. and Taylor, J. G. (1995). Internal Research Report.

[5] Baronne, P. and Joseph J-P. (1989), Experimental Brain Research, vol.78, pp: 447-464.

[6] Alexander, G. E., Crutcher, M. D. (1990), Trends in Neuroscience, vol. 13, No.7, pp: 266-271.

[7] Monchi, O. and Taylor, J. G. (1995), submitted to I.C.A.N.N.'95.

[8] Knight, R.T. and Grabowecky, M. (1995), in *The Cognitive Neurosciences* MIT press.pp:1357-70.

[9] Wilson, C. J. (1990), in *The synaptic Organisation of the brain*. O.U.P. pp: 278-316.

[10] Jones, E. G. (1981), International Review of Physiology. vol. 23, pp:173- 245.

Computational Modelling of Visual Similarity Effects on Object Categorisation and Naming: A Study of Face Learning

Toby J. Lloyd-Jones[1], Glyn W. Humphreys[2] and Noellie Brockdorff[2]

1. Cognitive Neuroscience Research Centre, Department of Psychology, University of Kent, Canterbury, Kent CT2 7LZ, U.K. Email: T.J.LloydJones@ukc.ac.uk. Tel: +441227 827611
2. Cognitive Science Research Centre, School of Psychology, University of Birmingham, Edgbaston, Birmingham B15 2TT, U.K.

Abstract

We report a series of experiments which investigate the effects of visual similarity on naming and categorising schematic faces. Three categories of faces were constructed where each face was composed of five binary dimensions (e.g. eyes: black or white; nose: round or triangular). Categories were constructed to be either 'visually similar' or 'visually dissimilar' within category, whilst maintaining across category visual dissimilarity. Subjects were asked either to learn numbers specific to each face (identity learning) or to learn to categorise one set of faces as belonging to a separate category from the remaining faces (category learning). For visually dissimilar faces, number association learning was faster and more accurate than for visually similar faces. For categorisation, the opposite result was found; for visually dissimilar faces, category learning was slower and less accurate than for visually similar faces. These results were modelled using feedforward, interactive activation and competition (IAC), and interactive activation and competition with learning (IACL) parallel distributed processing models of object identification and categorisation. We discuss the implications of the results for models of object processing and their relation to multidimensional scaling approaches to category and identification learning (e.g. Nosofsky, 1986).

Introduction

Accounts of visual object and face processing have stressed the role that visual similarity between exemplars plays in the recognition process. For example, in studies of object processing, Humphreys, Riddoch and Quinlan (1988) reported that living items (e.g. animals, fruit and vegetables) take longer to name than artefacts (e.g. clothing, furniture and tools). They attributed this naming advantage for artefacts to those items belonging to categories with visually dissimilar exemplars, whereas exemplars from living categories tend to be visually similar (e.g. having similar global shapes and parts in common). Humphreys et al. proposed that there is competition between objects from 'visually similar' categories, which slows down access to individual representations relative to when categories have visually dissimilar exemplars. In contrast to this, visual similarity between category exemplars may facilitate responses that are based on information computed across the category, such as super-ordinate categorisation. Consistent with this, objects from living categories are typically categorised faster than artefacts.

Similar results have been found also for face processing. In tasks requiring either recognition memory for previously shown faces, recognition of familiar faces, or face familiarity decisions (e.g. Valentine & Bruce, 1986), faces that are visually distinctive (i.e. visually dissimilar from their perceptual neighbours) are advantaged relative to those that are visually more typical (and hence more similar to their perceptual neighbours). In contrast, in tasks requiring only that intact faces are discriminated from jumbled ones, typical faces are advantaged relative to distinctive faces. These results can be linked to the work on object processing if it is assumed that tasks such as recognition memory for unfamiliar faces, familiar face recognition and face familiarity decisions all require access to individual stored face representations, whereas discriminations between real and jumbled faces can be based on activity across sets of face representations. For the former tasks, within-category visual similarity is detrimental, as it is for object naming, where there needs to be access to individual stored representations. Within-category similarity is helpful only when it correlates with the category-level responses (e.g. super-ordinate categorisation).

However, although the data suggest that within-category visual similarity plays a major role in object processing, previous experiments are not without their problems. In particular, estimates of within-category visual similarity have been based either on ratings (e.g. of facial distinctiveness, or of the number of parts shared between category members) or on global measures of visual similarity (e.g. the percentage of shared contours across a normalised set of category members; see Humphreys et al. 1988). These measures also commonly correlate with other factors, such as the semantic similarity between category members (at least with objects) or the familiarity of typical relative to distinctive faces. With such stimuli it is difficult to show that variations in visual similarity within categories is sufficient to generate the contrasting pattern of results, since any effects may at least in part be due to the co-varying factors. These problems may be overcome to some degree by using artificial stimuli, where variations in visual similarity can be controlled and other co-varying factors (e.g. semantic similarity) can be eliminated. The present study aimed to do this, by studying human learning of sets of schematic face stimuli that varied in their degree of within-category visual similarity. In Experiment 1, subjects were set to learn either general category-level responses to the stimuli or individual responses to particular faces. We proposed that visual similarity between exemplars within a category is sufficient to generate a cross-over interaction across identification and categorisation tasks, consistent with the object and face processing literature. High within-category similarity should facilitate category learning, but disrupt identity learning. In Experiments 2-4 we showed how these results can be captured naturally by connectionist models of human learning and object processing, including ones which specifically attempt to match the architecture of the human object processing system.

The present experiments, on the learning of schematic faces, resemble many others in the literature on category learning (e.g. Nosofsky, 1986,). Nosofsky, in particular, has argued that category and identity learning can be determined by similarity relationships between the stimuli to-be-learned. These effects have been modelled using nonmetric multidimensional scaling (MDS) procedures. In MDS models, similarity relations between entities are represented in terms of points in a dimensionallyorganised metric space. Similarity judgements, confusion matrices, joint probabilities and other measures of pairwise-similarity between stimuli can serve as inputs to the MDS routine, which produces a geometric model of the data with each stimulus represented as a point in n-dimensional space. The distance between the points in space is inversely related to the pairwisesimilarity between objects.

Within this approach, it is assumed that subjects store individual category exemplars in memory, and that categorisation and identification responses are based on the similarity of a target object to other stored exemplars. Identification responses are based on a measure of the absolute similarity between the target and the memory representation associated with the response, relative to the summed similarity between the target and all other memory representations. Categorisation responses are based on a measure of the similarity of the target to all stimuli within one category relative to the similarity of the target to all stimuli within the other category. In addition to this, Nosofsky has proposed that subjects differentially distribute attention over the psychological dimensions so as to maximise performance. The effect of this differential attention weighting is to alter the similarity relationships across identification and categorisation tasks. For example, to optimise categorisation, subjects may attend to a dimension that unites stimuli within one category and that distinguishes them from stimuli in other categories.

Nosofsky's work has shown how categorisation and identification accuracy for individual stimuli varies as a function of (1) similarity relative to other exemplars (for identification) and (2) within-relative to betweencategory similarity (for categorisation). However, the work has not shown how identification and categorisation vary across categories of item (rather than individual items), and whether variations in within-category visual similarity are sufficient to produce the patterns of performance for 'visually similar' and 'visually dissimilar' categories across identification and categorisation tasks observed with human subjects. This was tested in the present study.

Results

Evidence from both human subjects and two different connectionist model architectures (a feedforward three-layer network, an IAC model, and an IAC model with learning, using a modified Hebbian update function; see Burton 1994) converges on the same results: (1) learning semantic categories of objects is easier than learning to associate names to objects and (2) high visual similarity between category exemplars aids category learning but hinders identity learning. For visually similar groups of schematic faces, category learning is easier but learning to associate a name to an individual face is more difficult than for a visually dissimilar group of faces. The modelling results endorse the proposed theoretical explanation for this category difference. In the present simulations the effects of visual similarity can be attributed to co-activation of a wider range of units, from the same group, for visually similar faces. Since similar input units feed into the same semantic unit, the co-activation of input units facilitates semantic classification. In contrast, for identification, the co-activation of input units means that a corresponding number of output units are co-activated providing more competition to the eventual winning Name unit. Within the IAC framework, the more competing units that are active, the longer it takes a particular unit to emerge as overall winner; hence identification takes longer for visually similar categories of faces.

Conclusions

The present research has shown that variations in within-category visual similarity are sufficient to generate opposite patterns of results in human category and identity learning. This mirrors results in the literature on both object and face processing, although of course it does not show that variations in within-category similarity necessarily cause the effects with objects and faces. The IAC model further emphasises that the effects of within-category visual similarity vary as a function of the differentiation required to complete a given task successfully. Identification requires differentiation between category members and so is impaired by high levels of visual similarity between category members. Categorisation requires detection of common features within a category and so is facilitated by within-category sharing of features. The idea of within-category differentiation can be used to account for a variety of other results on object processing, including the effects of surface detail and effects of priming (e.g. Lloyd-Jones & Humphreys, submitted). We suggest that the present data are a natural consequence of dynamic information processing systems, such as the IAC model simulated here, in which processing between levels of representation is not discrete but operates continuously. In such continuous processing systems, competition between representations at one level (e.g. to establish a semantic representation) is fed-forward to influence subsequent response levels (e.g. for naming). Whether partial information fed-forward from one processing stage to another is beneficial or detrimental depends on whether the response requires individuating information. When it does not require such information, partial information is beneficial. However, when individuating information is required, partial information can impair performance since it can prime competing representations.

Showing that IAC models can capture the human data, and that this holds when learning is introduced, demonstrates the generality of the phenomena, and provides an existence proof that variations in physical similarity are sufficient to determine some category effects in object recognition performance.

References

Burton, A.M. (1994). "Learning new faces in an interactive activation and competition model." *Visual Cognition*, 1, 2/3, 313-348.

Humphreys, G.W. Riddoch, M.J. and Quinlan, P.T. (1988). "Cascade processes in picture identification." *Cognitive Neuropsychology*, 5, 67-103.

Lloyd-Jones, T.J. & Humphreys, G.W. (submitted). "Perceptual differentiation as a source of category effects in object processing: evidence from naming and object decision."

Nosofsky, R.M.(1986). "Attention, similarity, and the identificationcategorisation relationship." *Journal of Experimental Psychology: General*, 115, 39-57.

Valentine, T & Bruce, V (1986). "Recognising familiar faces: The role of distinctiveness and familiarity." *Canadian Journal of Psychology*, 40, 300305.

THE CREATIVE PROCESS (ESPECIALLY IN TECHNOLOGY):
A KNOWLEDGE LEVEL COGNITIVE MODEL AND ITS IMPLICATIONS

Subrata Dasgupta
The Center for Advanced Computer Studies
University of Southwestern Louisiana
Lafayette, Lousiana 70504
e-mail: dasgupta@cacs.usl.edu

In one of his *Dialogues,* Plato, in the guise of his dead teacher Socrates, speaks of poetry-making as a divine dispensation, a kind of madness sent down from heaven. His audience of one, Ion, was thus pleased to be assured that when he recited the Homeric epics, he was possessed by the gods. In the centuries that followed, many poets, composers, scientists and artists would express rather similar views about their own powers of creation.The theme of this paper is that contrary to the 'divine dispensation' theory -- or the notion that the creative process is ineffable -- the judicious marriage of historical studies and modern ideas from cognitive science and artificial intelligence can yield a great deal of insight into the character of the creative process. The nature of this insight is discussed here with reference to one significant domain of the human enterprise, viz., *technology*.

Technology -- that is, the conceiving and making of artifacts intended for practical use -- has, of course, existed since the Lower Paleolithic era. It is as old as the first hominids. And yet, perhaps because its economic, social and historical aspects tend to dominate any discussion of the topic, there is a propensity to overlook the fact that technology is a *cognitive* activity. It involves the use of *knowledge*, and the faculties of *reasoning, remembering* and *understanding*. Moreover, technology entails *invention* -- the bringing into being of artifacts that are *original* in some significant sense. It is this aspect of technology -- invention as a creative, cognitive process -- that has occupied my recent attention and that I wish to address in this paper. It is my claim that we may indeed be able to uncover, and give an account of, some *universal* and *timeless* characteristics of the creative process in technology at some appropriate level of cognitive description. Let me call such an account a *theory of technological creativity*.

The Knowledge Level Model of Cognition

The caveat 'appropriate level of description' is important here for, as we well know, one of the hallmarks of complex systems is that it admits of multiple levels of description, each such level being appropriate for a particular kind of enquiry [7]; and, of course, the cognitive system is arguably amongst the most complex naturally occurring entities we are aware of. Thus, some cognitive scientists have come to acknowledge -- on the basis of both theoretical and empirical reasons -- the existence of multiple description levels for cognition, these levels being approximately associated with distinct time scales of mind-brain events.

The neural level is, obviously, one such level. But the most appropriate for our purpose is what Newell [5] termed the *knowledge level* wherein cognition is described in terms of goals, (mental) actions, knowledge, and intendedly rational behavior. There are two reasons for choosing this level: (*a*) The time scale of the knowledge level of cognition ranges from minutes through days, weeks to even months, and this is precisely the time scale at which technological creativity seems to be manifested; (*b*) Technology is fundamentally a goal-oriented activity -- it entails actions that strive to meet goals. This is precisely what the knowledge level model of cognition addresses.

In [4] a detailed model of the technologist as a cognitive being has been presented. This draws upon Newell's knowledge level model [5], related work by Simon on bounded rationality [8], the idea of connecting knowledge of various sorts by means of conceptual networks as described by Thagard [9], and the well-known concept of spreading activation [1] from cognitive psychology. Space does not allow me to present the details of this model except to note that it leads to the notion of a *knowledge level process* defined as a structured sequence of *actions* the input to which is a symbol structure representing *goals* or some token of knowledge from the cognitive agent's *knowledge body*, and the output of which is a symbol structure representing the *achievement of the goal* (the design or form of an artifact) and/or symbol structures denoting newly obtained knowledge. The actions constituting the process entail retrieval of knowledge tokens from the knowledge body through spreading activation and association, and the performance of a variety of *inferences* (including generalization, instantiation, abduction, analogical inference, and deduction). In the remainder of this paper, I present the principal *consequences* of this model, namely a set of four general propositions that, I claim, characterize the creative process in technology and, thus, the inventive mind across historical time, geographic space, and cultures. These propositions constitute the beginnings of a theory of technological creativity. I also cite some 'experiments' conducted in order to test the theory. These experiments use, as 'data', significant inventions drawn from the history of technology.

The Operational Principles Hypothesis

The creative technologist is armed with a rich body of interconnected, dynamically changing knowledge. Some of this is not specific to technology at all but is common to all thinking beings -- eg., general heuristics such as means-ends analysis or the rules of inference used in commonsense reasoning. Knowledge specific to the technologist -- *technological knowledge* -- is itself heterogeneous; it includes, at least in the past two centuries, the basic sciences, mathematics and the body of knowledge called engineering theory.

However, the knowledge that links technologists through historical time from the age of stone tools some two-and-a-half million years ago to the present era of microelectronics is not science, nor mathematics, nor engineering theory (for, as just noted, these entered technology only in relatively recent times), but what Polanyi first called *operational principles* [6], which we may define as follows: For a given class of artifacts, an operational principle is any proposition, rule, procedure, or frame of reference about artifactual properties or characteristics that facilitate action for the creation, manipulation and modification of artifactual forms and their implementations. This leads us to frame the

> *Operational Principles Hypothesis:* The essence of what characterizes a technologist is
> that his or her cognitive acts of creation are driven by knowledge of operational principles.

In [4], I have shown how even in the most modern of inventions, the electronic computer, in which the main participants were university trained physicists, mathematicians and electrical engineers, operational principles dominated the sources of ideas.

The Knowledge Level Hypothesis on Ideation

All acts of creation invoke, at the very least, certain momentous cognitve events called 'ideations'. Most writers on creativity have traditionally treated the question of ideation with extraordinary reverence: They have tended to leave unanswered the question: *What happens in ideation?* It is in this regard that the knowledge level model of cognition has proved to be particularly useful, for it allows us to advance the following

> *Knowledge Level Hypothesis on Ideation:* Let G be a technological goal for which S is a
> solution produced by an agent A, and let P be the cognitive process that resulted in S.
> Furthermore, let S be original in some significant sense. Then P can be specified in terms of
> a knowledge level process with G as input and S as output.

In [3], I have constructed, using available documentary and other forms of historical evidence, a detailed knowledge level process as a plausible explanation of how, in 1951, M.V. Wilkes may have been led to the idea of the microprogrammed control unit for digital computers. A similar process has been presented in [4] to explain how R. Stephenson arrived at the idea of the tubular bridge as the basis of the Britannia Bridge designed and built between 1844-47.

The Hypothesis Law of Maturation

Any significant act of creation in technology entails far more than ideation. Beginning with a goal, the inventor or designer enacts a knowledge level process that may engender one or more moments of ideation; eventually, an artifactual form reaches a state of *maturation*. In [4], I have argued that this total process from goal to the emergence of a mature form satisfies

> *The Hypothesis Law of Maturation:* A design process that reaches maturation does so
> through one or more cycles of hypothesis creation, testing and modification.

In [2], I have given an account of a detailed corroboration of this law using the historical records on the design of the Britannia Bridge by R. Stephenson and W. Fairbairn in the mid-19th century. Another corroborative test, presented in [4], involves the development of the first high-temperature, creep-resistant alloys in the 1930s.

The Phylogeny Law

One essential kind of knowledge that pervades acts of technological creation is historical knowledge. Artifacts, of even the most innovative kind, have an *evolutionary* past consisting of a linked network of earlier mature artifactual forms. One may liken this phenomenon to that of *phylogeny* in biology, a term which refers to the evolutionary history of a lineage, pictured as a series of adult stages. These observations lead to

The Phylogeny Law: Every act of invention or design has a phylogenic history.

Using historical records pertaining to the origins of the atmospheric steam engine invented by Thomas Newcomen in 1712, and to the birth of the first general purpose electronic digital computer (the ENIAC) in the 1940s by Eckert and Mauchly, I have shown the presence in each case of a distinct phylogenic history [4].

Conclusions

We have stated here the elements of a theory of technological creativity that is rooted in a relatively abstract (viz., knowledge level) model of cognition. An interesting implication of this theory is that, if correct, it sheds some light on the behavioral features demanded of any *artificial* creative system. Thus, if one desires to design a neural network-based computational system that exhibits the capacity to invent and design then, it seems, *such a system must exhibit emergent behavior that is in accordance with the theory outlined here.* I believe this is a conjecture worth investigating within the neural network paradigm.

References

[1] Collins, A.M. and Loftus, E.F., "A Spreading Activation Theory of Semantic Processing", *Psychological Review*, 82, 1975, pp 407-28.

[2] Dasgupta, S., "Testing the Hypothesis Law of Design: The Case of the Britannia Bridge", *Research in Engineering Design*, 6, 1, 1994, pp 38-57.

[3] Dasgupta, S., *Creativity in Invention and Design*, Cambridge University Press, New York, 1994.

[4] Dasgupta, S., *Technology and Creativity*, Oxford University Press, New York, 1996 (In Press).

[5] Newell, A., *Unified Theories of Cognition*, Harvard University Press, Cambridge, MA, 1990.

[6] Polanyi, M., *Personal Knowledge*, University of Chicago Press, Chicago, 1962.

[7] Simon, H.A., "The Architecture of Complexity", *Proceedings of the American Philosophical Society*, 106, Dec., 1962, pp 167-82.

[8] Simon, H.A., *Models of Bounded Rationality*, Vol. 2, MIT Press, Cambridge, MA, 1982.

[9] Thagard, P. *Conceptual Revolutions*, Princeton University Press, Princeton, NJ, 1992.

Novel Results Session

Neural Network Applications

NEUROCONTROL TECHNOLOGY FOR THE LOFLYTE TESTBED AIRCRAFT

Saeks, R., Lewis, C., Pap, R., Priddy,K., & Cox, C.

Accurate Automation Corporation
7001 Shallowford Rd.
Chattanooga, TN 37421

Abstract

Accurate Automation Corporation is leading the LoFLYTE advanced development program demonstrating the benefits of neural networks.. This is a multi-phase effort to develop the technologies necessary to design, fabricate, and flight test a Mach 5 waverider aircraft. Phase I of the program consisted of a feasibility study. Phase II is the critical design phase to construct a subsonic remotely piloted aircraft that will demonstrate the low speed characteristics of a waverider. During Phase II, a number of innovative technologies will be validated.. Included in this phase is the neurocontroller system test for this aircraft. Prototype actuator and sensor hardware has been developed and tested with our MIMD neural network hardware.

INTRODUCTION

Accurate Automation, working with Lockheed Martin Tactical Aircraft Systems and Mississippi State University, is currently developing a "waverider bodied" subsonic testbed aircraft termed "LoFLYTE" [Kandebo, 1995]. This program will lay the foundation for demonstrating a fully autonomous neural network controlled actuator and flight control system on a hypersonic aircraft configuration, and will serve as the initial testbed for both the inner and outer loop neurocontrollers.

The "LoFLYTE" vehicle will support two parallel control systems a baseline digital control system and our neurocontrol system. A sensor suite sufficient to support both control systems and the remote piloting system is part of the testbed.

Construction of the 100" wind tunnel model of the LoFLYTE waverider configuration, shown in Figure 1, was completed in the fall of 1994, and subsequently tested in late 1994 and early 1995.

Figure 1: 100" LoFLYTE Wind Tunnel Model

The waverider model has undergone extensive wind tunnel testing at NASA Langley Research Center in their 12 foot and 30 by 60 foot wind tunnels. A 100" neurocontrolled RC model version of the waverider is presently under construction. One area where neurall networks are used on LoFLYTE is for the inner and outer loop controls.

INNER LOOP CONTROL

The *hybrid inner loop controller (designed at AAC for LoFLYTE) uses a "classical" adaptive controller to train a neural network* with the network eventually learning to anticipate the response of the adaptive controller. This yields a hybrid neural/adaptive controller which:

- responds much faster to new commands or changes in the flight regime and system dynamics than the underlying adaptive controller, while

- retaining the stability, robustness, and generiticity of the adaptive controller.

Although we believe that the use of an adaptive controller to train a neurocontroller is new to the present program, Kwato, et al.[1988 and 1990] has used a classical (non-adaptive) controller to train a neurocontroller.

The core of our neural/adaptive joint controller is an adaptive joint controller developed by Seraji [1989]. This is a generic model reference adaptive controller which robustly tracks a prescribed set of trajectories assuming only that the actuator system can be modeled as a set of second order differential equations with positive "slow-varying" mass. Indeed, modulo this minimal set of constraints, the adaptive controller is generic, automatically adapting itself to the actuator and control surface dynamics.

Not surprisingly, given the generic and adaptive nature of this controller, the required feedback laws are both computationally intensive and cannot anticipate changes in system dynamics. In our hybrid implementation, neural networks are used to resolve both of these issues. A Functional Link network is used to implement the feedback laws thereby facilitating a parallel implementation of this computationally intensive process. Secondly, a neural network is trained to anticipate the feedback gains which would be produced by the adaptive controller and to initialize the adaptive controller with these gains at the start of each move. Indeed, we believe that this hybrid approach yields the best of both worlds.

- The neural network greatly speeds up the response of the adaptive controller, while

- the adaptive controller remains in the loop to guarantee stability and robustness, and to

- retrain the neural controller whenever the flight regime, or actuator dynamics change.

NEURAL/ADAPTIVE CONTROL ARCHITECTURE
ADAPTIVE CONTROL STRATEGY

The starting point for our hybrid neural/adaptive controller is a generic decentralized adaptive controller developed by Seraji [1989]. To this end it is assumed that the plant to be controlled is modelled by a second order system of nonlinear differential equations with positive slow varying mass and a small "disturbance" term. In all other respects, the algorithm is completely generic. No a-priori information about the dynamic pressure seen at the control surface, actuator and control surface dynamics, or the Reynolds number of the flight regime is required.

The architecture of our hybrid neural/adaptive controller is shown in Figure 1. The functional link adaptive controller is just the adaptive controller described above but implemented via a functional link neural network rather than numerical integration. The key to the architecture is the

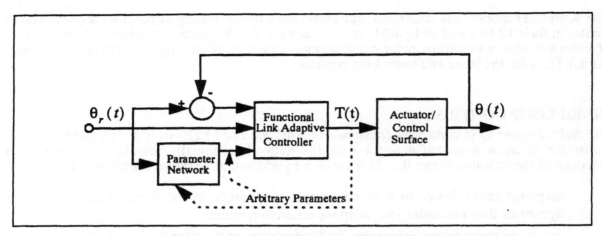

Figure 2: Hybrid Neural/Adaptive Control Architecture.

parameter network of Figure 2, which adjusts the arbitrary parameters (f(0), k_j(0), q_j(0), w's, δ's, α's, γ's, ρ's, β's, and λ's) in the adaptive controller algorithm for each reference input based on the prior performance of the adaptive controller under the same circumstances.

However, the adaptive controller remains in the loop guaranteeing asymptotic stability and robust asymptotic tracking independently of the choice of the arbitrary parameters. As such, if the pressure distribution varies on the control surface or its dynamics change, the adaptive controller guarantees that the prescribed performance criteria will be achieved, while simultaneously producing a response that can be used to update the neural controller's training.

PARAMETER NETWORK

The key to the performance of the architecture is the parameter network which is *trained by the adaptive controller to tune its initial coefficients for each command reference*. The parameter network is designed to find accurate solutions for the initial coefficients required by the adaptive controller for each actuator. This represents a significant improvement over the previous solution to the problem [Seraji, 1989] where a course approximation to an auxiliary term was made based on a priori knowledge of the system dynamics. Since the parameter network learns as the controller goes about its tasks, it needs no a priori knowledge and it continually improves its estimate of the initial coefficients. It can account for unexpected nonlinearities after it encounters them and it has a capacity to generalize. This approach has resulted in a significant reduction in both the maximum and average absolute tracking errors achieve by the controller.

STABILIZING AERODYNAMICS CONTROL

An Adaptive Critic (i.e., approximate dynamic programming) learning algorithm [Werbos, 1993] is used in implementing a learning controller. This algorithm represents a particular implementation of a reinforcement learning control algorithm in which the system is operated in a series of "training runs", then uses reinforcement learning [Barto, Sutton, and Anderson, 1983; Barto, 1993] to improve the performance of the system with each run. In its most general form, reinforcement learning control can be applied to linear or nonlinear systems and used to implement either quantitative or qualitative performance criteria. The primary constraint is that the control used in each training run must be "well behaved" (usually interpreted as stable) while the learning process should be designed to improve the performance of the system as the training process proceeds.

This outer loop control strategy differs fundamentally from the above described actuator controller in two respects. Since we assume a linear plant model, some type of gain scheduling program is required for the actuator controller as LoFLYTE passes through its various flight regimes, whereas the inner loop controller adapts automatically to changing flight regimes. Secondly, the actuator controller learns interactively in a mission simulator or in flight, while the inner loop controller learns in a fully autonomous mode. The aerodynamics controller, however, can deal with systems of arbitrary complexity while the actuator controller is restricted to second order systems.

NEURAL NETWORK HARDWARE

The design of the control system demonstrates that the neurocontrol method will control the actuators in flight. One of the primary problems is to demonstrate how the implementation can be accomplished to run in real time. Our design is implemented around the Accurate Automation Neural Network Processor which is based upon an Multiple Instructio /Multiple Data architecture described in Saeks et al [1994]. This equipment allows the actuator and aerodynamics controllers to be realized in hardware and tested. Presently, the neurocontrol hardware is attached to a simulated cockpit that is controlling hardware in the loop with sensors as well as an actuator and a wing operating in our lab.

ACKNOWLEDGMENTS

This work is sponsored by the National Aeronautics and Space Administration Small Business Innovation Research Program under Langley Research Center Contract NAS1-20404. The authors wish to express their appreciation to the United States Air Force and National Science Foundation for their support. We also wish to express our appreciation to Lockheed Martin Fort Worth, Mississippi State University and Pratt & Whitney for their assistance.

REFERENCES

Barto, Andrew G. (1993). Reinforcement Learning and Adaptive Critic Methods. In *Handbook of Intelligent Control: Neural, Fuzzy, and Adaptive Approaches*. White and Sofge, eds. New York: Van Nostrand Reinhold.

Barto, A.G., Sutton, R.S., and C.W. Anderson, (1983). "Neuronlike Adaptive Elements that can Solve Difficult Learning Problems", *IEEE Trans on Systems, Man, and Cybernetics*, Vol. SMC-13, pp. 834-846.

Kandebo, S.W. (1995). "Waverider to Test Neural Net Control", *Aviation Week & Space Technology*, April 3, 1995, pp. 78-79

Kwato, M., Setayama, T., and R. Suzuki, (1988). "Feedback Error Learning of Movement by Multilayer Neural Network", *Proc. of the 1st Annual Meeting of the Inter. Neural Networks Soc.*, p. 342.

Kwato, M., (1990). "Feedback Error Learning Neural Network for Supervised Motor Learning", In *Advanced Neural Computers* (ed. R. Eckmiller), Amsterdam, North Holland, pp. 365-372.

Pao, Yoh-Han, (1989). *Adaptive Pattern Recognition and Neural Networks*, Addison-Wesley, Reading.

Saeks, R, Priddy, K., Schneider, K and Stowell S. (1994). "On the Design of an MIMD Neural Network Processo", *Proceedings on the Congress on Neural Networks*, San Diego, CA, June 1994.

Seraji, H., (1989). "Decentralized Adaptive Control of Manipulators: Theory, Simulation, and Experimentation", *IEEE Trans. on Robotics and Automation*, Vol. 5, pp. 183-201.

Werbos, Paul J. (1993). Neurocontrol and Supervised Learning: An Overview and Evaluation. In Handbook of Intelligent Control: Neural, Fuzzy, and Adaptive Approaches. White and Sofge, eds. New York: Van Nostrand Reinhold.

Ultra-High-Speed Relay Fault Detection
Using Dynamic Models and Neural Network Classifiers[†]

Monica P. Carley, B. Eugene Parker, Jr.[‡] and Michael J. Szabo

BARRON ASSOCIATES, INC.
3046A Berkmar Drive
Charlottesville, VA 22901-1444

Abstract

The work described herein addresses the problem of discriminating, on a time scale of microseconds, between normal load and fault transients in three-phase shipboard power distribution systems. The solution approach relies on dynamic modeling to extract information from the line-to-line voltages, and subsequently, on a neural network classifier to distinguish between normal and fault transients based on dynamic model features.

1   Introduction

This paper discusses a relay algorithm that achieves rapid (i.e., microsecond time scale) and reliable fault detection in three-phase shipboard power distribution systems. Relays must react reliably and quickly to detect and isolate faults. Reliability is necessary to avoid both "false-alarm" tripping of circuit protection devices (CPDs) and "failed-to-trip" situations. High speed is needed for fight-through capability to avoid momentary power interruptions that can cause sensitive loads to shut down and to avoid under-voltage conditions (i.e., voltage degradation below 80 percent of the nominal voltage), which are the nemeses of combat system loads [4]. The difficulty of this task is exacerbated by the use of increasingly complicated loads (e.g., switched-mode, harmonic-producing loads, such as rectifiers and converters), that can cause loads to look electrically like faults. Switched-mode power supplies used in radar systems, for example, produce harmonic currents and transient glitches in the input voltage waveforms [9].

The approach described herein is based on the extraction of detection features from the line-to-line voltages, and use of such features in a classification neural network to distinguish normal from fault *voltage* transients. Note that only the voltage waveforms are utilized to make this discrimination, reducing significantly the instrumentation burden.

Several techniques for extracting detection features directly from the line-to-line voltages will be described. In general, the features can be derived by estimating the magnitude and phase of each of the three voltages individually, or by estimating the total magnitude and phase angle of the three voltages projected onto a single phasor. The same basic information regarding the phase balance of the system is exploited in both cases. A new approach, presented here, is to first dynamically model the line-to-line voltages and then use the prediction errors, or model residuals, as signals from which detection features are extracted; alternatively, model coefficients estimated on line may be used to distinguish normal from fault transients. It is noted, however, that performing on-line parameter identification generally requires more time than does residual generation, since a minimum number of data samples must be available after inception of a transient event to adapt parameter estimates sufficiently. Significant residuals, on the other hand, can generally be observed based on fewer transient sample measurements. The on-line computational burden is also reduced in the case of residual generation, since parameter identification algorithms may be executed off-line, prior to on-line implementation.

Previous work [1, 2, 7, 8] has demonstrated that phase information is the most reliable indicator of a fault. The advantage of the dynamic model-based approach is that the critical phase information is contained

---

[†]This work was supported by the Naval Surface Warfare Center, Carderock Division, Annapolis Detachment, under Contracts N00167-92-C-0004 and N00167-94-C-0083, and by the Naval Sea Systems Command, under Contract N00024-94-C-4205.

[‡]Author to whom all correspondence should be addressed; e-mail: parker@bai.mhs.compuserve.com, telephone: 804-973-1215.

specifically in the moving average residuals from an autoregressive moving average (ARMA) model; more sophisticated models, such as nonlinear ARMA models and neural networks, may also be utilized.

The detection features are next supplied to a *polynomial neural network (PNN) classifier* [3] which makes the fault/no-fault decisions. These PNNs are trained off-line on a database containing features computed over a wide range of normal operating conditions and representative fault scenarios. On-line, the trained network can be interrogated quickly using features extracted from voltage measurements. Using the dynamic modeling approach for feature extraction, and the classifier PNN for fault detection, the overall processing is relatively simple and can be accomplished in real-time. Related algorithms that have been developed to coordinate multiple relays on a time scale of microseconds are used subsequently to achieve selective fault isolation [5, 7, 8].

2   Data

The algorithms described herein were tested on data supplied by NSWC/Annapolis from recorded shipboard power distribution systems, as well as from computer simulations. The recorded shipboard power system data provided a variety of load transient examples, and numerous examples of line-to-line and three-phase bolted faults. The line-to-line voltages and line currents were sampled at 20 kHz. The types of loads consisted of resistive loads of varying levels of power, 20 HP motors, and pulsing rectifier and radar loads of varying power levels. Simulated data modeling a tiered, three-phase power distribution system was generated by NSWC/Annapolis using an *ACSL*-based software program. Examples of faults and normal load transients applied at various locations in the tiered system were simulated, with data samples recorded simultaneously at four different bus sites. The simulation data was sampled at 120 kHz. Three types of load turn-on transients were simulated: motors, RL loads, and rectifiers; faults were introduced both with and without other loads operating. Although the discrimination of transients may be enhanced by the inclusion of line currents, the voltage waveforms alone provided sufficient information for the present work.

3   Feature Extraction from Line-to-Line Voltages

In three-phase systems, phase differences between voltages have been found consistently to provide the most useful feature information for detecting faults and reliably discriminating normal load transients from faults [1, 2]. The following functions may be used to describe three-phase line-to-line voltages, where $\theta_1, \theta_3, \theta_5$ denote magnitudes, $\theta_2, \theta_4, \theta_6$ denote phases, and ω_0 denotes the nominal frequency:

$$V_{AB}(t) = \theta_1 \sin(\omega_0 t + \theta_2) \tag{1}$$

$$V_{BC}(t) = \theta_3 \sin(\omega_0 t + \theta_4) \tag{2}$$

$$V_{CA}(t) = \theta_5 \sin(\omega_0 t + \theta_6) \tag{3}$$

The features can then be computed as differences in phase: $\Delta_1 = |\theta_4 - \theta_2|$ and $\Delta_2 = |\theta_6 - \theta_2|$.

Methods for estimating the phases of the line-to-line voltages include nonlinear least squares, in which the θ coefficients of the sinusoidal models are estimated from the three measured voltages, and zero-crossing algorithms, in which the phases are computed based on the respective numbers of samples that elapse since the most recent zero-crossings. Although these features may provide sufficient information for reliable fault detection [1, 2], delays between fault inception and detection are inherent in both methods.

4   Park Transformation for Magnitude and Phase Features

The Park transformation [8] is a technique that can transform a balanced, three-phase AC system into the DC domain through use of a moving reference frame. By assuming a constant operating frequency, the amplitude and angular offset are transformed into constants that allow detection of two events: change in amplitude and loss of angular synchronization. Mathematically, the Park transformation is:

$$\begin{bmatrix} V_0 \\ V_d \\ V_q \end{bmatrix} = \sqrt{\frac{2}{3}} \begin{bmatrix} \frac{1}{\sqrt{2}} & \frac{1}{\sqrt{2}} & \frac{1}{\sqrt{2}} \\ \cos(\omega_0 t) & \cos\left(\omega_0 t - \frac{2\pi}{3}\right) & \cos\left(\omega_0 t + \frac{2\pi}{3}\right) \\ \sin(\omega_0 t) & \sin\left(\omega_0 t - \frac{2\pi}{3}\right) & \sin\left(\omega_0 t + \frac{2\pi}{3}\right) \end{bmatrix} \begin{bmatrix} V_{AB} \\ V_{BC} \\ V_{CA} \end{bmatrix} \tag{4}$$

The first equation is simply a check on the balanced condition; for any balanced set of three-phase voltages, this sum should be zero. The other two equations involve projecting the rectangular coordinate values onto the rotating reference frame. Given a constant operating frequency f_0 (e.g., 60 Hz) and a constant magnitude for all three voltages, the resulting constant vector in a two-dimension plane is:

$$V_{dq} = \left| \sqrt{\frac{3}{2}} V \right| \angle -\phi \tag{5}$$

V captures the system voltage level, whereas ϕ relates the start of the three-phase waveform pattern to the initial angle of the coordinate axes.

5 Dynamic Modeling for Residual-Based Features

Instead of relying on monitored system states (e.g., currents and voltages) directly to detect faults, model-based methods attempt to track the behavior of a system using predictions of measurable state variables. The basic approach is to use an analytic or black-box model to capture behavior considered to be "normal," and then to compare model estimates with the observed data over time. Parameters often reflect faults more dramatically and consistently than measured variables.

A dynamic modeling approach is outlined in which model inputs represent present and past measurements of the observable states; the model outputs represent predictions of state variables. The coefficients of the models can then be adapted either recursively on-line (e.g., using a sliding temporal window), or fixed, based on prior training on "normal" data. Detection relies then, respectively, on the occurrence of significant changes in the model parameters, or significant change in model prediction residuals. The residual-based approach provides for fastest real-time detection, since parameter adaptation is avoided; however, the normal dynamic characteristic behavior of the system must be captured adequately during training.

Linear, autoregressive, moving average (ARMA) models can be derived to describe AC power system voltage waveforms, taking into account the parameters of interest: magnitude, phase, and frequency. A linear model with two delays is sufficient to describe a sinusoidal signal at a constant frequency, such as an ideal 60 Hz voltage waveform. However, loads can introduce transient effects causing, for example, voltage sag, that should not be mistaken for faults. The autoregressive parameters capture the fundamental dynamic behavior of a system, whereas the moving average parameters capture changes due to varying inputs to the system. Although all of the ARMA model parameters are found to be important for detecting different types of voltage waveform disturbances, the moving average parameter(s) are particularly useful for detecting phase imbalance.

The filter coefficients for a basic sinusoid can be derived from the z-transform of the time domain expression for the waveform $v(t) = \sin(\omega t)$; this can be generalized further to include phase angle and damping, $v(t) = e^{-\zeta t}\sin(\omega t + \phi)$. The z-transform of this expression is

$$\frac{V(z)}{X(z)} = \frac{e^{-\zeta T}\sin(\phi) + z^{-1}e^{-\zeta T}\sin(\omega T - \phi)}{1 - 2z^{-1}e^{-\zeta T}\cos(\omega T) + z^{-2}e^{-2\zeta T}} \tag{6}$$

where T represents the sampling period. The resulting difference equation is the following linear autoregressive model with an exogenous-input (ARX):

$$a_0 v_k = a_1 v_{k-1} + a_2 v_{k-2} + b_0 x_k + b_1 x_{k-1} \tag{7}$$

where $a_0 = 1$, $a_1 = 2e^{-\zeta T}\cos(\omega T)$, $a_2 = -e^{-2\zeta T}$, $b_0 = e^{-\zeta T}\sin(\phi)$, and $b_1 = e^{-\zeta T}\sin(\omega T - \phi)$.

The autoregressive parameters, a_i, clearly contain no phase-angle information; they are functions of the damping factor, ζ, and frequency to sampling rate ratio, f/f_s (since $\omega T = \frac{2\pi f}{f_s}$). Therefore, changes in phase angle can only be monitored via the ARX b_i parameters, or in the case of ARMA models, via the moving average parameters.

To demonstrate the significance of individual parameters with regard to detection, a simple experiment was conducted to compare the effects of changes in voltage magnitude, phase angle, and line frequency. Four signals, sampled at $f_s = 6$ kHz, were generated in $MATLAB$: a 277 volt/60 Hz sinusoid with zero phase angle ϕ_0; the same signal (277 volt/60 Hz) except with a phase angle of $\phi_1 = 45$ degrees; a 185 volt/60 Hz signal (33 percent voltage sag) with zero phase lag; and finally a 277 volt/30 Hz sinusoid (half the frequency) with zero phase angle. Recursive Least Squares (RLS) was used to estimate the ARMA(2,1) model parameters over an interval of 2,000 samples; an RLS forgetting factor of $\lambda = 0.99$ was used. The final converged parameters are listed in Table 1. The estimated moving average parameters, $\hat{c}_i$, are intended to account

Table 1: Estimated ARMA(2,1) Parameters for Simulated Voltage Waveform: $v(t) = V\sin(2\pi f t + \phi)$

V	f	ϕ	$\hat{a}_1$	$\hat{a}_2$	$\hat{c}_1$
277	60	0°	1.9961	−1.0000	0.8301
277	60	45°	1.9961	−1.0000	−0.6190
185	60	0°	1.9961	−1.0000	0.8464
277	30	0°	1.9990	−1.0000	0.2097

for the overall discrepancy, due to noise and modeling error, between the observed output and the model estimated output, $e_k = v(k) - \hat{v}(k)$:

$$\hat{v}_k = \hat{a}_1 v_{k-1} + \hat{a}_2 v_{k-2} + \hat{c}_1 e_{k-1} \tag{8}$$

Although the ARX model parameter b_1 in Eq. 7 and the ARMA model parameter c_1 in Eq. 8 cannot be equated outright, they account for the same information (i.e., phase angle, as well as f/f_s). This is confirmed by the fact that the a_i coefficients in the ARMA model converge to the same values as those in the ARX model.

As expected, introducing a phase angle of 45 degrees in the second signal had minimal affect on the AR parameters, but a significant effect on the moving average parameter $\hat{c}_1$. Changing the frequency from f_0 (60 Hz) to f_1 (30 Hz) in the fourth signal affected both the AR and the MA parameters. The change from 1.996 to 1.999 is consistent with a change in frequency from 60 Hz to 30 Hz. Depending on the sampling rate f_s, the change in f/f_s may be insignificant. Similarly, the percentage of sag, or damping, would have to be large relative to the sampling rate for voltage sag to be evident in the parameters. Recall that damping is factored into the parameter estimates via the term $e^{-\zeta/f_s}$ and the damping factor, ζ, can only range between 0 and 1 (i.e., 0 percent to 100 percent damping). This is exemplified by the voltage sag from V_0 to V_1, which has a negligible effect on the parameters.

6 Neural Network Fault Classifier

In this work, a polynomial neural network (PNN) [3] classifier was synthesized using BAI's *CLASS* software to establish a discrimination function to distinguish successfully normal and fault transients based on the input features. *CLASS* fits the coefficients of a polynomial of specified degree and structure (i.e., additive terms only, cross terms only, or all terms), which is then used to compute the actual probabilities of class membership. In this application, one of only two possible classes can be assigned, normal or fault (i.e., binary classification). *CLASS* provides a statistically sound basis for tailoring the structure of discriminant functions, as well as for learning their coefficients; although the results show a very obvious separation in feature space, so that a simple linear discriminant is adequate, more complex decision surfaces may be needed upon examination of additional normal and fault transient data.

7 NSWC/Annapolis Data Results

Nominal ARMA(2,1) models, described by Eq. 8, were estimated dynamically using several cycles of pre-event data for each line-to-line voltage in each test. The models were then divided into their autoregressive and moving average parts to generate two separate predictions of the output, and hence two separate sets of prediction residuals:

$$\hat{v}_k^{AR} = \hat{a}_1 v_{k-1} + \hat{a}_2 v_{k-2} \tag{9}$$

$$\hat{v}_k^{MA} = \hat{c}_1 e_{k-1} \tag{10}$$

The prediction residuals are simply the difference between each of the above model predictions and the observed voltage time-series data. A standard method for separating dynamics and noise models is to use a prediction-error approach to model the autoregressive parameters, and then to use the resulting errors to fit the moving average coefficients [6]. The moving average prediction residuals, $v_k - \hat{v}_k^{MA}$, were found to be the most useful for discriminating load transients from fault events. These residuals are actually sinusoidal in nature because the model from which they are generated no longer contains the 60 Hz signal description captured by the autoregressive parameters of the complete model. Therefore, when the signal is effectively "filtered" through the model to produce predictions and residuals, the 60 Hz component remains.

The Park transformation was then applied to the set of three moving average residuals, transforming the three signals onto one phasor, having an associated magnitude and phase angle that were used as detection features. When the three voltage waveforms are perfectly balanced in phase and undistorted, the phase and magnitude features will be constant. Faults will result in features that deviate appreciably from their nominal values; for load transients, these deviations are less severe.

Fig. 1 shows a two-dimensional view of fault and load data for the simulated tiered distribution system, plotted in terms of the two detection features. An offset in the magnitude feature was removed throughout. The second feature shown in Fig. 1 is derived from the phase-angle feature; specifically, it is the difference between the minimum and maximum peak-to-peak values seen during the event in each test. Fig. 2 shows the same features resulting from evaluation of the shipboard data. For both simulated and shipboard data, normal vs. fault transient discrimination can clearly be made based upon these two features, as exemplified by the line separating the faults from the loads in both cases. Here, the simple linear discriminant shown is adequate for separating the two groups. In general, however, neural network classifiers can be used to derive appropriate discrimination surfaces.

8 Conclusions

Results on NSWC/Annapolis simulated and shipboard data demonstrate the concept of using dynamic models, learned off-line, to generate model residuals on-line for rapid discrimination between normal load and fault transients. The overall detection method described can be implemented in a real-time operating environment. Because the dynamic models are learned off-line, on-line processing requires implementation of: (1) a filter to generate one-step-ahead predictions and prediction residuals, (2) the Park transformation, by which two detection features are produced, and (3) a neural network detector. The discrimination surface between the normal and fault transients is learned off-line from training data; therefore, the on-line detection decision involves a quick interrogation of the network to make the class (normal vs. fault) assignment.

9 Acknowledgements

The authors thank Mr. Roger T. Cooley of NSWC/Annapolis for providing all of the simulation data used in these investigations. Gratitude is also expressed to Mr. David Clayton of NSWC/Annapolis for his support and guidance throughout this work. The helpful suggestions and technical support of Mr. W. Todd Shelton of BAI are also gratefully acknowledged.

References

[1] Carley, M.P., B.E. Parker, Jr., R.L. Barron, and D.G. Ward, *Improved Fault Detection and Clearing in Advanced Electric Distribution Systems for Ships*, Barron Associates, Inc., Final Technical Report, Contract N00167-92-C-0004, NSWC, Carderock Division, Annapolis Detachment, March 1993.

[2] Carley, M.P. and B.E. Parker, Jr., *Improved Fault Detection and Clearing in Advanced Electric Distribution Systems for Ships: Tasks B.1-B.4*, Barron Associates, Inc., Final Technical Report, Contract N00167-92-C-0004, Mod. P00001, NSWC, Carderock Division, Annapolis Detachment, August 1993.

[3] *CLASS: Algorithm for Synthesis of Polynomial Networks for Classification*, Users' Manual, Version 1.62, Barron Associates, Inc., June 1995.

[4] Goodnow, M.O., "Reply to 'Ships service electric power: enhanced survivability via early detection of incipient cable faults'," *Naval Engineers Journal*, May 1993.

[5] Larson, E.C. and B.E. Parker, Jr., "Pattern recognition-based coordination of ultra-high-speed relays," this conference.

[6] Ljung, L. *System Identification for the User*, Prentice-Hall: Englewood Cliffs, NJ, 1987.

[7] Parker, Jr., B.E. and N.A. Nigro, *Improved Fault Detection and Clearing in Advanced Electric Distribution Systems for Ships: Coordination of Multiple Circuit Breakers, Task B.6*, Barron Associates, Inc., Final Technical Report, Contract N00167-92-C-0004, Mods. P00002-P00004, NSWC, Carderock Division, Annapolis Detachment, June 1994.

[8] Shelton, W.T., M.P. Carley, B.E. Parker, Jr., and N.A. Nigro, *Improved Fault Detection and Clearing in Advanced Electric Distribution Systems for Ships, Task B.8: Fault Data Evaluation*, Barron Associates, Inc., Final Technical Report, Contract N00167-92-C-0004, Mod. P00005, NSWC, Carderock Division, Annapolis Detachment, January 1995.

[9] Williams, S.E. and B.D. Russell, "Ships service electric power: enhanced survivability via early detection of incipient cable faults," *Naval Engineers Journal*, May 1993.

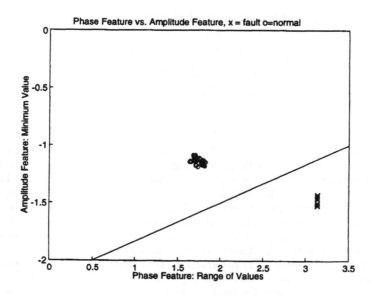

Figure 1: Normal and Fault Transient Discrimination of moving average Residuals (NSWC Simulated Data) in Feature Space

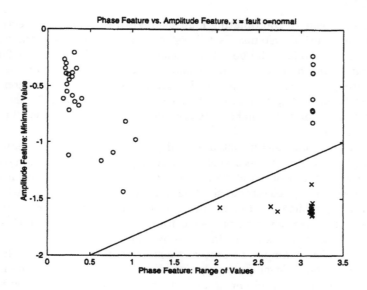

Figure 2: Normal and Fault Transient Discrimination of moving average Residuals (NSWC Shipboard Data) in Feature Space

Pattern Recognition-Based Coordination of Ultra-High-Speed Relays[†]

Edward C. Larson and B. Eugene Parker, Jr.[‡]

BARRON ASSOCIATES, INC.
3046A Berkmar Drive
Charlottesville, VA 22901-1444

Abstract

This work presents a pattern recognition relay algorithm that coordinates multiple ultra-high-speed (i.e., microsecond time scale) relays, without requiring inter-relay communication. Once the existence of a fault has been confirmed, a relay must attempt to identify the location of the fault as quickly as possible and, based on that knowledge, trip its associated circuit breaker (CB), if appropriate, so as to achieve *selective isolation* of the fault, shedding as little load as is necessary. In the absence of inter-relay communication, fault clearing requires that each individual relay be pre-assigned a specific *zone of protection*, such that if a fault originates inside that zone, the relay will trip its associated CB. With relay sensors located at one end of their protection zones, determining whether or not a relay should open its associated CB involves two steps: (1) determining the direction (up line or down line) of the fault relative to the location of the relay sensors, and (2) assuming that the fault is down line, determining whether the fault lies within the zone of protection of the relay. The algorithms discussed herein address both of these concerns.

1 Introduction

This paper addresses the problem of coordinating multiple high-speed circuit protection devices (CPDs) for use in shipboard power distribution systems. Fast decision-making by CPDs is critical because of the strict power quality requirements of modern shipboard equipment, such as electronic warfare systems. Such protection is particularly important in fault situations when it is vital that generation sources not be overloaded and that faults be isolated closest to their physical location. Continued operation under battle damage conditions is imperative to achieving a fight-through capability and is largely the reason that electrical power distribution systems for military combatants are being designed using distributed rather than radial or centralized architectures [9].

High-speed clearing of faults and power system reconfiguration is becoming a realizable goal because low conduction loss, ultra-fast switchgear is becoming more available. Solid-state power switches, for example, are being developed that are capable of switching power buses and feeders in several microseconds, which will enhance greatly the survivability of electronic shipboard systems. Examples of fast, high-power switching devices include MOSFET-Controlled Thyristors (MCTs) and Insulated Gate Bipolar Transistors (IGBTs). Such high-speed devices must themselves be protected from large current and voltage transients. Although solid-state devices such as inverters have built-in shut-down protection, such protection is insufficient from a systems-level perspective. For example, to protect themselves, inverters may shut down, shedding more load than is necessary when a fault develops in only one of the loads supplied by the inverter. More effective protection can be achieved under such circumstances if, instead, the CPD associated with the faulty load that is supplied by the inverter takes the load off-line, removing the fault and leaving the inverter and the remaining loads on-line. Given the high speed of inverter self-protection, if such action is to be accomplished, ultra-high speed relays are required.

Prior work by Barron Associates, Inc. (BAI) [8, 10] on the development of an ultra-high-speed (UHS) (i.e., microsecond time scale) directional comparison relay algorithm has sought to exploit transient voltage

---

[†]This work was supported by the Naval Surface Warfare Center, Carderock Division, Annapolis Detachment, under Contracts N00167-92-C-0004 and N00167-94-C-0083.

[‡]Author to whom all correspondence should be addressed; e-mail: parker@bai.mhs.compuserve.com, telephone: 804-973-1215.

and current signals resulting from the onset of a fault to determine its location relative to the relay sensors. Conventional directional comparison relay algorithms operate on a time scale of milliseconds [2, 5, 11] and effectively assume that all transients detected are fault transients. The conventional algorithm thus concerns itself mainly with the issue of relay coordination so as to ensure that a fault is isolated properly and that the appropriate circuit breaker (CB) takes action to clear the fault from the power distribution system. The conventional algorithm requires communication, in the form of a one-bit enable/disable signal, between a down-line relay to its up-line neighbor. The main drawback of this algorithm is the required inter-relay communication channel, which represents a potential point of failure. The communication signal can, of course, be superimposed on the power line itself, effectively eliminating the need for a separate communication channel, but this has the potential to introduce new problems.

This paper presents a pattern recognition relay algorithm that requires no inter-relay communication. The algorithm is based on neural network pattern recognition techniques to determine: (1) the relative direction (i.e., up line or down line) of a fault with respect to a relay, and (2) if the fault is within the "reach" (i.e., the spatial distance defining the protection zone) of a relay. The feasibility of such an approach has been demonstrated previously [7] for millisecond-time-scale operation and derives from the fact that the *zone of protection* (i.e., forward reach) of a relay can be set based on the voltage and current signals present during a fault event. Only the forward reach of the relay needs to be considered here, since faults lying within the reverse reach (i.e., up-line) of the relay can be eliminated based on the signs of the voltage and current transient signals [2, 5, 11]. As with the directional comparison relay algorithm implementations discussed above [8, 10], related techniques that have been developed to discriminate between normal and fault transients on a time scale of microseconds are employed prior to application of the present algorithm [1].

The main drawback of the pattern recognition algorithm is its requirement for a database of training examples, which are used to establish the reach of individual relays. Once established, the relay settings are then "good" only for a given circuit topology; if the circuit is changed, the relay reach settings may have to be re-established to ensure reliable performance. Robust behavior can, to a significant extent, be ensured through thorough training of the directional and reach neural networks under a variety of anticipated and potential operational scenarios.

Although the focus of the present work is on three-phase AC power systems, it is anticipated, based on earlier research conducted by one of the authors [8], that the pattern recognition approach outlined herein will apply equally to DC systems.

2 Pattern Recognition Relay Algorithm

2.1 Fault Direction Determination

The fundamental observables used by the direction identification algorithm are the signals $\Delta v(t)$ and $\Delta i(t)$, herein referred to as Δ-signals, and defined as:

$$\Delta v(t) = v(t)_{\text{measured}} - v(t)_{\text{predicted}} \tag{1}$$

$$\Delta i(t) = i(t)_{\text{measured}} - i(t)_{\text{predicted}} \tag{2}$$

where the "predicted" values are those that would occur under steady-state operation. These predicted signals may be obtained through use of sinusoidal templates that are maintained in a circular buffer one cycle in length. Immediately after normal or fault transient inception, the measured signals begin to deviate appreciably from the predicted signals. Discrimination between normal and fault transients is performed prior to fault direction determination and relay reach calculations; need for the latter processing steps is obviated if the transient disturbance does not represent a fault [1].

Past literature and inquiry into UHS directional comparison relay algorithms has not addressed the application of Δ-signal techniques to ungrounded electrical systems, such as delta-configured, three-phase naval systems, in which line-to-line voltage measurements only are generally available. Additionally, noise issues have not previously been addressed extensively. For reliable operation using Δ-signals, which are by their nature small quantities, robustness against noise is paramount, all the more so if products, differences, derivatives, and exponentiation of Δ-signals are used.

Past research has determined that the relative direction to a fault in AC systems can be determined by the helicity (sense of rotation) of the orbit swept out by the Δv and Δi signals immediately after a fault.

These trajectories, in general, have an offset along the Δi axis, which can be eliminated by differentiation [2, 5, 11]. It follows that the product $\Delta v \frac{d}{dt}(\Delta i)$ is able to identify orbit helicity and hence, fault direction. Attempts to generalize this result to a form applicable to delta-configured, three-phase systems has led to the finding that the following quantity consistently gives an unambiguous directional signature:

$$\Delta v_{BA} \cdot \frac{d}{dt}(\Delta i_B - \Delta i_A) + \Delta v_{CB} \cdot \frac{d}{dt}(\Delta i_C - \Delta i_B) + \Delta v_{AC} \cdot \frac{d}{dt}(\Delta i_A - \Delta i_C) \tag{3}$$

where v_{BA}, v_{CB}, and v_{AC} denote *line-to-line* voltages and i_A, i_B, and i_C represent phase currents. The summation in Eq. 3 includes all three line-to-line parameters, ensuring that the above "signature" is *phase invariant*, meaning that the input quantities are not affected by permutations of the A, B, C labeling. In other words, the three phases are treated identically. All findings reported herein are based on the analysis of simulation data (120 kHz sampling rate) provided by NSWC/Annapolis that reflect local voltage and current measurements made at two load relays that were situated on different buses in a tiered power distribution system.

The signature quantity (i.e., Eq. 3) was singularly able to distinguish up-line from down-line faults. In low-noise simulations, the distinction was so sharp that direction could readily be discerned by simple inspection without the aid of a formal discriminant function (e.g., neural network). All down-line faults exhibited a signature value that was positive and greater than a threshold value, whereas for up-line faults, the signature was either negative or of small absolute value (and more than an order of magnitude smaller than the threshold value). It is noteworthy that, using this signature, direction could be determined correctly based on the second sample after inception of a fault event.

2.2 Relay Reach Determination

In a hierarchical power distribution system, a given relay should trip its associated CB if and only if there exists a down-line fault that is within its zone of protection, meaning between it and its nearest down-line neighbor. In the problem of reach determination, no singularly decisive quantity analogous to the fault direction "signature" could be found. Data analysis proceeded on the assumption that there nevertheless exist more subtle patterns in the Δv and Δi signals that could accurately estimate reach with the aid of a neural network. Efforts were devoted to training a *classification polynomial neural network* for each relay to learn characteristics of Δ-signal behavior to distinguish near faults (i.e., those within reach) from far faults (i.e., those outside of the reach). As part of an overall fault-clearing policy for a given relay, these reach networks would be invoked immediately after a fault was detected *and* determined to be located down line of the relay in question.

As with fault direction determination, the reach problem mandates a binary decision: either the down-line fault is within reach and the relay therefore should open its associated CB (e.g., relay should output a logical 1), or the fault is not within reach and the CB associated with the relay should therefore remain closed (e.g., relay should output a logical 0). In accordance with established techniques for handling a C-class discrete output problem such as this ($C=2$ in the present context), relay reach classifiers were synthesized for each relay using BAI's *CLASS* [3] software program.

CLASS is an advanced inductive modeling tool that rapidly synthesizes feedforward polynomial neural networks for multivariate classification and decision-support applications. The user specifies the degree of nonlinearity desired in the classifier input layer. Arbitrary numbers of network inputs and classes are permitted. Proceeding from a numerical database of example classifications, *CLASS* determines the coefficients in the first layer using a numerical search that maximizes the log likelihood of correct classification (i.e., minimize the classifier logistic loss). All of the parameters in the network are adjusted simultaneously during the search. There are $C-1$ polynomial nodes in the first layer, where C is the number of classes represented in the database. The second (output) layer is a fixed nonlinear transformation that maps the outputs of the first-layer nodes into probabilities for each class; these probabilities always sum to unity.

Using *CLASS*, relay reach classifiers were synthesized separately for each relay. Training was performed using various pre-specified combinations of the local Δ-signals as inputs. Since each relay sensed different Δ-signals, the training databases were different for each relay. The pre-fabricated inputs were intermediate quantities computed directly from the raw Δ-signals, but were constructed expressly to incorporate phase invariance. Specifically, the quantities,

$$x_1 = (\Delta v_{BA})^2 + (\Delta v_{CB})^2 + (\Delta v_{AC})^2 \tag{4}$$

$$x_2 = \Delta v_{BA}(\Delta i_B - \Delta i_A) + \Delta v_{CB}(\Delta i_C - \Delta i_B) + \Delta v_{AC}(\Delta i_A - \Delta i_C) \tag{5}$$

$$x_3 = (\Delta i_B - \Delta i_A)^2 + (\Delta i_C - \Delta i_B)^2 + (\Delta i_A - \Delta i_C)^2 \tag{6}$$

$$x_4 = \frac{d}{dt}[(\Delta v_{BA})^2] + \frac{d}{dt}[(\Delta v_{CB})^2] + \frac{d}{dt}[(\Delta v_{AC})^2] \tag{7}$$

$$x_5 = \frac{d}{dt}[\Delta v_{BA}(\Delta i_B - \Delta i_A)] + \frac{d}{dt}[\Delta v_{CB}(\Delta i_C - \Delta i_B)] + \frac{d}{dt}[\Delta v_{AC}(\Delta i_A - \Delta i_C)] \tag{8}$$

$$x_6 = \frac{d}{dt}[(\Delta i_B - \Delta i_A)^2] + \frac{d}{dt}[(\Delta i_C - \Delta i_B)^2] + \frac{d}{dt}[(\Delta i_A - \Delta i_C)^2] \tag{9}$$

served as a sufficient set of inputs to linear nodal element polynomial neural network classifiers. The first three "features" (i.e., Eqs. 4-6) are phase-invariant quadratic combinations of the line-to-line voltage Δ-signals and *differences* in the current Δ-signals. The final three input features listed above (i.e., Eqs. 7-9) are the time derivatives of the first three.

Two methods were used to evaluate the reach-determining networks. The first method entailed partitioning the set of fault exemplars randomly into independent training and evaluation databases. Four different training-evaluation partitions were applied: 80-20 percent, 60-40 percent, 40-60 percent, and 20-80 percent. The second method, which is most useful when data are limited, involved use of *jackknife statistics*[§] [4].

The predictive accuracy of the networks were assessed by examining the training and evaluation *confusion matrices*, which give the number of observations assigned, both correctly and incorrectly, to each class. The confusion matrix results, for both the random partition and the jackknife methods, indicated that the neural networks produced correct decisions (i.e., zero missed detections and zero false alarms) without exception.

2.3 Pre-Fabricated Δ-Signal Input Combinations vs. Raw Δ-Signal Inputs

The results obtained above, for both fault direction determination and relay reach, using pre-fabricated combinations of Δ-signals, prompt the question of whether similar results can be obtained by providing the raw Δ-signals directly as inputs to neural networks. To answer this question, separate *CLASS* networks were synthesized for both direction and relay reach determination using the raw Δv and Δi signals, in conjunction with their time derivatives, as network inputs. In initial tests, different *linear* polynomial node *CLASS* networks were synthesized to determine fault directionality and relay reach. Although the resulting classifiers for both direction and reach passed the jackknife test with zero errors, even when time-derivative features were withheld, the same classifiers did not hold up when the original data were permuted in phase; that is, when an original observation, say $(\Delta v_{BA} = x, \Delta v_{CB} = y, \Delta v_{AC} = z)$, was permuted to form two new "observations," $(\Delta v_{BA} = y, \Delta v_{CB} = z, \Delta v_{AC} = x)$ and $(\Delta v_{BA} = z, \Delta v_{CB} = x, \Delta v_{AC} = y)$, which were appended to the database.

With use of a *second-degree* polynomial nodal element within *CLASS*, however, the training and evaluation errors went to zero. Just as in the case of the pre-fabricated analytic inputs (i.e., Eqs. 3-6), the resulting classifier was quadratic in the Δ-signals. This reinforces the earlier finding that quadratic combinations of Δ-signals are indeed necessary and sufficient features for learning directionality and reach. Moreover, it shows that permuting the original training data and then proceeding to construct classifiers that use raw input data only is equivalent to using pre-fabricated phase-invariant inputs.

The equivalence of the two techniques demonstrates the learning capability of *CLASS* neural networks and the robustness of the classifiers it synthesizes. The raw input method had the advantage that use of time derivatives was not necessary; this was true for both direction and reach determination. The absence of time derivatives means that the relay does not have to wait until the second post-fault sample to make a direction decision. Classifiers with 28 coefficients were needed for reach determination in each relay tested, compared to only seven coefficients each when the time derivatives were included in the candidate feature set. This modest complexity penalty is small, however, considering the robustness to noise that is gained by not utilizing products, differences, derivatives, and exponentiation of the Δ-signals.

[§]Here, a single fault exemplar is "jackknifed" out of the population set of fault exemplars and set aside, while the other exemplars are used for training. The lone omitted exemplar is then used to evaluate the performance of the network derived from the training. This process is repeated methodically, with each individual fault exemplar being isolated exactly once. In this way, a statistical ensemble of networks is obtained for each relay.

2.4 Noise Considerations

Consideration of noise effects in shipboard applications is paramount, due largely to the close spatial and electromagnetic proximity of generators and loads. As a result, ship cables are susceptible to substantial pickup from extraneous sources. A critical test of the above algorithms, therefore, is whether they hold up in noisy environments.

In initial investigations of noise effects on simulated data, Gaussian white noise was added to the Δ-signals. The spectrum of this noise was taken to be flat for frequencies up to the 120 kHz sampling rate; therefore, the noise levels superimposed on consecutive samples were uncorrelated. The noise was characterized by the root-mean-square (RMS) amplitude, which was a certain percentage of the RMS Δ-signal to which it was added (defined by averaging over the full set of experiments using the first 15 post-fault samples). This provided a well-defined signal-to-noise ratio (SNR).

Simulations involving additive white noise have shown that a noise level of 2 percent (i.e., SNR = 50) results in an evaluation error rate in both direction and reach decisions of about 2.5 percent, if network inputs are restricted to the first and second post-fault samples only. Waiting until the third sample eliminates training and evaluation errors in the presence of up to 3 percent noise. For 10 percent noise, elimination of error requires waiting until the sixth post-fault sample. In doing so, the the relay processor must compute running averages of the input variables used by the neural network.

Averaging over several samples in this way might not work, however, if the noise exhibits non-zero autocorrelation between samples. Correlated noise may be simulated by assuming that short-duration pulses of a certain well-defined shape are generated at random times. The pulse generation process is characterized by a mean arrival rate n, such that the probability of N pulses being generated over a time interval of length T is given by a Poisson distribution:

$$P(N,T) = \frac{(nT)^N e^{-nT}}{N!} \tag{10}$$

"Shot noise" synthesized in this way was simulated using an exponentially-decaying pulse waveform $e^{-t/\Delta}\theta(t)$, in which Δ is a time constant and $\theta(t)$ is the well-known Heaviside function. Positive and negative exponential pulses of identical shape were generated independently with a common mean arrival rate, $n = 40$ pulses per sampling interval. Δ was set to 2.5 sample periods. The autocorrelation function of such noise may be shown [6] to be

$$\phi(\tau) = n\Delta e^{-|\tau|/\Delta} \tag{11}$$

The correlation thus persists for a time duration on the order of $\Delta = 2.5$ samples. The noise amplitude may be characterized by the RMS value $\sqrt{\phi(0)} = \sqrt{n\Delta}$. For the specific values used, $\phi(0) = 10$. Comparison of this value to the RMS values of post-fault voltage and current Δ-signals encountered in the different experiments furnishes a well-defined SNR.

The robustness of the neural network fault direction algorithm described previously was tested with additive shot noise at different SNRs. Network inputs were all restricted to measurement at the second post-fault sample. The results indicated errors on both training and evaluation data based on a second-degree *CLASS*-generated neural network.

To combat shot noise in further tests with neural networks, the set of input features was enlarged to include averages over products of Δ-signals, viz., Δi_j^2, Δv_{kj}^2, $\Delta v_{kj}\Delta i_l$, where j, k, and l were instantiated to A, B, or C, arbitrarily, to represent line-to-line voltages and phase currents.

For a SNR of 20, the training and evaluation confusion matrices from averaging over five samples were $\begin{pmatrix} 123 & 3 \\ 3 & 249 \end{pmatrix}$ and $\begin{pmatrix} 123 & 3 \\ 3 & 249 \end{pmatrix}$, respectively, each showing three missed detections and three false alarms. Averaging over ten post-fault samples, the training and evaluation confusion matrices were $\begin{pmatrix} 5166 & 0 \\ 0 & 10332 \end{pmatrix}$ and $\begin{pmatrix} 126 & 0 \\ 0 & 252 \end{pmatrix}$, respectively. For a SNR of 10, values of $\begin{pmatrix} 5166 & 0 \\ 0 & 10332 \end{pmatrix}$ and $\begin{pmatrix} 115 & 11 \\ 3 & 249 \end{pmatrix}$ were obtained, respectively, averaging over five samples. Averaging over ten samples produced perfect training and evaluation results of $\begin{pmatrix} 5166 & 0 \\ 0 & 10332 \end{pmatrix}$ and $\begin{pmatrix} 126 & 0 \\ 3 & 249 \end{pmatrix}$, respectively. At a SNR of 5, values of $\begin{pmatrix} 4798 & 368 \\ 310 & 10022 \end{pmatrix}$ and $\begin{pmatrix} 106 & 20 \\ 15 & 237 \end{pmatrix}$ were obtained averaging over five samples, and $\begin{pmatrix} 5166 & 0 \\ 0 & 10332 \end{pmatrix}$ and $\begin{pmatrix} 123 & 3 \\ 3 & 249 \end{pmatrix}$ averaging over ten samples.

This illustrates that, as might be expected, for shot noise, one must wait longer to obtain results of similar quality to those obtained for white noise, due to the sample-to-sample correlation in the noise pattern. Because most of the input features were product combinations of Δ-signals, linear polynomial nodal elements only were used in these *CLASS* networks. It appears that providing *CLASS* with *quadratic input features averaged over time* was the key reason that linear *CLASS* networks achieved performance superior to those of the second-degree *CLASS* networks that were provided time-averaged raw Δ-signals only.

It is noted that these performance results were achieved using *static* (i.e., feedforward) neural networks, without use of time derivatives in the input feature set. *Dynamic* (i.e., recurrent) neural networks, which can be implemented using other BAI software and which takes into account the recent history of the input data, provide a capability for sophisticated averaging and filtering in the time domain, and can be made highly-adept at handling noisy data. The application of such networks should be explored further to enhance relay performance in low SNR environments.

3 Conclusions

Separate algorithms have been developed for identifying the relative direction to a fault and the zone of protection of a relay. Both algorithms have the advantages of fast, independent decision-making, ease of computation, and phase invariance. With a sampling rate of 120 kHz, sufficient information for resolving both direction and reach was found to be obtainable in less than 20 μsec (i.e., based on two post-fault sequential samples). The phase-invariance of both algorithms is key evidence of the robustness and portability of the methods discussed. The algorithms have been put to the test of superimposed noise, and have demonstrated that at the cost of a short time delay, they are able to provide correct decisions in noise levels significantly higher than that expected in practice. Further research is needed into the robustness of the pattern recognition relay algorithm under changing circuit topologies that are of practical interest.

4 Acknowledgements

The authors thank Mr. Roger T. Cooley of NSWC/Annapolis for providing all of the simulation data used in these investigations. Gratitude is also expressed to Mr. David Clayton of NSWC/Annapolis for his support and guidance throughout this work. The helpful suggestions and technical support of Mr. W. Todd Shelton of BAI are also gratefully acknowledged.

References

[1] Carley, M.P., B.E. Parker, Jr., and M.J. Szabo, "Ultra-high-speed relay fault detection using dynamic models and neural network classifiers," this conference.

[2] Chamia, M. and S. Liberman, "Ultra high-speed relay for EHV/UHV transmission lines," *IEEE Transactions on Power Apparatus and Systems*, Vol. PAS-97, No. 6, November/December 1978.

[3] *CLASS: Algorithm for Synthesis of Polynomial Networks for Classification*, Users' Manual, Version 1.62, Barron Associates, Inc., June 1995.

[4] Cherkassky, V., J. Friedman, and H. Wechsler, *From Statistics to Neural Networks*, Springer-Verlag: Berlin, 1991.

[5] Engler, F., O.E. Lanz, M. Hänggli, and G. Bacchini, "Transient signals and their processing in an ultra high-speed directional relay for EHV/UHV transmission line protection," *IEEE Transactions on Power Apparatus and Systems*, Vol. PAS-104, No. 6, June 1985.

[6] Heer, C.V., *Statistical Mechanics, Kinetic Theory, and Stochastic Processes*, Academic: New York, 1972.

[7] Novosel, D. and R.L. King, "Intelligent load shedding," *Neural Network Computing for the Electric Power Industry: Proceedings of the 1992 INNS Summer Workshop*, Stanford, CA, August 17-19, 1992.

[8] Parker, Jr., B.E. and N.A. Nigro, *Improved Fault Detection and Clearing in Advanced Electric Distribution Systems for Ships: Coordination of Multiple Circuit Breakers, Task B.6*, Barron Associates, Inc., Final Technical Report, Contract N00167-92-C-0004, Mods. P00002-P00004, NSWC, Carderock Division, Annapolis Detachment, June 1994.

[9] Petry, C.R. and J.W. Rumburg, "Zonal electrical distribution systems: an affordable architecture for the future," *Naval Engineers Journal*, May 1993.

[10] Shelton, W.T., M.P. Carley, B.E. Parker, Jr., and N.A. Nigro, *Improved Fault Detection and Clearing in Advanced Electric Distribution Systems for Ships, Task B.8: Fault Data Evaluation*, Barron Associates, Inc., Final Technical Report, Contract N00167-92-C-0004, Mod. P00005, NSWC, Carderock Division, Annapolis Detachment, January 1995.

[11] Vitins, M., "A fundamental concept for high-speed relaying," *IEEE Transactions on Power Apparatus and Systems*, Vol. PAS-100, No. 1, January 1981.

Finite Alphabets Least Relative Entropy Algorithm for Channel Equalization

Ning Li, Tülay Adalı, and Xiao Liu

Information Technology Laboratory, Department of Electrical Engineering
University of Maryland Baltimore County, Baltimore, MD 21228

Abstract

In this paper, we consider channel equalization by distribution learning introduced.in [1]. This formulation for channel equalization parametrizes the conditional probability mass function of the transmitted signal given the received signal by a neural network architecture and minimizes accumulated relative entropy (ARE) cost function. In this paper, we exploit the result that ARE minimization is equivalent to maximum partial likelihood (MPL) estimation to derive the least relative entropy (LRE) algorithm for finite alphabets. Simulation results are presented to demonstrate that the resulting algorithm can successfully equalize multipath channels.

1 Introduction

In the past decade, many linear adaptive equalization techniques have been successfully used to overcome the channel distortion and recover the transmitted symbols at the receiver end. Because of the increasing demand for very high speed efficient data transmission in communication systems, the need for sophisticated signal processing techniques to increase data communication rate has become more evident. In recent years, neural networks based on traditional mean square error (MSE) performance criterion have been proposed as a solution to this problem (see e.g. [6],[7]). A new formulation based on relative entropy cost function is introduced in [1] where the probability distribution function of the transmitted signal given the received signal is modeled by a sigmoidal perceptron. It is shown that this new perceptron based algorithm can successfully combat nonlinear channel distortions and rapidly adapt to an abrupt change after the convergence [2]. In [3] the formulation is extended to the finite alphabets case by using partial likelihood framework. It is shown that minimization of the accumulated relative entropy (ARE) cost function is equivalent to maximum partial likelihood (MPL) estimation under certain regularity conditions.

In this paper, conditional probability mass function (pmf) is modeled by multi-layer perceptron (MLP) for adaptive channel equalization for finite alphabets transmission. We derive the least relative entropy (LRE) by steepest ascent maximization of MPL cost function and present simulation studies to show its application for multipath channel equalization.

The paper is structured as follows: in section 2, we give the general problem formulation, LRE algorithm for finite alphabets is derived in section 3, and simulation results are presented in section 4.

2 Channel Equalization by Distribution Learning

The adaptive channel equalization problem by distribution learning is formulated as follows (consider Figure 1): A sequence of symbols $x(n)$ taking values from finite alphabets $\mathcal{S} = \{a_0, a_1, ..., a_M\}$ is transmitted through channel h. The neural network parametrizes the conditional probability mass function (pmf) and achieves learning by adjusting its weights based on the available information represented by the σ-field $\mathcal{F}_n$. The σ-field $\mathcal{F}_n$ is generated by events of the form $\mathbf{x}(n) = [x(n), x(n-1), ..., x(0)]$ and its time dependent covariates $\mathbf{z}(n) = [z(n), z(n-1), ..., z(0)]$ which are given by the observations (channel outputs) $y(n)'s$ for this case.

The conditional probability mass function is parametrized by a neural network as [3]:

$$P(x(n) = x|\mathcal{F}_n) = f(x, c(\boldsymbol{\theta}), g(\mathbf{z}_N(n), \boldsymbol{\theta})) \quad \forall x \in \mathcal{S} \tag{1}$$

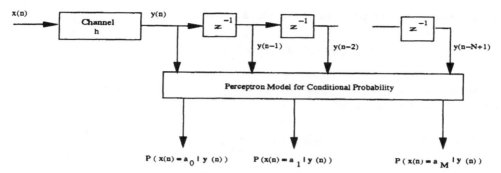

Figure 1: The Adaptive Equalization Problem

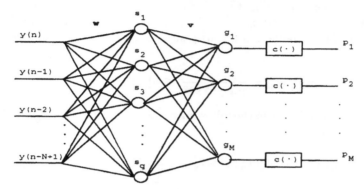

Figure 2: Neural Network Structure

where θ is the vector of network weights, $z_N(n)$ is a subset of $z(n)$ and contains most recent N values of $z(n)$, $g(z_N(n), \theta)$ is the output of the neural network, and $c(\theta)$ is the generalization function. We choose $c(\theta)$ and $f(\cdot)$ such that:

$$\sum_{x \in \mathcal{S}} p_{\theta}(x|\mathcal{F}_n) = 1 \quad \forall x \in \mathcal{S}. \tag{2}$$

The appropriate cost function we choose for this formulation is the accumulated relative entropy (ARE) given by:

$$\mathcal{I}_n = \sum_{i=1}^{n} \sum_{x \in \mathcal{S}} p^{true}(x_i|\mathcal{F}_i) \ln \frac{p^{true}(x_i|\mathcal{F}_i)}{p_{\theta}(x_i|\mathcal{F}_i)} \quad \forall x \in \mathcal{S}. \tag{3}$$

The aim is then to learn the parameters θ which minimize the performance criterion (3) under the observations $\mathcal{F}_1, \mathcal{F}_2, \cdots, \mathcal{F}_n$. However, the true conditional probability $p^{true}(x_i|\mathcal{F}_i)$ usually is not available. In [3], it is shown that the ARE minimization problem is equivalent to maximum partial likelihood (MPL) estimation problem under certain regularity conditions:

$$\theta_0 = arg(\min_{\theta} \mathcal{I}_n) = arg(\max_{\theta} \bar{\mathcal{L}}_n(\theta)) \quad \forall x \in \mathcal{S} \tag{4}$$

where $\bar{\mathcal{L}}_n(\theta) = \ln \mathcal{L}_n(\theta)$ is the partial log-likelihood function, and $\mathcal{L}_n(\theta) = \prod_{i=1}^{n} p_{\theta}(x_i|\mathcal{F}_i)$ is the partial likelihood function.

3 LRE Algorithm for Multi-Symbol Alphabets

In what follows, we assume that $x(n)$ is an independent sequence taking values from the finite alphabets $\mathcal{S} = \{a_0, a_1, ..., a_M\}$, and derive least relative entropy (LRE) algorithm by parametrizing the pmf with MLP. Figure 2 shows the network structure used as the probability distribution model.

Using (4) we can reformulate the problem as maximization of $\mathcal{D}_n$ given by:

$$\mathcal{D}_n = \bar{\mathcal{L}}_n(\theta) = \ln \mathcal{L}_n(\theta) = \ln \prod_{i=1}^{n} p_{\theta}(x_i|\mathcal{F}_i). \tag{5}$$

For finite alphabets, the conditional probability distribution can be represented by the M-output MLP in the following manner (see equation (1)):

$$p_{\theta}(x(n)|\mathcal{F}_n) = \sum_{m=1}^{M} f\left(d_m(x(n)), c\left(\varphi\left(\sum_{i=1}^{q} \varphi\left(\mathbf{y}_N^T(n)\mathbf{w}_i(n)\right) v_{mi}(n)\right)\right)\right) \tag{6}$$

In (6), $\mathbf{y}_N(n) = [y(n), y(n-1), ..., y(n-N+1)]^T$ is the observation vector containing the finite past of the received signal, $\mathbf{w}_i(n)$ is the N dimensional weight vector from the input layer to hidden node i, $(i = 1, 2, ..., q,$ where q is the number of hidden nodes) and v_{mi} $(m = 1, 2, ..., M)$ is the weight from the hidden node i to the output node m. $\varphi(\cdot)$ is a differentiable non-linearity such that $\varphi'(\cdot) > 0$. Here we choose the logistic activation function:

$$\varphi(\mathbf{y}_N^T\mathbf{w}_i) = \frac{1}{1 + e^{-\mathbf{y}_N^T\mathbf{w}_i}} \in [0, 1].$$

The generalization function $c(\cdot)$ is chosen in the following manner to ensure that $p_{\theta}(x(n) = a_m|\mathcal{F}_n) \in [0, 1]$ and that $\sum_{m=1}^{M} p_{\theta}(x(n) = a_m|\mathcal{F}_n) = 1$:

$$p_{\theta}(x(n) = a_m|\mathcal{F}_n) = c(g_m) = \frac{g_m}{\sum_{m=1}^{M} g_m}$$

where $g_m = \varphi(\mathbf{s}_q^T\mathbf{v}_m)$, and $\mathbf{s}_q^T = [s_1, s_2, ..., s_q]^T$ as defined in Figure 2.

The index function $d_m(x(n))$ corresponding to the mth symbol is defined as a function of $x(n)$ such that $d_m(x(n)) = 1$ when the channel input is the mth symbol and 0 when it is not. Then the cost function $\mathcal{D}_n$ (5) can be written as:

$$\mathcal{D}_n = \ln \prod_{m=1}^{M} p_{\theta}(x(n) = a_m|\mathcal{F}_n)^{d_m(x(n))}. \tag{7}$$

By the gradient ascent maximization of $\mathcal{D}_n$, the conditional probability model (6) results in the following algorithm with the parameter updates:

$$v_{mi}(n+1) = v_{mi}(n) + \mu_2 \left(d_m(n)\left(1 - g_m(n) - G_m(n)\right) - (1 - d_m(n))G_m(n)\right) s_i(n) \tag{8}$$

$$\mathbf{w}_i(n+1) = \mathbf{w}_i(n) + \mu_1\left(d_m(n)(1 - g_m(n) - \sum_{m=1}^{M} G_m(n)) - (1 - d_m(n))\sum_{m=1}^{M} G_m(n)\right)v_{mi}(n)s_i(n)(1-s_i(n))\mathbf{y}_N(n)$$

$$\tag{9}$$

where

$$G_m(n) = \frac{g_m(n)(1 - g_m(n))}{\sum_{m=1}^{M} g_m(n)}.$$

4 Simulation Results

The LRE algorithm derived in section 3 is applied to multipath channel equalization. We consider the four symbol alphabets $\mathcal{S} = \{-3, -1, 1, 3\}$ and the channel is chosen as the simple multipath $1.0 + 0.5z^{-1}$. For this case, the cost function can be written as:

$$\mathcal{D}_n = \ln \left(p_{\theta}(x(n) = -3|\mathcal{F}_n)^{d_1(x(n))} p_{\theta}(x(n) = -1|\mathcal{F}_n)^{d_2(x(n))} p_{\theta}(x(n) = 1|\mathcal{F}_n)^{d_3(x(n))} p_{\theta}(x(n) = 3|\mathcal{F}_n)^{d_4(x(n))}\right)$$

where the index function $d_m(m = 1, 2, 3, 4)$ is defined as follows for symbols $\{-3, -1, 1, 3\}$ respectively.

$$d_1(x(n)) = -(x(n)+1)(x(n)-1)(x(n)-3)/48, \quad d_2(x(n)) = (x(n)+3)(x(n)-1)(x(n)-3)/16$$

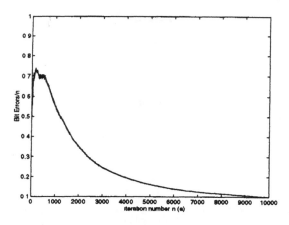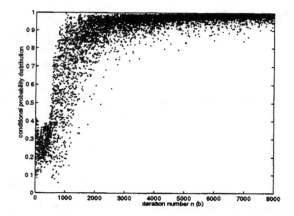

Figure 3: The Conditional Probability Distribution Learning

$$d_3(x(n)) = -(x(n) + 3)(x(n) + 1)(x(n) - 3)/16, \quad d_4(x(n)) = (x(n) + 3)(x(n) + 1)(x(n) - 1)/48$$

In Figure 3(a), the probability learning curve in terms of bit errors divided by the iteration number n shows that the LRE algorithm based on the conditional probability distribution model can equalize the multipath channel. Figure 3(b) shows that the estimated probability $p_\theta(x(n)|\mathcal{F}_n)$ converges to 1 as the algorithm iterates.

The same algorithm is also applied to the equalization of nonlinear multipath channel $1.0 + 0.5z^{-1}$ followed by the nonlinearity $0.5(\cdot)^3$, and similar results are obtained.

References

[1] T. Adalı and M. K. Sönmez, "Channel equalization with perceptrons: an information theoretic approach," *Proc. IEEE Int. Conf. Acoust., Speech, Signal Processing* (Adelaide, Australia), April 1994, vol.3, pp. 297-300.

[2] T. Adalı, M. K. Sönmez, and K. Patel, "On the dynamics of the LRE algorithm: a distribution learning approach to adaptive equalization," *Proc. IEEE Int. Conf. Acoust., Speech, Signal Processing*, (Detroit, MI), May 1995, vol.2, pp. 929-932.

[3] X. Liu and T. Adali, "Channel equalization by maximum partial likelihood estimation", *Conference on Information Science and System*, March 1995, Baltimore, MD, U.S.A.

[4] W. H. Wong, "Theory of partial likelihood, " *Ann. Statist.*, 14, pp. 88-123, 1986.

[5] H. White, "Learning in artificial neural networks: a statistical perspective", *Neural Computation*, vol. 1, pp. 425-464, 1989.

[6] G. J. Gibson, S. Siu, and C. F. N. Cowan, "The application of nonlinear structures to the reconstruction of binary channel equalization," *IEEE Trans. Signal Processing*, Aug. 1991, vol. 39, no. 8, pp. 1877-1884.

[7] G. Kechriotis, E. Zervas, and E. S. Manolakos, "Using recurrent neural networks for adaptive communication channel equalization," *IEEE Trans. on Neural Networks*, March 1994, vol. 5, no. 2, pp. 267-278.

A Neural Network Approach to the Optimal Data Association in Multi-Target Tracking

Yang-Weon Lee and Hong Jeong

Department of Electrical Engineering, Pohang University of Science and Technology, Pohang 790-784, Korea
Tel: +82-562-279-2223, E-mail:hjeong@hjstar.postech.ac.kr

Abstract

A neural network-based algorithm was developed for the data association problem in multi-target tracking (MTT). It is well known that the optimal association problem is a combinatorial problem. To cope with this problem, we proposed a new scheme that converts the uncertainty problem into an energy function. After then a neural network is used to compute the energy equation. It is shown that the new algorithm has the performance advantages over the JPDA.

I. Introduction

The primary purpose of a multi-target tracking(MTT) system is to provide estimates of target position and velocity, by using the measurement data within a specific gate of targets. Naturally, the performance of this system is limited by the measurement uncertainty; the detected location of the target is inaccurate. So, data preprocessing, so called *data association between targets and measurements* is needed before proceeding the target tracking.

Sengupta and Iltis [1] suggested the computation of the *a posteriori* probabilities for the joint probabilities data association(JPDAF) as a constrained minimization problem. However, the neural network developed in [1] has been derived from improper energy functions. Since the value of β_j^t's in the original JPDAF are not consistent with X_j^t of [1], these dual assumptions of no two returns from the same target and no single return from two targets should be used only in the generation of the feasible data association hypotheses, as pointed out in [2]. This resulted from misinterpretations of the properties of the JPDAF which the network was supposed to emulate. Furthermore, improper choices of the constant coefficients in the energy function in [1] make the situation worse.

To overcome this kind of defect, we propose a new energy equation for *data association* which is based on the Bayesian approach. It reflects the best natural constraints of the MTT *data association* problem. Also, the Hopfield neural network scheme is proposed for the new energy equation.

II. Constraints for Measurement-target relationship

Let m and n be the number of measurements and targets respectively, in a particular gate. For the purpose of solving the problem of data association of a large number of targets and measurements in a certain gate, we form a *validation matrix* [2] Ω for the n targets and m measurements. By definition, the validation matrix Ω is a $m \times (n+1)$ rectangle matrix is

$$\Omega = [\omega_{jt}] = \begin{pmatrix} 1 & \omega_{11} & \omega_{12} & \dots & \omega_{1n} \\ 1 & \omega_{21} & \omega_{22} & \dots & \omega_{2n} \\ \vdots & \vdots & \vdots & \vdots & \vdots \\ 1 & \omega_{m1} & \omega_{m2} & \dots & \omega_{mn} \end{pmatrix}, \tag{1}$$

where the first column denotes clutter and always $\omega_{j0} = 1 (j \in [1, m])$. For the other columns, $\omega_{jt} = 1 (j \in [1, m], t \in [1, n])$ if the validation gate of target t contains the measurement j and $\omega_{jt} = 0$ otherwise.

Based on the validation matrix Ω, data association hypothesis(or feasible events [3]) are generated subject to the following two restrictions:

$$\begin{cases} \sum_{j=1}^{m} w_{jt} = 1, & \text{for} \quad (t \in [1, n(j \in [1, m]]), \\ \sum_{t=0}^{n} w_{jt} = 1, & \text{for} \quad (j \in [1, m]). \end{cases} \tag{2}$$

Each *feasible event* $\mathcal{E}$ is represented by a *hypothesis matrix* $\hat{\Omega}$ [3], that has the same size as the validation matrix Ω. An element in $\hat{\Omega}$ is denoted by $\hat{\omega}_{jt}$ where $\hat{\omega}_{jt} = 1$ only if the measurement j is hypothesized to be associated with clutter ($t = 0$) or target t ($t \neq 0$). The generation of a *hypothesis matrix* leads to a combinatorial problem where the number of data association hypothesis increases exponentially with the number of targets and the number of measurements.

III. Constraints for Target Trajectories

Let's consider a particular situation of the gate for target t in Fig. 1. In this figure the position of the gate center of target t is represented by a vector $\mathbf{x_t}$. Also $\mathbf{y_j}$ means the the coordinate of the measurement j. Among the measurements included in this gate, at most one must be chosen as an actual target site. Note that the gate center is simply an estimate of this actual target position obtained by a prediction filter.

Since the target must change its direction smoothly, a possible candidate must be positioned on the site which is close to the trajectory as possible. As a measure of this distance, one can define the minimum distance between $\mathbf{x_t} = (x_t, y_t)$ and the measurement $\mathbf{y_j} = (x_j, y_j)$ as

$$||\mathbf{x_t} - \mathbf{y_j}||^2 \triangleq \frac{(x_j y_t - y_j x_t)^2}{(x_t^2 + y_t^2)}. \tag{3}$$

IV. Energy Function

Let's consider that $\hat{\Omega}$ is a parameter space and (Ω, Y, X) is an observation space. Then, *a posteriori* probability can be derived by the Bayes rule:

$$P(\hat{\Omega}|\Omega, \mathbf{y}, \mathbf{x}) = \frac{P(\Omega, \mathbf{y}, \mathbf{x}|\hat{\Omega})\mathbf{P}(\hat{\Omega})}{\mathbf{P}(\Omega, \mathbf{y}, \mathbf{x})}, \tag{4}$$

$$= \frac{P(\Omega|\hat{\Omega})P(\mathbf{y}, \mathbf{x}|\hat{\Omega})\mathbf{P}(\hat{\Omega})}{\mathbf{P}(\Omega, \mathbf{y}, \mathbf{x})}. \tag{5}$$

Here we assumed that $P(\Omega, \mathbf{y}, \mathbf{x}|\hat{\Omega}) = \mathbf{P}(\Omega|\hat{\Omega})\mathbf{P}(\mathbf{y}, \mathbf{x}|\hat{\Omega})$. That is the two variables (X, Y) and Ω are separately observed. This assumption makes the problem more tractable as we shall see later.

This relationship is illustrated in Fig. 2. From the parameter $\hat{\Omega}$, (X, Y) and Ω are observed. If the conditional probabilities describing the relationships between the parameter space and the observation spaces are available, one can obtain the MAP estimator

$$\Omega^* = \text{argmax}_{\hat{\Omega}} P(\hat{\Omega}|\Omega, Y, X). \tag{6}$$

We assume that the conditional probabilities are all Gibbs distributions:

$$
\begin{aligned}
P(\hat{\Omega}|\Omega, Y, X) &\triangleq \tfrac{1}{Z}\exp\{-E(\hat{\Omega}|\Omega, Y, X)\} \\
P(\mathbf{y}, \mathbf{x}|\hat{\Omega}) &\triangleq \tfrac{1}{Z_1}\exp\{-E(\mathbf{y}, \mathbf{x}|\hat{\Omega})\}, \\
P(\Omega|\hat{\Omega}) &\triangleq \tfrac{1}{Z_2}\exp\{-E(\Omega|\hat{\Omega})\}, \\
P(\hat{\Omega}) &\triangleq \tfrac{1}{Z_3}\exp\{-E(\hat{\Omega})\}, \\
P(\Omega, Y, X) &\triangleq \tfrac{1}{Z_4}\exp\{-E(\Omega, Y, X)\},
\end{aligned}
\tag{7}
$$

where $Z_s, (s \in [1, 2, 3, 4])$ and E denote partition functions and energy functions, respectively. Substituting (7) into (5) yields

$$E(\hat{\Omega}|\Omega, Y, X) = E(\mathbf{y}, \mathbf{x}|\hat{\Omega}) + \mathbf{E}(\Omega|\hat{\Omega}) + \mathbf{E}(\hat{\Omega}) - \mathbf{E}(\Omega, Y, X) \tag{8}$$

and the problem (6) becomes

$$\Omega^* = \text{argmin}_{\hat{\Omega}} E(\hat{\Omega}|\Omega, Y, X). \tag{9}$$

Since the optimization is executed with respect to $\hat{\Omega}$, the last term in (8) is a constant and one must ignore it.

The energy functions are the realizations of the constraints for the target trajectories and measurement-target relationships. The constraints in (2) and (3) are respectively represented by the energy functions in (10),(11) and (12).

$$E(\mathbf{y}, \mathbf{x}|\hat{\Omega}) \triangleq \sum_{t=1}^{n}\sum_{j=1}^{m} \frac{(x_j y_t - y_j x_t)^2}{(x_t^2 + y_t^2)} \hat{w}_{jt}, \tag{10}$$

$$E(\Omega|\hat{\Omega}) \triangleq \sum_{t=1}^{n}\sum_{j=1}^{m} (\hat{w}_{jt} - w_{jt})^2, \tag{11}$$

$$E(\hat{\Omega}) \triangleq \sum_{t=1}^{n}(\sum_{j=1}^{m}\hat{w}_{jt} - 1)^2 + \sum_{j=1}^{m}(\sum_{t=1}^{n}\hat{w}_{jt} - 1)^2. \tag{12}$$

Putting (10), (11) and (12) into (8), one get

$$E(\hat{\Omega}|\Omega, Y, X) = \frac{\mathbf{A}}{2}\sum_{t=1}^{n}\sum_{j=1}^{m} r^2 \hat{w}_{jt} + \frac{\mathbf{B}}{2}\sum_{t=1}^{n}\sum_{j=1}^{m}(\hat{w}_{jt} - w_{jt})^2 + \frac{\mathbf{C}}{2}\sum_{t=1}^{n}(\sum_{j=1}^{m}\hat{w}_{jt} - 1)^2 + \frac{\mathbf{D}}{2}\sum_{j=1}^{m}(\sum_{t=0}^{n}\hat{w}_{jt} - 1)^2, \tag{13}$$

where $r_{jt} \triangleq \frac{(x_j y_t - y_j x_t)}{\sqrt{x_t^2 + y_t^2}}$, and $\mathbf{A}, \mathbf{B}, \mathbf{C},$ and $\mathbf{D}$ are coefficients which can be adjusted to control the emphasis on different constraints and properties and $\mathbf{A}, \mathbf{B}, \mathbf{C},$ and $\mathbf{D} \geq 0$.

V. Neural Network Implementation

A Hopfield network with $m \times n$ neurons was considered. In Hopfield network, it is possible to verify that the energy function(Lyapunov function) given by

$$\mathbf{E} = -\frac{1}{2}\sum_{i}\sum_{j} W_{ij} X_i X_j - \sum_{i} I_i X_i. \tag{14}$$

necessarily admits local minima, corresponding to some vertices of the $m \times n$ dimensional hypercube defined by the condition $X_i = 0$ or 1 [4]. For the unipolar activation function, the Hopfield operational equation for the ith neuron is

$$\frac{dS_i}{dt} = -\frac{S_i}{\overline{d}} - \frac{\partial E}{\partial X_i}$$
$$= -\frac{S_i}{\overline{d}} + \sum_i W_{ij} X_j + I_i, \qquad (15)$$

where "$\overline{d}$" is a free parameter to be chosen, $\overline{t}$ is a time, W_{ij} is the connection weight from jth neuron to ith neuron and I_i is the external input data for the ith neuron.

The neurons in neural network MTT were subdivided into n target's columns of m neurons each. Henceforward we will identify each neuron with a double index, tl(where the index $t = 1, 2, \ldots, n$ relates to the target, whereas the index $l = 1, \ldots, m$ refers to the neurons in each column), its output with X_l^t, the weight for neurons tl and τp with $W_{\tau p}^{tl}$, and the external bias current for neuron tl with I_{tl}. According to this convention, we can extend the notation of the Lyapunov energy function (14) to two dimensions.

(13) can be written as

$$E_{AP} = \frac{1}{2} \sum_l \sum_p \sum_t \sum_\tau (B\delta_{t\tau}\delta_{lp} + C\delta_{t\tau} + D\delta_{lp}) X_l^t X_p^\tau + \sum_l \sum_t (\frac{A}{2} r_{lt}^2 - B\omega_{lt} - C - D) X_l^t + \frac{Cn + Dm}{2} + \sum_l \sum_t \frac{B}{2} \omega_{lt}^2. \quad (16)$$

We also can extend the notation of the Lyapunov energy function (14) to two dimensions:

$$\mathbf{E} = -\frac{1}{2} \sum_l \sum_p \sum_t \sum_\tau W_{\tau p}^{tl} X_l^t X_p^\tau - \sum_l \sum_t I_l^t X_l^t \qquad (17)$$

By comparing (16) and (17), it follows after some rejection of constant terms that $\mathbf{E} = E_{AP}$ if

$$W_{\tau p}^{tl} = -B\delta_{t\tau}\delta_{lp} - C\delta_{t\tau} - D\delta_{lp}$$
$$I_l^t = -\frac{A}{2} r_{lt}^2 + B\omega_{lt} + C + D \qquad (18)$$

With the specific values from (18), the equations of motion for the MTT become

$$\frac{dS_l^t}{dt} = -\frac{S_l^t}{\overline{d}} - B X_l^t - C \sum_p X_p^t - D \sum_\tau X_l^\tau + B\omega_{lt} + C + D - \frac{A}{2} r_{lt}^2. \qquad (19)$$

Fig. 3 sketches the resulting two-dimensional network architecture as a directed graph.

VI. Experiments

We consider that the performance of the algorithm is first evaluated for the data association problem and the two different tracking examples in the two-dimensional space are considered next. The performance of the present algorithm for MTT is compared to that of the JPDA algorithm. The data association and convergence of energy are shown in Fig. 4. The tracking performances of cross and parallel travelling target are shwon in Fig. 5 and Fig. 6. The tracking performance is compared with JPDA method. The proposed filter maintains the tracking both parallel and crossing targets even if the JPDA does not work in heavy clutter environment. It works 10% better than JPDA.

VII. Conclusion

In this paper, we proposed a new data association algorithm for MTT. We showed that this algorithm is stable and converges to the solutions very close to global minima. The convergence time is always less than the time constant of the networks processing element(neurons). This implies that fast solutions can be realized if the algorithm is implemented in hardware circuits. Also, the tracking performance works about 10% better than the JPDA algorithm in tracking accuracy.

References

[1] Sengupta,D., and Iltis, R.A., "Neural solution to the multitarget tracking data association problem," *IEEE Trans. on AES, AES-25*, pp. 96-108, Jan. 1989

[2] Y. Bar-Shalom, "Extension of probabilistic data associatiation filter in multitarget tracking," in Proc. 5th Symp. Nonlinear Estimation Theory and its Application, pp. 16-21, Sept. 1974

[3] T.E. Fortmann, Y. Bar-Shalom, and M. Scheffe,"Sonar Tracking of Multiple Targets Using Joint Probabilistic Data Association," *IEEE J. Oceanic Engineering*, Vol. OE-8, pp.173-184, July 1983

[4] Hopfield, J.J., and Tank, D.W., "Neural computation of decisions in optimization problems," Biological Cybernatics, pp. 141-152, 1985

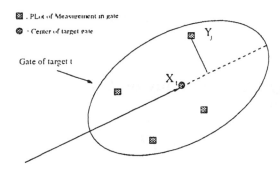

Fig 1　Target trajectory and the measurements

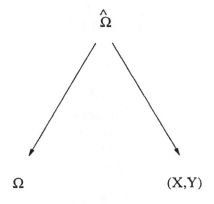

Fig. 2.　The parameter space and the observation space.

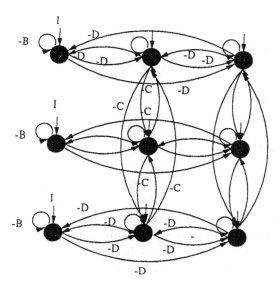

Fig. 3　Example of Hopfile MTT network configuration.

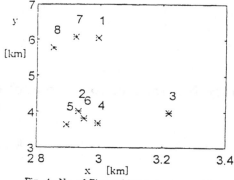

Fig 4a No. of Plots within gate at scan 10

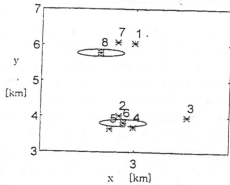

Fig. 4b Data association result at scan 10

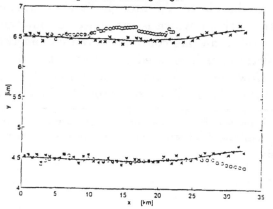

— : target trajectory
O : JPDA algorithm
∗ : Proposed algorithm

Fig.5 Tracking performance comparison
against the crossing target

Fig 6 Tracking performance comparison　against the parallel target

Fuzzy Neural Network Control of Complex Systems: A Study on Longitudinal Vehicle Control

Shinya Kikuchi [1]   and   Partha Chakroborty [2]

1 Introduction

Fuzzy logic control has proven to be a powerful tool in the control of complex, highly non-linear systems. Various applications have been reported [1]. Yet, Fuzzy logic control (FLC) has suffered from a major drawback — the lack of a feedback adjusting mechanism. In its traditional form the FLC algorithm could not be modified or tuned to obtain either a better control or a closer emulation of the human controller.

The drawback can be effectively remedied using Fuzzy Neural Networks (FNN). The construction of the network closely follows the structure of an FLC in that (1) FNNs naturally processes inputs parallelly, (2) the activation function works as possibility distributions or membership functions of FLCs, and (3) logical AND and OR can be represented through the nodes. By restructuring the FLC in the format of NNs, one can modify the FLC rules using the correction algorithms of NNs.

This paper discusses issues regarding representation of the FLC as FNNs. A case study on the longitudinal vehicle control using FNNs is presented as an example.

2 FNN Representation of an FLC Algorithm

A fuzzy logic control algorithm has the following basic structure:

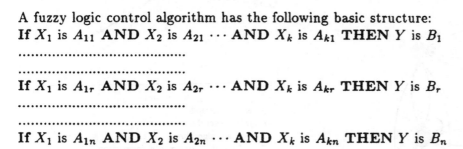

If X_1 is A_{11} **AND** X_2 is A_{21} $\cdots$ **AND** X_k is A_{k1} **THEN** Y is B_1

If X_1 is A_{1r} **AND** X_2 is A_{2r} $\cdots$ **AND** X_k is A_{kr} **THEN** Y is B_r

If X_1 is A_{1n} **AND** X_2 is A_{2n} $\cdots$ **AND** X_k is A_{kn} **THEN** Y is B_n

In the above X_1 through X_k are variables which characterize the state of the system and Y is the variable which is controlled to maintain a certain desired condition. (Note that there could be more than one controlled variable and that the X_i's are affected by the state of the Y.) This structure has been used extensively in various industrial control problems successfully.

However, there are certain issues which are still largely unresolved. These include: 1. Interpretation of the AND operator; 2. Combination of the actions suggested by the various rules; 3.

[1] Professor, Department of Civil Engineering, University of Delaware, Newark, DE 19716.

[2] Assistant Professor, Department of Civil Engineering, Indian Institute of Technology, Kanpur, Kanpur 208016, India

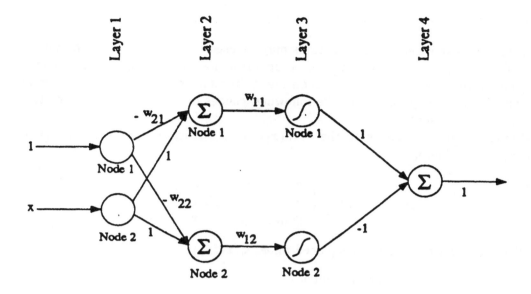

Figure 1: Representing membership functions in FNNs

Defuzzification procedure; 4. Definition of the membership functions for A_{11} through A_{kn} and B_1 through B_n.

Answers to these issues are relevant as they would largely affect the functioning of the control algorithm. In this paper the concentration is on the last issue. The idea is whether the approximate notion of A_{11} through A_{kn} and B_1 through B_n can be tuned so as to obtain a better "definition" of the membership functions.

In the past few years much work has been done on representing FLC as an FNN and using the modification algorithms of Neural Networks (NNs) to achieve tuning of membership functions. In the following we briefly present a representation technique including the representation of the Min and the Max operators in FNNs (these operators are generally avoided in FNNs as their derivatives are not continuous.), and weighted average technique of combining the different actions.

2.1 Membership function representation in FNNs

A powerful and convenient way of representing a membership function of the trapezoidal type is shown in Figure 1.

Using the above representation as the basic building blocks for membership functions, and combining their outputs suitably, FLC rules may also be represented in FNNs. An in-depth discussion on representations may be found in Horikawa et al [3,4].

2.2 Representation of the Min and Max operators

In the NN representation, one faces a problem of using the Min and Max operators because they are not continuously differentiable (note that gradient descent algorithms require information on the derivatives). To overcome this problem some continuously differentiable approximations of these operators were devised. These functions may be used to represent the Min and Max operators.

The $Min(x_1, x_2)$ and the $Max(x_1, x_2)$ operators have discontinuous derivatives at $x_1 = x_2$. The approximations try to avoid this discontinuity by approximating the operators in the vicinity of the equality of the operands. In the following, classes of functions which does this approximation effectively are presented.

First, the approximation to the $Min(x_1, x_2)$ is discussed. Let $g_{min}(x_1, x_2)$ represent the approximation. Where,

$$g_{min}(x_1, x_2) = \begin{cases} x_2 & \text{if } x_2 \leq x_1 - \epsilon \\ x_1 & \text{if } x_2 \geq x_1 + \epsilon \\ \phi_{min}(x_1, x_2) & \text{if } x_1 - \epsilon \leq x_2 \leq x_1 + \epsilon \end{cases}$$

The following constraints are placed on $\phi_{min}(x_1, x_2)$:

1. $\phi_{min}(x_1, x_2)$ should be symmetric

2. $\phi_{min}(x_1, x_2) = x_2$ at $x_2 = x_1 - \epsilon$

3. $\phi_{min}(x_1, x_2) = x_1$ at $x_2 = x_1 + \epsilon$

4. $\phi'_{min}(x_1, x_2) = 1$ at $x_2 = x_1 - \epsilon$

5. $\phi'_{min}(x_1, x_2) = 0$ at $x_2 = x_1 + \epsilon$

6. $\phi'_{min}(x_1, x_2)$ should be continuous

Functions of the following form were chosen.

$$\phi_{min}(x_1. x_2) = a(x_1^2 + x_2^2) + b(x_1 + x_2) + cx_1x_2 + d.$$

Using the restrictions stated above the following form was obtained:

$$\phi_{min}(x_1, x_2) = -\frac{1}{4\epsilon}(x_1^2 + x_2^2) + \frac{1}{2}(x_1 + x_2) + \frac{1}{2\epsilon}x_1x_2 - \frac{\epsilon}{4}.$$

Following similar logic and changing the restrictions we can obtain the approximations for $Max(x_1, x_2)$, $g_{max}x_1, x_2$. Where.

$$g_{max}(x_1, x_2) = \begin{cases} x_1 & \text{if } x_2 \leq x_1 - \epsilon \\ x_2 & \text{if } x_2 \geq x_1 + \epsilon \\ \phi_{max}(x_1, x_2) & \text{if } x_1 - \epsilon \leq x_2 \leq x_1 + \epsilon \end{cases}$$

and,

$$\phi_{max}(x_1, x_2) = \frac{1}{4\epsilon}(x_1^2 + x_2^2) + \frac{1}{2}(x_1 + x_2) - \frac{1}{2\epsilon}x_1x_2 + \frac{\epsilon}{4}$$

Note that by making ϵ arbitrarily small one can get progressively closer approximations of the Min and Max operators. These approximations have a few interesting interpretations while using it with the back-propagation algorithm. These may be found in Chakroborty [3].

2.3 Discussion on Weighted Average combination of actions

In general, the different actions suggested by the rules are combined through the union operation. The resulting fuzzy set is then defuzzified to obtain a crisp action.

Another way of combining the different actions would be through simple weighted average of the actions (this is essentially a linear interpolation). For example, in a two rule case, if τ_1 and τ_2 represent the truth of the premise of Rule 1 and Rule 2 under a given input condition, then

$$Ac\tilde{t}ion = \frac{\tau_1 \tilde{a_1} + \tau_2 \tilde{a_2}}{\tau_1 + \tau_2}$$

would give the combined action. $\tilde{a_1}$ and $\tilde{a_2}$ are the actions associated with the two rules.

This procedure has some inherent benefits:

1. FNN representation provides considerable simplification and has interesting ramifications on the modification of the membership functions using the back-propagation algorithm.

2. Computational efficiency increases because the arithmetic involved is considerably simpler.

3. The nature of $\tilde{a_1}$ and $\tilde{a_2}$ are reflected in $Ac\tilde{t}ion$. For example, if $\tilde{a_1}$ and $\tilde{a_2}$ are fuzzy numbers representing, say the approximate force to be applied under certain conditions to restore stability, then $Ac\tilde{t}ion$ will also be a fuzzy number. This is intuitively appealing since there is no reason why $Ac\tilde{t}ion$ should be a single number.

4. If defuzzified value is assumed to be that which yields the highest possibility then only the modal value for the fuzzy sets representing the actions from each of the rules needs to be represented in the FNN. This allows considerable simplification in the FNN representation.

In a case study of longitudinal vehicle control using fuzzy logic the weighted average technique was used [3]. The results obtained were very satisfactory, yet computationally, the process was very simple. In the following section the back-propagation algorithm and its implications on membership function modification will be discussed.

3 Back-propagation and Implementation of Some Bases of Rule Modification

The back-propagation or the delta rule has been utilized to modify the membership functions of an FLC. In this section, the basic effects of the delta rule on the modification of the membership functions is discussed. It is shown that the back-propagation algorithm does implement a set of logical bases for the modification of the membership functions.

Consider the following representation of an FLC:

1. The membership functions of the anticident variables are represented by the method shown in the previous section.

2. The **And** operator is represenened by the Min (or its approximation).

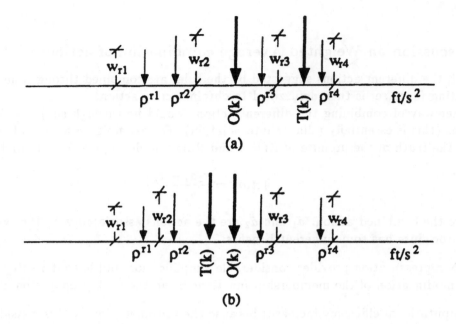

Figure 2: Possible outcome scenarios from an FLC

3. The actions of the various rules are combined using the weighted average technique discussed in the previous section.

In any prediction, as in the case at hand, one of the following three situations may arise: (1) The predicted value (action) is greater than the observed/desired value (action); (2) The predicted value (action) is less than the observed/desired value (action); and (3) The predicted value (action) is equal to the observed/desired value (action).

Any corrective algorithm should modify the membership functions of the rules such that the predicted action becomes closer to the observed or desired action (and if the predicted and the observed are equal then the rules should not be modified).

Figure 2 shows possible outcomes from an FLC. The idea of the rule modification algorithm would be to minimize the difference between $T(k)$ and $O(k)$. The notation used in the diagram is as follows:

- $T(k)$ represents the Target action (or the observed action) for input vector k and $O(k)$ represents the Output action (or predicted action) for the input vector k,

- ρ^r represents the action suggested by Rule r,

- $w_r(k)$ represents the truth value (or the degree of match) of the premise of Rule r for the input vector k.

It can be shown that the back-propagation algorithm implements the following correction mechanism:

1. Increase the ρ^r values if $T(k) > O(k)$ and reduce the values of ρ^r if $T(k) < O(k)$. For example, in Figure 2 (a) the values of of ρ^r should be increased and decreased in Figure 2 (b).

2. Increase the value of $w_r(k)$ if

$$(\rho^r - O(k)) \times (T(k) - O(k)) > 0$$

For example, $w_{r3}(k)$ and $w_{r4}(k)$ in Figure 2(a), and $w_{r1}(k)$ and $w_{r2}(k)$ in (b) should be increased.

3. Decrease the value of $w_r(k)$ if

$$(\rho^r - O(k)) \times (T(k) - O(k)) < 0$$

For example, $w_{r1}(k)$ and $w_{r2}(k)$ in Figure 2(a), and $w_{r3}(k)$ and $w_{r4}(k)$ in (b) should be decreased.

4. Do not modify the membership functions of Rule r if $w_r(k) = 0$.

5. Modify the membership function of that fuzzy set of the anticident which yields the value of $w_r(k)$. If more than one fuzzy set of the anticident yield values close to the $w_r(k)$ then modify the membership functions of all the sets.

This feature of the back-propagation algorithm is very appealing and provides a theoretical basis for using it to modify membership functions of the FLC.

4 Case Study: Longitudinal Vehicle Control

The longitudinal vehicle control problem has gained importance in the recent years with the emergence of the Intelligent Vehicle-Highway System(IVHS). In this problem when two vehicles are closely following one another, the behavior of a vehicle relative to the actions of the vehicle in front is studied. This is called car-following phenomenon. In general, the following vehicle attempts to maintain a "safe-distance" between the vehicles in response to the actions (acceleration and deceleration) of the leading vehicle.

The longitudinal control algorithm is supposed to deliver appropriate actions so that a safe distance and zero relative speed is eventually obtained. However, the safe distance headway is dependent on the velocity at which the following vehicle is traveling, and it is determined only by experience of individual drivers. This and other interdependencies of the variables make this a complex control problem. Discussions on this problem are found in many textbooks of traffic flow theory [5,6].

5 Implementation of the Control Algorithm using FNNs

An FLC was developed for the longitudinal control of vehicles. The results show that it provides an effective tool for explanation and simulation of driver (who are essentially controllers) behavior.

The FLC which we developed had 396 rules, 4 input parameters, and 1 output parameter. (It should be noted that out of the 396 rules only a few are utilized at any one time). The FLC is described in Kikuchi and Chakroborty [8]. For the FLC to be practically useful, it was necessary

Table 1: Number of Nodes in Each Layer

Layer	Number of Nodes
1	7
2	40
3	40
4	23
5	396
6	397
7	396
8	1

to introduce the ability to calibrate the FLC for different drivers so that the actions taken by the FLC conforms to those of the actual drivers. To introduce this calibration capability the FLC is represented by an FNN.

The FNN representation had eight layers (including the input and the output layer). The number of nodes in each layer are shown in Table 1. A detailed description of the FNN structure is found in Chakroborty [3].

6 Results and Discussion

The FLC and its FNN representation was used to study the effectiveness of the longitudinal vehicle control algorithm. Here, two noteworthy results are presented.

Figure 3 shows three situations. Each line in the figure shows the process of headway stabilization from three different initial distance headways where the FLC achieves control under the following condition:

1. Initially the vehicle pair is in an unstable situation (the vehicles in each of the three situations are too far apart or too close for the speed at which they were traveling).

2. The leading vehicle accelerates for 4 seconds at the rate of 5 ft/s^2.

Note that since the final velocity is same all the three lines (which represent different initial conditions) converge to the same state (i.e. zero relative speed and safe distance headway of 130 ft.).

Figure 4 shows how the FNN effectively tunes the membership functions of the FLC rules to obtain a better match between the observed control actions and predicted control actions. The asterisk on the figure mark data on acceleration/deceleration rates applied by a particular driver under a driving situation over a period of time. A band on the top figure represents the predictions from the untuned FLC (represented as an FNN). A band on the bottom figure represents the predictions from the tuned FLC (tuning being done using the back-propagation algorithm. As can

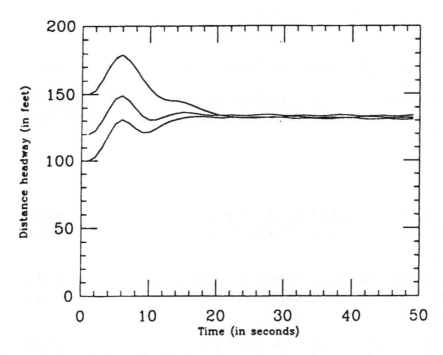

Figure 3: Result from the FLC implementation of longitudinal vehicle control

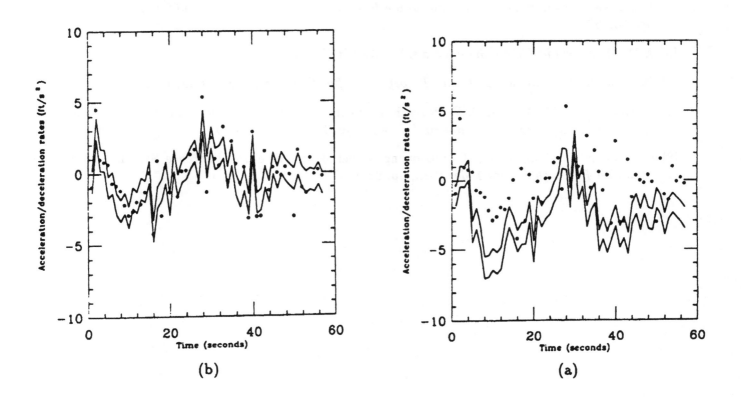

(b)

(a)

Figure 4: Result from the FNN implementation of longitudinal vehicle control

be seen, the band in the bottom figure includes more number of observed actions than the band (of equal width) in the top figure.

Chakroborty [3] tested tuning of the FLC by the FNN for 3 different controllers drivers successfully. The FNN representation of FLC is found to modify the controller so as to emulate the desired control actions.

References

[1] R. M. Tong. An Annotated Bibliography of Fuzzy Control. *Industrial Applications of Fuzzy Control,* Edited by Michio Sugeno, Elsevier Science Publishers, B.V. (North-Holland), 1985, pp. 249-269.

[2] R. J. Williams. The Logic of Activation Functions. *Parallel Distributed Processing: Explorations in the Microstructure of Cognition,* Volume 1, The MIT Press, Cambridge, Massachusetts, 1986, pp. 423-443.

[3] P. Chakroborty. A Model of Car-Following: A Fuzzy-Inference-Based System. *Ph.D. Dissertation,* University of Delaware, Newark, Delaware, 1993.

[4] Horikawa, S., T. Furuhashi, Y. Uchikawa and T. Tagawa. A study on Fuzzy Modeling using Fuzzy Neural Networks. *Proceedings of the International Fuzzy Engineering Symposium,* 1991, pp. 562-573.

[5] A.D. May. *Traffic Flow Fundamentals,* Prentice Hall, N.J., 1990.

[6] W. Leutzbach. *Introduction to the Theory of Traffic Flow,* Springer-Verlag, Berlin, 1988.

[7] R. Herman, E.W. Montroll, R.B. Potts, R.W. Rothery. Traffic Dynamics: Analysis of Stability in Car Following. *Operations Research,* Vol. 7, No. 1, 1959, pp. 86-106.

[8] S. Kikuchi, P. Chakroborty. Car-following Model Based on Fuzzy Inference System. *Transportation Research Record 1365,* 1992, pp. 82-91.

Fuzzy Logic oriented to Active Rule Selector and Membership Function Generator for High Speed Digital Fuzzy μ-Processor

Francesco Boschetti   Alessandro Gabrielli   Enzo Gandolfi   Massimo Masetti

Department of Physics University of Bologna Via Irnerio 46 40126 Bologna   Italy

FAX +39-51-247244 E-mail masetti@vaxbo.bo.infn.it

Abstract

This paper presents a Fuzzy Logic overview starting from the basic considerations throughout the implementation of a fuzzy rule based algorithm. The chosen method used to implement a fuzzy algorithm into a digital hardware architecture, such as an ASIC (Application Specific Integrated Circuit), highly affects the fuzzy system response both in terms of precision and speed. From this point of view, especially for high speed purposes, some hardware implementation solutions become crucial points in order to meet the constraints for modelling complex systems. One of these points is the rule inference process since, overall for large number of fuzzy rules, it plays a significant role on the global processing time. Here we present a trade-off solution to meet high speed constraints. Another point is the fuzzification process that directly affect the silicon area, especially in digital solutions. We have investigated these two points togheter since a good trade-off between them, in other words timing versus area, leads to high performance fuzzy μ-processores. The presented solution have already been mapped to 0.7 μm ES2 digital libraries and correctly simulated.

Introduction

Fuzzy Logic deals with *fuzzy variables, fuzzy sets, term sets, universes of discourse, degrees of membership (degrees of truth), fuzzification* and *defuzzification* methods and *inference processes*. Let us now have a brief overview over these terms.

Say that a generic *m*-dimensional *fuzzy variable* is a function that varies whithin the interval defined by its domain. This is said *universe of discourse* (included into R^m). Each *universe of discourse* is divided into several intervals that are allowed, or better have to, overlap each other. Over each interval is defined a *fuzzy set* named by a logical name and described by a *membership function* (MF): $f: R^m => [0,1]$. It is said that the *fuzzy set* is defined by the ordered pair $[x, f(x)]$. In addiction, all the *fuzzy sets* related to a *fuzzy variable* make the *term set*. This function, for each input value, returns the *degree of membership (degree of truth)* of its related *fuzzy set (Fuzzification Process)*. Many *degrees of truth* are combined together into each rule *premise* to give the global *premise degree of truth*. This can be done by fuzzy inference opeartors such as disjunction (minimum or product that are *t-norms*) and/or conjunction (maximum or sum that are *t-conorms*). So, each *fuzzy rule* is composed of a *premise* and a *conclusion* (IF *premise* THEN *conclusion*) and, depending on the *premise degree of truth*, the *conclusion* has a different effect in terms of strength: contribution to the final output variable. The way by which the *premise degree of truth* affects the *conclusion* of the related *fuzzy rule* is the *inference* method. Once all the *fuzzy rules* have been performed and the related rule contributions have been carried out, the final *defuzzification* method takes place. This step evaluates the output value taking into account all the single fuzzy rule contributions; the most used is a kind of weighted sum (*center of gravity*). All the previous definitions form the so-called *fuzzy algorithm* since it is able to 'describe' the problem while, to build either a software or hardware tool that is able to 'solve' the problem, the *fuzzy algorithm* needs to be implemented into a *fuzzy system*. To do this job, some decisions have to be made since there are several (many) methods to correctly implement the *t-norm*, the *t-conorm*, the *inference* and *defuzzification* processes. We wish to emphasize that the implementation of a *fuzzy algorithm* into a *fuzzy system* is one of the hardest jobs while designing a fuzzy architecture. In fact, if one deals just with fuzzy system design or simulation without considering hardware implementation, this problem does not appear. Nevertheless, particularly for ASIC design, the above mentioned decisions to make during the implementation of a *fuzzy algorithm* into a *fuzzy system* affect significantly the chip response in terms of timing, layout area, precision and reliability. A good fuzzy logic implementation is also well considered a universal approximator [1] [2] that is: a generic continuous *m*-dimensional function $H: R^m => R$ can be approximated up to any precision with a *fuzzy system*. Moreover, the following theorem asserts that:

Theorem: If $H: A => R$ is a continuous function on a compact A (included into R^m), $\forall\ \varepsilon > 0$
$\exists$ a *fuzzy algorithm* such that $\sup\{|\ H(x) - fuzzy\_algorithm(x)|$, x belongs to A$\} \le \varepsilon$.

As above mentioned, fuzzy logic based systems are useful to model complex systems where precision, speed and reliability have to be taken into account even if the knowledge base is not well defined. In fact, many methods have been proposed to implement a fuzzy rule system, starting from the human intelligence of an expert, to the artificial intelligence of neural networks [3] or genetic algorithms and hybrid expert systems [4]. Nevertheless, the design of the *fuzzy rules* is just one of the jobs to do while designing the global *fuzzy system*. Once the *fuzzy rules* have been selected to describe a specific problem, these have to be implemented into a hardware architecture and this leads to choices among several methodologies. That we present here is anyway always referred to digital specific architectures. Starting from this point, everyone is allowed to design his own *fuzzy algorithm* as long as he applies the right implementation method solutions. The most used, both in sofware tools and in hardware devices, is the Mamdani method, well known also as Min-Max method since it uses minimum and maximum operators as *t-norm* and *t-conorm* and the *center of gravity* as *defuzzification* method [5]. As regards the application fields in which high speed fuzzy processor can be required, we introduce the High Energy Physics Experiments [6] where high speed is always a big constraint. For this reason we have already designed and fabricated [7] a first release digital fuzzy processor with 1.0 μm technology. The two main problems we found while designing it were the generation of the MF and the selection of the active *fuzzy rules*. Actually these problems have not been solved yet but many solutions have been investigated and here we propose and describe the latest two.

In the first release of our fuzzy processor we used look-up tables to store the input variable MF shapes. They needed about 9 mm^2 to store a coded 4-bit MFs for four 7-bit input variables and this was about one third of the total layout area. Indeed, the system had to process the whole *fuzzy set of rules* before letting the *defuzzification* process start. Nevertheless, the global processing time was smaller than 2 μs. These solutions, until now, have been the most widly used [8] [9] [10] [11].

So far, especially for both small input variable and MF numbers, say up to 8 MF for 2 or 3 input variables, the look-up tables have been used to store the MF shapes. On the other hand, since we are going to design faster new release fuzzy processors also with larger input numbers, we can no longer use look-up tables because of their large layout area requirements, nor process all the *fuzzy rules*. So, two of the main aims are to reduce as much as possible the layout area corresponding to the MF generations and to select just *active fuzzy rules*. With *active fuzzy rules* we just mean the rules with a non-null contributions to the final result.

Active Rule Selector

So far, who has been dealing with Fuzzy Logic knows that the number (#) of allowed *fuzzy rules* increases exponentially as $\#fuzzy\_rules = \#MF^{\#variables}$ depending on the number of variables and the number of MF. Nevertheless, just a few *fuzzy rules*, which we call *active rules*, give a non-zero contribution to the final result; if one write all the possible *fuzzy rules*, the *active rules* to *fuzzy rules* ratio depends on the variable and MF numbers and how the MF releted to a given variable overlap each other. For a generic set of *fuzzy rules*, the number of *active rules* can vary depending on the actual input variable values. This is the reason why the active rule selection becomes a very significant point to face, particularly for large fuzzy rule numbers. In fact, a generic fuzzy system global processing time is nearly proportional to the number of processed *fuzzy rules* [12] that can either be *active rules* or null rules. It can be said that generally the whole set of *fuzzy rules* is mainly made of null rules [13].

Here we present a solution that we have developed and simulated for the selection of a fuzzy system *active rules* made of 7-MF N input variables. Hence, every fuzzy rule antecent is composed of N 3-bit groups to select the right MF of each input variable. We use the code '111' to reject the contribution of a given input variable to a given rule. For example if we had 3 input variables named *Var0, Var1, Var2* and the *fuzzy set* labels named from *0* to *7*, the fuzzy rule *if {(Var0 is 1) and (Var2 is 5)} then ...* would have as antecedent part: 001-111-101. Moreover, the solution we present refers to at most an overlap 2 that means that every input variable can involve one or two *fuzzy sets* (MF), as reported in Figure 1b.

Once the input variables have been read, the Active Rule Selector is able to recognize what interval and MF

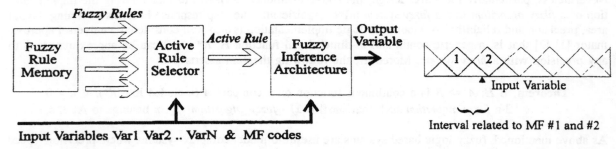

Figure 1 a) Fuzzy Processor and Active Rule Selector   b) Membership Function Selection

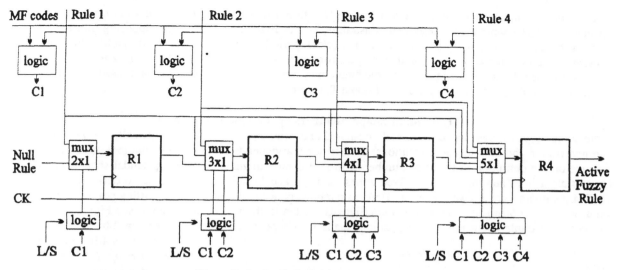

Figure 2 Active Rule Selector

are involved and, in particular, this is very easy to design since the two involved *fuzzy sets* are consecutive. After these intervals have been selected (see Figure 1b), each *fuzzy rule* can be differentiated from being active or null. This can be done in several way depending on the disjunction and/or conjunction fuzzy inference operators; for example in case of disjunction *minimum* operator, the selection is simply obtained by comparing the 3-bit antecedent rule codes with the selected interval ones. Any other architecture can be easly implemented instead of the *logic* blocks if it is preferred getting the Ci values in another way; this will not affect the behaviour of the active Rule Selector.

The proposed solution, reported in Figure 1a and Figure 2, applies this method to 4 *fuzzy rules* at a time so that, into a parallel architecture, at every clock period, we have 4 combinatorial architectures (*logic*) that give 4 selection bits named *C1, C2, C3 and C4*. These bits identify the *active rules* from the null ones. Depending on the combination of these selection bits, each of the 4 *fuzzy rules* is stored into one of the 4 shift registers *R1, R2, R3* and *R4* if it is an *active fuzzy rule*, or rejected if it is null *fuzzy rule*. The shift registers are always filled up from right to left; that is, if only one *fuzzy rule* out of 4 is active then it is stored into the shift register *R4*; if two *fuzzy rules* out of 4 are active then they are stored into the shift registers *R4* and *R3*; and so on. This is done by the multiplexer blocks reported in Figure 2. In case of having 4 null *fuzzy rules*, the architecture stores just a null rule into the register *R4*. The state of the circuit just described is said Loading Mode because the selected *active rules* have to be stored into the shift registers. Of course, to avoid loosing the active previously selected *fuzzy rules*, during the Loading Mode the shift registers must be empty. The second operating mode is called Shifting Mode that occurs when at least one of the shift registers, from right to left, *R3, R2* and *R1*, besides of *R4*, holds an *active fuzzy rule*. This means that the circuit is not yet ready to read 4 new *fuzzy rules* and it needs other Shifting Mode periods. This lasts up to the period just before the next Loading Mode, that is when the shift registers *R1, R2* and *R3* are empty while *R4* holds the last *active rule* of the 4 previously loaded. We wish to emphasize that at every clock cicle this circuit gives a *fuzzy rule* on output even if this is not necessarely an *active* one. As just described, if the Loading Mode gets 4 null *fuzzy rules*, the circuit cannot avoid putting out a null rule itself, before loading other 4 *fuzzy rules*.
In this way, the Loading and Shifting Modes (L/S in Figure 2) occur alternatively allowing the circuit to process 4 *fuzzy rules* at a time and, since most of the *fuzzy rules* are null, this solution allows rejecting most of them, decreasing significantly the global processing time. It should be noted that the speed-up depends both on the *fuzzy system* in terms of *fuzzy rules* and their implementation solutions, and on how the *fuzzy rules* are sorted inside the Fuzzy Rule Memory. If possible, it is reasonable to sort them in such a way that, for any combination of input variable actual values, potential *active fuzzy rules* are not close to each other.

Let us now give an example of speed-up calculation. Let us say we have #*rule*=1024 *fuzzy rules* stored inside the Fuzzy Rule Memory, #*active*=256 *active fuzzy rules* at a time, #*module*=4 parallel loading blocks, #*input*=8 input variables, #*mf*=7 MF for each input variable and an overlap 2 (any input variable value belongs at most to two different consecutive *fuzzy sets*). Within this configuration, we have the following *Minimum* and *Maximum Processing Cicles*:

$$Minimum\ Processing\ Cicles \quad = \#rule/\#module = 1024/4 = 256$$
$$Maximum\ Processing\ Cicles \quad = ((\#module-1)*\#active+\#rule)/\#module = (3*256+1024)/4 = 488$$

Let us then compare these results with those we would get if we had a traditional architecture that would process, with the same above described constraints, all the 1024 *fuzzy rules* even supposing into a pipelined structure that processes one *fuzzy rule* at a time (clock period). With this solution the global inference processing time is reduced by a factor that ranges from 56% = (1-448/1024) to 75% = (1-256/1024).

As regards the area required for the implementation of this solution, we have used 0.7 μm digital libraries obtaining a standard cell area of about 0.65 mm².

Trapezoidal-Shape Membership Function Generator

The solution we propose has been already designed and simulated. It reduces dramatically the layout area in comparison to the look-up table solutions, by a factor that depends on the size of the look-up table and, of course on the definition in terms of number of bits. It approximates a generic trapezoidal shape function by two straight lines and three strictly fixed zones for High and Low levels. Of course, to define a trapezoidal MF, 4 parameters are anyway required. Here, as parameters, we have used the two starting points of the *Rising* and the *Falling Straight Lines* and two coefficients related to the two desired slopes (see Figure 3). To give a generic example about how the trapezoidal shape is generated, let suppose to have a 8-bit *fuzzy variable*, and a 4-bit *degree of membership* (16 values). As reported in Figure 3, it is easy to understand that the two *Low Zones* and the *High Zone* can be generated by implementing digital comparators. For each zone the related comparators check whether the input value is included or not; this means that the *degree of membership* has to be carried out by choosing it between low and high logic level or, in other words, the *degree of membership* is put either to 0 or 15.

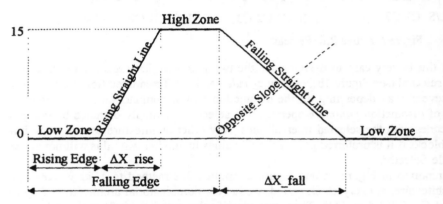

Figure 3 Trapezoidal-Shape Generic Membership Function

The *Rising Zone* and the *Falling Zone* have to be computed in another manner. Let now consider the *Rising Zone*: the circuit must generate a straight line from the *Rising Edge* to the beginning of the *High Zone*. This straight line must rise up linearly from 0 to 15. In short terms, the architecture related to this job executes the equation 2 without performing neither any division nor any multiplication computation that, as well known, are big time consuming operations. In the following equations we give some more details about this fast solution. In particular, as reported in Figure 2, ΔX_rise and ΔX_fall are the intervals under which rispectively the rising and the falling straight lines are defined. For example let $\Delta X\_rise(fall)$ be lower than 256 (taking into account that the *universe of discourse* of x is 256 [0,255]). Let define in the below equations some parameters related to the input variables, such as *Rise*, *Fall*, *A* and *B*. The parameters *Rise* and *Fall* are allowed to vary wherever into the *universe of discourse* while *A* and *B* can assume integer values.

$$Rise = x - Rising\_Edge \quad Fall = x - Falling\_Edge \quad A=256/\Delta X\_rise \quad B=256/\Delta X\_fall$$
$$Rise(Fall) \text{ belongs to } [0,255] \quad A(B) \text{ belongs to } [1,2,3, ... 256]$$

Using the previous terms the straight line equation becomes:

$$\alpha = (\Delta Y/\Delta X\_rise)*Rise; \quad 16*\alpha = 16*(\Delta Y/\Delta X\_rise)*Rise; \quad 16*\alpha = (256/\Delta X\_rise)*Rise$$

$$16*\alpha = A*Rise; \qquad \alpha = (A*Rise)/16 \tag{1}$$

Here ΔY is put to 16 and is directly the *degree of membership*. Nevertheless, the right ΔY should be 15 but, since $15/\Delta X\_rise$ is a non-integer number and must be rounded anyway, the approximation is really reasonable. The same reasoning can be extended to the number 255 that is replaced with 256.

So far, we have not been dealing with the hardware implementation of Formula 1. Nevertheless, to carry out this operation is required just a multiplication between the operands *A* and *Rise*. The operand *A* stands for a 8-bit slope parameter while the *Rise* one is the shifted-input variable. The division by 16 does not take effect at all since it is a division by a power of 2 (truncation operation).

Finally, the rising and falling straight line generation solutions are very similar since just the output α-values are different. As reported in Figure 3, the α-values related to the falling straight line are the complement to 1 of the α-values of another straight line with opposite slope. This feature allows to generate the two straight lines by sharing most of the applied hardware reducing again the global layout area.

For example, for a 7-bit *fuzzy variable*, 4-bit *degree of membership* and 1 bit of precision, we have obtained a standard-cell layout area of about 0.3 mm^2 and it works properly within 20 ns.

Conclusion

As regards the Membership Function Generator, we can say that its implementation does not depend significantly on the parameter bit numbers, so that it can be extended to slightly larger ones without affecting too much the timing performances and area features. We have designed this generator with 0.7 μm digital technology obtaining about 0.3 mm^2 standard cell area and the circuit has been pipelined within a 20 ns clock cicle. The same timing relations have been obtained by simulating the Active Rule Selector so that, for these reasons, we propose their implementation in fast fuzzy architectures.

For HEPE trigger purposes, where a decision about good event detection and noise rejection must be made within few μs, these solutions are going to take place [14] [15]. In fact, as well described in the introduction, *fuzzy logic* can be applied to complex sistems such as pattern (trajectory) recognition, with good timing-area features for future applications to HEPE where hard trade-off solutions are required.

References

[1] L. X. Wang - *Fuzzy Systems are Universal Approximators*
Proceedings of Fuzzy-IEEE '92 San Diego March 8-12 1992 (pag. 1163-1170)
[2] J. Castro - *Fuzzy Logic Controllers are Universal Approximators*
Technical Report #DECSAI-93101, 6-1993 University of Grenada Department of Computer Science
[3] Saman Halgamuge Glesner
A Fuzzy Neural Approach For Pattern Classification With The Generation Of Rules Based On Supervised Learning
Neuro Nimes 1992 November 2-6 1992 Nimes France
[4] Surmann Kanstein Goser - *Self-Organizing and Genetic Algorithms for Automatic Design of Fuzzy Control and Decision Systems*
Proceedings of the First European Congress on Fuzzy and Intellingent Technologies, EUFIT '93 Aachen September 7 - 10 1993 (pag. 1097-1104)
[5] Kruse Gebhardt Klawonn - *Foundation on Fuzzy Systems*
1994 John Wiley & Sons
[6] D'Antone, Gandolfi, Masetti, Vitullo - *A Fuzzy System to Detect and Count Parallel Noised Tracks*
1994 ACM Simposium on Applied Computing: Track on Fuzzy Logic in Application, pp. 166-169
[7] Gandolfi, Gabrielli, D'Antone, Spotti, Masetti
Architecture of a 50 MFIPS Fuzzy Processor and related 1.0 μm VLSI CMOS digital circuits
Microneuro IEEE 94 Inter. Con. on Microel. for Neural Net. and Fuzzy Systems Torino 1994 - pp. 125-133
[8] Pagni, Poluzzi, Lo Presti, Rizzotto - *Automatic Syntesis Analysis Implementation of a Fuzzy Controller*
Second IEEE International Conference on Fuzzy Systems 1993 San Francisco (pag. 105-110)
[9] Neichfeld, Klinche, Menke, Nolles, Kunemund - *A General Purpose Fuzzy Inference Process*
Microneuro IEEE 94 Inter. Con. on Microelectronics for Neural Networks and Fuzzy Systems Torino 1994
[10] Ungering, Bauer, Goser - *Architecture of a Fuzzy processor based on a 8-bit microprocessor*
Third IEEE International Conference on Fuzzy Systems 1994 Orlando (pag. 297-301)
[11] Miki, Matsumoto, Ohto, Yamakawa
Silicon Implementation for a Novel High Speed Fuzzy Inference Engine: Mega-Flips Analog Fuzzy Processor
Journal of Intelligent and fuzzy System Vol. 1 (1) pag. 27-42 1993 John Wiley & Sons
[12] Ikeda, Kisu, Hiramoto, Nakamura
A Fuzzy Inference Coprocessor Using a Flexible Active-Rule-Driven Architecture
IKE IEEE 1992 pp 537-544
[13] Ansgar, Ungering, Goser - *Architecture of a 64-bit Fuzzy Inference Processor*
Third IEEE International Conference on Fuzzy Systems 1994 Orlando (pag. 1776-1780)
[14] P. Ribarics - *A Second Level Neural Network Trigger in the H1 Experiment at HERA*
1992 IEEE Nuclear Science Symposium and Medical Imaging Conference
[15] C. S. Lindsey, B. Demby, H. Haggerty - *Drift Chamber Tracking with Neural Network*
1992 IEEE Nuclear Science Symposium and Medical Imaging Conference

GENET and Tabu Search for
Combinatorial Optimization Problems

Dr. J. F. Boyce, C. H. D. Dimitropoulos, G. vom Scheidt, Prof. J. G. Taylor
Wheatstone Laboratory, King's College London, Strand, London WC2R 2LS, U.K.
jfb@physig2.ph.kcl.ac.uk, vom@phlim.ph.kcl.ac.uk, hcd@phalpha.ph.kcl.ac.uk, udah057@kcl.ac.uk

Abstract. Constraint satisfaction problems are combinatorial optimization problems which involve finding an assignment to a set of variables that is consistent with a set of constraints. In this paper the use of two local search techniques, namely GENET and Tabu Search for constraint satisfaction optimization problems and partial constraint satisfaction problems is investigated. These methods are compared by application to a difficult partial constraint satisfaction optimization problem, namely the Radio Links Frequency Assignment Problem (RLFAP).

1 Introduction

A constraint satisfaction problem consists of finding an assignment to a set of variables that is consistent with a set of constraints. In this paper we assume that the number of variables is finite and the respective domains are also finite and discrete. Constraints restrict the configurations which may be assigned to subsets of the variables. There are many real-world problems that can be described within this formalism, for example scheduling, labeling in vision, bin-packing, and frequency assignment problems.

Constraint Satisfaction Problems: A CSP is a finite set V of variables, a function D which maps every variable to a set of domains, and a set C of constraints.

Constraint Satisfaction Optimization Problems: In many real-world instances, it is not sufficient to find just any assignment which satisfies all constraints. If there is a multitude of valid solutions to a problem, *i.e* more than one assignment which violates no constraints, additional requirements on the minimization process may be introduced. In some circumstances one solution is as good as any other, but in scheduling or frequency assignment problems, solutions will vary in resource usage of some form and hence an optimal solution should also minimize these secondary costs. Constraint satisfaction optimization problems may be modeled as a special case of PCSPs, as defined below.

Partial Constraint Satisfaction Problems: In some instances of constraint satisfaction problems, the nature of the problem may only require a subset of the constraints to be met, or may be so over-constrained that only a subset of the constraints can be met, *i.e* no complete solution exists. In either case a partial solution will be accepted, but an objective-function or cost-function may be introduced to grade these solutions with respect to secondary objectives, such as resource usage, or importance of constraints. A PCSP is a finite set of variables, a set of finite domains for the variables, a finite set of constraints on an arbitrary subset of variables, and an objective-function which maps every assignment for the set of variables to a scalar. An optimal solution to a PCSP is an assignment which satisfies a subset of the constraints and minimizes the objective-function. The objective-function may contain weights for violating certain constraints and any number of additional terms dependent on the variable assignments.

2 GENET and Tabu Search

Combinatorial optimization problems and especially partial CSPs may be hard to tackle using complete methods like branch-and-bound due to the vast parameter space to be examined. Heuristic methods that produce acceptable approximate results in a short time and improve on them if more time is available are therefore an important alternative approach. Many of them are based upon a local search technique which employs some form of hill-climbing to find local minima, combined with an escape technique to try to leave their basins of attraction.

Genet and Tabu Search both fit into this paradigm and for our experiments both use a very similar local search method, while employing different escape techniques. During minimization, at each iteration a local neighbourhood (the set of states that can be reached by adjusting *one* variable) is examined and the resulting 1-optimal move is made.

Both Tabu Search and Genet deform the cost surface as the search proceeds. Tabu search imposes hard limits on the possible search itineraries using the taboo list, while Genet uses a scheme of dynamic local penalization to fill up local minima and discourage incompatible assignments. Both approaches will be explained in the next sections.

2.1 GENET

2.1.1 Introduction

Genet is a connectionist approach to CSPs developed by Tsang and Wang [1]. The problem representation in Genet derives from its neural network interpretation. A recurrent network with weighted inhibitory connections encodes the variables and constraints characterizing the problem instance. The network alternatingly settles into stable states corresponding to minima of the cost-surface and modifies connection strengths during the "learning" phase of the algorithm to escape from local minima.

2.1.2 Problem Modeling

Variables are represented by clusters of nodes with binary-valued activations. Each node of a cluster corresponds to one value in its variable's domain, and only one node is active at any time, indicating the current assignment. For instance if a variable had a domain consisting of the values (10,20,30,40,50) and was assigned to a value of 40, the corresponding nodes would have activations (0,0,0,1,0).

Constraints are modeled as inhibitory connections linking incompatible nodes. All connections are initially weighted with '-1'. During "learning" this inhibition can be strengthened, as the algorithm tries to discourage certain assignments. The weights can be stored as a $n \times m$ matrix for each constrained variable-pair, where n and m are the respective domain sizes. As a generalization it can be assumed that all nodes are linked to all other nodes, with connections corresponding to unconstrained assignments set to a weight of '0'. The network is then fully connected.

2.1.3 Network Dynamics

Initially all variables are assigned to random values in their domains (one node in each cluster is set to one, all others to zero) and all weights connecting incompatible nodes are initialized to '-1'. Then the activation of all nodes is computed by summing over the weighted activations of all incoming connections,

$$a_{ik}^{(n+1)} = \sum_{l=1}^{|V|} \sum_{j=1}^{|D_l|} w_{ijkl}^{(n)} \cdot a_{jl}^{(n)} \qquad (1)$$

where a_{ik} and a_{jl} are activations of nodes, w_{ijkl} are the weights between them and $|V|$ and $|D_l|$ are the number of variables and their domain sizes.

Then in each cluster the node with the highest (least negative) input is activated and all others are inactivated. The active node represents the new assignment. This process is repeated until the network reaches a fixed point and no further updates occur. If the network has reached a global minimum, the algorithm stops. Otherwise Genet's "learning" rule is applied and the algorithm tries to escape from the local minimum by imposing additional penalties on connections between active nodes corresponding to violated constraints:

$$w_{ijkl}^{(n+1)} = w_{ijkl}^{(n)} + a_{ik}^{(n)} \cdot a_{jl}^{(n)} \cdot w_{ijkl}^{(0)} \qquad (2)$$

Note that the product on the right-hand side will be zero for connections between unconstrained nodes and '-1' if a constraint is violated, i.e both nodes are active and incompatible.

2.1.4 Extension to PCSPs and CSOPs

Genet can be described as a hill-climbing technique choosing 1-optimal moves in a cost-surface deformed by penalizations. The original formulation of Genet does not solve CSOPs or PCSPs. In Genet all constraints are treated as equal and no secondary objectives are taken into account. But by weighting constraints and adding layers to the cost-surface that correspond to secondary objectives like resource usage, the original Genet has been extended to handle CSOPs and PCSPs [2].

The input to a node can be separated into two terms: a constant 'compatibility' term $w_{ijkl}^{(0)}$ which is '-1' if nodes i and j of variables k and l are incompatible and '0' otherwise, and a monotonically decreasing 'inhibition' term $h_{ijkl}^{(n)}$, which contains the penalties that a constraint accumulates during the search. The cost-function then becomes

$$c(n) = -\frac{1}{2} \sum_{k \in V} \sum_{i=1}^{|D_k|} \sum_{l \in V} \sum_{j=1}^{|D_l|} a_{ik}^{(n)} \cdot a_{jl}^{(n)} \cdot w_{ijkl}^{(0)} - \frac{1}{2} \sum_{k \in V} \sum_{i=1}^{|D_k|} \sum_{l \in V} \sum_{j=1}^{|D_l|} a_{ik}^{(n)} \cdot a_{jl}^{(n)} \cdot h_{ijkl}^{(n)} \qquad (3)$$

which yields the number of violations plus their penalties. By augmenting this cost-function with additional terms corresponding to secondary objectives and using weights proportional to the importance of constraints, the search is directed towards minima of a cost-function with these additional terms:

$$c(\vec{x}) = -W - H(n) - A(\vec{x}) \qquad (4)$$

The law (1) then becomes gradient descent on (3) in the activity $a_{ik}^{(n)}$. Here W includes the 'compatibility' terms, $H(n)$ includes the 'inhibition' terms (the penalties) and $A(\vec{x})$ any additional terms, such as the number of frequencies used in a RLFAP, evaluated at position $\vec{x}$.

2.2 Tabu Search

Tabu Search is a modern heuristic method which was introduced by Glover [3, 4] as an efficient way of finding high quality solutions to hard combinatorial optimization problems.

The name "Tabu" derives from the implementation of search guidance by the imposition of restrictions, either by direct exclusion of some moves or by modified probabilities for possible moves. The rules which govern the restrictions codify the a priori knowledge of the problem class. They depend both on the current structure of the neighbourhood of the solution and its history. The rules themselves may vary dynamically during the course of a search both in response to recent search behavior and to the number of search moves since initiation.

The rules are based on the interaction between *restriction* and *aspiration*, where the former seeks to limit the moves available at any search state whilst the latter permits the overriding of restrictions if the search appears to be trapped in a local minimum.

2.2.1 Implementation

The RLFAP implementation of Tabu Search outlined below [1] requires three parameters to run: the size of the tabu list ($|T|$), the patience parameter (p), and the ratio parameter (N).

1. Begin with a *random assignment* of values to variables.

2. Consider all variables within $N\%$ of the maximum number of violations,

    (a) Check all values for each variable,

    (b) Check for TABU and ASPIRATION.

3. Select the best move for the iteration & go to (2).

4. Store the best move so far and update *tabu list* [2] and *aspiration criteria*. [3]

5. Repeat from step (2), until a solution is found or until there is no improvement in the cost for more than p iterations.

---

[1] For a detailed description of this implementation see [5].

[2] The new move is added to the *recency* based tabu list, which means that for the next $|T|$ iterations this move will be *tabu*. Recency based tabu was all that was required to find feasible assignments in most cases. However, on some occasions the same link would be repeatedly selected for assignment on each iteration and tabu search would cycle with different frequency assignments for the same link. To prevent this cycling and to diversify the search a *frequency* based tabu is imposed on that link for a fixed number of iterations.

[3] A simple type of aspiration criteria is employed: a candidate move is licit (non-tabu) if the assignment yields a solution with a cost better than the best found so far. Hence, the updated aspiration value is $A := min(A, cost - 1)$.

3 The Radio Links Frequency Assignment Problem

We now assess the performance of GENET and Tabu Search for the Radio Links Frequency Assignment Problem (RLFAP), by application to a set of realistic instances, the CELAR problems [4]. Part of the work presented in this section is a result of the *Combinatorial Algorithms for Military Applications (CALMA)* project, where funding for King's College London was provided by the DRA in the EUCLID Framework [6].

The radio links frequency assignment problem occurs in many civil and military applications [7, 8]. The main objective is to assign radio frequencies to a number of transmitters, subject to a number of constraints, so that a minimum of interference occurs. However, it may be impossible to satisfy all constraints, in which case trying to minimize the number of violated constraints (*i.e.* the interference) is a more realistic goal. The problem is NP-complete, and is a variant of the general T−graph coloring problem, as introduced by Hale [9].

3.1 The CELAR data set of problems

In the CELAR problems, a set of possible frequencies is given to operate the radio links. Each of the radio links has to be assigned to one of the frequencies, while satisfying a usually large number of constraints of the following type: for any two "neighbouring" links i and j, if f_i (resp: f_j) is the frequency assigned to link i (resp: to link j) then $|f_i - f_j| > c_{ij}$ for 'Inequality' constraints, and $|f_i - fj| = c_{ij}$ for 'Equality' constraints. The concept of "neighbouring" links, here, not only depends on the fact that the links lie geographically close to each other, but also on various electromagnetic characteristics (such as propagation, transmission power, etc ...) which may result in electromagnetic incompatibility (at certain frequencies) between the links.

In some of the eleven CELAR scenarios there are many solutions and hence all constraints have to be met while minimizing resource usage (scen01–scen05,scen11), and in others there are no solutions and certain constraints have higher priority than others combined with restrictions on assignment mobility (scen06–scen10). So the CELAR data contains examples for CSPs, PCSPs, and CSOPs of varying size and difficulty.

Each variable(link) can be assigned to a frequency from its respective domain of frequencies. The optimization criteria are:

- **scen01–03**: multiple solutions, minimize the number of distinct frequencies used.

- **scen04**: multiple solutions, minimize the frequency span.

- **scen05**: multiple solutions, minimize the highest frequency used.

- **scen06–08**: no solutions satisfying all constraints,
  but a subset of *hard* constraints has to be satisfied
  and *soft* constraints have varying penalties for violation.

- **scen09,10**: as above, but variables also have varying mobility
  and reassignment of variables incurs varying penalties.

- **scen11**: multiple solutions, no secondary objectives.

3.2 Results

The following results for the CELAR data set were obtained using a C-implementation of Tabu Search and a C++-implementation of the extension of Genet, both running on a 130 MHz DEC Alpha. Genet was optimized to use a minimal-neighbourhood change propagation scheme to accelerate the local search.

Both Tabu Search and Genet are able to find good solutions to problems scen01–03. Note that the Genet results given for these problems are sample values, since they are subject to a time/quality tradeoff. Problems scen04 and scen05 are more tightly constrained and consequently much harder to solve. Here both methods benefit significantly from a pre-processing stage which exploits arc-consistency. Across all instances to which they were applied, both methods also perform well in comparison with other search techniques investigated in the *Calma* project.

---

[4] The data was provided by the French "Centre d'Electronique de l'Armement"(CELAR).

CELAR	variables/ constraints	best known cost	best found		found optimum		average time	
			TABU	GENET	TABU	GENET	TABU	GENET
scen01	916/5548	16	18	16	n.a.	20%	3hrs	75s
scen02	200/1235	14	14	14	70%	100%	4min	9s
scen03	400/2760	14	14	14	20%	10%	34min	32s
scen04	680/3968	46	n.a.	46	n.a.	100%	n.a.	12s
scen04arc	680/3968	46	46	46	100%	100%	10s	0.24s
scen05	400/2598	792	n.a.	792	n.a.	30%	n.a.	8min
scen05arc	400/2598	792	792	792	40%	100%	7min	2s
scen06	200/1322	3623	9180	3852	—	—	14min	10min
scen07	400/2865	374705	6541695	435132	—	—	46min	18min
scen08	916/2744	293	1745	366	—	—	6hrs	32min
scen09	680/4103	15716	16873	n.a.	—	—	18min	n.a.
scen10	680/4103	31517	31943	n.a.	—	—	2hrs	n.a.
scen11	680/4103	0	0	0	60%	60%	54min	25s

4 Conclusions

Both methods are effective and flexible ways for solving partial constraint satisfaction and combinatorial optimization problems as present in the *Celar* set of Radio Link Frequency Assignment Problems. Genet appears to be much faster than Tabu Search. However, some of this may be due to its extensive optimization and hence it is difficult to directly compare the processing times. Experiments on small but tightly constrained frequency assignment problems for which Tabu Search almost always finds the optimal solution while Genet consistently fails, indicate that there may be a class of hard problems to which Genet is not applicable in the current implementation. Both methods were also tested for their behavior under perturbations of the problems, which occur if additional constraints or variables are introduced or existing ones removed. Since they employ local search and use a dynamic escape technique, they perform well under perturbations and can benefit from any previously found solutions.

For their financial support, CHD would like to thank the *DRA*, and GvS would like to thank the *German National Scholarship Foundation*.

References

[1] E.P.K. Tsang and C.J. Wang. A generic neural network approach for constraint satisfaction problems. In J.G. Taylor, editor, *Neural network applications*, pages 12–22. Springer-Verlag, 1992.

[2] G. vom Scheidt. Extension of GENET to partial constraint satisfaction problems and constraint satisfaction optimisation problems. Master's thesis, King's College London, U.K., 1995. Dept. of Mathematics.

[3] F. Glover. Tabu search part I. *ORSA J. Comput.*, 1:190–206, 1989.

[4] F. Glover. Tabu search part II. *ORSA J. Comput.*, 2:4–32, 1990.

[5] A. Bouju, J.F. Boyce, C.H.D. Dimitropoulos, G. vom Scheidt, and J.G. Taylor. Tabu search for the radio links frequency assignment problem. In *Applied Decision Technologies, London [ADT'95]. UNICOM Conf.*, 1995.

[6] W. Hajema, M. Minoux, and C. West. Request for proposals on the CALMA project. Technical appendix: Statement of the radio link frequency assignment problem, 1993.

[7] A. Raychaudhuri. Optimal multiple interval assignments in frequency assignment and traffic phasing. *Discrete Applied Mathematics*, 40:319–332, 1992.

[8] K.Chiba, F. Takahata, and M. Nohara. Theory and performance of frequency assignment schemes for carriers with different bandwidths under demand assignment SCPC/FDMA operation. *IEICE Trans. Commun.*, E75-B, No.6:476–486, 1992.

[9] W.K. Hale. Frequency assignment: Theory and applications. *Proc. IEEE*, 68:1497–1514, 1980.

MOTION ESTIMATION USING A COMPOUNDED SELF ORGANIZING MAP-MULTI LAYER PERCEPTRON NETWORK

Bernd Michaelis, Olaf Schnelting, Udo Seiffert and Rüdiger Mecke

Institute for Process Measurement Technology and Electronics
Otto-von-Guericke University of Magdeburg (Germany)
39106 Magdeburg, Universitätsplatz 2
schnell@ipe.uni-magdeburg.de

Abstract

In this paper the utilization of Artificial Neural Networks (ANN) for motion estimation is considered. With simple neural structures it is possible to improve the reliability and accuracy of block matching algorithms (BMA) by a postprocessing of the similarity criterion. The ANN dimensions the appropriate structures. An associative memory realizes an adaptive choise of these filtering structures depending on the image contents. The fundamental idea and some first results will be described. The performance capability of the proposed method is shown for selected real world two-dimensional measuring situations which are not solvable with conventional BMA.

1 Introduction

In recent years interest in image processing has been directed towards applications in the field of image sequence analysis. Particularly, methods of motion estimation are increasing in their practical importance. Global object displacements as well as whole displacement vector fields are interesting. Well known application fields are e. g. image data compression for the digital video telephone, automatic traffic control, interpretation of satellite image data, automatic manufacturing, ecology and medical diagnostics.

Nevertheless, there are some unsolved problems which require innovative solutions. One example is the determination of complex object displacements in distorted industrial environments, e. g. bad image acquisition conditions such as extreme illumination changes, overlapping movements or noise. The employment of neural structures to solve these problems is such an innovative way. There are only a few investigations known on this field [1, 2].

2 Problem Description and System Model

Considering the performance capability of biological systems in movement perception it seems to be useful to apply existing neurophysiological knowledge about natural information processing to "technical vision". The aim is not the modeling of biological systems, rather it is planned to solve technical problems following such prototypes. Essential results in the investigation of biological vision come from researches on insects, whose neural signal processing is easy to understand. Compared to such biological originals [3, 4] some simplifications are introduced. The starting point of investigation is the system model shown in Fig. 1. In the first step it realizes the well-known block matching method by comparison of consecutive image pairs.

In addition to usual methods of motion estimation, a-priori information about the image scene is taken into consideration. The ANN (Fig. 1, subsystem 3) diminishes errors in the displacement vector field.

Subsystem 2 corresponds to the widely known block matching algorithm [6]. The Mean Absolute Difference (MAD) is used as similarity criterion. Traditional matching algorithms exclusively perform a MAD minimum search for displacement detection.

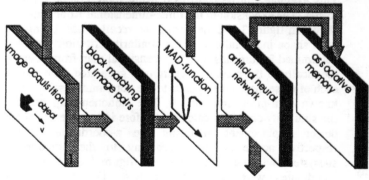

displacement vectors

Fig. 1: System model for motion analysis with a neurobiologically based structure

However, there are some problems for motion determination in the case of image acquisition in distorted environments (e.g. illumination changes, overlapping movements in one block, textured foreground or background and noise) and if high spatial resolution (block dimension 8x8 pixel or smaller) is required. One reason for this is the deformation of the similarity criterion. Particularly in the region of the MAD minimum it can cause wrong measuring results. Besides, the emergence of multiple similar minima can prevent the unique correspondence between the object movement and the coordinates of location.

The idea based on the system model (Fig. 1) is the postprocessing of the MAD function in subsystem 3. This is realized using object-specific a-priori information. The associative memory reloads the weights in subsystem 3 in dependence on the current image block. The main aim is the suppression of the disturbances mentioned above.

3 Classification of similarity criterion groups

Because most industrial applications of motion estimation have been directed towards certain classes of measuring objects, it can be assumed that information about object-specific parameters are known in advance. Investigations have shown, that essential object parameters are reflected in a characteristic form of the similarity criterion. In complexe scenes Obviously many classes result in complexe scenes. The fundamental problem is to reduce the variety of these classes. Particularly in case of small block dimensions it is possible to reduce the variety of object-specific forms of similarity criteria to a number of significant basic patterns.

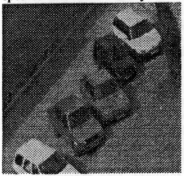

Fig. 2:   Image scene

Practical investigation on real pattern image scenes (Fig. 2) confirm this statement. It seems efficient, starting from the similarity on the MAD level, to take a division of the objects or parts of them in blocks with respect to the corresponding MAD functions into determined classes. Aside from empirical procedures for the division into classes some researches using of self-organizing Kohonen-Maps were done [2, 5]. These neural structures have the capability to group objects according to their similarity into local zones in a feature map.

For minimization of the computational overhead the local independence of the shape of the similarity criterions in the range of the extremum is assumed. With that the Kohonen-Map shown in figure 3 can be reduced to an one-dimensional map during the training phase. As input signals two-dimensional similarity criterions were used, which were calculated in the sense of an auto-correlation function using 16 x 16 pel. blocks of the scene shown in figure 2. A maximum displacement of +/- 4 pel. is assumed. Using a 512 x 512 pel. image there are 961 different input similarity criterions the size 9 x 9. The adjusted weights after about 20 epochs are depicted in figure 4.

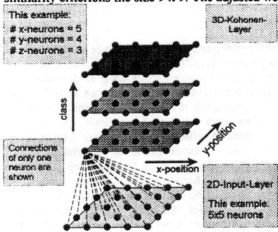

Fig. 3:   Three-dimensional Kohonen-Map for classification of object specific similarity criterions in the recall phase

The number of about 1000 different MAD-functions is divisible into only 4 significant classes (classes a-d). Figure 4 „no class" proves, that, although there are some unused classification neurons left, no improvement of the class arrangement can be achieved. Hence it follows that a reduction to a limited number of feature classes is possible. This example can be confirmed using more complex image scenes. The expansion to the three-dimensional Kohonen-Map shown in figure 3 is done during the recall phase. Using the local shape independence of the similarity criterion for each determined feature class a two-dimensional map from neurons identically to the classifing neurons is generated. The size of each of these maps corresponds to the maximum displacement known as a-priori information. The Kohonen-Map decodes the similarity criterions calculated before independently of the object displacement analysing the z-coordinate of the respective active neuron. According to the function of subsystem 4 in the system model in figure 1 the other local coordinates were not used at first. For this, further investigations are planed, which are directed at immediately finding the object displacement and which are using the additional local information for a prediction to minimize the postprocessing overhead (hierarchical systems).

4 Improvement of Motion Estimation

The employment of neural structures specifically for the improvement of motion estimation has not been investigated much up to now. This task has been transfered to the ANN (Fig. 1, subsystem 3). The trained knowledge about concrete objects or parts of them in blocks is used for the determination of the minimum position of the MAD function.

In first fundamental investigations of the application of ANN for the solution of the above mentioned problems simple backpropagation networks were used. They were trained for the recognition of certain MAD forms using supervised learning. It is possible to restrict the consideration to one output neuron because the weight distribution of the system is locally independent. This essentially simplifies the network structure and reduces the necessary calculations. The training vectors are created according to the MAD function (Fig. 5) for motionless objects in identical images in the sense of a auto-correlation function. The use of the MAD function in this manner is based on different aspects. One of these is the fact, that the image contents is reflected in the form of the MAD function. Another one is the feature of local invariance regarding the object position. That means the form of the MAD minimum is independent of the object displacement in the case of undistorted images. The training phase is done off-line. The result of the training procedure are the matrix of weights W and the bias B. The postprocessing of the distorted MAD function can be done on-line according to the transfer properties of the neural network. The postprocessed MAD function originates from the distorted similarity criterion. Ideally, this has the value zero at the detected position.

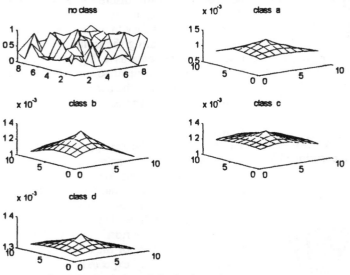

Fig. 4:   Weight data sets of the Kohonen-Map

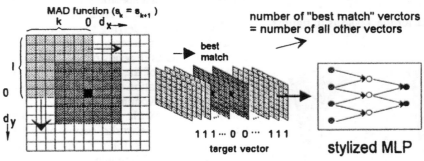

Fig. 5:   Structure of the training data set and simplified architecture of neural network

For the described employment a classification of object-specific MAD functions is done according to section 3. The trained Kohonen-Map is suited to address the weight data sets (weight matrices), stored in an associative memory (Fig. 1, subsystem 4). The number of weight data sets corresponds to the number of classified feature groups.

5 Selected Example

The procedure explained in section 3 and 4 shall be illustrated by a selected example. Fig. 6 shows a used real image scene. The corresponding MAD functions are depicted in Fig. 7. The clear correspondence of the existing minima to the actual object movement is not possible by conventional means. The superimposing between the foreground texture and the moving measuring object visible in Fig. 6 (left side) leads to the creation of two minima (see Fig. 7). The minimum that corresponds to the fixed foreground texture is dominant. In dependence on the technological problem, this overlapping is usually distorting and a separation of both movements is desired. The resulting correspondence problem can be solved by the utilization of a-priori information about the measuring situation. The a-priori information is represented by the MAD function of the non-distorted motionless measuring object (Fig. 6, right side). This function is calculated in a previous off-line process.

The neural networks used were trained to the form of the MAD function according to the procedure, shown in Fig. 5. The postprocessed MAD functions calculated according to the network transfer properties showe, that the minimum corresponding to the foreground texture (position dx=dy=0) is greatly suppressed. By contrast, the interesting minimum is emphasized.

A fundamental problem for real practical applications of the discribed method is the calculation time needed for the off-line training phase. For this reason investigations with reduced training data sets were done. The idea is to use a statistically selected subset of the complete traning data set. It bases on the fact that the ANN interpolates between the locally discrete MAD function during the training phase.

Furthermore it is easy to understand that the method of generating the training vector set (see section 3) contains a high information redundancy. A comparison of the results shows that reducing the complete data set up to 90% yields correct vector fields.

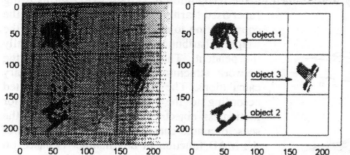

Fig. 6: Probing sequence (left) and non-distorted measuring object (right)

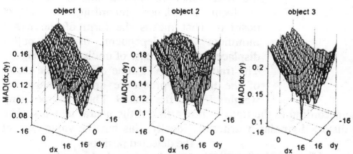

Fig. 7: Distorted similarity criterions for the 3 objects in figure 6

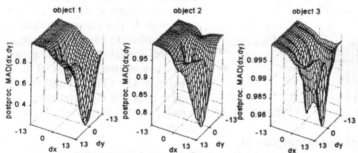

Fig. 8: Postprocessed similarity criterions showing the exact displacements

Conclusions

The described results show, that the structure according to Fig. 1 makes a considerable improvement of the motion estimation in the case of the above mentioned distorted measuring situations possible. This improvement is achieved by the utilization of object specific a-priori information. A further improvement of the efficiency of the procedure can be expected using more efficient classifiers using multiple layers of neurons [7, 8].

In practical realizations it is not possible to assign each object a specific set of weights of the ANN. Therefore a creation of a small number of classes referring to object specific MAD functions is necessary. The sufficient. number of classes depends on the block size containing parts of the objects. It is efficient to analyze the creation of classes by means of self-organizing Kohonen Maps [2, 5]. A combination with the described backpropagation networks seems useful to find new approaches for a feature adaptive motion estimation in complex scenes.

This work was supported by the LSA grant 1441/A0083 and the DFG (Mi 377/3-2).

References

[1] Convertino, G.; et. al.: Hopfield: Neural Network for Motion Estimation and Interpretation. Proc. ICANN' 94, Sorrento, Italy, 26-29 May 1994, Vol. 1, pp. 78-81.

[2] van Deemter, J. H.; Masterbroek, H. A. K.: A statistical correlation technique and a neural network for the motion correspondence problem. Biological Cybernetics 70 (1994), pp. 329-344.

[3] Zaagman, W.H.; et. al.: On the Correlation Model: Performance of a Movement Detecting Neural Element in the Fly Visual System. Biological Cybernetics 31 (1978), pp. 163-178.

[4] Poggio, T.; Reichart, W.: Considerations on Models of Movement Detection. Kybernetik 13 (1973), pp. 223-227.

[5] Seiffert, U.; Michaelis, B.: Estimating Motion Parameters from Image Sequences by Self-Organizing Maps. Proc. 39. IWK 27-30 Sept. 94, Vol. 2, pp. 75-82. Verlag E. Weisspflug, Grossbreitenbach (Thuer.).

[6] Musmann, H.-G.; Pirsch, P.; Grallert, H.-J.: Advances in Picture Coding. Proc. IEEE 73 (1985) No.4, pp. 523-530.

[7] Schnelting, O.;Michaelis, B.; Mecke, R.: Artifical Neural Networks for Motion Estimation. Proc. ICANNGA 95, Ales, France, 19-21 April 1995, Springer Verlag Wien New York, pp. 136-139.

[8] Schnelting, O.;Michaelis, B.; Mecke, R.: Motion Estimation by Using Artifical Neural Networks. IEEE NIPS 95, Neos Marmas Halkidiki, Greece, 20-22 June 1995.

Device-Independent Color Correction for Multimedia Applications Using Neural Networks and Abductive Modeling Approaches

Vasant Shastri[1], Egondu Onyejekwe[2], and Luis C. Rabelo[3]

[1]Computer Science Department, Ohio University, Athens, Ohio 45701
[2]The Ohio State University, Columbus, Ohio 43220
[3]Stocker Center, Ohio University, Athens, Ohio 45701, FAX (614) 593-0778, rabelo@bobcat.ent.ohiou.edu

Abstract

Although color has appeal for developers and consumers alike, color reproduction poses a major problem in many computer-based applications including multimedia and desktop publishing. The problem arises because of device independence color, and the way each device processes color. However, matching the appearance of the monitor and print images may be impossible, and achieving satisfactory results is complex. Not only are there fundamental differences between computer screen (additive) and printers (subtractive), but subtractive color is in general more prone to errors due to dye inadequacies. In order to control the error in porting color, different traditional techniques have been applied. In this paper, the utilization of neural networks as well as abductive modelling approaches to color error reduction are introduced from an RGB (Red Green Blue) color model perspective. Analysis of the results and on-going research issues are discussed.

INTRODUCTION

A major challenge occurs in color reproduction [4,8,9,10,11]. This involves moving color for example from a device that records color information, red, green and blue (RGB) additively, to one that records color information, cyan, magenta, yellow (CMY) and sometimes black as well (CMYK) subtractively. A computer display device would display a color image whose composition is constituted by an additive mechanism through which all colors are derived by adding RGB combinations. In order to print the same image, the printer would use a subtractive mechanism that uses CMY dyes to subtract colors from the image. To print a color image seen on the computer screen to be perceived as a true-color reproduction when printed on a paper, the red, green, and blue data values that drive the display must be transformed into data that control the amounts of cyan, magenta, yellow and black on the printer. The difference in the way display and print images are produced have important consequences for the transformation.

Matching the appearance of the monitor and print images may be impossible, and achieving satisfactory results is complex. In order to control the error in porting color, different traditional techniques have been applied. These traditional techniques include mainly some form of calibration using either trial and error, or polynomial regression, and neural networks [2,5] (strictly) for CIE color models.

In this paper, the problem of device independence and error minimization in color reproduction are addressed using two data-driven techniques: artificial neural networks and a non-parametric modeling technique which integrates concepts of regression and hierarchical /distributed processing of neural networks (i.e., abductive reasoning). Two sets of experiments were performed. The first set of experiments involved the use of a synthetic simulation of error using the non-linear technique of error diffusion. The second set of experiments utilized a procedure by feeding back an image to the computer after it had been printed and scanned. There was a random assignment of images in each training and testing class. These experiments were performed based on the "natural" RGB color model.

The remainder of this paper is organized as follows. First, the basic principles of the techniques utilized are outlined. Second, the different experiments performed and results are provided. Finally, the main conclusions and a short outlook are presented.

OVERVIEW OF THE DATA DRIVEN TECHNIQUES UTILIZED

Among the characteristics of color reproduction problems are imprecision, nonlinear functions, and noisy data. Color error correction does not readily subject itself to linear mathematical solutions, hence there is the need to find other techniques. So, color error correction is a good candidate for techniques which are capable of non-linear modeling, noise resistant, and fuzzy schemes. This study therefore, proposes the use of neural networks and abductive reasoning for controlling color error in multimedia applications.

Neural Networks

These exploratory experiments were mainly developed using standard backpropagation to implement the neural networks. Initial studies utilized other supervised paradigms. However, backpropagation yielded higher generalization levels.

In this research several approaches were utilized, when using the standard backpropagation paradigm, in order to achieve fast convergence and select an appropriate architecture. First, a minimum hidden units architecture is selected according to "reasonable" RMS and Maximum Output errors. Second, sensitivity analysis is utilized to prune input variables. Third, the final architecture is achieved by a weight pruning training process.

a) Number of Hidden Units: To help find an appropriate number of hidden units an interactive addition of nodes was performed. A new node is added to the hidden layer(s) if the root mean square (RMS) error curve has flattened out to an unacceptable level. This process is stopped when the desired performance has been achieved. This training mechanism yielded an architecture of 16 hidden units upon completion of several trials.

b) Eliminating Input Variables: It is possible to evaluate the significance of each input by examining their impact on the output. This was done by utilizing a measure of the impact expressed as [7]:

$$\text{Impact of } I_i = (1/N) \; \Sigma \; ASE((1/N)\Sigma I_{ij}) - ASE \; (I_i)$$

where I_{ij} is the ith input of the jth training sample, N is the total number of training samples, ASE is the average square error. The analysis of the input variable indicated that, to predict accurately R values, three inputs were needed R G B. Therefore, the elimination of input variables reinforced the initial model of using three inputs and not using a single input model.

c) Weight Pruning Techniques: In this research, the elimination of weights was performed as described by Weigend et al. [12]. This technique has the following objective function:

$$Ep = 1/2\Sigma(t_i-o_{il})^2 + l \; \Sigma \; (w_i/w_o)^2/(1+ (w_i/w_o)^2)$$

This weight elimination process increased the performance of the networks. However, this increase in performance was not so dramatic as expected. Weight elimination reduced the number of weights by a small quantity. In addition, to speed convergence behavior, the dynamic selection of parameters such as learning rates and momentum factors were utilized.

Abductive Modeling

The statistical learning algorithm used in this research is an innovative non-parametric modeling technique developed by AbTech Corporation (Charlottesville, VA 22903) and incorporated in its modeling software AIM [1]. The manner by which AIM arrives at a solution, is much like a regression analysis than a neural network. AIM takes each independent variable and creates a third degree polynomial, the coefficients of which are computed such that the polynomial gives the best fit to the independent variable. After testing each independent variable alone, polynomials of all pairs, then all triples [6]

$$(i.e., W_0 + W_1x_1 + W_2x_2 + W_3x_3 + W_4x_1^2 + W_5x_2^2 + W_6x_3^2 + W_7x_1^3 + W_8x_2^3 + W_9x_3^3 + W_{10}x_1x_2 + W_{11}x_1x_3 + W_{12}x_2x_3 + W_{13}x_1x_2x_3)$$

are tested. The best polynomials found in the first pass are further combined into polynomials of polynomials. This process is repeated for several levels in a search for the best polynomial solution (i.e., hierarchical modeling). At each stage, the goodness of fit of the model to the learning set is measured (very similar to a evolutionary computation-based algorithm). A complexity penalty which is small for simple expressions and large for complicated expressions is added to the fitting square error (FSE), rewarding simple expressions and penalizing complicated ones (to develop a tradeoff between training and generalization errors). Therefore, the modeling criterion (Predicted Square Error (PSE)) could be expressed as follows [3]:

$$PSE = FSE + KP$$

where KP is the term utilized to penalize complex networks and could be further decomposed as follows:

$$KP = CPM((2K/N) * Sp^2)$$

where CPM is a complexity penalty multiplier, K is the total number of network coefficients, N is the number of training samples, and Sp is an a priori estimate of the optimal model's error variance based on each variable.

Building a model with AIM involves four simple steps: importing a database of examples, synthesizing a model, analyzing its performance, and using the resulting model. The user interface leads the user through this process logically. Once the user has imported a database, and the user specifies specific input and unused-input, and one-output parameter, AIM automatically develops abductive network models.

EXPERIMENTS AND RESULTS

The experimental design was a 2*2*4*3 - using two techniques, two sources of error, four different training sets , and the three primary color values (defining the correct output), R, G, and B, for both the training and testing patterns. The input to the systems consisted of the RGB values of each image (error diffused or scanned). There were five groups of images (four groups for training and one group for testing). The first group consisted of only one image, and therefore 256 sets of RGB values (i.e., 256 training patterns). The second group of images consisted of five images and therefore a multiple of 256 three dimensional RGB pattern values - hence consisted of 1280 RGB training patterns. The third group of images consisted of ten images, and 2560 RGB training pattern, and the fourth group consisted of fifteen images and a multiple that generated 3840 RGB training patterns. Five independent images were used for testing (with 256 testing patterns each one - the testing error was an average of the individual errors of each testing image).

The experiment for the printed/scanned images followed a different image preparation procedure. The image is obtained through scanning of the printed image. Both techniques yielded good results. However, AIM outperformed the backpropagation neural networks in each of the testing cases studied (Figure 1). Reproduction of pictures was accomplished successfully using both techniques (quantitatively and qualitatively). In addition, AIM had faster training sessions (for the larger size files AIM had training sessions of 250 seconds against one hour for backpropagation - using a Pentium @90mhz computer)

CONCLUSIONS

The empirical results show the effectiveness of the proposed neural network and abductive modeling methods. Unlike usual methods of transforming RGB data into CIE tri-stimulus values and CIE-CMYK data for the printer, in this research, we have eliminated the need to go through this step, making the system device-independent. Currently, other neural networks schemes (e.g., general regression neural networks) and their possible integration with abductive modeling are being investigated.

REFERENCES
[1] AIM User's Manual, AbTech Corporation, Charlottesville, Virginia.
[2] Chang, Gao-Wei, and Chang Po-Rong, "Neural Plant Inverse Control Approach to Color Error Reduction for Scanner and Printer," IEEE International Conference on Neural Networks Vol. III, 1993, p.1979-1983.
[3] Drake, K.C., "Highly-automated, non-parametric statistical learning for autonomous target recognition," Proceedings of the SPIE 20th Applied Imagery Pattern Recognition Workshop-October 1991, McLean, Virginia.
[4] Gentile, Ronald, S., "Device independent color in PostScript," SPIE, Vol. 1913, 1994, p. 419-432.
[5] Kang, R. and Anderson Peter, G., "Neural Network Application to the Color Scanner and Printer Calibrations," Journal of Electronic Imaging, Vol. 1, No. 2, 1992, p. 125-135.

[6] Montgomery, G. , "Abductive Diagnostics," American Institute of Aeronautics and Astronautics, Inc., 1989 by AbTech Corporation.

[7] Moody, J., and Utans, J. "Principled Architecture Selection for Neural Networks: Application to Corporate Bond Rating Prediction," ADVANCES IN NEURAL INFORMATION PROCESSING SYSTEMS 4, Morgan Kaufmann.

[8] Petschchik, Benno, "Color Hard Copy - a self-tuning color correction algorithm based on a colorimetric model," Printing Technologies for images, Gray Scale, and Color, Proc. SPIE, Vol. 1458, 1991, p. 108-114.

[9] Robertson, A. R., "COLOR PERCEPTION," PHYSICS TODAY American Institute Of Physics, December, 1992, p. 23-29.

[10] Roetling, P., "The Physics of Digital Color," PHYSICS TODAY American Institute of Physics, December, 1992, p. 23.

[11] Starkweather, Gary K., "A Color-Correction Scheme for Color Electronic Printers," COLOR research and application, Supplement Vol. 11, 1986, p. 67-72.

[12] Weigend, A., Rumelhart, D., and Huberman, B., "Generalization by Weight Elimination with Application to Forecasting," ADVANCES IN NEURAL INFORMATION SYSTEMS 3, 1991, Morgan Kaufmann.

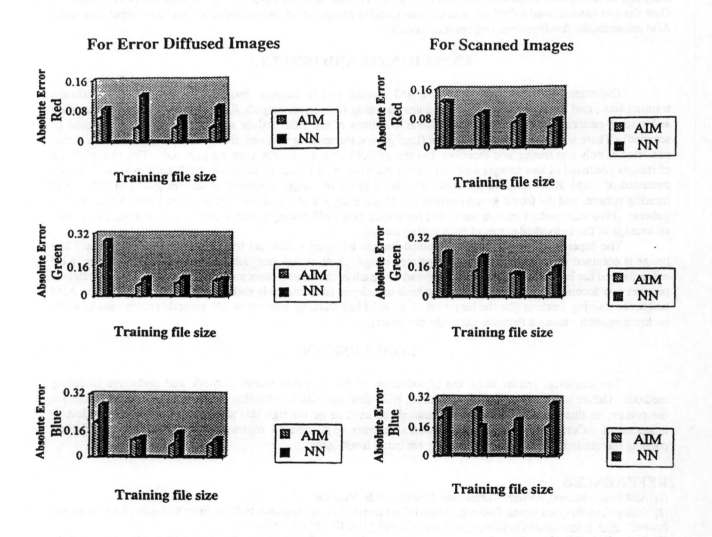

Figure 1. Results using the testing images

Time Delay Neural Networks
for NO$_X$ and CO Prediction in Fossil Fuel Plants

Bora Bakal*, Tülay Adalı*, M. Kemal Sönmez†, and Reza Fakory‡

*Information Technology Laboratory, Department of Electrical Engineering
University of Maryland Baltimore County, Baltimore MD 21228
†Institute for Systems Research, University of Maryland, College Park. MD 20742
‡Simulation, Systems & Services (S3) Technologies Company, Columbia MD 21045

Abstract

This paper presents a time delay neural network (TDNN) model designed for the prediction of NO$_X$ and CO emissions from a fossil fuel power plant. NO$_X$ and CO emissions of the plant are determined as a function of other related time-series such as air flow rates, oxygen levels that are measured during the system operation, using data obtained from a coal burning fossil fuel power plant in Sweden. Correlation analysis is performed on the data to determine the spread of cross-correlation between pairs of variables, and this information is used to design a variable-length variable-position window TDNN structure. We introduce a preprocesser which employs an iterative regularization scheme to recover unavailable portions of CO data (that are clipped due to saturation of the measuring device). Prediction after training with the restored data set has proven to be significantly more accurate.

1 Introduction

Fossil fuel power plants are urged to install highly sophisticated equipments in order to monitor, control and minimize their gaseous emissions. This necessity adds considerably to the complexity and cost of installation, operation and maintenance of power plants. Therefore, a cost effective solution for modeling and controlling these emissions carries great industrial significance. Especially, after the passage of 1990 Clean Air Act, plants are required to limit their gaseous emissions such as NO$_X$ which is believed to be a major contributor to acid rains [10]. One significant cause of increased NO$_X$ emissions is the excess air in the boiler during combustion. The furnace temperature from the heat of the combustion can also affect NO$_X$ emissions of a fossil fuel plant. In order to minimize these effects, there is a variety of possible low-NO$_X$ control strategies [6] most of which are industrially funded projects under the U.S. Department of Energy (DOE) Clean Coal Technology (CCT) Program [5]. Obviously, availability of effective control technologies will assist utilities and industry in meeting the requirements of the Clean Air Act Amendments of 1990.

In this paper, we present a time delay neural network (TDNN) model to predict the NO$_X$ and CO emissions of a fossil fuel power plant. In our experiments, we use real plant observations of the system variables from a coal burning fossil fuel power plant in Sweden. The rest of the paper is organized as follows: Section 2 explains the neural network structure. In section 3, a cross-correlation analysis is presented for efficient TDNN implementation. Section 4 and 5 concentrate on the procedures for the prediction of NO$_X$ and CO, respectively. Finally, conclusions are drawn in Section 6.

2 Time Delay Neural Networks (TDNN)

Whenever the patterns possess temporal information, and cannot be represented with static input-output mappings, the learning neural network requires some form of memory. One way to introduce memory is to turn the temporal sequence into a spatial input pattern, that is, to unfold the temporal sequence in time. This is accomplished by incorporating tapped delay lines at the input of a multi-layer perceptron (MLP), thus obtaining a time delay neural network (TDNN) structure (Fig. 1). This structure can extract the temporal correlation yielding accurate predictions. The efficiency of a TDNN is mostly dependent on the

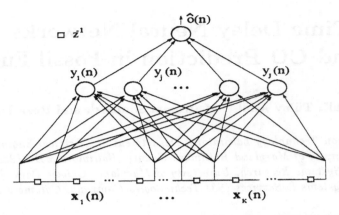

Figure 1: Time Delay Neural Network (TDNN) Structure

number of the delay units, i.e. the window size. As will be explained in the next section, a cross-correlation analysis is performed on the data to obtain the most suitable window size for each variable for efficiency in implementation.

We introduce the following notation for the variable window size TDNN implementation. Let $\mathbf{x}_k(n)$ be a variable length input vector such that

$$\mathbf{x}_k(n) = \begin{bmatrix} x_k(n - C_k - \frac{W_k-1}{2}) \\ \vdots \\ x_k(n - C_k - 1) \\ x_k(n - C_k) \\ x_k(n - C_k + 1) \\ \vdots \\ x_k(n - C_k + \beta) \end{bmatrix}$$

where W_k is the proposed window size for the kth input variable, C_k the center of the window is defined as the time delay at which the correlation between the target variable and the kth input variable is maximum, and

$$\beta = \min\left\{C_k, \frac{W_k - 1}{2}\right\} \tag{1}$$

introduces a constraint on the window size to ensure causality, a condition that has to be satisfied for on-line plant applications. Based on the above definitions, the propagation of the signal is represented as

$$y_j(n) = \tanh\left(\sum_{i=1}^{I} z_i(n)v_{ij}(n)\right) \qquad \hat{o}(n) = \tanh\left(\sum_{j=1}^{J+1} y_j(n)w_j(n)\right),$$

where

$$\mathbf{z}(n) = \begin{bmatrix} \mathbf{x}_1(n) \\ \vdots \\ \mathbf{x}_K(n) \\ 1 \end{bmatrix},$$

$z_{I+1}(n)$ and $y_{J+1}(n)$ are assigned to unity, the bias of the neurons, J is the number of neurons in the hidden layer, $v_{ij}(n)$ is the connection weight from the ith node in the input layer to the jth neuron in the hidden layer, $w_j(n)$ is the connection weight from the jth neuron in the hidden layer to the output, K is the number of input variables, and I is defined as the total length of the input vector under the constraint introduced by (1). We consider a single output structures shown in Fig. 1 Learning is achieved by training the weights with backpropagation such that the mean square error is minimized.

3   Cross-correlation Analysis

The time sequences we use in our implementation are obtained from a coal burning fossil fuel power plant in Sweden. There are five variables –measured during the system operation– which are sampled with 1 Hz. (This sampling frequency produces 23808 samples for the day-time data set and 50688 samples for the night-time data set.) These variables are; NOX (Nitrogenoxide emission), CO (Carbonmonoxide emission), O2 (Oxygen), PRBS (Pseudo Random Binary Sequence), and TOTFL (Total Air Flow Rate).

The cross-correlation functions between the target variables (NOX and CO) and the input variables are computed under the assumption of stationarity under normal plant operating conditions. PRBS, which is a pseudo random binary sequence, controls the air flow rate (TOTFL) which in turn affects the oxygen level (O2) in the combustion furnace. Consequently, the effect of the variation in O2 level reflects on the NOX production. Since PRBS and TOTFL are disturbances that affect the target variables with a certain time delay, the peaks of the cross-correlation functions occur with certain time delays. However, since the effect of O2 reflects on the target variables almost immediately due to the fast nature of the chemical reaction taking place, the correlation peaks at almost zero time delay. These plots are shown for the NOX target variable in Fig. 2.

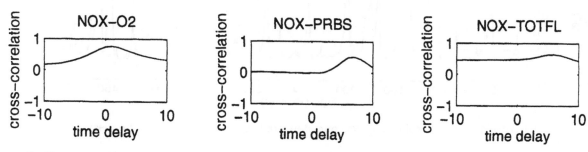

Figure 2: Cross-correlation characteristics for NOX and O2 (left), NOX and PRBS (middle), and NOX and TOTFL (right).

4   Prediction of NO$_\mathbf{X}$ Emissions

The analysis of the cross-correlation curves suggest the choices $C_1 = 1$ (O2), $C_2 = 6$ (PRBS), and $C_3 = 6$ (TOTFL). Furthermore, the slowly decaying correlation characteristics for O2 and TOTFL suggests a larger window size for these inputs, whereas concentrated nature for PRBS suggests a smaller window size. For our TDNN model the suitable window sizes are chosen as; $W_1 = 41$, $W_2 = 5$, and $W_3 = 13$.

The data set is formed as follows: 8 subsets of data are formed, each consisting of 400 samples half of which are chosen from the night-time data set and the remaining half from the day-time data set. Prediction results are shown in Fig. 3.

5   Prediction of CO Emissions

Prediction of CO emissions presents a more difficult statistical challenge as the available CO data have clipped portions due to the saturation of the measuring apparatus. Thus, the training data have to be preprocessed before they can be presented to the network. It is not feasible to discard the clipped portions since they are frequent and spread. Removing them would destroy the temporal integrity of the time series resulting in a drastic decrease in the amount of usable training data. They convey a limited amount of useful information as well.

Our approach is to restore the data by estimating the clipped portions using an iterative regularization scheme. Main idea is to estimate a complete time series for the entire data which minimizes the mean square error for unclipped portions while enforcing a regularity criterion for the whole dataset. The imposed

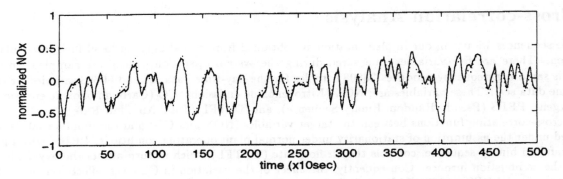

Figure 3: Actual (solid line) vs. one-step predicted (dotted line) NOx emissions.

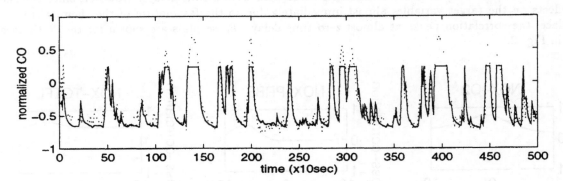

Figure 4: Actual (solid line) vs. one-step predicted (dotted line) CO emissions.

regularity criterion is implicit in the overall technique, i.e. the use of a fixed architecture net. The iteration works as follows:

Step 0: Train the TDNN using only the unclipped portion of the data.

Step 1: Predict CO samples one-step into the future with the weights obtained from the previous step, and replace each clipped sample by the predicted value if the predicted value is greater than the saturation level, otherwise leave samples unchanged.

Step 2: Train the TDNN using the time-series obtained in **Step 1** as the target signal, and goto **Step 1**.

Step 0 initializes the weights of the net to model the time series. In **Step 1**, the net model is used to generate an estimate for the whole time series. This estimate is then utilized in **Step 2** to improve the net model by using it as the target in training. A new estimate is then produced by the net model obtained this way to be used in further model improvement. This iteration is carried out a number of times until a regular estimate with an acceptable amount of MSE over the unclipped portions is obtained. It is hard to define a stopping criterion which embodies the regularity constraint, but in practice several iterations of the algorithm result in plausible and useful estimates for the restored data. Prediction after training with the restored data set has proven to be significantly more accurate.

After the preprocessing stage, training and testing is done with the same window sizes and the window centers as in Section 4, since the cross-correlation peaks for CO occur at the same time delays as in Fig. 2 The results obtained with this implementation are illustrated in Fig. 4.

6 Conclusions

In this paper we present a TDNN for "one-step into the future" prediction of NOX and CO emissions. We exploit the cross-correlation functions between the target variables and the input variables to determine the window sizes and the window centers for the tapped delay line at the input of the TDNN. Basically, two features of the cross-correlation functions aid the selection of these quantities: the time delay at which the cross-correlation peak occurs (window center), and the rate of decay of correlation between variables (window size). We also present a neural network preprocesser to recover CO data which is distorted due to the saturation of the measurement device. TDNN can extract the information on CO emissions from the healthy portions of the data and yield a realistic estimate of the CO emissions which are distorted in the original data.

References

[1] T. Adalı, B. Bakal, R. Fakory, D. Komo, M. K. Sönmez, and C. O. Tsaoi, "Dynamic System Modeling with Neural Networks," *Proc. GSE Systems Users Conf.*, (Columbia, MD), Sept. 1994.

[2] B. Bakal, T. Adalı, R. Fakory, D. Komo, M. K. Sönmez, and C. O. Tsaoi, "Modeling Core Neutronics by Recurrent Neural Networks," submitted to *World Congress on Neural Networks*, (Washington, DC), July 17-21, 1995.

[3] N. V. Bhat and T. J. McAvoy, "Determining Model Structure for Neural Models by Network Stripping," *Computers and Chemical Engineering*, vol. 16, no. 4, pp. 271-281, 1992.

[4] K. Chakraborty, K. Mehrotra, C. K. Mohan, and S. Ranka, "Forecasting the Behavior of Multivariate Time Series Using Neural Networks," *Neural Networks*, vol. 5, pp. 961-970, 1992.

[5] "Update on NO_x Control Technologies," *PETC Review*, Spring 1995.

[6] V. Dupont, M. Pourkashanian, A. Williams, and R. Woolley, "The Reduction of NO_x Formation in Natural Gas Burner Flames," *Fuel*, vol. 72, no. 4, pp. 497-503, 1993.

[7] C. R. Gent and C. P. Sheppard, "Predicting Time Series by a Fully Connected Neural Network Trained by Back Propagation," *Computing & Control Engineering Journal*, pp. 109-112, May 1992.

[8] S. Haykin, *Neural Networks: A Comprehensive Foundation*. New York: Macmillan College Publishing Company, 1994.

[9] K. S. Narendra and K. Parthasarathy, "Identification and Control of Dynamical Systems using Neural Networks," *IEEE Trans. on Neural Networks*, vol. 1, no. 1, March 1990.

[10] D. J. Smith, "NOx Emission Control Demands a Range of Solutions," *Power Engineering*, July 1992.

[11] Z. Tang, C. Almeida, and P. A. Fishwick, "Time Series Forecasting Using Neural Networks vs. Box-Jenkins Methodology," *Simulation*, vol. 57, no. 5, pp. 303-310, 1991.

Wavelet Aided Assembly Line Inspections

Sheng Zhong[*], Harold Szu[†], Qing-Yun Shi, Francis Chin[‡]
Lei Xu, Min-Teh Cheng, Huisheng Chi, Ke Chen, Che Li

Dept. of Mathematics, National Lab on Machine Perception
Peking University, Beijing 100871, China

[†] Naval Surface Warfare Center, Dahlgren Division
Silver Spring, MD 20903-5000, USA

[‡] Dept. of Computer Science, Univ. of Hong Kong, Hong Kong

Abstract

Automated Assembly Line Inspections(AALI) can benefit from the multiresolution wavelet transform(WT) preprocessing followed with a neural network(NN) fault detection postprocessing. Specially, we have demonstrated the point singularity detection in a card-box food/drink packaging automation, which is essential for hygienic purpose. The pin-holes on the box were detected as singularities through continous WT(CWT). Their shapes were restored by a multiresolution discrete WT(DWT) shape-from-shading(SFS) technique. And then a neural network was employed to further distinguish pin-hole singularities from other non pin-hole singularities.

Keywords: automated assembly line inspections, wavelet transform, multiresolution analysis, shape from shading, neural networks

1 Introduction

In industry automation, product quality control requires efficient and robust inspections. In assembly line environments, real-time inspections are very important techniques. AALI prefers fast and reliable inspections. A lot of work has been done in this area. Szu[1] addresses the problem of automatic fault recognition(AFR) using an imaging correlation technique with the help of simulated annealing and neural network(NN). Villalos, et al[2] and Glover[3] also made use of NNs for inspections/fault diagnosis of machine surfaces and Coke bottle filling-up process.

Real time image and signal processing techniques are the keys to fast and reliable inspections. In this paper, we demonstrate that wavelet transform(WT) can facilitate AFR through the example of card-box food/drink packaging assembly line. The boxes with microscopic pin-holes should be dectected to prevent bacteria from entering them and corrupting the food or drink such as milk. The pin-holes can be detected as singularities in the image or 1D signal. In addition, the box surface irregularities mingled with noise bury the pin-hole singularities and make the image or 1D signal very singular and hard to show the pin-holes obviously. Szu, Zhong, *et al.* [5] proposed a multiscale CWT method to distinguish shape singularities from noise. Zhong, Shi and Cheng[6] proposed a wavelet based SFS technique to recover the shape information. To further distinguish the pin-hole singularities from other shape singularities, an NN postprocessing process is adopted using the shape information as input. The wavelet multiresolution preprocessing and NN postprocessing accelerate the time-consuming shape recovering process and fault identification process and improve system performance.

Our goal is not to replace human inspection, rather to reduce the amount of in-situ human inspection so that the food/drink packaging process can be sped up, i.e., the goal of the WT-NN techniques is to minimize the samples that need human inspection by branching off only those potential defect samples from packaging station.

2 Smart eye preprocessing

One of the important reasons that WT is considered for AALI applications is that wavelet multiresolution analysis can model the human visual system very well. It is known that visual information is processed in

---

[*]visiting HKU, current address: Dept. of Compt. Sci., Univ. of Hong Kong, HK; email: zhsh@csd.hku.hk

different channels at the early stages of human vision. These channels have different frequencies and actually act as band-pass filters. The responses of the receptive fields of the eye are similar to wavelet filters such as the Mexican hat and Morlet wavelets. Multiscale/multiresolution WT can thus be employed to simulate the smart eye preprocessing.

Supppose the process of looking at a car. We first get the sketch of the whole car, and then futher into details such as the door, the window, the bars and etc.. This coarse to fine process can be well simulated by multiresolution DWT. The attentive fixation on a moving object can be interpreted as a coarse to fine multiresolution process too.

In practice, the more accurate we model the brain-style intelligence, the more we demand WT to model human eyes for multiresolution input. Computationally speaking, the coarse to fine strategy makes the interesting feature easy to follow and thus be detected more accurately and rapidly. Thus, CWT and DWT are employed in the preprocessing of AALI. Fig.1 shows the diagram of the the whole AALI process.

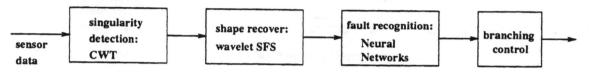

Figure 1: AALI diagram

3 1D model of the convey belt assembly line inspection

In a card box food/drink packaging assembly line, an 1D line-by-line scanning system is preferred to a 2D imaging system because a sequence of images has to be processed to extract correct class features from individually variable features[1] in 2D imaging system which is a tough task plagued with the oversensitivity to errors compounded from multiple degrees of freedom. The U.S. Postal Printing Office and Federal Bureau of Printing Office have selected the line-by-line anolog scan to search on-line for imperfections or flaws of stamps and dollars bills.

In a manufactory assembly line setup, we can control the scanning light and parts without occlusion on the convey belt as ideally as possible. Fig.2 illustrates an inspection setup. An overhead light and sensor(scanner) acquires the line-by-line data while the card box is conveyed on the belt. The line raw data are feeded to the computer where the inspection is being carried out and a control signal is sent for branching the box once a decision can be made.

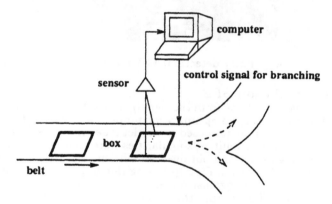

Figure 2: AALI setup

The challenge is to detect microscopic pin-holes on a drink/food card box container. The task becomes difficult because of the presence of noise and other non-pin-hole shape singularities and the requirements from real-time on-line processing. We can demonstrate this by a typical 1D signal which implies a rooftop shape with a singularity at the top. In Fig. 3, (a) is the shape of the rooftop, which is employed to emulate the shape singularities on the surface of the card box. The shapes of the pin-holes and the abrupt convexes or concaves on the surface are different in nature, which will be feeded to NNs for further identification later. Here we do not differentiate them just to elucidate the effect of noise. Without noise, the senor data of (a) is illustated in (b), and with nonzero mean noise, in (c).

First, noisy points should not be declared as singularities. Second, shapes of the singularities should be recovered to further distinguish pin-holes and other surface irregularities. And finally, all the processing should

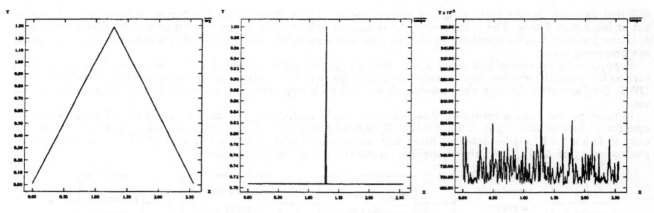

Figure 3: (a). roof-top (b). sensor data (c). noisy sensor data

be fast and suited to real time realization.

4 WT Preprocessing

WT is employed to detect singularities from the sensor data and to restore shapes of the card surface(line by line) because of the reasons stated in section 2.

4.1 Singularity detection using CWT

Because the behavior of a shape singularity is different from that of a noisy point when the signal is convolved with wavelets at different scales, the shape singularity can be detected by checking the evolution of the CWT magnitudes across scales. In Fig. 4, the magnitudes of the CWT coefficients of the signal shown in Fig. 3(c) across scales are displayed. Here we make use of the Morlet wavelets, which was proven able to locate the shape singularity buried among the noise[5]. CWT can be implemented efficiently by parallel computing.

Figure 4: Singularity detection: CWT across multiple scales

4.2 Wavelet based multiresolution SFS

It is an ill-posed problem to recover the shape from the signal/image. With smoothness constraint and boundary conditions, Brooks and Horn[4] modeled it as an optimization propsed problem and proposed an iterative solution, which is time-consuming. Zhong, Shi, et al [6] proposed a wavelet aided multiresolution fast algorithm for SFS. To overcome the drawback of SFS that discontinuities/singularities were round-off, Szu, Zhong, et al.[5] integrated the knowledge from the detected singularity and obtained an efficient feature-preserving SFS method. Fig. 5(a) gives the restored shape from the signal shown in Fig. 3(c) using this technique. The shape of the singularity(roof-top) is preserved. And the method is robust against noise. It was shown that the wavelet based multiresolution analysis and singularity detection helped accelerate the shape recovering greatly.

Fig. 5(b) is an illutration of the shape of a typical card box line, which contains a pin-hole recognized as the deepest hole. Automatic extraction of knowledge about the singularity[7] is essential for the success of the automatic fault inspections.

5 NN Postprocessing

In product quality control systems, false alarms of product quality should be avoided. After the above WT preprocessing, shape information of the singularities is obtained. It is feeded to NNs to identify pin-holes from non-pinhole singularities. Because more obviously different features are presented in the shape information, the NNs can differentiate the pin-holes and non-pin-hole singularities more easily and accurately using the shape information as input than using the 1D sensor raw 1D signal directly. Furthermore, the effect of noise is graetly decreased on the shape information domain. These can be demonstated by comparing Fig. 5(b) to Fig. 3(c).

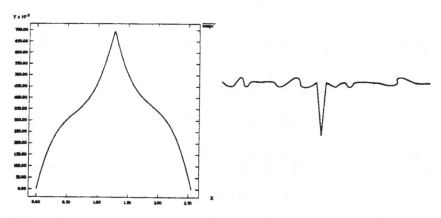

Figure 5: (a). shape from Fig. 3(c)   (b). typical card surface shape

Also in [8], Telfer, Szu and *et al.* have demonstated that the direct use of raw data as input to the NN is inferior to the use of wavelet patches of the raw data.

As to the NNs employed, a multilayer perceptron trained by backpropagation can perform the classification very well.

6 Discussion and conclusion

We have demonstrated the efficiency of the wavelet aided AALI scheme. The success of the wavelet based method is because of the several reasons. First, wavelet-based multiresolution analysis such as the CWT and DWT can perform as the smart eye processing, which results in accurate singularity detection in noisy environment and accurate shape information suited to fault/defect identification. Second, NN can efficiently distinguish the shapes of different singularities, which makes the assembly line inspection robust. Third, all involved techniques have efficient implementations, e.g., CWT can be parallel implemented and DWT is fast and accelerates the SFS process.

Shapes of singularities are the key to a robust and efficient AALI system. Thus, automatic extraction of knowledge about the singularity is a very essential technique for shape restoration. Such a technique is being further developed[7] using an automatic correction scheme to approach accurate singularity information.

References

[1] H. Szu, "Automatic fault recognition by image correlation neural network techniques, " *IEEE Trans. Indu. Elect.*, Vol. 40, No.2, pp. 197-208, April 1993.

[2] L. Villalos and S. Gruber, "A system for neural network-based inspection of machine surfaces," *J. Neural Network Computing*, Vol. 2, no. 2, pp. 18-30, fall 1990.

[3] D. E. Glover, "Optical processing and neurocomputing in automated inspection systems," *J. Neural Network Computing*, Vol. 1, no. 1, pp. 5-18, Summer 1989.

[4] M. J. Brooks and B. K. P. Horn, "Shape and source from shading, " in *Int. Joint Conf. Artificial Intelligence*, LA, CA, pp. 932-936, August 1985.

[5] H. Szu, S. Zhong, Lei Xu, Qing-Yun Shi, Min-Teh Cheng, Ke Chen, Huisheng Chi, Che Li, "Multiresolution wavelet techniques for noisy inverse sensing problems," *Proc. SPIE*, Vol. 2491, *Wavelet Appl. II*, pp. 481-489, Orlando April 17-21, 1995.

[6] S. Zhong, Qing-Yun Shi, Min-Teh Cheng, "Fast shape from shading based on wavelet transform," *Proc. SPIE*, Vol. 2242, pp. 169-178, Orlando, April 4-8, 1994.

[7] S. Zhong, H. Szu, et al., "Wavelet based feature-preserving shape from shading," unpublished.

[8] B. A. Telfer, H. Szu, et al., "Adaptive wavelet classification of acoustic backscatter and imagery", Opt. Eng., Vol. 33, no.7, pp. 2192-2203, July 1994.

Neural Networks for Optimal Data Association in Detection of Hot Plate

Jung-Gu Kim and Hong Jeong

Department of Electrical Engineering, Pohang University of Science and Technology
Pohang 790-784, Korea, Tel: +82-562-279-2223, E-mail:hjeong@hjstar.postech.ac.kr

Abstract

This paper introduces an algorithm for boundary detection in IR image, that consists of tracking filter and data association. The major achievement of this paper is the introduction of the new data association algorithm. We define the data association as a constrained optimization and derive a neural network as an efficient solution.

I. Introduction

In steel plate rolling, the front end of the plate may bend upward or downward on leaving the roll gap primarily due to unbalanced rolling. Front end bending may cause serious drawbacks both in productivity and in quality of the steel products. So far, only inaccurate curvatures estimated from the physical conditions such as temperature, thickness, speed difference of the upper and lower roll has been used. In this paper, we solve this problem by image processing technique and derive a new algorithm based upon neural networks.

Due to the characteristics of the imaging conditions, we prefer to the IR image. Also, the noise contained in the image makes it hard to use binary images. The conventional algorithms such as contour following, Hugh transform, edge detection are not working for this type of images.

Starting with the IR image, our goal is then to find the exact contour of the object. We define the task as a target tracking problem that consists of tracking filter and data association. Especially we introduce a new data association algorithm that shows better performance than the conventional ones.

II. Description of the Overall System

Fig. 1 shows overall boundary detection system which is divided into two subsystems: acquisition and tracking which further consists of data association and data filtering. In the first phase,

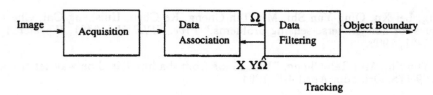

Fig. 1. Boundary detection system.

appropriate positions of the object boundaries are estimated by the acquisition system. Starting from these initial positions, the boundaries are traced by the tracking system. Inside the tracking system, the data association between tracks and the observed boundary points are responsible for the data association system. Using this information and the observation data the tracking filter updates the estimated boundary positions and predicts the centers of the next gates. This information is used again by the data association and the loop repreates until some termination condition is reached. The purpose of this paper is to develop the data association using neural network algorithms.

III. Data Association

A. Problem Formulation

Suppose that there are T object boundaries and N number of measurement data in validation gates[1]. The problem is that when a set of measurement data is received, it has to be determined that which measurements are to be used for each boundary. The relationships of these measurements and boundary are best described by $N \times (T+1)$ validation matrix[1].

$$
\Omega = [\omega_{ij}] = \begin{bmatrix}
\omega_{10} & \omega_{11} & \omega_{12} & \cdots & \omega_{1T} \\
\omega_{20} & \omega_{21} & \omega_{22} & \cdots & \omega_{2T} \\
\vdots & \vdots & \vdots & \vdots & \vdots \\
\omega_{N0} & \omega_{N1} & \omega_{N2} & \cdots & \omega_{NT}
\end{bmatrix}. \tag{1}
$$

The elements of the validation matrix is binary, that is, $\omega_{ij} = 1$ if the ith measurement originated from jth object, and $\omega_{ij} = 0$ otherwise. The first column of this matrix is considered as noise and others as object boundary and all rows are regarded as measurement data.

For the purpose of solving the problem of a large number of measurements and objects, we find the data association matrix. The data association matrix for different gates and measurements can be formulated based on the validation matrix (1). And the task of finding this feasible association matrix is viewed as a constrained optimization problem. We define this problem by the MAP estimate: $\hat{\omega}^* = \arg\max_{\hat{\omega}} P(\hat{\omega}|\omega, y, x)$, where y, x and ω are measurement data in validation gate, center of the gate, and initial validation matrix, respectively.

B. Energy Function

The posterior probability becomes

$$
P(\hat{\omega}|y, x, \omega) = \frac{P(\omega|\hat{\omega})P(y, x|\hat{\omega})P(\hat{\omega})}{P(y, x, \omega)}. \tag{2}
$$

For the pdfs of (2), we assume Gibbsian distribution, $\frac{1}{Z}\exp(-E)$ for some partitian function Z and energy function E and the following properties for the energy function.

$$
E(\hat{\omega}|y, x, \omega) = E(\omega|\hat{\omega}) + E(y, x|\hat{\omega}) + E(\hat{\omega}). \tag{3}
$$

The first term $E(\omega|\hat{\omega})$ in (3) stands for the relationship of matching between ω and $\hat{\omega}$, and their distance is usually modeled as a Gaussian distribution. The energy is therefore can be written as the following form

$$
E(y, x, \omega|\hat{\omega}) = \alpha \sum_{i=1}^{N} \sum_{j=1}^{T} (\omega_{ij} - \hat{\omega}_{ij})^2, \tag{4}
$$

where α is a constant.

Let's consider an arbitrary trajectory with data y_i within validation gate. Using simple vector operation, the direction of arbitrary trajectory and perpendicular distance between data and the trajectory can be calculated. Here, we assume that the energy for measurement located close to the trajectory has to be low than that of data located far from the trajectory.

The energy function for this distance relationship with data association can be thought as

$$E(y, x|\hat{\omega}) = \beta \sum_{i=1}^{N} \sum_{j=1}^{T} \frac{(x_i y_j - y_i x_j)^2}{x_j^2 + y_j^2} \hat{\omega}_{ij}, \tag{5}$$

where x_i, y_i are the x and y components of the measurement, x_j, y_j are the x and y components of center of the validation gate of boundaries, and β is a constant.

It is reasonable that the only one measurement data is considered for a specific object at each time. Therefore the energy must be low for only those solutions that produce a single 1 in each column and a single 1 in rows from the second column in association matrix. Then the energy function for these constraints can be obtained by

$$E(\hat{\omega}) = \lambda \sum_{i=1}^{N} (\sum_{j=0}^{T} \hat{\omega}_{ij} - 1) + \gamma \sum_{j=1}^{T} (\sum_{i=1}^{N} \hat{\omega}_{ij} - 1). \tag{6}$$

Here λ are γ are constant.

The total energy function is then

$$E(\hat{\omega}|y, x, \omega) = \alpha \sum_{i=1}^{N} \sum_{j=1}^{T} (\omega_{ij} - \hat{\omega}_{ij})^2 + \beta \sum_{i=1}^{N} \sum_{j=1}^{T} \frac{(x_i y_j - y_i x_j)^2}{x_j^2 + y_j^2} \hat{\omega}_{ij} + \lambda \sum_{i=1}^{N} (\sum_{j=0}^{T} \hat{\omega}_{ij} - 1) + \gamma \sum_{j=1}^{T} (\sum_{i=1}^{N} \hat{\omega}_{ij} - 1)$$

$$\tag{7}$$

C. Hopfield Neural Network

Given total energy (7), we find the efficient solution using Hopfield neural network. To find the weight and input bias of Hopfield neural network we rearranged the energy function as

$$E = \sum_{i=1}^{N} \sum_{k=1}^{N} \sum_{j=0}^{T} \sum_{l=0}^{T} \{\alpha \delta_{ik} \delta_{jl} (1 - \delta_{0j}) + \gamma[\delta_{ik} + \delta_{jl}(1 - \delta_{0j})]\} \hat{\omega}_{ij} \hat{\omega}_{kl} \tag{8}$$

$$- \sum_{i=1}^{N} \sum_{j=0}^{T} \{2\alpha(1 - \delta_{0j})\omega_{ij} - \beta(1 - \delta_{0j}) \frac{(x_i y_j - x_j y_i)^2}{(x_j^2 + y_j^2)} + 2\gamma(2 - \delta_{0j})\} \hat{\omega}_{ij}$$

$$+ \sum_{i=1}^{N} \sum_{k=1}^{N} \sum_{j=0}^{T} \sum_{l=0}^{T} \alpha \delta_{ik} \delta_{jl} (1 - \delta_{0j}) \omega_{ij} \omega_{kl} + \gamma(N + T),$$

where $\sum_{i=1}^{N} \sum_{k=1}^{N} \sum_{j=0}^{T} \sum_{l=0}^{T} \delta_{ik} \delta_{jl} (1 - \delta_{0j}) \alpha \omega_{ij} \omega_{kl}$ and $\gamma(N + T)$ are constant.

Finally, the weight and the input bias are obtained by

$$w_{ikjl} = -2\{\alpha \delta_{ik} \delta_{jl} (1 - \delta_{0j}) + \gamma[\delta_{ik} + \delta_{jl}(1 - \delta_{0j})]\}, \tag{9}$$

$$I_{ij} = 2\{\alpha(1 - \delta_{0j})\omega_{ij} - \beta(1 - \delta_{0j}) \frac{(x_i y_j - x_j y_i)^2}{2(x_j^2 + y_j^2)} + 2\gamma(2 - \delta_{0j})\}. \tag{10}$$

The overall architecture of Hopfield neural network for computing data association matrix is shown in Fig. 2. In this figure, the inputs for the first column of neurons are

$$I_{i0} = 2\gamma, \tag{11}$$

and inputs for others are

$$I_{ij \neq 0} = 2\alpha \omega_{ij} - \beta \frac{(x_i y_j - x_j y_i)^2}{x_j^2 + y_j^2} + 4\gamma. \tag{12}$$

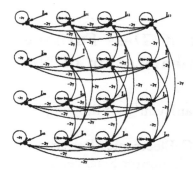

Fig. 2. Hopfield neural network architecture for data association.

IV. Experimental Result

To evaluate the effectiveness of proposed method for finding optimal boundary of hot plate in IR image, an experiment was performed. The experiments are provided for data association, and filtering systems. The test images have been taken from mono CCD camera and IR filter of wavelength of 1050 nm.

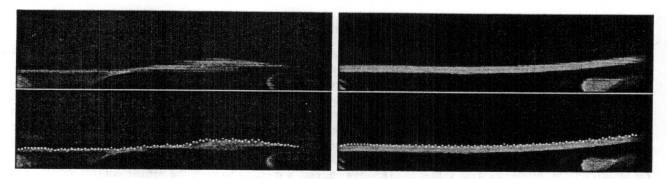

Fig. 3. Input IR images of hot plate(upper) and upper boundary(lower).

We showed two IR images of hot plate and the upper boundary found using proposed method in Fig. 3.

V. Conclusion

In this paper we introduced an algorithm for boundary detection of hot plate in IR image that consists of tracking filter and data association. We defined the data association problem as a constrainted optimization and derived the Hopfield neural network as an efficient solution. We showed experimental results for finding upper boundary.

REFERENCES

[1] T. E. Fortmann, Y. Bar-Shalom and M. Scheffe, "Sonar tracking of multiple targets using joint probability data association," *IEEE Journal of Oceanic Engineering*, Vol. OE-8, No. 3, pp. 173-183, July, 1983.

[2] J. J. Hopfield and D. W. Tank, "Neural computation of decisions in optimization problems," *Biological Cybernetics*, 52, pp. 141-152, 1985.

[3] D. Sengupta and R. A. Iltis, "Neural solution to the multitarget tracking data association problem," *IEEE Trans. on Aerospace and Electronic Systems*, Vol. AES-25, No. 1, pp. 96-108, Jan. 1989.

[4] P. Smith and G. Buechler, "A branching algorithm for discriminating and tracking multiple objects," *IEEE Trans. on Automatic Control*, Vol. AC-20, pp. 101-104, Feb. 1975.

[5] H. M. Sun and S. M. Chiang, "Tracking multitarget in cluttered environment," *IEEE Trans. on Aerospace and Electronic System*, Vol. AES-28, No. 2, pp. 546-559, April, 1992.

Control of Glass Furnace System
using the Linearization of Neural Network

SunnaKim*, HyeranByun[†], YillbyungLee[†], and BuhakHan[‡]

* LG Electronics Research Center
† Dept. of Computer Science, Yonsei University
‡ Samsung Corning Co. Ltd.

Department of Computer Science, Yonsei University
134 Shincheon-Dong, Seodaemun-Gu, Seoul 120-749, KOREA
TEL: +82-2-361-2713 FAX: +82-02-365-2579
E-mail: sunna@cordoba.crl.goldstar.co.kr,
yblee@csai.yonsei.ac.kr

Abstract

In this paper, the control method for GFS(Glass Furnace System) using neural network is proposed. The GFS is a melting process to produce TV glass bulbs. We simulate the GFS with MLP(Multi-Layer Perceptrons). The input of MLP is a set of control values for the operation of GFS and the output is a defect rate of products. With the proposed upper bound defect rate by the expert operators, we extract the control values through the approximation of a MLP by a SLP(Single-Layer Perceptron) and the training of SLP. MLP is converted into SLP by the linearization of nonlinear model. And the SLP that is converted to change control values in the limit range produces the new control values. It is tested whether the generated defect rate that is less than the proposed one. By the repetition of transforming MLP into SLP and training SLP in the limit range, we could extract the proper control values of GFS. We suggest a method to seek the proper control values that the defect rate smaller than that proposed by the expert operator of GFS and prove the validity of the method through the experiments.

1 Introduction

In this paper, the control method of GFS(Glass Furnace System) using neural network is proposed. The GFS is a melting process to produce TV glass bulbs. The GFS is controlled to reduce the defect of products. It is difficult to control GFS because GFS is a nonlinear dynamic system and there are many control variables for controlling GFS. Before our research is proposed, the GFS is controlled by the method that obtains the control values using Taylor Expansion Equation. But the result of a method using Taylor Expansion Equation is not good, because that method did not solve the problem of calculating the inverse value in the many-to-one mapping, The method that proposed in this paper obtains approximately the inverse value of the many-to one mapping in the control of GFS, appling the learning algorithm of neural network that modified partially. We apply the modified learning algorithm to get the new control value, exchanging the input vector and the weight vector before learning the neural network. Thus, instead of the weight vector, the input vector is updated during learning. In our method, the information of the current state of GFS is given to the control process. There are the current control values and the current defect rate of the products and the upper bound defect rate that proposed by expert operators of GFS. With these information, the control process of GFS calculate the new control values that reduce the defect rate. If the new defect rate predicted by the new control values is not less than the upper bound defect rate, the controller repeats the process. We use the linearization of nonlinear model to control GFS in neural network architecture, since the linear model is more apt to get the inverse value than the nonlinear model. When we convert nonlinear model to linear model, this linearization satisfied the limit condition in which the converted linear model approximate the nonlinear model with accuracy. Our control method undergoes 3 steps in neural network model. Until the result of the process meets the given condition, these steps are repeated.

We describe 3 steps of the control process using neural networks and present the experimental results. Finally we summarize the results of our work in section 4.

2 Neural network model and Control Process of GFS

The first step of the control process of GFS is training MLP to obtain the input-output mapping of the GFS control. Given the current control values, we can predict the defect rate using the trained MLP.

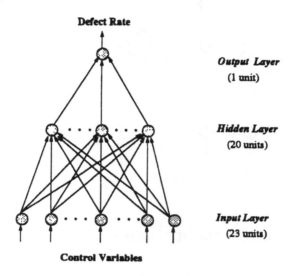

Figure 1: MLP for simulating GFS

The input vector of MLP is the control values and the output is the defect rate of the produced TV glass bulbs. In step 2, the trained MLP is transformed to SLP(Single-Layer perceptron), by (1) and (2). Let O_j be the output value of mode j, and ϕ be the bias term of node j. a_j and b_j are the coefficients of the linearized sigmoid fucntion where $f(x) = a \times x + b$ in node j. And W_{ki} is the connection weight from node i to node k. W'_{ki} and ϕ'_k are the weight and the bias in the converted SLP[13].

$$W'_{ki} = \Sigma_j W_{kj} a_j W_{ji} \tag{1}$$

$$\phi'_k = \Sigma_j W_{kj}(a_j O_j + b_j) + \phi_k \tag{2}$$

Therefore, the nonlinear model is approximated by the linear model. In the last step, the transformed SLP is trained after the input vector and the weight vector are exchanged.

The desired output(O-β) which is less than the current output is related to the limit condition of the linearization of nonlinear model. After the training of SLP, the updated input vector I' is satisfied only if the MLP outputs the defect rate that is less than the upper bound defect rate proposed by expert operators of GFS, when it is inputed to MLP. Unless the new input vector is satisfied, we go back to step 2.

3 Experimental Results

We trained the MLP with the monthly GFS data of Samsung Corning Co. Ltd. The input vector is a set of 23 control variables and the output is the defect rate of the products. Using the proposed method, we obtained the proper control values that produce a smaller defect rate than the upper bound defect rate. Moreover, the results satisfied the GFS control rule that the variation of each control variable must be small. Table 1. shows

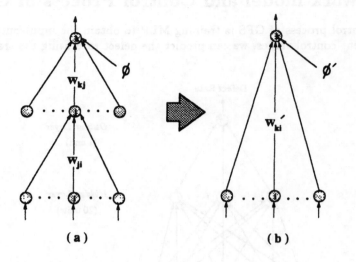

Figure 2: The MLP and the transformed SLP

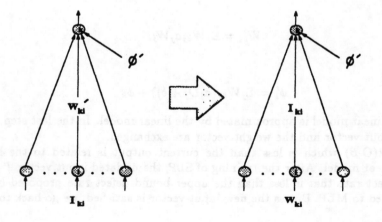

Figure 3: The exchanging of input vector and weight vector

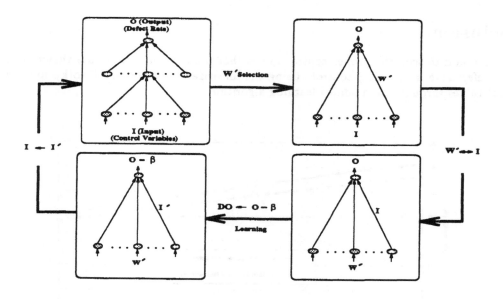

Figure 4: The flow of the GFS control process

Table 1: Example of the result(the new control value)

	current	new		current	new
control no. 1	518.81	522.92	control no.13	362.39	364.70
control no. 2	2374.47	2347.11	control no.14	4807.20	4773.00
control no. 3	4045.85	4049.48	control no.15	6188.63	6182.26
control no. 4	3958.03	3963.14	control no.16	5834.51	5826.57
control no. 5	2462.12	2464.72	control no.17	3876.81	3906.57
control no. 6	580.06	581.04	control no.18	1543.11	1488.90
control no. 7	635.12	633.81	control no.19	4805.74	4796.52
control no. 8	664.77	665.03	control no.20	6183.05	6198.67
control no. 9	362.19	364.74	control no.21	5827.80	5825.71
control no.10	580.34	579.27	control no.22	3879.86	3908.93
control no.11	636.37	633.17	control no.23	1543.98	1493.46
control no.12	666.21	666.21	Defect Rate	27.90(%)	15.37(%)

an example of the result that the new defect rate predicted by the new control values is less than the current defect rate.

We set the value of β in training SLP to 0.0001 according to the experiment that studied the relation of β and the accuracy of linearization and also the relation of β and the execution time.

4 Conclusion

We suggest a method to seek the proper control values that produce the defect rate that is smaller than the upper bound defect rate in the GFS control. Using the linearization in neural network model, we obtain the proper control values through the modified learning algorithm.

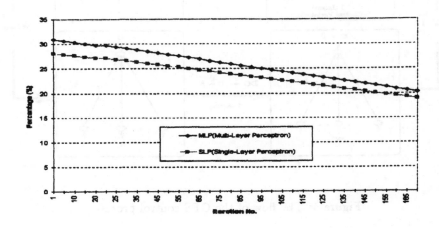

Figure 5: The decreasing of the defect rate in MLP and SLP

Fig.6 obtained in the analysis of the result shows that the input vector calculated to reduce the defect rate in SLP makes the MLP output the defect rate which was reduced too. It is that Even though the output of SLP and the output of MLP are not perfectly equal with about the same input, the difference of SLP and MLP decrease in increasing the number of repetition of process. This show the validity of our approximation to control GFS using the converted SLP that is the linearized neural network, instead of the MLP that is the non-linear neural network.

References

[1] James A. Freeman, David M. Skapura, *Neural Networks - Algorithms, Applications, and Programming Techniques*, Addison-Wesley, 1991.

[2] W. Thomas Miller,III, Richard S. Sutton, and Paul J. Werbos, *Neural Networks for Control*, The MIT Press, 1990.

[3] A. Cichocki, R. Unbehauen, *Neural Networks for Optimization and Signal Processing*, Wiley, 1992.

[4] Nicolaos B. Karayiannis, Anasstasios N. Venetsanopoulos, *Artificial Neural Networks - Learning Algorithms, Performance Evaluation, and Applications*, Kluwer Academic Publishers, 1993.

[5] Jin Seol Yang, Sung Joo Park, "Neural Network Approach to Dynamic Process Control:*Application to Manufacturing and Traffic Systems*",

[6] K. J. Hunt, D. Sro, R. Zbikowski, and P. J. Gawthrop, "Neural Networks for Control Systems - *A Survey*," *Automation*, Vol.28, No.6, pp.1083-1112, 1992.

[7] Richard L. Burden, J. Douglas Faires, *Numerical Analysis*, PWS-KENT, 1988.

[8] Yasuhiro Wada, Mitsuo Kawato, "A Neural Network Model for Arm Trajectory Formation Using Forward and Inverse Dynamics Models," *Neural Networks*, Vol.6, pp.919-932, 1993.

[9] Kumpati S. Narendra, Snehasis Mukhopadhyay, "Adaptive Control of Nonlinear Multivariable Systems Using Neural Networks," *Neural Networks*, Vol.7, No.5, pp.737-752, 1994.

[10] Yutaka Maeda, "Learning Rules of Neural Networks for Inverse Systems," *Electronics and Communications in Japan*, Part 3, Vol.76, No.4, pp.17-24, 1993.

[11] Jenq-Neng Hwang, Chi-Hou Chan, Robert J. Marks II, "Frequency Selective Surface Design Based on Iterative Inversion of Neural Networks," *IJCNN, San Diego*, Vol.1, pp.39-44, 1990.

[12] A. Linden, J. Kindermann, "Inversion of multilayer nets," *IJCNN, Whashington D.C.*, Vol.2, pp.425-430, 1989.

[13] Kang-Mo Jung, Kang-suk Lee, "A Decision Support System using Neural Networks in a Glass Furnace Process," *IJCNN, Nagoya*, Vol.3, pp.2795-2798, 1993.

Neural Networks, Simulation, Genetic Algorithms, and Machine Learning for Manufacturing Scheduling

Luis Carlos Rabelo
Dept. of Industrial and Systems Engineering, Ohio University, Athens, Ohio 45701, USA, rabelo@bobcat.ent.ohiou.edu
Albert Jones
National Institute of Standards and Technology, Gaithersburg, Maryland 20899, USA
Yuehwern Yih
School of Industrial Engineering, Purdue University, West Lafayette, Indiana 47907, USA

Abstract. To respond to the complex nature of manufacturing systems scheduling, a framework is developed displaying the capabilities of learning and self-improvement which provides the necessary adaptive scheme . This proposed framework uses a hybrid architecture that integrates neural networks, discrete-event simulation, genetic algorithms, and machine learning. Neural networks are used to quickly evaluate and select a small set of candidate sequencing or scheduling rules from some larger set of heuristics. Genetic algorithms are applied to this remaining set of rules to generate a single "best" schedule using simulation to capture the system dynamics. A trace-driven knowledge acquisition technique (symbolic) is used to generate rules to describe the knowledge contained in that schedule. The derived rules are then added to the original set of heuristics for future use.

1. Introduction

To efficiently and effectively control manufacturing systems, intelligent, computer-based decision aids are needed. Typically, decisions are generated from the knowledge contained in a knowledge base. The first step in developing the required knowledge base is knowledge acquisition. In most cases, knowledge sources are "human experts" who describe or explain the process of decision making. However, there is a problem with manufacturing scheduling due to the lack of available expertise. As a consequence of this problem, we often resort to a "computer-based expert" to help us analyze the impact of scheduling rules on system performance. In this approach, simulation results can be used to form the knowledge base through inductive learning processes. However, it is impractical to study all the scheduling policies and their combinations through simulation.

To shorten the lead time for developing intelligent scheduling aids, it is imperative that the knowledge acquisition process be quick and easily refined, as new knowledge becomes available. In addition, this process must fit into an overall framework for real-time scheduling. In this paper, we describe a methodology which integrates neural networks, simulation, genetic algorithms, and machine learning technniques. The integrated system determines the start and finish times of the jobs assigned to any module in a hierarchical shop floor control architecture [3]. Since a hierarchy decomposes the global scheduling problem into multiple levels, this methodology 1) never needs to solve very large problems, and 2) can react to delays on the manufacturing shop floor in a manner which is not disruptive to the rest of the system. Moreover, by exploiting the parallel processing and modeling capabilities of neural networks, simulation, and genetic algorithms it has the potential to be extremely fast and highly adaptable to customer needs. Finally, the use of a learning technique provides the additional capability to learn what works and what does not work in a variety of situations and to utilize that knowledge at a later time.

2. The Hybrid Framework

We now describe a methodology for solving the real-time sequencing and scheduling (s/s) problems. This method consists of a four step refinement process. The first step is to generate a set of candidate s/s rules from a much larger set of heuristics. We have used single-performance, neural networks as discussed in section 2.1. We then evaluate these candidates against all of the performance measures dictated by the higher elements of the hierarchy (i.e., supervisors). The last step is to use the top candidates from that ranking as input to a genetic algorithm to determine the "best" sequence or schedule. This is discussed in section 2.2. In section 2.3, a technique for extracting the knowledge contained in that schedule for future use is described.

2.1. Candidate Rule Selection

The first step in this process is to select a small list of candidate rules from a larger list of available rules . For example, we might want to find the best five scheduling policies (e.g., dispatching rules) from the list of all known scheduling policies so that each one maximizes (or minimizes) at least one of the performance measures, with no regard to the others. To carry out this part of the analysis, we have used neural networks. Neural networks have shown good promise for solving some classic, textbook job shop scheduling problems. These implementations have been based on relaxation models (i.e., pre-assembled systems which relaxes from input to output along a predefined energy contour). The neural networks are defined by energy functions in these approaches. However, due to a large number of variables involved in generating a feasible schedule, it has been difficult for these approaches to solve realistic job shop scheduling problems with multiple objectives. It is even difficult to get a good sub-optimal solution when attempting to solve problems in real-time.

There are four reasons to select neural networks as candidate rule selectors. First, due to the decomposition that results from the hierarchical control architecture used, we never have to solve the global shop floor scheduling problem all at once. Since it is decomposed into several scheduling and sequencing problems. Second, it is no longer necessary to resolve the global problem each time a minor delay occurs or a new job is put into the system. Local rescheduling and resequencing can be done with little impact on the overall shop floor schedule. Third, as discussed below, each neural network is designed (i.e., they are presented with training sets of representative scheduling instances and they learn to recognize these and other scheduling instances) to optimize a single objective (e.g., minimization of work-in process inventory). Neural networks in our approach are utilized as pattern recognition machines. Neural networks assign a given shop floor status to a specific rule with some degree.

In this research, initial efforts have focused on backpropagation neural networks. As indicated above, this approach to developing the actual rule selector is to have a backpropagation neural network trained to rank the available rules for each individual performance measure of interest (multiple performance evaluation comes in the next section). The weights for each of these networks are selected after a thorough training analysis. To carry out this training, we used two methodologies 1) off-line training and 2) on-line training.

a) Off-Line Training

In off-line training, training data sets for each of the performance measures need to be geneerated from simulation studies. Suppose we wanted to train a neural net to minimize the maximum tardiness and we wanted to consider the following dispatching rules: SPT (Shortest Processing Time), LPT (Longest Processing Time), FIFO (First In First Out), LIFO (Last In First Out), SST (Shortest Set Up Time), LST (Longest Set Up Time), CR (Critical Ratio), etc. After simulating each of these rules off-line under a variety of input conditions, we would be able to rank them to determine the best rule for this measure (The example in this section gives some of these simulation results.). These results are used to train a neural network.

b) On-Line Training

In on-line training, adaptive critics concepts are utilized to train (in real-time) the neural network structures [1,5]. Q-learning (a derivation of adaptive critics) [4] is used to predict a scheduling policy to meet the required performance criterion for a given queue status and for an undefined period of operation. This performs as an effective candidate rule selector. The key idea of Q-learning is to assign values to state (shop floor status)-action (scheduling policy) pairs. Q-learning does not need an explicit model of the dynamic system which underlies the decision problem. It directly estimates the optimal Q values (i.e, ranking) for pairs of states and admissible actions. The optimal Q value for state i (shop floor status) and action u (a scheduling heuristic) is the cost of executing action u in state i. Any policy selecting actions that are greater with respect to the optimal Q values becomes the optimal policy. Actions are ranked based on the Q values. On the other hand, ranking through an evaluation function requires more information like immediate costs of state action pairs and state transition probabilities. Instead of state transition probabilities, Q-learning requires a random function to generate successor states. The Q-value of the successful action is updated with learning parameters, although the other admissible actions, Q values remain the same. Q-learning learns to accurately model the evaluation function. For a given state x, the system (e.g., a neural network) chooses the action a, where the utility util(x,a) is maximal. Q-learning consists of two parts: a utility function and a stochastic action selector. The utility function implemented using a neural network based on backpropagation works as both evaluator and policy maker . It tries to model the system by assigning values to action-state pairs

We have initiated this training for a wide range of performance measures and dispatching rules for a single machine sequencing and multiple machine scheduling problems. We anticipate using these results for robots, machine tools, material handling devices and inspection devices. They will form the lower level of the two-level scheduling system which we are developing. The output from the rule selector phase will be a collection of R matched pairs - {(performance measure, best rule)$_1$, ..., (performance measure, best rule)$_R$}. These pairs form the candidates which are passed on to the next phase for more detailed analysis.

2.2 Genetic Algorithms

No matter how the utility function described above is constructed, only one rule from the candidate list can be selected. This causes an undesirable situation whenever there are negatively correlated performance measures, because no one rule can optimize all objectives simultaneously. Conceptually, one would like to create a new "rule" which 1) combines the best features of the most attractive rules, 2) eliminates the worst features of those rules, and 3) simultaneously achieves satisfactory levels of performance for all objectives. To do this, we propose to use a genetic algorithm approach.

The compromise analysis process carried out by a genetic algorithm can be thought of as a complex hierarchical "generate and test" process. The generator produces building blocks which are combined into schedules. At various points in the procedure, tests are made that help weed out poor building blocks and promote the use of good ones. To reduce and support uncertainty management of the search space, the previous steps will provide partial solutions and building blocks to the problem of compromise analysis.

2.3 Inductive Learning Algorithm - TDKA

Now that this new schedule has been generated, we want to extract the knowledge contained in that schedule for future use. To do this, we must derive a "new rule" which can be used to regenerate schedules in the same way that other dispatching rules like SPT are used. This new rule will not, however, be a simple dispatching rule. To do this, we will use a technique developed in by Yih [6]. TDKA is a method that extracts knowledge from the actual results of decisions rather than statements or explanations of the presumed effects of decisions. There are three steps in the process of trace-driven knowledge acquisition: *data collection*, *data analysis*, and *rule evaluation*.

The core of the TDKA lies in the step two- data analysis. There are two types of rules involved -- decision rules and class assignment rules. If the state space is viewed as a hyper plane, class assignment rules draw the boundaries on the hyper plane to define the areas of classes. For each class, a single production rule is used to determine what to do next. These rules are in the form of

"If [state Œ class i] then apply R_i* "

In data analysis, the records collected are used to define classes and to select a single rule for each class. The rule formation algorithm can be described by three steps as follows.

> *I. Initialize*
> Determine state variables
> Determine decision rules
> Set initial value for acceptance level (L)
> Determine initial class C_1
> Obtain a trace (a set of records) from simulation
>
> *II. Vote*
> Each record in this class (C_i) votes for all the decision rules that will result in the same decision as in the record
> Summarize the vote results in percentage (No. of votes / No. of records)
>
> *III. Form rules*
> The decision rule (R_k*) with the highest percentage wins.
> If the percentage is higher than L, then form the following rule
> > **If [state Œ C_i] then apply R_k***
> > else
> > > Split class C_i into two classes based on selected state variable (V_p*) and threshold (Th_i*).

Add two class assignment rules.

$$\text{IF } [\text{state } \mathcal{E} \; C_i] \text{ and } [V_{p}\text{*}<Th_i^{*}] \text{ THEN } [\text{state } \mathcal{E} \; C_{i1}]$$
$$\text{IF } [\text{state } \mathcal{E} \; C_i] \text{ and } [V_{p}\text{*}\_Th_i^{*}] \text{ THEN } [\text{state } \mathcal{E} \; C_{i2}]$$

Repeat Steps II and III for classes C_{i1} and C_{i2}.

IV. Stop

This iterative process will stop whenever the rule formation is completed. That is, the state space has been properly divided into several classes and a single production rule is selected for each class .

3. A Comprehensive Example

Consider a single machine sequencing problem with 7 types of jobs. Each job-type has its own arrival time, due date, and processing time distributions. The set-up time is sequence dependent. The objective is to determine a sequence which minimizes mean flow time (where the goal is to minimize the mean flow time of the jobs (i.e., Finish Time - Arrival Time) to be scheduled) and maximum tardiness . Assume that we are to generate a sequence for the 10 jobs in the input queue of the machine as described in Table I.

Job #	Job Type	Mean Processing Time	Arrival Time	Due Date
1	7	5	154	203
2	3	5	154	193
3	4	3	159	194
4	3	5	160	208
5	2	4	166	194
6	1	4	170	202
7	3	5	185	231
8	2	4	186	221
9	7	5	192	243
10	7	5	200	250

Current Time : 200
Previous Job Type executed : 3

Rule	Votes	%
SPT	5	55%
LPT	5	55%
FIFO	5	55%
LIFO	1	11%
SST	6	67%
LST	5	55%
SPST	6	67%
LPST	3	33%
EDD	6	67%
LDD	1	11%
mSLACK	6	67%
MSLACK	1	11%
CR	5	55%

Number of records = 9

Table I. Job description for the example problem   **Table II. Voting strategy**

The candidate rule selector implemented, using backpropagation neural networks (previously trained by off-line training), uses the system status and the performance criteria (mean flow time and maximum tardiness) in order to select a small set of candidates from the 13 rules available. Each neural network has six inputs, 12 hidden units in the hidden layer, and 13 outputs (one for each dispatching rule). Each neural network (one for mean flow time and the other for mean tardiness) in parallel ranks all rules. The networks developed in the C programming language takes less than 10 mS (486 PC compatible @ 33 MHz) to give an answer to the problem. The neural network for mean flow time ranks the higher SPST (Shortest Processing and Shortest Set-upTime first) and SST (Set-up Time first). On the other hand, the neural network for maximum tardiness ranks the higher EDD (Earliest Due Date first) and mSLACK (Smallest Slack first).

A genetic algorithm is utilized having as initial populations the selected schedules and some randomly generated schedules. The fitting function is a combination of all performance measures with the coefficients (e.g, a and b - see Equation [20]) reflecting the "importance" and the magnitude of each measure according to the imposed criteria expressed as follows (these coefficients are changed during each genetic iteration when more information is known about the possible values - limits - for each measure):

$$a \text{ (Mean Flow Time)} + b \text{ (Maximum Tardiness)}$$

where

a: coefficient for "Mean Flow Time"
b: coefficient for "Maximum Tardiness"
and $a + b <= 1; a > 0.0; b > 0.0$

The crossover mechanism utilized is based on "order Crossover" as developed by Syswerda [20]. The genetic algorithm takes eleven iterations with an average time of less than 700 mS on a 486 PC @ 33 MHz. The new schedule compromises both measures with an acceptable degree of success (**Mean Flow Time = 73.5** and **Maximum Tardiness = 6**). In order to verify the answers, a program that generates all possible solutions to the sequencing problem was utilized (10!), which took approximately 2 hours of cpu time of the 486 PC @ 33 MHz. The "new" schedule generated by the genetic algorithm is superior (based on the combined performance criteria) to the initial schedules selected by the neural networks. The output is (2 3 6 5 1 4 7 8 10 9). This sequence performs better than EDD for maximum tardiness while maintaining good performance in mean flow time (better than the third ranked rule-SPT). The exhaustive search procedure indicated that the solution of the GA is very good (actually, sequences with Mean FlowTime that are less than 73.5 with Maximum Tardiness that are less than 6 do not exist!). This schedule is selected to be applied to the manufacturing system.

We now show how to use TDKA to generate a new sequencing rule. Using the GA sequence (2 3 6 5 1 4 7 8 10 9), we first obtain the trace from simulation in the following format.

(Q, NT, MT, AT, VP, VS) ---> Action where
Q: number of jobs in the queue
NT: number of tardy jobs
MT: maximum tardiness
AT: mean tardiness
VP: variance of processing times
VS: variance of set-up times
Action: job identification number to be selected next

For instance, the trace from simulation is:

(10, 4, 10, 7.25, 0.50, 1.17) ---> 2
(9, 4, 14, 9.75, 0.53, 1.00) ---> 3
(8, 4, 17, 11.3, 0.27, 0.13) ---> 6
(7, 3, 14, 13.0, 0.24, 0.24) ---> 5
(6, 2, 16, 16.0, 0.17, 0.67) ---> 1
(5, 2, 16, 9.5, 0.20, 1.20) ---> 4
(4, 1, 8, 8.0, 0.25, 1.00) ---> 7
(3, 1, 13, 13.0, 0.33, 0.00) ---> 8
(2, 0, 0, 0.0, 0.00, 0.00) --->10

Each record in the trace will vote for the rules that could yield the same decision as in the sequence. The summary of votes is listed in Table II.

We start with one class, called Class 1. If we are satisfied with the accuracy of 67%, that is 67% is higher than the acceptance level (L), we may arbitrarily choose SST, SPST, EDD or mSLACK and form the following rule.

"If [state Œ Class 1] then apply SST"   (1)

If we would like to obtain higher accuracy, the variable MT (maximum tardiness) can be used to split Class 1 into two subclasses, Class 11 and Class 12.   Class 11 includes the states with MT _ 10, and Class 12 has the remainder. Then, rules will be formed.

"If [MT _ 10] then state Œ Class 11"   (2)
"If [MT < 10] then state Œ Class 12"   (3)

After splitting into two classes, the voting process repeats within each class.
The following rule for Class 12 could be formed with 100% accuracy with LPT, SST, or SPST.

"If [state Œ Class 12] then apply SPST"   (4)

In Class 11, if we are satisfied with the accuracy of 86%, we may form the following rule with EDD or mSLACK.

"If [state Œ Class 11] then apply EDD"   (5)

However, if we would like to achieve higher accuracy, MT is used again to split Class 11 into Class 111 and Class 112 with threshold of 17. The following rules are formed.

"If [state Œ Class 11] and [MT _ 17] then state Œ Class 111"   (6)
"If [state Œ Class 11] and [MT < 17] then state Œ Class 112"   (7)

After splitting, two rules may be formed with 100% accuracy as follows.

"If [state Œ Class 111] then apply SPT"   (8)
"If [state Œ Class 112] then apply EDD"   (9)

Finally, rules (2), (3), (4), (6), (7), (8), and (9) will be included in the rule base and this set of rules is able to generate sequences based on the strategy embedded in the sequence derived from the GA.

4. Conclusions

In this paper, we have described a methodology to solve sequencing and scheduling problems which integrates neural networks, simulation, genetic algorithms, and machine learning techniques. By exploiting the parallel processing and modeling capabilities of the neural networks, simulation, and genetic algorithms it has the potential to be extremely fast and highly adaptable to customer needs. The preliminary results are very encouraging.   However, extensive computational experiments are needed to benchmark against current methodologies and evaluate the robustness of this hybrid approach.

References
[1] A. Barto, "Reinforcement learning and adaptive critic methods," in *Handbook of Intelligent Control: Neural, Fuzzy, and Adaptive Approaches*, edited by D. White and D. Sofge, Van Nostrand Reinhold Publication, 1992.
Ph.D. Dissertation, University of Missouri, 1990.
[2] L. Rabelo, "A hybrid artificial neural network and expert system approach to flexible manufacturing system scheduling", Ph.D. Dissertation, University of Missouri-Rolla, 1990.
[3] L. Rabelo, Y. Yih, A. Jones and G. Witzgall, "Intelligent FMS scheduling using modular neural networks", in *Proceedings of ICNN*, 1993, pp. 1224-1229.
[4] C. Watkins, "Learning from delayed rewards", Ph.D. Dissertation, Cambridge University, Cambridge, England, 1989.
[5] P. Werbos, "Approximate dynamic programming for real time control neural modelling," *handbook of intelligent control: neural, fuzzy, and adaptive approaches.*, *edited by D.* White and D Sofge, Van Nostrand Reinhold Publication, 1992, pp. 493-525.
[6] Y. Yih, "Trace-driven knowledge acquisition (TDKA) for rule-based real-time scheduling systems," *Journal of Intelligent Manufacturing*, 1, 4, pp. 217-230, 1990.

Recognition of Protein Coding Regions and Reading Frames in DNA Using Neural Networks

Artemis Hatzigeorgiou and Martin Reczko
German Cancer Research Centre
Im Neuenheimer Feld 280
69120 Heidelberg, Germany
email: hatzigeorgiou@dkfz-heidelberg.de

Neural networks have been successfully applied to the recognition of protein coding regions and functional sites in DNA since several years. Our approach addresses both the recognition of coding regions (exons) and the identification of the correct reading frame in each exon. With this information a reliable translation into the corresponding amino acid sequence of the protein is possible for each tentative coding region. In connection with a prediction of mRNA splice sites the assembly of complete genes using only information from the DNA is much more feasible.

The input information to the network is a direct translation of the nucleotides within a window of the DNA sequence into a local code (A:0001, C:0010, G:0100, T:1000). A window of 91 nucleotides is hence represented by the activations of 364 input neurons. The activation of a single output neuron indicate whether the nucleotide in the center of the window belongs to an exon or to untranslated DNA. This is the main difference to the neural networks employed in the 'Xgrail' system [Ueberbacher et al. 1991] where a set of statistical properties is extracted from the sequence and then used as input to a neural network classifier. The approach of [Brunak et al. 1991] is more related to this study but is focused only on the prediction of mRNA splice sites.

The exon examples used for training the neural networks are generated by sliding a window of 91 nucleotides over the coding part of the mRNA of 30 human genes without alternative splicing with an increment of 3 nucleotides. This ensures that the first nucleotide of a exon window is always the first nucleotide of a codon for one amino acid. The examples representing non-exons are generated by sliding a window of the same size over the non-coding region of the DNA with an increment of 2 nucleotides.

The generalisation performance of the networks are tested using the patterns extracted from 15 other human genes. This performance is tested every 10 presentations of the complete training set. The training is stopped if this performance is not improving anymore. The Backpercolation algorithm [Jurik,1991] is used for training the neural networks. The main difference to the wellknown Backpropagation algorithm (Rumelhart et al. 1985) is the assignment of an individual error information to each neuron in the network. The networks trained with Backpercolation tend to have connection strengths with smaller absolute values resulting in better generalisation performance when compared with networks trained with Backpropagation.

At the end of the training the performance is tested on each nucleotide of 4 additional genes that are neither contained in the training set nor in the test set. These results show that the network recognises the correct open reading frame in every coding region of these genes. The reading frame is identified using the periodicity of the output activities of the network.

A high activity occurs at the first nucleotide of a codon followed by two low activities. The high activity occurs with a periodicity of three nucleotides.

In the intron regions there are also some positions with a high activity but without this regularity.

In order to define the border of the exons the results of this network are recorded along the sequence and a window of 30 consecutive outputs is then used as input into a second network. The results of this second network decrease the level of false positive recognition when compared to the output of the first network. In a test with 3 Gens (14.690 Bp) 14th of the 15th exons are predicted with 5 false positive exons.

The exact location of the start and end of an exon is determined by prediction of the donor and acceptor sites. This recognition is trained using the cascade correlation learning algorithm (Fahlman et al. 1990). This algorithm is able to add neurons to a network to optimize the architecture and the connection strength in a network simultaneously.

The recognition of the correct open reading frames of succesive exons offers additional constraints for their verification since any splicing occuring within a codon already defines the reading frame of the next exon. The exact location of the start and end of an exon is determined by prediction of the donor and acceptor sites. This recognition is trained using the cascade correlation learning algorithm (Fahlman et al. 1990). This algorithm is able to add neurons to a network to optimize the architecture and the connection strength in a network simultaneously. The patterns used to identify donorsites contain 10 nucleotides, with 3 nucleotides from the exon and 7 from the intron. For the acceptor sites a window of 18 nucleotides is used with again 3 nucleotides in the exon and 15 in the intron. This asymetric extraction of the windows is used because most conserverd splicing signal is extending more into the intron region. The donor classification is correct for 100 of all nucleotides are classified as donors but are not. On the same sequences, the acceptor classification is correct for 83.33 of all nucleotides are classified as false positive acceptor sites.

The recognition of the correct open reading frames of succesive exons offers additional constraints for their verification since any splicing occuring within a codon already defines the reading frame of the next exon.

The collection of these networks does not require the calculation of any additional statistical features. Once all networks are trained, the processing of a new sequence is performed by forward propagation of the sequence information. This requires only a fixed number of multiplications and additions for each nucleotide and can be performed very fast even on low-end workstations.

References:

[Ueberbacher:91] Proc.Natl.Acad.Sci. USA.Vol. 88, p.11261-11265, 1991

[Brunak:91] J.Mol.Biol. Vol.220, p. 2-17,1991

[Rumelhart:86] D. E. Rumelhart et al. 1986, Parallel Distributed Processing, Vol. 1, D. E. Rumelhart and J. L. McClelland (Eds.) MIT Press, Cambridge, Massachusetts

[Fahlman:90] Fahlman, S. E. and Lebiere, C. in Advances in Neural Information Processing systems II, by D.S. Touretzky, p. 524-532 ,1990,Morgan Kaufmann, San Mateo, California.

[Jurik:91] Backpercolaction, paper distributed by Jurik Research and Consulting, PO 2379, Aptos, CA 95001, USA

Novel Results Session

Theory and Architecture

A Comparative Study of Gabor and Pixel Representations in Original and PC Spaces

Ladan Shams, Jean-Marc Fellous, Christoph von der Malsburg
{lshams, fellous, malsburg}@selforg.usc.edu
Center for Neural Engineering
University of Southern California,
Los Angeles, CA 90089-2520

Abstract

We investigate the relative strengths of two possible models of primary visual cortex simple cells: Gabor jets, and Principal Component (PC) masks of gray-level pixel patches. We assess the robustness of these two approaches with respect to rotation in depth. Possible higher level representations such as projections of jets in their PC space are also explored. The methods and results of the experiments are evaluated and their biological plausibility discussed. We conclude that the Gabor-jet representation serves as a more biologically plausible representation because it possess a better identity discrimination power than the original gray-value input, and it can allow for an intermediate representation which is more robust than the pixel-PC masks with respect to rotation in depth.

1 Introduction

Analytical Principal Component Analysis (PCA) or its equivalent neural network implementations have been shown to produce center-surround and oriented operators if applied to images or correlated random noise patterns (Sanger, 1989) (Rubner, 1990). The first few principal components (PCs) derived consist in an isotropic gaussian followed by a pair of orthogonal edge/bar detectors. Baddeley and Hancock showed that, while PCs of gaussian-blurred random noise also include orthogonal oriented filters, the orientation is random (Baddeley, 1991). Their study suggested that the horizontal and vertical pair produced by natural images is due to the underlying structure of the natural images. Similar set of filters were developed also by Liu et. al (Liu, 1994), using circular patches of natural scenes as inputs to a neural net, and by King and Xu (King and Xu, 1995), using analytical PCA on square patches of images of faces.

All methods mentioned above produce a pair of oriented orthogonal filters (horizontal and vertical in case of natural scenes) followed by more complex patterns similar to derivatives of gaussian operators. Although this is in agreement with the somewhat higher percentage of simple cells with horizontal and vertical sensitivity found in the primate visual cortex, this finding fails to provide an explanation for the formation and existence of receptive fields of other orientations in the visual cortex. The PCs derived from natural images capture their statistical structure, decrease their abundant redundancy, leading to significant data compression, and have been shown to be simply computable by unsupervised learning using feedforward neural networks. While PCA provides a plausible developmental (due to the simple neural net implementations) and functional (due to the data compression) model of receptive fields, Gabor functions have been shown to be the most appropriate descriptors of simple cell responses. The Gabor filters not only fit the simple cell responses with good accuracy, but also suggest that the redundancy resulting from their overlapping receptive fields may prove necessary for further processing in the higher areas of the visual path. In this paper, we begin to explore the relative virtues of these methods experimentally. We look at four different methods of representation, apply them to a highly important transformation dealt with by animals in real life (rotation in depth), and compare their performances. The patches of pixels will approximate the retinal input, while the PCs of pixel-patches as well as the Gabor functions will provide two possible approximations of V1 simple cells properties, and finally we will consider the PCs of Gabor jets as a possible intermediate representation used by higher levels of visual processing.

2 Experiments and Results

2.1 Background

One of the major problems in studying the possible ways of coding incoming visual information lies in its intrinsic variability. A given object such as the face of a given person, can be easily perceived in spite of numerous visual distortions such as changes in luminosity, size, contrast, or orientation in depth. One is therefore led to hypothesize that such robustness to changes might not be solely operational (due to the sophisticated high-level processing), but possibly representational (based on the neural representation in early visual stages). What could be the nature of a code for objects which would intrinsically present invariances or robustness to a certain range of visual input distortions ?

The seminal studies of Hubel and Wiesel (Hubel & Wiesel, 1962), as well as others, have shown that a large number of cells in the primary visual cortex (V1) can be characterized by their receptive field, determined by their response to the presentation of an oriented bar or gratings at a given spatial frequency. Numerous mathematical descriptions of these receptive fields were then proposed as models of the activity of the cells involved in the initial processing stages of vision. Among these various formulations, Gabor functions were quickly regarded as an acceptable model of the receptive fields of such cells (Marcelja 1980)(Daugman 1980)(Jones & Palmer 1987).

In first approximation, such Gabor functions can be parametrized with respect to their orientation and center spatial frequency. Orientation is encoded by the plane wave component of the Gabor functions while spatial frequency is coded by the width of their gaussian envelop. V1 receptive fields can therefore be characterized by a Gabor function G(O,F) of 2 parameters: their orientation (O, in degrees) and their size (or center spatial frequency, F, in radians).

In the 2 dimensional plane swept by a position vector P, the function can be written (see (Lades et al 1993 for details)):

$$G(O,F) = \frac{K^2}{s} * e^{\left(-\frac{K^2 . P^2}{2s}\right)} * (e^{iK.P} - e^{-\frac{s}{2}}) \qquad \text{with} \qquad K = Fe^{iO}$$

Because of the linear behavior of V1 simple cells, the response of a cell tuned to a preferred orientation O, and spatial frequency F to a visual stimulus such as a face can be modeled by the magnitude of the complex coefficient resulting from the convolution of G(O,F) with the image. In effect, such a filtering amounts to extracting regions presenting edges oriented in a certain direction and of a certain 'thickness', discarding all other information.

To account for the fact that, at a fixed locus of the visual field, many V1 cells respond differently according to their preferred orientation and spatial frequency, the activation of V1 at each visual spatial location is modeled by a 16-dimensional vector (called a Gabor-Jet) of such coefficients, resulting from the convolution of the image with 16 Gabor functions taken at 2 different spatial frequencies (the lowest frequency modeling a receptive field of about 25x25 pixels, in our 128x128 images) and 8 orientations separated from each other by Π/8. Jets, therefore, are 16 dimensional vectors of positive components.

2.2 Extraction of the Principal Components

We used fifty 128x128 pixel images of faces of 256 gray values to extract 2000 arbitrary Gabor-jets and rectangular pixel patches (21x21 pixels each). The points of data extraction were all within the head, and the jets and pixel patches were extracted at the same positions. These 441-dimensional patches and 16-dimensional jets were used to compute the PCs. Using the Kaiser criterion to determine statistical significance, we identified the first twenty two and the first four vectors as PCs for the patches and jets, respectively. As can be clearly seen in Figure 1, the PCs of the first pixel patches are in accordance with the previous studies, except for the fact that the vertical filter (the second PC) precedes the horizontal one (the third PC) in our case, which may be

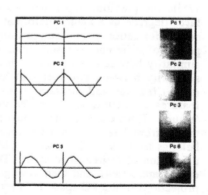

Figure 1: Left: Jet PCs (2 frequencies separated by vertical bars, orientations: vertical first). Right: Pixel PCs.

due to the structure of our stimulus set (faces). To verify the dependence of the pixel-PCs on the structure of the data as opposed to the edges of the patches, we rotated the patches by ninety degrees and computed their PCs. The PCs also rotated by the same amount.

Figure 1 reveals a clear correspondence between the two types of PCs. The first PCs are isotropic in both cases. As the second and sixth PCs of the patches resemble vertical and oblique edges, the second and third PCs of the jets also show peaks of highest sensitivity to the vertical and oblique orientations respectively.

2.3 Rotation in depth

The objective of this experiment is to investigate the robustness of the four different representations with respect to rotation in depth. Ultimately, we would like to assess the relative strengths and weaknesses of the four coding methods for all important transformations posed to the visual system such as change in illumination, change in size, noise, etc. We chose rotation in depth as the starting point for two reasons. First, the mammalian visual system is bound to address this difficulty since the mobility of the animal requires not only for the animal to recognize objects at different viewpoints but also to do so reasonably fast. Second, rotation in depth has been one of the more difficult distortions posed to machine vision, requiring sophisticated and yet not so successful engineering approaches.

Ten faces were selected, and 21x21 pixel patches and 16-D jets were extracted at three facial loci for four different view points of each face. External corner of the right eye, vertical edge of the right nostril, and right corner of the mouth constituted the facial loci, and the degrees of rotation were approximately: 0 (frontal: F), 22 (quarter profile: Q), 45 (half profile: H), and 90 (profile: P) degrees. Similarities between the same points, viewed at different angles were computed taken the frontal view as the reference, and averaging over the faces and over the facial points yielding a curve of similarities for each of the coding methods. The coding schemes were the original pixel patches and jets (441-D, and 16-D vectors), the projected patches and jets in the object-based PC space (22-D, and 4-D vectors). In all cases, we transformed the distance d between two vectors into similarity s by

$$s = (max-d)/max$$

where max is the maximum distance between any two random vectors obtained experimentally. This transformation yields a real number between zero and one.

To measure dissimilarity (distance) between two jets (in both original and PC space) we used the angle between the two vectors, computed as

$$d(J1, J2) = acos((J1 . J2)/(\|J1\| * \|J2\|))$$

where J1 and J2 are two jets, and $\|.\|$ denotes the Euclidean norm. We used Euclidean distance as the measure of dissimilarity (d) for the pixel-based representations.

Figure 2 shows the results of this experiment.

2.4 Identity Discrimination

While the previous experiment explored how the similarities between the same facial features of the same faces degrade as a natural deformation such as rotation in depth is introduced, it did not address how effective such information is in distinguishing the same features of different faces. In other words, the discriminatory power of different representations is yet unknown. To test for this property we need to examine how the similarity between two identical features of a given face changes, as the face rotates, in comparison with the similarity between two identical features of different faces (i.e., identities). To do this, we used the same (three) features and the same (ten) faces as in the previous experiment, but this time we treated the frontal features as models stored in the memory and for each rotated feature, we found the best matching frontal feature. Thus, each feature is now compared with all ten stored frontal features, and the identity corresponding to the frontal feature with the highest similarity is treated as the best matching identity. If the best match belongs to the same face, we consider it as being correctly recognized. Figure 3 shows the recognition rate as a function of degree of rotation. The rates are derived by averaging the correct matches over the examples of each feature (ten), and then averaging over the features. The testing of the discrimination performance of the projections in the PC space is in progress and will not be discussed here.

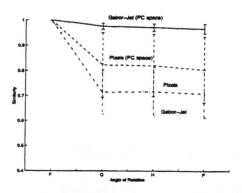

Figure 2 : Rotation in Depth

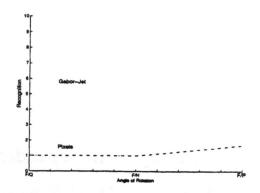

Figure 3: Discrimination

3 Discussions and Conclusions

In this paper, we used rotation in depth as a transformation in relation to which we compared the robustness of different coding methods. We used faces as objects of interest, and will use the results of psychophysical experiments performed on faces to evaluate the performance of the methods under study. It has been shown that the recognition of human faces becomes increasingly difficult as the degree of rotation between two compared faces is increased. Bruce et. al. showed that the response time for the task of discriminating two faces monotonically grows as we deviate from frontal view to the maximum rotation of profile view (Bruce et al., 1987). This clear indication of increase in difficulty suggests an absence of rotation-invariant representation in early stages and a need for further processing by the visual system in order to achieve the apparent view-invariant recognition. Higher error rates in identity discrimination have been also shown to be a function of rotation when subjects are given small amount of time for judging (Kalocsai et al., 1994), suggesting a decrease or reliable discrimination with rotation in depth.

Gabor-jet representations, as a model of early visual representation, not only demonstrates a substantial improvement over the original pixel input in terms of identity discrimination power, but also present a monotonic degradation of recognition as the angle of rotation increases (Figure 3). While this behavior matches the performance of the early stages of the biological visual system (as mentioned above), the further processing of the information encoded with initial representations should potentially lead to a view-point robust (or reasonably insensitive) recognition. We investigated the PCs of jets as a possible higher level of representation, and examined the robustness of the similarities based on this method, contrasting it with another commonly used representation such as PCs of pixels. As can be seen in Figure 2, the jet-PCs clearly show less degradation, and less variability (lower standard deviations), thus more robustness than the pixel PCs. The Gabor-jets, therefore, are not only adequate models of V1 simple cells, but also may allow for view-point robust representations at higher levels of visual processing.

References

Baddeley, R. J., and Hancock, P.J.B. (1991). "A statistical analysis of natural images matches psychophysically derived orientation tuning curves." *Proc. R. Soc. Lond. B*, 219-223.

Kalocsai, P., I. Biederman and E. E. Cooper (1994). *To What Extent Can the Recognition of Unfamiliar Faces be accounted for by the Direct Output of Simple Cells?* ARVO, Sarasota, FL.,

King, I. and L. Xu (1995). *Using Global PCA generated receptive fields for face recognition.* World Congress on Neural Networks, Washington, DC, L.E.A Publishers.

Liu, Y., and Shouval, H. (1994). "Localized principal components of natural images--an analytic solution." *Network: Computation in Neural Systems*, 317-324.

Rubner, J., and Schulten, K. (1990). "Development of Feature Detectors by Self-Organization: A Netwok Model." *Biological Cybernetics*, 193-199.

Sanger, T. D. (1989). "Optimal Unsupervised Learning in a Single-Layer Linear Feedforward Neural Network." *Neural Networks*, 2: 459-473.

Long–term dependencies in NARX networks

Tsungnan Lin [1,2], Bill G. Horne [1], Peter Tiño [1,3] and C. Lee Giles [1,4]

[1] NEC Research Institute, 4 Independence Way, Princeton, NJ 08540
[2] Department of Electrical Engineering, Princeton University, Princeton, NJ 08540
[3] Dept. of Computer Science and Engineering, Slovak Technical University,
Ilkovicova 3, 812 19 Bratislava, Slovakia
[4] UMIACS, University of Maryland, College Park, MD 20742

June 14, 1995

Abstract

It has recently been shown that gradient descent learning algorithms for recurrent neural networks can perform poorly on tasks that involve long–term dependencies [2]. In this paper we explore the long–term dependencies problem for a class of architectures called NARX networks, which have powerful representational capabilities [11]. We have previously reported that gradient descent learning is more effective in NARX networks than in recurrent networks that have "hidden states" on problems including grammatical inference and nonlinear system identification [5]. We show that although NARX networks do not circumvent the problem of long–term dependencies, they can greatly improve performance on such problems. We present some experimental results which show that NARX networks can often retain information for two to three times as long as conventional recurrent neural networks.

1 Introduction

Recurrent Neural Networks (RNNs) are capable of representing arbitrary nonlinear dynamical systems [12, 13]. However, learning simple behavior can be quite difficult using gradient descent. Recently, it has been demonstrated that at least part of this difficulty can be attributed to *long–term dependencies*, i.e. when the desired output at time T depends on inputs presented at times $t \ll T$. This was noted by Mozer [9], and recently formalized by Bengio [2], who argue that for many practical applications the goal of the network must be to *robustly latch information*, i.e. the network must be able to store information for a long period of time in the presence of noise. More specifically, they argue that latching of information is accomplished when the states of the network stay within the vicinity of a hyperbolic attractor, and robustness to noise is accomplished if the states of the network are contained in the *reduced attracting set* of that attractor, i.e. if the eigenvalues of the Jacobian are contained within the unit circle. When a system is robustly latch information, then the fraction of the gradient due to information n time steps in the past approaches zero as n becomes large. This effect is called the problem of *vanishing gradient*. Bengio *et al.* claim that the problem of vanishing gradients is the essential reason why gradient descent methods are not sufficiently powerful to discover long–term dependencies.

In this paper, we propose an architectural approach to deal with long–term dependencies. We focus on a class of architectures based upon Nonlinear AutoRegressive models with eXogenous inputs (NARX models), and are therefore called *NARX networks* [3, 10]. This is a powerful class of models which has recently been shown to be computationally equivalent to Turing machines [11]. Furthermore, We have previously reported that gradient descent learning is more effective in NARX networks than in recurrent neural network architectures with "hidden states" when applied to problems including grammatical inference and nonlinear system identification [5]. Typically, these networks converge much faster and generalize better than other networks. The results in this paper give an explanation of this phenomenon.

2 NARX networks

An important class of discrete–time nonlinear systems is the *Nonlinear AutoRegressive with eXogenous inputs* (NARX) model [3, 7, 8, 14].

$$y(t) = f\left(u(t - D_u), \ldots, u(t-1), u(t), y(t - D_y), \ldots, y(t-1)\right),$$

where $u(t)$ and $y(t)$ represent input and output of the network at time t, D_u and D_y are the input and output order, and f is a nonlinear function. When the function f can be approximated by a Multilayer Perceptron, the resulting system is called a *NARX network* [3, 10].

An intuitive reason why output delays can help long–term dependencies can be found by considering how gradients are calculated using the BPTT. BPTT involves two phases: unfolding the network in time and backpropagating the error through the unfolded network. When a NARX network is unfolded in time, the output delays will appear as jump–ahead connections in the unfolded network. Intuitively, these jump–ahead connections provide a shorter path for propagating gradient information, thus reducing the sensitivity of the network to long–term dependencies. However, this intuitive reasoning is only valid if the total gradient through these jump–ahead pathways is greater than the gradient through the layer–to–layer pathways.

It is possible to derive analytical results for some simple toy problems to show that NARX networks are indeed less sensitive to long–term dependencies. Here we give one such example, which is based upon the latching problem described in [2].

Consider the one node autonomous recurrent network described by, $x(t) = \tanh(wx(t-1))$ where $w = 1.25$, which has two stable fixed points at ± 0.710 and one unstable fixed point at zero. The one node, autonomous NARX network $x(t) = \tanh\left(\sum_{\tau=1}^{D} w_\tau x(t - \tau)\right)$ has the same fixed points as long as $\sum_{i=1}^{D} w_i = w$.

Assume the state of the network has reached equilibrium at the positive stable fixed point and there are no external inputs. For simplicity, we only consider the Jacobian $J(t, n) = \frac{\partial x(t)}{\partial x(t-n)}$, which will be a component of the gradient $\nabla_w C$. Figure 1a shows plots of $J(t, n)$ with respect to n for $D = 1$, $D = 3$ and $D = 6$ with $w_i = w/D$. These plots show that the effect of output delays is to flatten out the curves and place more emphasis on the gradient due to terms farther in the past. Note that the gradient contribution due to short term dependencies is deemphasized. In Figure 1b we show plots of the ratio $\frac{J(t,n)}{\sum_{\tau=1}^{n} J(t,\tau)}$, which illustrates the percentage of the total gradient that

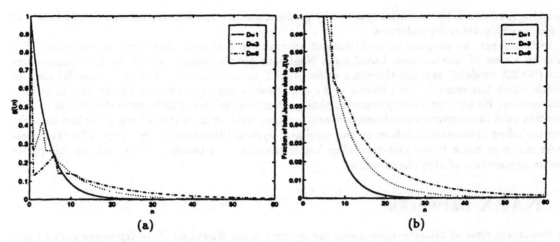

Figure 1: Results for the latching problem. (a) Plots of $J(t, n)$ as a function of n. (b) Plots of the ratio $\frac{J(t,n)}{\sum_{\tau=1}^{n} J(t,\tau)}$ as a function of n.

can be attributed to information n time steps in the past. These plots show that this percentage is larger for the network with output delays, and thus one would expect that these networks would be able to more effectively deal with long-term dependencies.

3 Experimental results

3.1 The latching problem

We explored a slight modification on the latching problem described in [2], which is a minimal task designed as a test that must necessarily be passed in order for a network to robustly latch information.

The task is to classify the class of a string based on the first three inputs. The following inputs are irrelevant to determine its class. We use uniform random noise in the range $[-0.155, 0.155]$ while Gaussian random noise was used in [2].

We fixed the recurrent feedback weight to $w_\tau = 1.25/D$, which gives the autonomous network two stable fixed points at ± 0.710, as described in Section 2. It can be shown [4] that the network is robust to perturbations in the range $[-0.155, 0.155]$. Thus, the uniform noise in $e(t)$ was restricted to this range.

For each simulation, we generated 30 strings from each class, each with a different $e(t)$. The initial values of h_i^j for each simulation were also chosen from the same distribution that defines $e(t)$. For strings from class one, a target value of 0.8 was chosen, for class two -0.8 was chosen.

The network was run using a simple BPTT algorithm with a learning rate of 0.1 for a maximum of 100 epochs. (We found that the network converged to some solution consistently within a few dozen epochs.) If the simulation exceeded 100 epochs and did not correctly classify all strings then the simulation was ruled a failure.

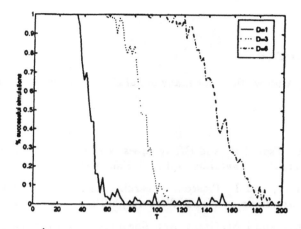

Figure 2: Plots of percentage of successful simulations as a function of T, the length of the input strings, for different number of output delays.

We varied T from 10 to 200 in increments of 2. For each value of T, we ran 50 simulations. Figure 2 shows a plot of the percentage of those runs that were successful for each case. It is clear from these plots that the NARX networks become increasingly less sensitive to long-term dependencies as the output order is increased.

4   Conclusion

In this paper we considered an architectural approach to dealing with the problem of learning long-term dependencies, i.e. when the desired output depends on inputs presented at times far in the past, which has been shown to be difficult for gradient based algorithms. We explored the ability of a class of architectures called NARX recurrent neural networks to solve such problems. We found that although NARX networks do not circumvent this problem, it is easier to discover long-term dependencies with gradient descent in these architectures than in architectures without output delays. This has been observed previously, in the sense that gradient descent learning appeared to be more effective in NARX networks than in recurrent neural network architectures that have "hidden states" on problems including grammatical inference and nonlinear system identification [5].

We presented an analytical example that showed that the gradients do not vanish as quickly in NARX networks as they do in networks without multiple delays when the network is contained in a fixed point. We also presented two experimental problems which show that NARX networks can outperform networks with single delays on some simple problems involving long-term dependencies.

We speculate that similar results could be obtained for other networks. In particular we hypothesize that any network that uses tapped delay feedback [1, 6] would demonstrate improved performance on problems involving long-term dependencies.

Acknowledgements

We would like to thank Andrew Back for many useful discussions on this material.

References

[1] A.D. Back and A.C. Tsoi. FIR and IIR synapses, a new neural network architecture for time series modeling. *Neural Computation*, 3(3):375–385, 1991.

[2] Y. Bengio, P. Simard, and P. Frasconi. Learning long-term dependencies with gradient is difficult. *IEEE Transactions on Neural Networks*, 5(2):157–166, 1994.

[3] S. Chen, S.A. Billings, and P.M. Grant. Non-linear system identification using neural networks. *International Journal of Control*, 51(6):1191–1214, 1990.

[4] P. Frasconi, M. Gori, M. Maggini, and G. Soda. Unified integration of explicit knowledge and learning by example in recurrent networks. *IEEE Trans on Knowledge and Data Engineering*, 1993. (in press).

[5] B.G. Horne and C.L. Giles. An experimental comparison of recurrent neural networks. In *Advances in Neural Information Processing Systems 7*, 1995. To appear.

[6] R.R. Leighton and B.C. Conrath. The autoregressive backpropagation algorithm. In *Proceedings of the International Joint Conference on Neural Networks*, volume 2, pages 369–377, July 1991.

[7] I.J. Leontaritis and S.A. Billings. Input–output parametric models for non–linear systems: Part I: deterministic non–linear systems. *International Journal of Control*, 41(2):303–328, 1985.

[8] L. Ljung. *System identification : Theory for the user*. Prentice-Hall, Englewood Cliffs, NJ, 1987.

[9] M. C. Mozer. Induction of multiscale temporal structure. In J.E. Moody, S. J. Hanson, and R.P. Lippmann, editors, *Neural Information Processing Systems 4*, pages 275–282. Morgan Kaufmann, 1992.

[10] K.S. Narendra and K. Parthasarathy. Identification and control of dynamical systems using neural networks. *IEEE Transactions on Neural Networks*, 1:4–27, March 1990.

[11] H.T. Siegelmann, B.G. Horne, and C.L. Giles. Computational capabilities of NARX neural networks. Technical Report UMIACS-TR-95-12 and CS-TR-3408, Institute for Advanced Computer Studies, University of Maryland, 1995.

[12] H.T. Siegelmann and E.D. Sontag. On the computational power of neural networks. *Journal of Computer and System Science*, 50(1):132–150, 1995.

[13] E.D. Sontag. Systems combining linearity and saturations and relations to neural networks. Technical Report SYCON-92-01, Rutgers Center for Systems and Control, 1992.

[14] H.-T. Su, T.J. McAvoy, and P. Werbos. Long–term predictions of chemical processes using recurrent neural networks: A parallel training approach. *Industrial Engineering and Chemical Research*, 31:1338–1352, 1992.

Parameter Adaptation using a Meta Neural Network

Colin McCormack,
Dept. of Computer Science,
University College Cork,
Ireland.
colin@odyssey.ucc.ie

Abstract

A method of using a Meta Neural Network to alter the values of learning rule parameters during training is proposed. The Meta Neural Network is trained using results derived from previous training on a problem local to or disparate from the domain the MNN will be applied to. Experiments are undertaken to see how this method performs by using it to adapt a global parameter of the Quickpropagation learning rule.

1 Introduction

Two of the major shortcomings in the implementation of neural networks is the erratic nature of the quality of the solution (where quality can be defined as the speed of convergence and the accuracy of the resultant network) and the waste of the resources used in training a network. The quality of the solution is heavily dependant on the initial network parameters (weights, architecture, etc.) and the selection of the most suitable learning rule parameters. The waste of computational resources results from extensive training with incorrect parameters or the unsuitability of parameters found to be optimal for previously solved problems when applied to new problems (this applies to both network and learning rule parameters).

The main series of developments in overcoming this is in the selection of optimal learning rule parameters for a specific learning task. The problem of parameter selection has been examined [1] and methods have been proposed to find a general method of parameter selection by means of adapting current learning rule parameters during the training process, the most successful of these seems to be a method known as RPROP [1].

The function of this paper is to investigate another method of parameter adaptation which involves the use of a separate neural network (called a Meta Neural Network) to adapt a parameter, specifically the ε parameter of the Quickpropagation learning rule.

1.1 Quickpropagation

Quickpropagation [2] has been selected as the basis for this study since it is one of the most effective and widely used adaptive learning rules. There is only one global parameter making a significant contribution to the result, the ε parameter, so the method of adjustment of this parameter can be studied and the impact of such adjustment can be ascertained in isolation from other factors.

Quickpropagation uses a set of heuristics to optimise Backpropagation, the condition where ε is used is when the sign for the current slope and previous slope for the network is the same. In this situation the update rule for each weight is stated to be:

$$\Delta w(t) = \frac{S(t)}{S(t-1) - S(t)} \cdot \Delta w(t-1) + \varepsilon.S(t)$$ where S(t) and S(t-1) are the current and previous values of

the slope $\delta E / \delta w$.

The value of ε is split by dividing it by the number of inputs to each unit. This helps ε stay in a useful range since the accumulated $\delta E / \delta w$ values are proportional to the fan-in and this results in an improvement in performance.

2 Experimental Description

Experiments were undertaken using three different methods of ε selection. The first method used fixed ε values, the purpose of this was to establish the impact of varying the initial ε value and ascertain whether there was an optimal ε value suitable for the particular circumstances.

Another method of improving a networks performance is to evaluate several possible parameter values for the next epoch and choose the value that will lead to the greatest reduction in error. This is done in the second set of experiments, which uses a method known as backtracking because it allows the learning rule to back away from parameter values that do not lead to a short term decrease in error value.

The third method was to use a Meta Neural Network. A Meta Neural Network (MNN) is a form of supervisor neural network which makes suggestions to a conventional learning rule on the values of various parameters. The earliest work on MNN's [3] proposed a system which made suggestions for weight and parameter values, however this system was limited to a fixed architecture and to problems of the same problem domain as that used to train the MNN. We use two forms of MNN, one which uses its experience of learning on the same problem domain as the network it is aiding and one which has experience of learning on a different problem domain.

2.1 MNN Methodology

The scheme comprises three stages. In the first stage data for training the MNN is created, in the second stage the MNN is trained and in the third stage the MNN is used to guide a conventional learning rule.

In stage 1 a backtracking system was set up which allowed a learning algorithm to see the results of the selection of the next ε value. At each epoch potential ε values are evaluated and the ε value leading to the greatest reduction in error in the training set was chosen and the learning process continued. The value of ε is limited to six values (in the range 0.1 to 0.000001) and at each step ε is allowed to increase or decrease by a factor of 10 or remain at the current value, these three ε values are then evaluated. A set S is created which contains the current slope, the previous slope and the action which produced the best value of ε.

In stage 2 the set S is used as a training set for a MNN, where the inputs are: current slope, previous slope, and the output is a single value which indicates whether the value of ε was increased, decreased or remained the same.

In stage 3 at each epoch the conventional neural network passes the value of the current slope and the previous slope to the MNN which suggests an increase/decrease or no change in the value of ε. The MNN does this by calculating a range for the decision to increase/maintain/decrease the ε value using the upper and lower bounds of the results obtained from the trained MNN. The learning rule used to train the MNN was Quickpropagation, as described above.

2.2 Error reporting description

The set of examples is divided into three sets: the training set is used to train the network, the validation set is used to evaluate the quality of the network during training and to measure overfitting (this is known as cross validation). Finally the test set is used at the end of training to evaluate the resultant network. In the series of experiments undertaken 50% of the total available examples are allocated for the training set, 25% for the validation set and 25% for the test set.

The error measure, E, used was the squared error percentage [4], this was derived from the normalisation of the mean squared error to reduce its dependence on the number of coefficients in the problem representation and on the range of output values used:

$$E = 100 . \frac{o_{max} - o_{min}}{N.P} \sum_{p=1}^{P} \sum_{i=1}^{N} (o_{pi} - t_{pi})^2$$ where o_{min} and o_{max} are the minimum and maximum values

of the output coefficients used in the problem, N is the number of output nodes of the network and P is the number of patterns in the data set.

The Generalisation Loss (GL) at epoch t is defined as the relative increase of the validation error over the minimum so far: $GL(t) = 100 . \left(\frac{E_{va}(t)}{E_{opt}(t)} - 1 \right)$ where $E_{va}(t)$ is the current validation error and the value $E_{opt}(t)$

is defined as being the lowest validation set error obtained in the epochs up to t: $E_{opt}(t) = \min_{t' \leq t} E_{va}(t')$.

The GL value represents a measure of the level of overfitting of the network.

Training progress P is measured after a training strip of length k, which is a sequence of k epochs numbered n+1,...,n+k where n is divisible by k:

$$P_k(t) = 1000 . \left(\frac{\sum_{t' \in t-k+1...t} E_{tr}(t')}{k . \min_{t' \in t-k+1...t} E_{tr}(t')} - 1 \right)$$, where E_{tr} is the training set error.

2.3 Benchmark Problem description

The Thyroid problem is a classification problem with 7200 examples in total, variations on the data set have been used in comprehensive studies [4,5]. Each element is described by a vector of 21 input values and a correct classification which is one of three classes. The architecture used for the experiments using the Thyroid problem is 21-7-3 with the error classification percentage calculated according to the 40-20-40 rule.

The Building problem is an approximation problem and represents the prediction of energy consumption in a building. There are 14 inputs and 3 outputs with 4208 examples. The data set is obtained from problem A of 'The Great Energy Predictor Shootout - the first building data analysis and prediction problem' contest organised in 1993 for the ASHRAE meeting in Denver, Colorado. The architecture used for this problem is 14-16-3.

The Thyroid and Building problems used in this paper are taken from the PROBEN1 set of benchmarks [4] and known therein as the 'Thyroid a' and 'Building a' problems. The results in this paper will not be compared with previous studies since this paper seeks to establish the effectiveness of the use of a MNN not its optimality, another factor is the irreproducibility of the initial parameters of other benchmark problems so comparison would be made on an unequal basis.

3 Results

3.1 Experiments with all parameters fixed

The first set of experiments is performed using all the parameters (learning rule and architecture) fixed. Experiments are performed for various values of ε to investigate the result of its variation. The results of these can be seen in table 1. Results for the Thyroid problem are under the column heading 'Th' and for the Building problem under the column heading 'Bl'. The results for a MNN trained using the set S obtained from a backtracking training run on the Thyroid problem (see section 2.1) are shown under 'Thyroid MNN' and those for the MNN trained using the Building problem backtracking results are listed under 'Building MNN'. Those results obtained for the backtracking method described in section 2.1 are given under 'Backtracking'. Final training, validation and test set errors are shown, percentage classification error is shown for the Thyroid problem under the column heading '%'. 'Duration' is the number of epochs which elapsed before progress, P, dropped below 0.1 (the learning termination condition). 'Relevant' is the epoch at which the best validation error was reported (this means that epochs after this point were overfitting). 'Final GL' is the GL value obtained at the final epoch and represents a measure of the overfitting.

ε value	Training		Validation		Test		%	Duration		Relevant		Final GL	
	Th	Bl	Th	Bl	Th	Bl	Th	Th	Bl	Th	Bl	Th	Bl
0.1	.33	.09	.97	.61	.96	.53	1.46	1413	1331	560	1264	13.1	1.65
0.01	.35	.07	.96	.65	.99	.53	1.43	1007	935	567	521	21.7	4.35
0.001	.26	.08	.94	.74	.77	.53	1.09	2624	361	2242	353	6.7	1.82
0.0001	.26	.07	.8	.83	.78	.57	1.07	2296	899	1719	892	19.0	.44
0.00001	.41	.59	.79	2.94	.93	1.7	1.35	1016	18	429	8	17.0	120
0.000001	.31	.59	.79	2.94	.8	1.7	1.17	1384	22	212	12	8.3	120
Thyroid Meta	.21	.077	.75	.605	.67	.50	1.04	1112	726	1016	398	0.26	1.52
Building Meta	.32	.079	.84	.698	.93	.54	1.31	2652	477	2223	442	12.3	1.06
Backtracking	.38	.08	.81	.77	.88	.56	1.17	1186	734	963	92	9.77	29.2

Table 1: Results for Thyroid and Building problems using fixed parameters.

For the conventional values of ε used, the results displayed in table 1 show that the best result for the Thyroid problem is that for $\varepsilon=0.001$ and for the Building problem it is 0.1. The performance evaluation criteria in this case are the training, validation and test set error and the degree of overfitting. For the Thyroid problem the Thyroid MNN outperforms all the conventional results and the Building MNN puts in a reasonable performance. For the Building problem the Thyroid MNN again outperforms the conventional results and the Building MNN outperforms the majority of them. Backtracking performs very poorly in spite of the fact that at every epoch it selects the ε value which will reduce the error the most.

3.2 Experiments with varying weight sets

A further series of experiments were made to check the capabilities of a MNN under different initial parameter conditions. The initial weight set was varied for a series of experiments and the best result, average of the results and standard deviation for the results are presented in table 2. The best performing ε values for the Thyroid and Building problems obtained from the experiments in section 3.1 are used ($\varepsilon=0.001$ and 0.1 respectively) and their results are reported under 'Normal' in table 2.

	Training		Validation		Test		%	Duration		Relevant		Final GL	
	Th	Bl	Th	Bl	Th	Bl	Th	Th	Bl	Th	Bl	Th	Bl
Normal													
Best Result	0.24	**0.07**	0.78	**0.71**	0.77	**0.54**	1.13	1654	**862**	1323	**752**	1.73	**3.82**
Average	0.27	**0.081**	0.862	**0.722**	0.87	**0.57**	1.27	1497	**831**	742	**707**	23.44	**2.56**
Std Dev	0.07	**0.007**	0.082	**0.048**	0.09	**0.023**	0.14	461	**162**	356	**247**	21.73	**2.39**
Thyroid MNN													
Best Result	0.21	**0.071**	0.79	**0.66**	0.7	**0.51**	1.04	1884	**822**	883	**800**	13.66	**0.4**
Average	0.24	**0.073**	0.802	**0.706**	0.79	**0.532**	1.15	1900	**725**	999	**574**	21.29	**1.55**
Std Dev	0.05	**0.002**	0.086	**0.037**	0.07	**0.016**	0.10	591	**182**	789	**254**	7.24	**1.43**
Building MNN													
Best Result	0.21	**0.067**	0.6	**0.67**	0.8	**0.52**	1.19	1574	**1006**	1571	**484**	0.16	**4**
Average	0.26	**0.072**	0.778	**0.754**	0.82	**0.544**	1.21	1476	**814**	1079	**679**	7.69	**1.94**
Std Dev	0.04	**0.004**	0.111	**0.087**	0.05	**0.023**	0.08	545	**220**	482	**210**	6.14	**1.36**

Table 2: Results for experiments using the Thyroid and Building problems with a varied weight set.

For the results for the Thyroid problem, the best overall result is obtained using a Building MNN. Both MNN's outperform the normal Quickpropagation (which used the best identifiable ε). The Thyroid and Building MNN's produce a lower average error and standard deviation than the normal learning method.

For the Building problem, the best result is produced using a Thyroid MNN, however both the Building and Thyroid MNN again outperform conventional Quickpropagation.

For both problems the average results are better using a MNN and the standard deviation is lower indicating that the MNN are consistent performers. No one MNN shines out as superior, the Building MNN is actually better when applied to the Thyroid problem and vice versa. Each MNN improves on the conventional method by acquiring some general knowledge about the method of adaptation of the parameter.

4 Conclusion

Meta Neural Networks are a new method of augmenting conventional learning rules and of reusing training process results which have no other value. Parameter value optima's can be determined for individual cases but a MNN is more consistent at outperforming conventional methods. We have seen that a MNN training using knowledge derived from a different problem domain can outperform the selection of the optimal ε parameter obtained by trial and error.

Judd [6] shows that it is practically impossible to arrive at an optimal result by trial and error and therefore to improve the capabilities of neural networks it may be worthwhile considering the incorporation of MNN's into learning rules so they can be more flexible, more generally applicable and produce a better quality solution. This contrasts with the alternative approach of developing more general learning rules which may not be suitable for every type of problem or developing specialised learning rules which are only suitable for specific types of problem.

References

[1] **Riedmiller, M.** Advanced supervised learning in multi-layered perceptrons: From backpropagation to adaptive learning algorithms. *Computer Standards and Interfaces.* vol 16 part 3. 265-278. (1994)

[2] **Fahlman, S.** Faster-Learning variations on Back-Propagation: An Empirical Study. *Proceedings of the 1988 Connectionist Models Summer School.* Morgan Kaufmann. (1988)

[3] **Naik, D.K.** Meta-Neural Networks that learn by learning. *International Joint Conference on Neural Networks 90.* I 437-442. (1990)

[4] **Prechelt, L.** PROBEN1: A set of neural network benchmark problems and benchmarking rules. *Technical Report, Dept. of Informatics, University of Karlsruhe, Germany.* URL:ftp://ftp.ira.uka.de/pub/neuron/proben1.tar.gz. (1994)

[5] **Schiffmann, W.** Optimisation of the Backpropagation Algorithm for training multilayer perceptrons. *Technical report, Dept of Physics, University of Kobelnz, Germany.* URL:ftp://archive.cis.ohiostate.edu/pub/neuroprose/schiff.bp_speedup.ps.Z (1993)

[6] **Judd, S.** Learning in Networks is Hard. *Proc. IEEE First Conference on Neural Networks*, San Diego. II 685-692. (1987)

SONNET 2: A New Unsupervised Neural Network for Segmentation

Albert Nigrin
Department of Computer Science and Information Systems
The American University
Washington DC 20016
nigrin@american.edu

June 2, 1995

Abstract

This paper presents a neural network called SONNET 2. Unlike other unsupervised neural networks that implement winner-take-all strategies, SONNET 2 can segment input patterns using multiple winners. It can also form stable categories under both fast and slow learning. One principal difference between SONNET 2 and most other networks is the manner by which competition is implemented. Instead of category nodes competing to classify input signals, in SONNET 2, competition is implemented by having signals on input lines compete to activate their respective classifying nodes. This paper describes the basic structure of SONNET 2 and presents simulations that illustrate the properties of the network.

1 Introduction

In many real-world conditions, objects can only be defined by their relation to other objects. Unfortunately, current unsupervised neural networks (Carpenter and Grossberg, 1991; Fritzke, 1994; Kohonen, 1988) are winner-take-all networks that can only attend to one input pattern at a time. Thus, even if an input pattern contains many classifiable subpatterns, such networks can learn and categorize only a single subpattern at a time, rather than *simultaneously* learning and categorizing each of the subpatterns in context. (This is true about virtually all networks that use competitive learning, even those operating under supervised learning.) However a new **Self-Organizing Neural NETwork** called SONNET 2 is able to use unsupervised learning to segment input patterns using multiple winners.

Winner-take-all (WTA) networks are entirely adequate for input patterns with unambiguous boundaries. For example, suppose a network that has been trained to recognize the letters of the alphabet is presented the patterns in Figure 1a. Since a clear segmentation exists, it is possible to classify either letter in the input, delete that letter from the input representation, and then classify the other letter. Unfortunately, this approach is not adequate for the pattern in Figure 1b. Here, although the best single representation for the pattern is the letter O, that category does not account for all the information in the input pattern. Thus, it would be preferable to segment the input as the letters E and F, which do account for all the input.

The reason current networks have difficulties with multiple winners may have to do with the manner by which they implement competition. *In most current networks, classifying nodes compete for the right to classify signals on their input lines. However in SONNET 2, it is the input signals that compete, and do so for the right to activate the classifying nodes.* (See also Reggia, Peng, and Bourret (1991).) This type of competition will be termed 'input competition', in contrast to the 'category competition' used by most other competitive neural networks. The simplest implementation of SONNET 2 uses two fully connected layers, $F^{(1)}$ and $F^{(2)}$, where input patterns are represented at $F^{(1)}$ and output categories at $F^{(2)}$. The jth $F^{(1)}$ node is labeled s_j while the ith $F^{(2)}$ node is labeled χ_i.

In addition to being able to operate with multiple winners, SONNET 2 achieves other desirable properties including: operation under unsupervised or supervised learning; stable category coding under either fast, intermediate or slow learning; the ability to use a vigilance parameter to regulate the coarseness or tightness of categories; the ability to operate under noise; the ability to operate in pseudo real-time; the ability to use feedback to disambiguate possible choices; and the ability for learning time to scale well to large numbers of patterns (Nigrin, 1993; Page, 1993).

(a) I5   (b) EF

Figure 1: Input scenes consisting of various letters. (a) The letters I and S can be properly classified by WTA networks since clear boundaries exist. (b) Although the category for O does not account for all the input, that category would be improperly chosen by WTA networks since it forms the single best representation available.

2 Criteria for Classification

WTA networks categorize input patterns by finding the best single existing category to represent an input (by whatever metric is chosen). However, when multiple winners are allowable, that criteria should be extended to allow the network to choose a collection of categories that together best represent the input. There are many possible measures for optimality. Factors that may influence segmentation include: higher level context, probability of occurrence of individual categories, importance of detection of individual categories, recency of occurrence of categories, etc. Whichever criteria are appropriate is entirely dependent on the application.

Therefore, rather than hardwiring one criteria or another into the network, we will attempt to use a minimal measure that will most likely be applicable in many different areas. Additional criteria can then easily be added to the network to provide specialization. The main criteria that SONNET 2 will attempt to satisfy is that *as much of the input pattern as possible should be exclusively accounted for using the existing categories at* $F^{(2)}$. The phrase exclusive allocation means that the same portion of an input pattern will not be able to activate different categories simultaneously. For example, if the input pattern is $CARGO$, then the network can segment the pattern either as χ_{CARGO} or as χ_{CAR} and χ_{GO} (Marshall, 1995).

However, this criteria alone is not sufficient for acceptable behavior. For example, a one-to-one mapping from input to output cells will trivially satisfy this criteria with no useful benefit. Therefore, a second criteria in SONNET 2 is that when some input pattern is equally well represented by a single larger category or by multiple smaller categories, then the network will activate the larger category over the smaller categories. (Categories representing larger and smaller numbers of input nodes will be referred to as larger and smaller categories respectively.) In the example above, if the network has categories for χ_{CAR}, χ_{GO} and χ_{CARGO}, then $CARGO$ will activate χ_{CARGO}, rather than χ_{CAR} and χ_{GO}. (While necessary in unsupervised learning, this preference could be overridden by supervision or context (Nigrin, 1993).)

Simulation 1, shown in Table 1, demonstrates that when multiple categories are in competition, the active categories represent as much of the input as possible. (However, it is possible to regulate the trade-off between accounting for all the input vs. choosing larger categories, as Section 3 shows.) The network used fast learning to categorize the 11 binary patterns AB, BC, BCD, $BCDEF$, CD, DE, DEF, $DEFG$, DF, EF, and GH, each in a single trial. The network was then presented the patterns shown in Table 1. As can be seen from the table, the active categories were consistent with one another and accounted for as much of the input as possible. Notice that a single category activated rather than multiple categories with the same coverage. For example, $BCDEFGH$ was classified by χ_{BCDEF} and χ_{GH} rather than by χ_{BC}, χ_{DEF}, and χ_{GH}. The fact that the segmentations operate correctly for different numbers of categories consisting of different size patterns demonstrates that the parameters have not been optimized for a single situation. Additional simulations are presented in Nigrin (1995), which tests many possibilities and shows that network operation is dependent only on the relative sizes between patterns.

3 Organization of SONNET 2

In most competitive networks, category nodes compete for the right to classify signals on active input lines, as shown in Figure 2a. However, Nigrin (1995) explains why the use of 'category competition' makes it extremely difficult for learning systems to be generalizable to operation with multiple winners. An alternative approach, called 'input competition' is shown in Figure 2b. Here, it is the inputs to the category nodes that compete for the right to activate the category nodes (although the competition is still based on the activity

Input Pattern	Active Categories	Input Pattern	Active Categories
$BCIJKLM$	x_{BC}	$BCDEF$	x_{BCDEF}
B	x_{BC}	$BCDEFG$	x_{BC}, x_{DEFG}
BC	x_{BC}	$CDEFGH$	x_{CD}, x_{EF}, x_{GH}
BCD	x_{BCD}	$BCDEFGH$	$x_{BCDEF}. x_{GH}$
$BCDE$	x_{BC}, x_{DE}	$ABCDEFGHL$	$x_{AB}, x_{CD}, x_{EF}, x_{GH}$

Table 1: Classifications formed by the network for various binary input patterns when categories exist for the binary patterns AB, BC, BCD. $BCDEF$, CD, DE, DEF, $DEFG$, DF, EF, and GH.

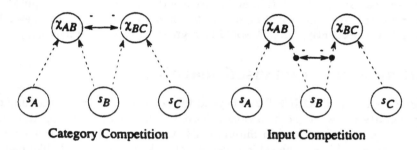

Category Competition   Input Competition

Figure 2: Different types of competition (a) Category competition (b) Input competition. The area of locality on a link indicated by the small black circles will be referred to as p cells.

of the category nodes).

This competition will be implemented at an area of locality called p cells, with the p cell on the link from s_j to χ_i being referred to as p_{ji}. (The nodes in Figure 2 may be viewed either as separate neurons or as a set of internal circuit pathways within a single neuron.) Each p cell competes only with the p cells of other assemblies that receive input from the same $F^{(1)}$ cell. For example, if s_B sends signals to both χ_{AB} and χ_{BC}, then $p_{B,AB}$ will compete only with $p_{B,BC}$. Those links will provide the only competition for the system, since the links emanating out of s_A and s_C will not compete either with each other or with the links out of s_B. If a p cells wins the competition with other p cells, it is allowed to fully transmit its excitatory signal, while if a p cell loses the competition it emits little or no excitation. Thus, only those $F^{(2)}$ nodes connected to winning p cells fully activate. This highly selective type of interaction is the main advantage of input competition, since it restricts competition to precisely the areas that should be competing. (The current implementation uses $O(n^2)$ links by funnelling all the inhibition to interneurons, which then output the *max* of the signals back.)

For example, suppose $F^{(2)}$ contains two categories χ_{AB} and χ_{ABC} and that the pattern ABC is active at $F^{(1)}$. Initially, the competition will start out roughly equal between $p_{A,ABC}$ and $p_{A,AB}$ and also between $p_{B,ABC}$ and $p_{B,AB}$. However, since $p_{C,ABC}$ receives no inhibition from other cells, it will reach high levels and activate χ_{ABC} to above that of χ_{AB}. Consequently $p_{A,ABC}$ and $p_{B,ABC}$ will output more inhibition and gain a competitive advantage over $p_{A,AB}$ and $p_{B,AB}$. Eventually χ_{ABC} will fully activate and χ_{AB} will be almost fully inhibited. Conversely, if AB were presented to this classification field, then χ_{AB} would win the competition because the input to the category cells are divided by the size of the categories, and χ_{ABC} would receive only about 2/3 of the input received by χ_{AB}. Consequently, $p_{A,AB}$ and $p_{B,AB}$ would gain a competitive advantage, causing χ_{AB} to activate instead of χ_{ABC}.

Now let us expand the discussion to three cells in the competition, by adding the category χ_{CD} to the categories χ_{AB} and χ_{ABC}. For the patterns AB and ABC, the network will behave similarly to that discussed above with χ_{AB} activating for AB and χ_{ABC} activating for ABC. In the latter case, since χ_{CD} did not receive its full input, it would only partially activate and the minor amount of inhibition from $p_{C,CD}$ to $p_{C,ABC}$ would not be enough to change the outcome of the competition. However, if $ABCD$ were presented,

| (3) | (3) | (6) | (15) | (4) | (9) | (4) | (5) | (4) |

Figure 3: The categories that were combined into input patterns and then extracted when presented together in all possible pairs. The number in parenthesis indicates the epoch upon which the pattern was categorized.

χ_{CD} would receive its full input and indeed alter the segmentation. Initially, just as in the previous cases, the initial competitive balance between competing p cells would start out roughly equal. However since $p_{D,CD}$ did not receive any inhibition, χ_{CD} would activate more quickly than the other cells (similar to the case when χ_{ABC} competed against χ_{AB} for ABC), and consequently $p_{C,CD}$ would very quickly turn off $p_{C,ABC}$. After this had occurred, the situation would be similar to when χ_{AB} and χ_{ABC} competed by themselves for the input pattern AB. Consequently, $ABCD$ would be segmented by χ_{AB} and χ_{CD}.

4 Fast and slow unsupervised learning

Since the dynamics of learning in SONNET 2 is beyond the scope of this paper, the discussion is restricted to describing in generality a few of the behaviors achieved. The network can operate under a variety of learning speeds. First, as was illustrated in Simulation 1, the network can use fast learning to categorize a patterns in a single trial. This is achievable because unlike learning methods like backpropagation, the learning of new patterns does not erode previously formed representations. One other note in regard to fast learning. With certain choices of a vigilance parameter (used to regulate the coarseness of the categories), it is possible for the output nodes to learn to classify only those portions of the input field that are not yet currently represented by any output node. For example, suppose χ_i has categorized BC, χ_j has categorized FG and the input pattern $ABCDEFGHIJ$ is presented. If the vigilance parameter has been set to a low value, then a new category node will learn the remainder of the input pattern, $ADEHIJ$. This type of behavior is possible mainly because of the extremely specific nature of the input competition.

Besides being able to use fast learning, the network is also able to use slow learning to discover significant subpatterns that are embedded within an input. The patterns in Figure 3 were presented to the network in all possible pairs (32 different input patterns in total). Because each of these input patterns contained subpatterns that occurred in different contexts, SONNET 2 created categories for all the patterns shown in Figure 3. This occurred with 15 epochs (an epoch is one presentation of the 32 input patterns), even though none of the patterns in Figure 3 appeared in isolation, but were instead presented in conjunction with other patterns. Thus, the network was forced to deal with multiple subpatterns in parallel. Furthermore, although this simulation demonstrates only two subpatterns presented together at a time, additional simulations have shown that correct operation also occurs when the input patterns contain additional numbers of classifiable subpatterns.

5 Supervised learning

By using a set of small abstract problems, the previous simulations have demonstrated that SONNET 2 extends the range of applicability of unsupervised networks. However, it is also necessary to test the network's behavior on real-world data. Unfortunately, a framework for supervised learning that exploits the full power of SONNET 2 has yet to be designed. Thus, a simple framework was constructed that is sufficient to test the network on presegmented input patterns. The basic method used is similar to k-means clustering, where a set of uncommitted nodes are set aside for each different output. Then during training, unsupervised learning is used within each cluster with the restrictions that (1) uncommitted cells in incorrect clusters are not allowed activate and (2) when a committed cell in an incorrect cluster incorrectly activates, inhibition to uncommitted cells in the correct cluster is disregarded. After training, all cells are allowed to activate freely and the cluster containing the cell with highest confidence is considered the output of the network.

The data consisted of recorded examples of the 11 steady-state vowels of English spoken by 15 speakers and is available from the Carnegie-Mellon University connectionist benchmark collection at ftp.cs.cmu.edu in the file /afs/cs/project/connect/bench/vowel.data. The speech signals were preprocessed. yielding input vectors of size 10. Each speaker provided 6 samples for each of the 11 vowels giving 990 frames of data. Robinson (1989) separated that data into 528 frames for training (4 males and 4 females) and used the remaining 468 frames for testing (4 males and 3 females). He examined the performance of a variety of networks including single-layer perceptron (33% correct), multilayer perceptrons (44–51% correct), Modified Kanerva Model (43–50% correct), Radial basis networks (48–53% correct), Gaussian node networks (45–55% correct), Square node network (50–55% correct), and the traditional nearest neighbor algorithm (56% correct). In addition Fritzke (1994), achieved rates of up to 67% with his network.

Preliminary simulations with SONNET 2 have achieved 54% correct on the data using 92 hidden nodes (after 4 epochs of the training data), a result comparable with the neural networks tested by Robinson. Although Fritzke's network achieved better results, that network does not seem to be applicable to areas in which multiple winners are necessary. Furthermore, future versions of SONNET 2 will allow category nodes to represent different amounts of variance at different input dimensions and thus may be able to narrow the difference in error rates.

6 Discussion

There are two major types of learning systems currently available: (1) error reduction methods like backpropagation, and (2) competitive learning systems like ART or Kohonen maps. In the past the error reduction systems have had a great advantage because of their ability to make and use distributed representations. Unfortunately, no adequate theory exists on how to use the error reduction methods to provide unsupervised learning. This is a major weakness when modeling biological organisms and also when trying to apply the networks to domains in which correct answers are not known a-priori.

Conversely, previous networks that used competitive learning were able to use unsupervised learning but were unable to form distributed representations. This resulted in the 'grandmother cell' dilemma, and also prevented segmentation of input patterns based on global context. SONNET 2 provides a first step towards partially alleviating these problems because of its ability to learn and use multiple winners in the category layer. As shown in Nigrin (1995), it exhibits a global context-sensitive constraint satisfaction behavior, with small contextual changes in an input pattern dramatically altering the manner by which input patterns are segmented. Finally because SONNET 2 achieves a host of other properties (alluded to at the end of the introduction section), it may form a good basis for modeling perception in biological organisms and may also be useful for technological applications.

References

Carpenter G., Grossberg S., and Rosen D. (1991). Fuzzy ART: fast stable learning and categorization of analog patterns by an adaptive resonance system. *Neural Networks*, 4(6):759-772.

Fritzke B (1994). Growing cell structures – A self-organizing network for unsupervised and supervised learning. *Neural Networks*, 7(9):1441–1460.

Kohonen, T. (1988). *Self-Organization and Associative Memory*. Springer-Verlag, New York.

Marshall J. (1995). Adaptive perceptual pattern recognition by self-organizing neural networks: Context, uncertainty, multiplicity, and scale. *Neural Networks*, 8(3):335–362.

Nigrin, A. (1993). *Neural Networks for Pattern Recognition*. MIT Press, Cambridge, MA.

Nigrin, A. (1995). *SONNET 2: An unsupervised neural network for learning multiple subpatterns in context*. Submitted for publication.

Page M. (1993). *Modelling aspects of music perception using self-organizing neural networks*. Unpublished doctoral dissertation, University of Wales.

Reggia J. A., Peng Y., & Bourret P. (1991). Recent applications of competitive activation mechanisms. In E. Gelenbe, Ed., *Neural Networks: Advances and Applications*. Elsevier Science Publishers B.V. North Holland.

Robinson, A. J. (1989). Dynamic error propagation networks. PhD thesis, Cambridge University.

ADAPTIVE VOTING FAULT TOLERANT SYSTEMS
BASED ON A NEW TRAINING RULE

Dr. Nikos Gaitanis

NCSR "Democritos "
Inst. of Inform.& Telecom
153 10 Aghia Paraskevi, Attiki
Tel : +(301) 6520847 , Fax : +(301) 6532175
Email : nikos@iit.nrcps.ariadne-t.gr

ABSTRACT

Adaptive voting is a Fault Tolerant technique in which , for modules i , the two valued voter inputs ni (nti= 1, -1) are weighted by the factor ati at the clock time t . In the pure form of adaptive voting the decision is based on the sum or discriminant function (Σ(ati)(nti)) using a threshold detector

$$D[(\Sigma(ati)(nti)) > 0] = \begin{cases} 1 & \text{if true} \\ -1 & \text{if false} \end{cases}$$

The factors ati are modified here over time by the accumulated history of agreements between the detector output Dt and the corresponding voter input (nti) using a new simple and effective , non supervised training rule .

INTRODUCTION

Since the early 1940's when the first relay computers were developed, the question of how to insure reliable computer operation has been an important one . Today, when computers are used in critical space missions, millions of miles from their human operators and in biomedical systems where the human life depends on their correct operation, even a small computing error could result in the loss of a life or millions of dollars of equipment and years of research. Under such conditions the design of computing systems which can operate correctly in spite of hardware of software failures is important . Such systems are called Fault Tolerant Systems and they are characterized by their ability to execute specified algorithms correctly regardless of hardware and/or software failures [1]

Fault Tolerant systems are usually designed by the use of Modular Redundancy (MR) techniques. The module to be made Fault Tolerant is replicated a number of times. Replication can be Hardware (with the same hardware structure such as PC or Microprocessors or Memory units) or software (with the same input-output operation such as classifiers trained with the same training rule to distinguish the same prototype elements).

These replicas constitute the executive organ of the Fault Tolerant System and the number of replicas defines the degree of redundancy . The restoring organ is made up of the additional circuit necessary to perform the function of software or hardware fault masking and/or recovery over the executive replicas . Fault masking and recovery is performed using a majority voting system whose output agrees with the majority of module (replicas) outputs.

In the case of N-Modular Redundancy (NMR) where the executive organ consists of N replicas (N is odd number) we can tolerate (N-1)/2 module failures . Though the corrective action of NMR systems is immediate and the faulty module never affects the output , the fault masking ability deteriorates as more copies fail. The faulty modules eventually outvote the good modules However, an NMR system could continue to function if the known bad modules could be discounted in the vote . This can be achieved when upon the occurrence of a failure the NMR structure reconfigure itself so that the contribution of the failed module to be reduced or eliminated. Pierce[2] was the first to propose a scheme of this type using an adaptive restoring organ . The system output is a weighted vote of the module outputs . The weight depends on the error probability of the corresponding module. A weighted -input vote-taker is implemented with linearly separable Boolean Functions using threshold gates. Adaption circuits estimate the error probability of each of the modules and use the estimate to set the vote-weight . The threshold vote-taker and the adaption circuitry make up the restoring organ called <u>decision element</u> by Pierce . For the implementation of a system like this three questions arise :

1) What vote-weight to use
   a) Continuous
   b) Quantized
2) How to estimate the error probability
   a) Using reliability information generated in the source
   b) Counting the errors occurred in a time cycle and setting the weight accordingly
   c) Counting the errors periodically and incrementing the previous cycle data
   d) (for quantized vote-weights) Disconnect a channel whenever the error count exceeds
     a given threshold.
3) How to detect errors
   a) From conditions in the module itself
   b) By comparison with the externally supplied correct answer
   c) By comparison with the output of the restoring organ
   d) By comparing the outputs of the modules with one another.

All the implementations of adaptive voting proposed till now by Pierce [2] , Goldberg,et al [3] Losq [4], Devaney[5] and deSousa_Mathur[6] answer to 1(b) 2(d) and 3(c, or d)

In this paper we present new answers in Adaptive Voting 1(a) , 2(b or c) and 3(c) using an algorithmic and systematic process (training rule) for the calculation of vote-weights The weights are modified here over time by the accumulated history of agreements between the vote taker and the corresponding input using a new simple and efficient non supervised training rule . In this case NMR systems which at the first time can tolerate up to $(N-1)/2$ faulty modular units finally they can tolerate $(N-1)$ faulty modular units

STRUCTURE

The structure of the adaptive voting systems consists of the executive organ with N (where N= odd number) hardware or software replicas of a given module, with two valued outputs $nti=$ 1 or -1 for every module $i= 1,2,3,..,N$ at a particular clock time $t=1,2,..$. These output lines are multiplied by the corresponding weight number ati and the sum $\Sigma(ati)(nti)$ is compared with a constant threshold number $T= 0$ in the threshold detector $Dt= D[\Sigma(ati)(nti) > 0]$. In cases where the sum $\Sigma(ati)(nti)$ is

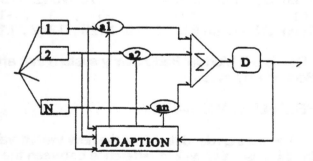

greater than 0 then the result is Dt= D[Σ(ati)(nti) > 0]= 1 and when the sum Σ(ati)(nti) is not greater than 0 then the result is Dt= D[Σ(ati)(nti) > 0] = -1 .

Each of the module outputs nti at this time t , is compared with the threshold detector output Dt=D[Σ(ati)(nti) >0] in the <u>weight adaption</u> circuit which determines the new weight values a(t+1)i for the next time (t+1)

TRAINING RULE

Let (n1)= (n11, n12, n13, .., n1N)   be the first input state from the modular units M1,M2, .. ,MN applied to the adaptive voter , at the clock time t=1

Let (a1)= (a11, a12, a13, ... a1N) with a11=a12=a13= .. =a1N = (1/N) be the first state of weight values

Then the output D1= D[Σ(n1i)(a1i) > 0] of threshold detector at the clock time t=1 will be D1=1 when the discriminant output Σ(n1i)(a1i) is greater than 0 and D1= -1 when the discriminant output D1= D[Σ(n1i)(a1i) >0] is not greater than 0 .

We define the <u>agreement value</u> of an input state (nt) applied at the clock time t=1,2, .. to be the number . R(nt)= Σ(1+(Dt)(nti))/2 which is equal to the number of modular units which agree with the majority Dt

Then the new state of weight values (a2)= (a21, a22, ..., a2N) for the clock time t=2 is obtained as follows

$$a2i = a1i + [(1+(D1)(n1i))/2] [1/ R(n1)] \text{ with } i= 1,2,3, .. N$$

In general for a given state of weight values (at) = (at1, at2, ... atN) at the clock time t the new state of weight values a(t+1) = (a(t+1)1, a(t+1)2, ... , a(t+1N) for the clock time t+1 is obtained as follows

$$a(t+1)i = ati + [(1+(Dt)(nti))/2] [1/ R(nt)]$$

where   R(nt) = Σ(1+(Dt)(nti)) /2 and
             Dt   = D[Σ(nti)(ati) >0]

EXAMPLE

Let N= 7   with (a1)=(0.142, 0.142, 0.142, 0.142, 0.142, 0.142, 0.142) for t=1
Let   (n1)=(1 ,   1 ,   -1 ,   1 ,   -1 ,   1 ,   1   )
Then D1=1 with (a2)=(0.342, 0.342, 0.142, 0.342, 0.142, 0.342, 0.342)   for t=2
Let   (n2)=(-1 ,   -1 ,   -1 , -1 ,   1 ,   1 ,   -1)
Then D2=-1 with (a3)=(0.542, 0.542, 0.342 , 0.542, 0.142, 0.342, 0.542)   for t=3
Let   (n3)=(1 ,   1 ,   -1 ,   1 ,   -1 ,   -1 , -1)
Then D3= 1 with (a4)=(0.875, 0.875, 0.342 , 0.875, 0.142 , 0.342,0.542)   for t=4
Let   (n4)=(-1 , -1 ,   1 ,   -1 , -1 ,   1 ,   1   )
Then D4=-1 with (a5)=(1.125, 1.125 , 0.342 , 1.125, 0.392 , 0.342,0.542)   for t=5

This is a 7 Modular Redundancy system that after 4 tryals   reconfigures into a 3 Modular Redundancy system

RELIABILITY AND SAFETY

This training rule determines the new weight values based on the agreement value 1/R(nt) In this case the weight difference between the modular units increases rapidly when the number of agreements decreases or when the number of disagreements increases . This operation increases the Reliability of the system but not the safety .

In general Reliability (RE) of NMR systems is defined as the probability that the system produces correct output at a particular clock time t and Safety(SA) is defined as the probability that the system output at a particular clock time t, is either correct or that the error at the output is detectable. In practice any Modular Redundancy system must be chosen which meets not only the Reliability requirement but also the safety requirement.

Safety of a Modular Redundancy system increases when we use the disagreement value $G(nt)$ instead of the agreement value $R(nt)$. Where _disagreement value_ of an input state (nt) applied at the clock time $t=1,2,\ldots$ is the number $G(nt)= \Sigma(1-(Dt)(nti))/2$ which is equal to the number of modular units which do not agree with the majority Dt.

In this case the weight diference between the modular units increases rapidly when the number of agreements increases or when the number of disagreements dencreases. This operation increases the safety of the system since the contribution of Modular units in the majority voting is eliminated very fast which do not agree with a large number of Modular units.

EXAMPLE

Let N= 7   with (a1)=(0.142, 0.142, 0.142, 0.142, 0.142, 0.142, 0.142)   for t=1
Let   (n1)=(1 , 1 , -1 , 1 , -1 , 1 , 1)
Then D1=1 with (a2)=(0.642, 0.642, 0.142, 0.642, 0.142, 0.642, 0.642)   for t=2
Let   (n2)=(1 , -1 , -1 , -1 , 1 , 1 , -1)
Then D2=-1with (a3)=(0.642, 0.975, 0.475 , 0.975, 0.142, 0.642, 0.975)   for t=3
Let   (n3)=(1 , 1 , -1 , 1 , -1 , -1 , -1)
Then D3= 1with (a4)=(0.892, 1.195, 0.475 , 1.195, 0.142 , 0.642,0.975)   for t=4
Let   (n4)=(-1 , -1 , 1 , -1 , -1 , 1 , 1)
Then D4=-1with (a5)=(1.125, 1.528, 0.475 , 1.528, 0.475 , 0.642,0975)   for t=5

CONCLUSIONS

A new adaptive voting technique has been developed for increasing the reliability and safety of critical application systems. This technique is based on a simple and effective training rule which calculates a numerical weight for each of the replicas of a given prototype. The weights are modified here over time by the accumulated history of agreements or disagreements between the vote taker and the corresponding input .

REFERENCES

1] Avisienis , A. " Fault Tolerant computing- An Overview " IEEE Trans. Comp.m, Vol. 4 , January 1971 , pp. 5-8.
2] Pierce, W. H. " Adaptive Vote-Takers Improve the Use of Redundancy," In Redundancy Techniques for Computing Systems, pp.229-50. Edited by R.H. Wilcox and W.C. Mann Washington : Spartan Books,1962.
3] Goldberg, J. K., et al " Techniques for the realization of Ultrareliable Spaceborn Computers ," Final-Report Phase 1, Stanford Research Institute Project 5580, Menlo Park , California ,Sept. 1966.
4] Losq, J. " A Highly Efficient Redundancy Scheme: Self-Parging Redundancy ," IEEE Trans. Comp., Vol.C-25,June 1976, pp.569-578
5] Devancy, M.J. " Fault Diagnosis and Self Repair in Operational Synchronous Digital Systems, " Ph.D Dissertation, Univ. of Missouri-Columbia, June, 1971

Nonlinear Correlation in Neural Networks and
Its Effects on Learning Efficiency *

Zhong Zhang   Xiaozhong Li   Shuo Bai

National Research Center for Intelligent Computing Systems
Academia Sinica, P.O.Box 2704, Beijing 100080, P.R.China

Abstract

This paper examines nonlinear correlation among neurons in neural networks and its effects on learning efficiency. A measure of learning efficiency of neural networks is first presented. And then, learning efficiency of feed-forward neural networks with hidden layers is analyzed theoretically and the general learning efficiency expression for a second-order three-layer network is derived. Finally, the effects of nonlinear correlation on learning efficiency are discussed under certain conditions. The results show that an improvement of training speed of the network is dramatic, which is consistent with previous numerical simulation experiments.

I. Introduction

The back-propagation algorithm[1] is a classical neural network learning algorithm which has been successfully applied in training neural networks. However, the training speed of the back-propagation algorithm is too slow to be practical, since it usually takes several thousands of iterations in training to guarantee the convergence of the network. Furthermore, the connections among neurons of a multi-layer neural network are almost of first-order linear correlation, and thus this network is quite ineffective in solving complex classification and pattern recognition problems. The problems of how to speed up the learning process and how to enhance pattern recognition capabilities have consequently attracted much attention, and new efficient learning algorithms have been continuously put forth. Another alternative approach is to increase the nonlinear connection between neurons of the neural network, from which high order neural networks[2], functional-link neural networks[3] and complex-valued neural networks[4] have been proposed. In our previous work [5], we found that these models are effectively different expressions of nonlinearity in neural networks.

In this paper, we first give an outline of the nonlinear correlation in neural networks. And then, we define a measure of learning efficiency of neural networks, and analyze quantitatively how the nonlinear correlation in neural networks affects learning efficiency. Finally, we discuss the learning efficiency under certain conditions. Our results show that there is a surprising improvement in training speed of the network when the nonlinear correlation is taken into account. The system error of the network decreases exponentially over iteration times. These conclusions are consistent with previous numerical simulational experiments [2-4].

*This project is supported in part by National Natural Science Foundation of China.

II. Nonlinear Correlation in Neural Networks

Generally speaking, nonlinearity in neural networks means nonlinearity of the threshold function of a neuron, and neurons are linked by linear correlation. Dynamical behavior and chaotic effects of neural networks are caused by nonlinearity of the threshold function. As is well known, there are many complex and exotic examples of nonlinearity in nature. Nonlinear properties of the connected structure of neurons in neural networks are manifested mainly in three forms: high order neural networks, functional-link neural networks and complex-valued neural networks[5].

In this paper, "nonlinear correlation in neural networks" refers to the nonlinear property of connected structures and link weights of neurons in the network. These nonlinear properties will lead to important influences on the learning behavior of neural networks.

III. Theoretical Analysis of Learning Efficiency

We define a measure of learning efficiency of neural networks as follows:

Definition 1. *Suppose the system error of a neural network is E_i after the ith training iteration, and the system error is E_{i-1} prior to it, then the increase of the system error on the ith iteration is $\Delta E_i = E_i - E_{i-1}$. The learning efficiency of the ith iteration is*

$$\eta_i = -\frac{\Delta E_i}{E_{i-1}} = 1 - \frac{E_i}{E_{i-1}} \tag{1}$$

This is a dynamic measure of learning efficiency, which changes according to iteration step i.

Definition 2. *Initial system error of the network is E_0, and the system error is drops to E_M after M training iterations. The learning efficiency of the entire training process is*

$$\eta = 1 - \frac{E_M}{E_0} = 1 - \prod_{i=1}^{M}(1 - \eta_i) \tag{2}$$

The energy function of the system error of the network is

$$E_i = \frac{1}{2}\sum_{k=1}^{p}(y_k^i - T_k)^2 \tag{3}$$

where, y_k^i is the actual output of output-layer neuron k after the ith training iteration, T_k is the kth component of the expected output, and p is the number of outputs of the network.

Let output error be $\delta_k^i = y_k^i - T_k$, and $y_k^i = y_k^{i-1} + \Delta y_k$. Δy_k is the increase in output y_k through iteration step i. If the second-order small term Δy_k^2 is omitted, we obtain

$$\eta_i \approx -\frac{2\sum_{k=1}^{p}\Delta y_k \delta_k^{i-1}}{\sum_{k=1}^{p}\delta_k^{i-1^2}} \tag{4}$$

The total learning efficiency for M iterations is

$$\eta = 1 - \prod_{i=1}^{M}\left(1 + 2\frac{\sum_{k=1}^{p}\Delta y_k \delta_k^{i-1}}{\sum_{k=1}^{p}\delta_k^{i-1^2}}\right) \tag{5}$$

For the sake of simplicity, a second-order three-layer neural network is used as an example to analyze the nonlinear correlation effects on learning efficiency. The results may easily be extended to more complex network models.

Consider a second-order three-layer neural network: let x_i denote the state of input-layer neuron i ($i = 1, 2, \cdots, m$), z_j denote the state of hidden-layer neuron j ($j = 1, 2, \cdots, n$), and y_k denote the state of output-layer neuron k ($k = 1, 2, \cdots, p$). The link weight between neuron i of the input-layer and neuron j of the hidden layer is V_{ij}, and the second-order link weight is V_{lij}. The link weight between neuron j of the hidden layer and neuron k of the hidden layer is W_{jk}, and the second-order link weight is W_{ijk}.

The output state of output-layer neuron k is

$$y_k = g\left[\sum_{j=1}^{n}(W_{jk}z_j + \sum_{i \neq j}^{n}W_{ijk}z_iz_j)\right] \qquad (k = 1, 2, \cdots, p) \tag{6}$$

The output state of hidden-layer neuron j is

$$z_j = g\left[\sum_{i=1}^{m}(V_{ij}x_i + \sum_{l \neq i}^{m}V_{lij}x_lx_i)\right] \qquad (j = 1, 2, \cdots, n) \tag{7}$$

The threshold function of a neuron is the sigmoid function: $g(x) = 1/(1 + e^{-x})$.

Through a training iteration, the new output state of neuron k is

$$y_k' = g\left\{\sum_{j=1}^{n}[(W_{jk} + \Delta W_{jk})(z_j + \Delta z_j) + \sum_{i \neq j}^{n}(W_{ijk}i + \Delta W_{ijk})(z_i + \Delta z_i)(z_j + \Delta z_j)]\right\} \tag{8}$$

in which, ΔW_{jk}, ΔW_{ijk}, Δz_j are the respective increase.

In the case of a small signal, Eq.(8) is extended in Taylor series expansion, and take only first-order terms, we obtain

$$\Delta y_k \approx y_k(1 - y_k)\sum_{j=1}^{n}[\Delta W_{jk}z_j + \Delta z_j(W_{jk} + 2\sum_{i \neq j}^{n}W_{ijk}z_i) + \sum_{i \neq j}^{n}\Delta W_{ijk}z_iz_j] \tag{9}$$

In a similar way, extending Eq.(7) obtains

$$\Delta z_j \approx z_j(1 - z_j)\sum_{i=1}^{m}(\Delta V_{ij}x_i + \sum_{l \neq i}^{m}\Delta V_{lij}x_lx_i) \tag{10}$$

The learning rules of the back-propagation algorithm in the neural network are

$$\begin{cases} \Delta W_{jk} = -\alpha d_k^m z_j, & \Delta W_{ijk} = -\beta d_k^m z_iz_j \\ \Delta V_{ij} = -\alpha d_j^h x_i, & \Delta V_{lij} = -\beta d_j^h x_lx_i \end{cases}$$

where, α is the first-order learning factor, β is the second-order learning factor, $d_k^m = y_k(1 - y_k)\delta_k$, and $d_j^h = z_j(1 - z_j)\sum_{l}^{p}(W_{jl} + \sum_{i \neq j}^{n}W_{jil}z_i)d_l^m$.

For a single-output network $p = 1$, substituting these equations into Eq.(4) gives

$$\eta_i = \eta_i^1 + \eta_i^2 \tag{11}$$

$$\begin{cases} \eta_i^1 = 2y_k^2(1 - y_k)^2\delta_k^{-1}\sum_{j=1}^{n}z_j^2(\alpha + \beta\sum_{i \neq j}^{n}z_i^2) \\ \eta_i^2 = 2y_k^2(1 - y_k)^2\delta_k^{-1}\sum_{i=1}^{m}x_i^2(\alpha + \beta\sum_{l \neq i}^{m}x_l^2)\sum_{j=1}^{n}z_j^2(1 - z_j)^2(W_{jk} + \sum_{q \neq j}^{n}W_{jqk}z_q)^2 \end{cases}$$

This is the general expression of the dynamic learning efficiency of the multi-layer network, in which η_i^1 is the learning efficiency resulting from the ith modifying link weights between the hidden layer and the output layer, and η_i^2 is the learning efficiency resulting from the ith modifying link weights between the input layer and the hidden layer.

IV. Discussion and Conclusion

When the high order nonlinear terms in Eq.(11) is omitted, we obtain the linear learning efficiency as follows:

$$\eta_i^l = \eta_i^{l1} + \eta_i^{l2} = 2\alpha y_k^2 (1 - y_k)^2 \delta_k^{-1} [\sum_{j=1}^{n} z_j^2 + \sum_{i=1}^{m} x_i^2 \sum_{j=1}^{n} z_j^2 (1 - z_j)^2 W_{jk}^2] \tag{12}$$

On the assumption that there are an approximate relationship $\beta \sim \alpha$, $W_{ijk} \sim W_{jk}$ in most simulation experiments, we can obtain the approximate expression of the statistical average value of the nonlinear learning efficiency as follows:

$$\bar{\eta}_i^{nl} \approx (1 + \frac{n}{4})\eta_i^{l1} + (1 + \frac{m}{4})(1 + \frac{n}{2})^2 \eta_i^{l2} \tag{13}$$

In general, $\eta_i^2 \gg \eta_i^1$, and in the case where the number of input-layer neurons m and the number of hidden-layer neurons n are large numbers, there is the following relationship:

$$\bar{\eta}_i^{nl} \propto m n^2 \bar{\eta}_i^l \tag{14}$$

Eq.(14) gives the relationship between the nonlinear learning efficiency and the linear learning efficiency in a training iteration. From Eq.(2) and Eq.(14), it can be seen that the nonlinear learning efficiency increases with iteration times more than the linear learning efficiency by an exponential factor. On the other hand, the error function of the network for taking into account nonlinear correlation decreases with iteration times exponentially faster than that of the linear correlation network. These results are consistent with previous numerical simulational experiments [2-4].

The focus of previous research work has been numerical simulation experiments. In this paper, we have first carried out theoretical analyses of the effects of the nonlinear correlation on learning efficiency of neural networks. In the case of a small signal, we obtained the general expression of the learning efficiency. Under certain conditions, we analyzed the quantitative relationship between linear learning efficiency and second-order nonlinear learning efficiency, and our results may be used to interpret and understand previous numerical simulation experiments[2-4]. In addition, we intend to study influences of the nonlinear correlation on local minima in neural networks, as well as on attraction domains of neural networks in the near future.

References

[1] D.E.Rumelhart, et al., "Learning internal representations by error propagation", *Parallel Distributed Processing*, MIT Press, Cambridge, MA, 1986.

[2] C.L.Giles and T.Maxwell, *Applied Optics, Vol.26, No.23*, pp.4972-4978, 1987.

[3] Y.H.Pao, ADAPTIVE PATTERN RECOGNITION AND NEURAL NETWORKS, Chapter 8, *Addison-Wesley Publishing Company, Inc.*, 1989.

[4] G.R.Litter, et al., *Applied Optics, Vol.29, No.11*, pp.1591-1592, 1990.

[5] Zhong Zhang and Shuo Bai, ADVANCED PROGRESS IN ARTIFICIAL INTELLIGENCE, *Tsinghua University Press*, pp.348-355, 1994.

Toward a Model of Consolidation:
The Retention and Transfer of Neural Net Task Knowledge

Daniel L. Silver and Robert E. Mercer
Department of Computer Science, University of Western Ontario
London, Ontario, Canada   -   June 14, 1995

Keywords: artficial neural networks, consolidation, learning to learn, task knowledge transfer

Introduction

Theoretical and empirical artificial neural network (ANN) research has focused on the *tabula rasa* approach of inducing a model of a classification task given a set of supervised training examples. Consequently, most ANN learning systems do not take advantage of previously acquired task representation when considering a potentially related task. There has been little work done on the storage of task knowledge (representation) after it has been induced, its integration with previously learned tasks of the same problem domain, and its recall to facilitate the learning of a new task. This can be considered a major aspect of the problem of "learning to learn". Our research investigates systems of artificial neural networks which use acquired task representations to decrease learning time for a new task. This paper introduces an architecture of two feed-forward back-propagation neural networks and associated software, which we collectively refer to as a *consolidation system*. We demonstrate the system's ability to retain, consolidate, and transfer representations over the domain of simple boolean functions. [McCl94] contains an important discussion of consolidation which has influenced the work presented here.

Problem Statement: To design an architecture of artificial neural networks which is capable of using the knowledge of previously learned task representations to generate a *good initial representation* from which to start learning a new task. More specifically, the problem is to develop an architecture which is capable of iteratively: (1) Retaining and consolidating task representations of learned tasks in a meta-knowledge database; (2) Using the meta-knowledge database to generate a *good initial representation* from which to start learning a new task. The term *good initial representation* is defined as a set of weights which statistically performs better than random sets of initial weights. Performance is measured by comparing the average initial training error (total sum of squared error over all examples), the average number of training iterations to convergence (until training error is below a defined level), and by observing the graphs of the training error versus number of iterations. The tasks we consider in this paper are the class of 16 2-variable boolean logic functions. Henceforth, the terms task and function should be considered synonymous.

Background: Learning to learn, an area of intense inquiry since 1990, can be subdivided along several themes: catastrophic interference and methods of knowledge transfer between a learned *source* task and a new *target* task [Shar94, Prat93], priming of neural networks with symbolic knowledge [Shav92, Towe91], compositional learning which advocates first learning sub-tasks of a more complex function [Sing92], learning search information during the training of source tasks and the use of this information to reduce the training time on a target task [Thru94, Nail93, Fren94], and learning task representation, the focus of this paper. Previously, Baxter [Baxt95] has shown how a set of source tasks chosen from a fixed distribution can be used to simultaneously learn a common internal representation (the weights in the common portion of a neural network) of the task domain. The representation can then be used to speed up the learning of a new target task (only the unique weights in the new network require training). However, to our knowledge, no one has developed a method of sequentially learning source tasks using a neural network architecture such that the system retains learned task representations and uses that knowledge to predict a good set of initial weights from which to begin learning a new task.

Hypothesis: Our working hypothesis has been as follows: The neural network representation (ie. connection weights) of functions within a problem domain can be forced to form a structured *function of functions* at a meta-knowledge level. Just as task level examples can be used to develop a generalized model using a neural network, examples of function representation can be used to develop a generalized model of the function of functions. Thus, previous function representations within the "locality" of a new function can be generalized over to estimate a good initial starting point for learning. This estimation can be considered an interpolation over the space of hypotheses outlined by previously learned function representations.

The Model

Figure 1 provides a block diagram of the consolidation system. There are two feed-forward back-propagation neural networks which interact with one and the other during two different phases of operation: *query* and *training*. This cycle of interaction is intended to force a structure on the function of functions at the meta-knowledge level.

The Networks: Both networks employ the standard back-propagation of error algorithm (each node uses a sigmoid activation function) with a momentum term [Hert91]. The task network (TN) is used to learn each new boolean function. The TN accepts the supervised boolean function examples (I_T) and produces an estimate of the function output (O_T). It is, at a minimum, a two-layer network, composed of 2 passive input nodes and 1 output node. At specified times, the connection weights are extracted from the TN to produce a set of *signature weights* for a task or the final converged set of weights. The signature weights can be seen as a representation of the training examples for a function after a fixed number of iterations starting from a known set of initial weights. The signature weights are used as input to the meta-level network during both the query and training phases.

The experience network (EN) acts as a generalized database of previously learned function representations. If there are n weights in the TN, then the EN will be composed of n input nodes, $\lceil n + \sqrt{n} \rceil$ hidden nodes, and n output nodes. The EN accepts a set of signature weights supervised with the converged weights for each of the previously learned functions (I_E). It produces an estimate of the converged weights (O_E) which we will refer to as the set of *generated weights*. The back-propagation learning algorithm for this network includes a weight cost term [Hert91] which forces an amount of generalization to occur.

The Query Phase: **Step 1 - TN produces signature weights.** The TN is initialized with a known set of weights and then trained on the I_T for a new function. At the end of a fixed number of iterations, all TN weights are extracted to produce a set of signature weights. **Step 2 - Query EN using signature weights.** The signature weights are tranformed into a *query example* for the EN network. The EN network accepts the query example as input (I_E) and outputs (O_E) a set of generated weights. **Step 3 - Prime TN with generated weights.** The set of generated weights produced by the EN is transferred into the TN replacing the signature weights.

The Training Phase: **Step 4 - TN produces converged weights.** Using the set of EN generated weights as the starting point, the TN is trained to convergence (until total sum of squared error is below an acceptable level). After training has completed, all TN weights are extracted to produce a set of converged weights. **Step 5 - Consolidate the representations of all learned tasks.** This is the critical step in the consolidation system. The signature weights and converged weights for the most recently learned task are paired together as input attributes and target outputs, and added to the set of training examples (I_E) for the EN. The EN is then

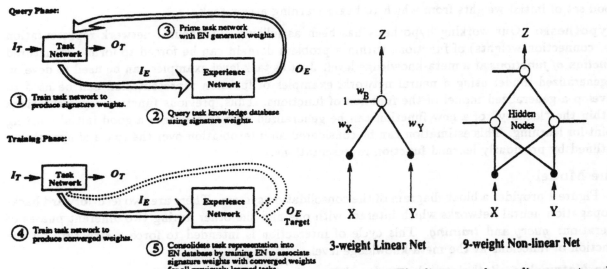

Figure 1: A block diagram of the consolidation system model.

Figure 2: The linear and non-linear networks used in the studies.

trained to convergence.

The objective is to produce a generalized model of the function of functions, or more accurately a function of their TN representations. The expectation is not to be able to perfectly recall a set of converged weights, but to generate a good set of starting weights much closer to the desired than a random draw would likely provide. The success of the EN producing a good initial representation for a new task depends on the EN's ability to associate the signature weights for the task to an appropriate position in weight space. If the function space is continuous and the EN contains representation knowledge within the locality of the new function then it should be able to generalize to a better than random initial representation; that is, the TN training time, on average, will be reduced. If the EN does not have representation knowledge within the locality of the new function then it is possible that the generated weights will have a detrimental effect on TN learning; that is, the training time will be longer on average than for a random set of TN weights.

Preliminary Results

We have conducted two studies in the fixed problem domain of boolean functions of 2 variables. In each case the performance of a TN initialized with generated weights from an EN was compared to a randomly initialized TN. To ensure statistical accuracy, all experiments were conducted seven times using different pseudo-random seed values, and various ranges of random initial weights. The averages and standard deviations were calculated. To be fair, the statistics for the TN initialized with EN generated weights include the number of iterations required to produce the signature weights. The training of the EN is considered a background task, therefore it's computational cost is not included.

There are 16 boolean functions of 2 variables each having a total of 4 training examples. Consider the set of training examples for the AND function (inputs X and Y, output Z): (0 0, 0), (0 1, 0), (1 0, 0), (1 1, 1). Based on the output sequence, we will refer to this as the $f0001$ function. During the course of the studies various graphical tools were used to visualize the functions produced by the TN. The surface of the function was rendered in 3-dimensions (X,Y,Z), the movement of the TN hyperplane(s) was(were) animated, and 3-dimensional scatter plots were used to show the position of the TN weights. These visualization techniques helped greatly in the analysis of the consolidation system.

Simple Linear TN with 1 Node and 3 Weights. The first experiment examined the simple two-layer TN composed of 2 passive input nodes and 1 active output node (see Figure 2). This network had in total 3 connection weights, 2 input-to-output node weights w_X, w_Y, and 1 bias weight w_B. This TN is capable of learning all 14 linearly separable boolean functions (XOR = $f0110$ and NXOR = $f1001$ are excluded). The associated EN was a three-layer network composed of 3 passive input nodes, 5 hidden nodes, and 3 output nodes. For each new task the TN was run for 35 iterations before generating a set of signature weights. For both networks the weight step size was 0.1, the momentum term was 0.9. The acceptable level of error was set at 0.00001 for the TN and 0.0001 for the EN. The EN had a weight cost term of 0.0007.

Figure 3 is a diagram of the 3-dimension weight space used by the TN. It shows the position of all 14 of the boolean functions according to their w_X, w_Y, w_B weights after reaching an error level ≤ 0.01. Notice the symmetry in the position of the various tasks. It is this regularity of structure that makes it possible for the EN to predict a good initial representation (starting weights) for a new task given representation knowledge of adjacent tasks. Although, this is not necessarily a function of the EN for this low dimensional weight space (the same regularity can be produced if small initial random weights in the range -0.5 to 0.5 are chosen), we believe that by using the consolidation system the same structure can be forced on higher dimensional weight spaces.

Various numbers and sequences of functions were used to train and test the consolidation system. Certain sequences were found to build a good base of task representation knowledge for training subsequent functions. For example, if $f0010$ and $f1010$ were "experienced", then the training time for $f1011$ to reach an error < 0.01 was reduced, on average, from 460 iterations to $35+240 = 275$. The EN generated weights were $w_X = 2.71, w_Y = -5.44, w_B = 0.28$. The converged set of weights were $w_X = 5.44, w_Y = -5.44, w_B = 2.17$. Conversely, if $f1101$ and $f0100$ were experienced, then the time to train $f1011$ increased to an average of $35+2360$ iterations. The EN generated weights were $w_X = -5.42, w_Y = 5.42, w_B = 0.00$. Observing Figure 3, we see that $f0010$ and $f1010$ are close to $f1011$ and are able to provide representational information which is better than random, while $f1101$ and $f0100$ are some distance away and produce a poor initial representation for $f1011$. An animation of the movement of the hyperplane created by the output node confirms this intuition. The EN generated weights initialize the TN with a hyperplane which moves rapidly from approximately the $f1010$ position to the $f1011$ position.

One of the more successful sequences of "experienced" functions was $f0001, f1101, f1011, f1110$. After the consolidation of the representation of these functions within the EN, all functions (except $f0000$) required from 5% to 40% fewer training iterations. Observing Figure 3 it can be seen that these 4 functions span a large portion of the volume created by the 14 functions and, thus, provide a wide spectrum of representational knowledge. Even more interesting are the positions of the TN hyperplanes associated with these functions. Each of the four functions partitions off one of four training examples in input space. The results of our experiments indicate that once the representation of theses hyperplanes are consolidated in the EN, the EN can generalize over this knowledge to predict a better than random starting representation for the remaining tasks. The $f0000$ function does not do as well since it is the greatest "distance" from the 4 consolidated representations.

Non-linear TN with 2 Hidden Nodes and 9 Weights. The second experiment examined the more complex three-layer TN composed of 2 passive input nodes, two hidden nodes, and 1 output node. This network has in total 9 connection weights: 4 input-to-output node weights,

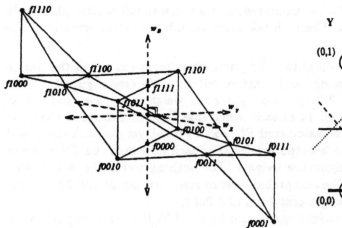

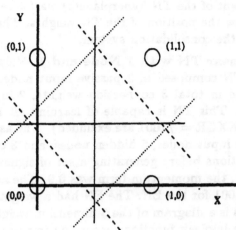

Figure 3: Weight space for the simple one node network. Each point represents a boolean function.

Figure 4: Hyperplanes created by the hidden nodes of the non-linear network.

2 hidden-to-output weights, and 3 bias weights to each of the active nodes. This TN is capable of learning all 16 boolean functions. The associated EN was a three-layer network composed of 9 passive input nodes, 12 hidden nodes, and 9 output nodes. For each new task the TN ran for 105 iterations before generating a set of signature weights. The weight step size, momentum term, weight cost term, and acceptable levels of error were set as per the first experiment.

As in the first experiment, various numbers and sequences of functions were used to train and test the consolidation system. Again, the order in which the functions were learned affected the consolidation system's ability to initialize a new TN with a better than random set of weights. The results generally agreed with the simpler linear network of 3 weights. An animation of the movement of the 2 hyperplanes created by the hidden nodes, as well as surface renderings of the actual output of the network, show the performance advantage provided by the EN generated weights after consolidation of adjacent functions.

The most successful sequence of "experienced" functions was $f0110, f0011, f1001, f0101$. After consolidating the representation of these functions within the EN, all functions on average (excluding $f0000$ and $f1111$) required 85.3% fewer training iterations. As an example, the average training time for the $f0100$ function was reduced from an average of 2090 to 152 iterations. Graphs of training error versus numbers of iterations show that functions begin with lower initial error rates, and follow a rapid gradient descent to a global minimum error. Thus, empirical results indicate that, depending upon those tasks which have been previously consolidated, the EN is able to initialize the TN with a representation that is much better on average than a random set of weights.

Discussion

The preliminary results provide evidence that our model of consolidation constrains the choice of initial weights for a new task to a region of weight space defined by the previously learned tasks. If the new task resides within this region of previous experience, then the likelihood of the EN generating a good initial representation is high. Conversely, if the new task to be learned falls some distance outside of the region of experience then the EN generated weights will likely produce prolonged training times. This indicates that the order of task consolidation is very important.

The results for the non-linear TN are particularly impressive. The reason for this is perhaps the most important conjecture produced by our research: *by learning the more complex non-linear boolean functions first, the consolidation system acquires the necessary representation for many of the simpler boolean functions as well.* Observe Figure 4. In order to create a model of the non-linear XOR = $f0110$ or NXOR = $f1001$ functions, two hyperplanes must be positioned by the TN as shown by either the dashed lines or the dotted lines. One hyperplane must be positioned horizontally or vertically as shown by the solid lines in order to create a model of the linear functions $f0011$ or $f0101$, respectively. In combination with the hidden to output layers of the TN these hyperplanes can be used to generate all boolean functions except $f0000$ and $f1111$. These two functions require that both hyperplanes be moved out of the area of the examples. This can take many iterations. The weights which represent the hyperplanes and the hidden-to-output layer connectivity are interleaved during EN training. Subsequently, EN generated weights for any of the remaining functions (excepting $f0000$ and $f1111$) are positioned to rapidly fall into their required positions.

We have identified a number of questions about our hypothesis and system which deserve closer examination. Will our method of generating the signature weights remain valid over larger and more complex problem domains? Is it reasonable to assume that the signature weights will be unique? What are the theoretical problems of training the EN to associate the signature weights to converged weights? How can the trade-off between generalization to new task representations and the accurate recall of previously learned representations be over-come? Our future research direction includes answering these questions, as well as testing the consolidation system against other families of functions (*eg.* polynomials, boolean equations of n variables).

References

[Baxt95] Jonathan Baxter, Learning internal representations, *Proceedings of the Eighth International Conference on Computational Learning Theory*, ACM Press, Vol. (to appear), Santa Cruz, CA, 1995.

[Fren94] Robert M. French, Interactive tandem networks and the sequential learning problem, *CRCC Technical Report*, Center for Reserach on Concepts and Cognition, Indiana Univeristy, 1994.

[Hert91] J. Hertz, A. Krogh, and R.G. Palmer, Introduction to the Theory of Neural Computation, Adddison-Wesley Pub. Co., Redwood City, CA., 1991.

[McCl94] James L. McClelland, Bruce L. McNaughton, and Randall C. O'Reilly, Why there are complementary learning systems in the hippocampus and neocortex: Insights from the successes and failures of connectionist models of learning and memory, *Technical Report PDP.CNS.94.1*, Department of Psychology, Carnegie Mellon University, Pittsurgh, PA 15213, 1994.

[Nail93] D.K. Nail and Richard J. Mammone, Learning by learning in neural networks, *Artificial Neural Networks for Speech and Vision; ed: Richard J. Mammone*, Chapman and Hall, London, 1993.

[Prat93] Lorien Y. Pratt, Discriminability-Based transfer between neural networks, *Advances in Neural Information Processing Systems 5*, Morgan Kaufmann, Vol. 5, pp. 204–211, San Mateo, CA, 1993.

[Shar94] Noel E. Sharkey and Amanda J.C. Sharkey, Understanding catastrophic interference in neural nets, *Dept. of Computer Science Research Report CS-94-4*, University of Sheffield, UK, 1994.

[Shav92] Jude Shavlik, Integrating Explanatory and Neural Approaches to Machine Learning, *Computational Learning Theory and Natural Learning Systems, Constraints and Prospects*, MIT Press, Cambridge, Mass., 1992.

[Sing92] Satinder P. Singh, Transfer of learning by composing solutions for elemental sequential tasks, *Machine Learning*, 1992.

[Thru94] Sebastian Thrun, A Lifelong Learning Perspective for Mobile Robot Control, *Proceedings of the IEEE Conference on Intelligent Robots and Systems*, IEEE, September, 1994.

[Towe91] Geoffrey G. Towell and Jude W. Shavlik, Interpretation of Artificial Neural Networks: Mapping Knowledge-Based Neural Networks into Rules, *Advances in Neural Information Processing Systems 4*, Morgan Kaufmann, Vol. 4, pp. 977–984, San Mateo, CA, 1991.

Stability and Bifurcation Analysis of Fixed Points in Discrete Time Recurrent Neural Networks with Two Neurons

Peter Tiňo

Department of Computer Science and Engineering
Slovak Technical University
Ilkovicova 3, 812 19 Bratislava, Slovakia
Email: tino@decef.elf.stuba.sk

Bill G. Horne and **C. Lee Giles***

NEC Research Institute
4 Independence Way
Princeton, NJ 08540
Email: {horne,giles}@research.nj.nec.com

ABSTRACT

The position, number and stability types of fixed points of a two–neuron recurrent network with nonzero weights are investigated. We partition the network state space into several regions corresponding to stability types of the fixed points. If the neurons have the same mutual interaction pattern, i.e. they either mutually inhibit or mutually excite themselves, a lower bound on the rate of convergence of the attractive fixed points towards the saturation values, as the absolute values of weights on the self–loops grow, is given. When both neurons self-excite themselves and have the same mutual interaction pattern, the mechanism of creation of a new attractive fixed point is shown to be that of saddle node bifurcation.

1   Introduction

In this contribution, the issues concerning fixed points of discrete–time recurrent neural networks consisting of two neurons are addressed. Assuming nonzero weights, we partition the network state space into several regions corresponding to stability types of the fixed points.

Hirsh [2] proved that when all the weights in a recurrent network with exclusively self-exciting (or exclusively self-inhibiting) neurons are multiplied by larger and larger positive number (neural gain), attractive fixed points tend to saturated activation values. In case of two–neuron network, under the assumption that the neurons have the same mutual interaction pattern[1], we give a lower bound on the rate of convergence of the attractive fixed points towards the saturation values as the absolute values of weights on the self–loops grow.

Furthermore, the position and the number of fixed points is discussed. A similar approach to determining the number and position of fixed points in continuous–time recurrent neural networks can be found in [1].

Under some conditions on weights, the saddle node bifurcation is shown to be responsible for creation of a new attractive fixed point.

---

*Also with UMIACS, University of Maryland, College Park, MD 20742
[1]they either mutually inhibit or mutually excite themselves

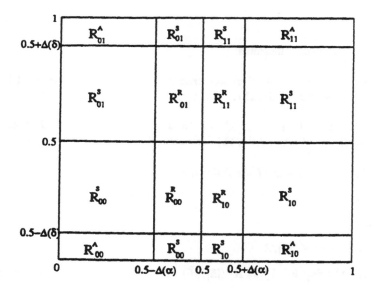

Figure 1: Partitioning of the network state space according to stability types of the fixed points.

2 Qualitative analysis

The iterative map under consideration can be written as follows:

$$(x_{n+1}, y_{n+1}) = (g(ax_n + by_n + t_1), g(cx_n + dy_n + t_2)),$$ (1)

where $(x_n, y_n) \in (0,1)^2$ is the state of the network at the time step n, $a, b, c, d \in \Re \setminus \{0\}$ and $t_1, t_2 \in \Re$ are weights and bias terms respectively. g is a sigmoid function $g(\ell) = 1/(1 + e^{-\ell})$. Since the neuron activations x_n and y_n are positive, signs of the weights determine the type of the corresponding connections: a *connection* is *exciting* and *inhibiting* if its weight is positive and negative respectively.

The aim of this section is to partition the state space $(0,1)^2$ of neurons' activations into several regions according to stability types of fixed points of (1).

For $u > 4$, define

$$\Delta(u) = \frac{1}{2}\sqrt{1 - \frac{4}{u}}.$$

For $\alpha > 4, \delta > 4$, the regions of the (x, y)–space

$$\left(0, \frac{1}{2} - \Delta(\alpha)\right) \times \left(0, \frac{1}{2} - \Delta(\delta)\right),$$

$$\left(\frac{1}{2} - \Delta(\alpha), \frac{1}{2}\right] \times \left(0, \frac{1}{2} - \Delta(\delta)\right) \cup \left(0, \frac{1}{2} - \Delta(\alpha)\right) \times \left(\frac{1}{2} - \Delta(\delta), \frac{1}{2}\right]$$

and

$$\left(\frac{1}{2} - \Delta(\alpha), \frac{1}{2}\right] \times \left(\frac{1}{2} - \Delta(\delta), \frac{1}{2}\right]$$

are denoted by $R^A_{00}(\alpha, \delta)$, $R^S_{00}(\alpha, \delta)$ and $R^R_{00}(\alpha, \delta)$ respectively. Regions symmetrical to $R^A_{00}(\alpha, \delta)$, $R^S_{00}(\alpha, \delta)$ and $R^R_{00}(\alpha, \delta)$ with respect to the line $x = 1/2$ are denoted by $R^A_{10}(\alpha, \delta)$, $R^S_{10}(\alpha, \delta)$ and $R^R_{10}(\alpha, \delta)$ respectively. Similarly, let $R^A_{01}(\alpha, \delta)$, $R^S_{01}(\alpha, \delta)$ and $R^R_{01}(\alpha, \delta)$ denote the regions symmetrical to $R^A_{00}(\alpha, \delta)$, $R^S_{00}(\alpha, \delta)$ and $R^R_{00}(\alpha, \delta)$ with respect to the line $y = 1/2$. Finally, $R^A_{11}(\alpha, \delta)$, $R^S_{11}(\alpha, \delta)$ and $R^R_{11}(\alpha, \delta)$ denote regions that are symmetrical to $R^A_{01}(\alpha, \delta)$, $R^S_{01}(\alpha, \delta)$ and $R^R_{01}(\alpha, \delta)$ with respect to the line $x = 1/2$ (figure 1).

Denote $a - bc/d$ and $d - bc/a$ by $\bar{a}$ and $\bar{d}$ respectively.

In [3], we proved the following theorems:

Theorem 1: *If $bc > 0, |a| > 4, |d| > 4$, then all attractive fixed points of (1) lie in $\bigcup_{i \in \mathcal{I}} R_i^A(|a|, |d|)$, where $\mathcal{I}$ is the index set $\mathcal{I} = \{00, 10, 01, 11\}$.*

Theorem 2: *If $bc < 0, ad < 0, |a| > 4, |d| > 4$ and $|ad| \geq |bc|/2$, then all fixed points of (1) lying in $\bigcup_{i \in \mathcal{I}} R_i^A(|a|, |d|)$, $\mathcal{I} = \{00, 10, 01, 11\}$ are attractive.*

Theorem 3: *If $|\bar{a}|, |\bar{d}| > 4$ and one of the following conditions is satisfied*

- $bc > 0$ *and* $ad < 0$

- $bc < 0$ *and* $ad > 0$

- $bc < 0, ad < 0$ *and* $|ad| \leq |bc|/2$

then all fixed points of (1) lying in $\bigcup_{i \in \mathcal{I}} R_i^A(|\bar{a}|, |\bar{d}|)$, $\mathcal{I} = \{00, 10, 01, 11\}$ are attractive.

For an insight into a bifurcation mechanism (explored in the next section) by which attractive fixed points of (1) are created (or dismissed), it is useful to have an idea where other types of fixed points can lie. For the case when both neurons are either self-exciting, or self-inhibiting ($ad > 0$), and their mutual interaction is of the same character ($bc > 0$), we have the following theorem [3]:

Theorem 4: *Suppose $ad > 0, bc > 0, |a| > 4, |d| > 4$. Then,*

- *attractive points can lie only in $\bigcup_{i \in \mathcal{I}} R_i^A(|a|, |d|)$, $\mathcal{I} = \{00, 10, 01, 11\}$.*

- *if $ad \geq bc/2$, then all fixed points in $\bigcup_{i \in \mathcal{I}} R_i^S(|a|, |d|)$ are saddle points; repulsive points can lie only in $\bigcup_{i \in \mathcal{I}} R_i^R(|a|, |d|)$.*

- *if $|ad - bc| < 4\min\{|a|, |d|\}$, then there are no repellors.*

3 Quantitative analysis

In this section we are concerned with the actual position of fixed points of (1). (x, y) corresponding to fixed points should lie on curves $y = f_{a,b,t_1}(x)$ and $x = f_{d,c,t_2}(y)$, where

$$v = f_{s,r,t}(u) = \frac{1}{r}\left(-t - su + ln\frac{u}{1-u}\right).\qquad(2)$$

$ln(u/(1-u)): (0, 1) \to \Re$, is a monotonically increasing function with $\lim_{u \to 0^+} ln(u/(1 - u) = -\infty$ and $\lim_{u \to 1^-} ln(u/(1 - u) = \infty$.

The constant term $-t$ is responsible for a vertical shift of the whole function. If $s > 4$ then the term $-su$ causes the function $-su - t + ln(u/(1-u))$ to "bend" so that on $[1/2 - \Delta(s), 1/2 + \Delta(s)]$ it is decreasing, while it still increases on $(0, 1/2 - \Delta(s)) \cup (1/2 + \Delta(s), 1)$. $-su - t + ln(u/(1-u))$ is always concave and convex on $(0, 1/2)$ and $(1/2, 1)$ respectively. The coefficient r scales the whole function and flips it around the u-axis, if $r < 0$.

Using the results from the previous section, in case of self-exciting neurons with the same mutual interaction pattern[2], reasoning about the stability type of the fixed points can be based on the knowledge to which monotonicity intervals of the functions $f_{a,b,t_1}(x)$ and $f_{d,c,t_2}(y)$ they correspond. The intersection pattern can allow for up to 9 fixed points. Attractive fixed points can lie only on the intersection of the outer branches of f_{a,b,t_1} and f_{d,c,t_2}. Whenever the the middle branch of f_{a,b,t_1} intersects with an outer branch of f_{d,c,t_2} (or vice-versa), it corresponds to a saddle point of (1). The usual scenario of creation of a new attractive fixed point is that typical of the saddle-node bifurcation in which a pair attractive + saddle fixed point is created. Attractive fixed points disappear in a reverse manner: an attractive point coalesces with with a saddle and they

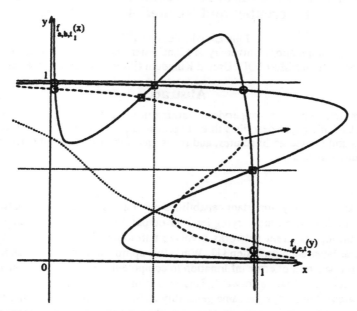

Figure 2: Geometrical illustration of saddle-node bifurcation in a recurrent neural network with two state neurons. Saddle and attractive points are marked with squares and circles respectively. $a, d > 0$, $b, c < 0$.

are annihilated. This is illustrated in figure 2. $f_{d,c,t_2}(y)$ shown as dashed curve intersects $f_{a,b,t_1}(x)$ in three points. By increasing d, f_{d,c,t_2} bends further (solid curve) and intersects with f_{a,b,t_1} in five points[3]. Note that as d increases attractive fixed points move closer to vertices $\{0, 1\}^2$.

This tendency, in the context of networks with exclusively self-exciting (or exclusively self-inhibiting) recurrent neurons, is discussed in [2]. Our result stated in Corollary 1, assumes two-neuron recurrent network. It only requires that the neurons have the same mutual interaction pattern ($bc > 0$) and gives a lower bound on the rate of convergence of the attractive fixed points of (1) towards some of the vertices $\{0, 1\}^2$, as the absolute values of weights on the self-loops grow.

Corollary 1: *Assume* $bc > 0, |a| > 4, |d| > 4$. *Then all attractive fixed points of (1) lie in the* ε-neighborhood *of vertices of unit square, where*

$$\varepsilon = \sqrt{\left(\frac{1}{2} - \Delta(|a|)\right)^2 + \left(\frac{1}{2} - \Delta(|d|)\right)^2}.$$

References

[1] R.D. Beer. On the dynamics of small continuous–time recurrent networks. Technical Report CES–94–18, Case Western Reserve University, Cleveland, OH, 1994.

[2] M.W. Hirsch. Saturation at high gain in discrete time recurrent networks. *Neural Networks*, 7(3):449–453, 1994.

[3] P. Tiňo, B.G. Horne, and C.L. Giles. Fixed points in two–neuron discrete time recurrent networks: Stability and bifurcation considerations. Technical Report UMIACS-TR-95-51, Institute for Advance Computer Studies, University of Maryland, College Park, MD 20742, 1995.

---

[2]and $ad \geq bc/2$

[3]At the same time, $|c|$ has to be also appropriately increased so as to compensate for the increase in d so that the "bended" part of $f_{d,c}$ does not move radically to higher values of x.

Parallel Formulations of Real-Time Recurrent Learning for Hypercubes and Related Architectures

John Lloyd (Member IEEE)

Department of Computation, University of Manchester Institute of Science and Technology

Manchester M60 1QD, United Kingdom (jlloyd@ap.co.umist.ac.uk)

Abstract

Real-time recurrent learning is a powerful supervised learning procedure for training recurrent networks to perform temporal association tasks. This paper describes three approaches for parallelising the real-time recurrent learning algorithm on hypercubes and related architectures, and investigates their theoretical performance and scalability on hypercube-connected multicomputers.

1. Introduction

Recurrent neural networks have many important capabilities not found in feedforward networks, including attractor dynamics and the ability to deal with time-varying input or output through their own natural temporal operation. A popular technique for training recurrent networks involves unfolding the network into a multilayer feedforward network that grows by one layer each time step [1]. While this approach, known as back propagation through time (BPTT), uses backward propagation of error information to compute the error gradient, an alternative approach is to propagate activation gradient information forward. This results in an algorithm called real-time recurrent learning (RTRL) [2]. The RTRL algorithm enjoys the same generality as BPTT while not suffering from its growing memory requirement in arbitrarily long training sequences. However, the storage and computational requirements for training an n-neuron network are quite severe, being $\Theta(n^3)$ and $\Theta(n^4)$ respectively. Fortunately, the inherent parallelism of the algorithm allows us to pursue an implementation on parallel computers.

While many parallel formulations have been proposed for other neural network algorithms, particularly back propagation [3, 4], relatively little seems to have been done on the RTRL algorithm. This paper describes three approaches for parallelising the RTRL algorithm on hypercube-connected parallel computers. The main difference between these approaches is the level of granularity at which parallelism is exploited: the first exploits parallelism at the neuron level, the second at the weight level, and the third at an even finer level – the derivative level. Although these schemes are natural for hypercube architectures, they are equally well-suited to fat-tree-based architectures such as the Meiko CS-2 and Connection Machine CM-5.

The remainder of this paper is organised as follows. Section 2 describes the RTRL algorithm. Section 3 describes the three parallel formulations of RTRL and derives expressions for their parallel execution times on hypercube-connected multicomputers. Section 4 compares the performance and scalability of the three schemes. Section 5 contains some conclusions and suggestions for further work.

2. Real-Time Recurrent Learning

Consider a fully-connected recurrent network with the following activation dynamics:

$$y_i(t+1) \;=\; f(u_i(t)) \;=\; f\left(\sum_{j=1}^{n} w_{ij} y_j(t) + x_i(t)\right) \qquad i = 1, 2, \ldots, n \qquad (1)$$

Starting from the initial condition $\pi_{ij}^k(0) = 0$, the RTRL algorithm computes the activation derivatives $\pi_{ij}^k(t) \equiv \partial y_k(t)/\partial w_{ij}$ at each time step using the recursion

$$\pi_{ij}^k(t+1) = f'(u_k(t))\left(\sum_{l=1}^{n} w_{kl} \pi_{ij}^l(t) + \delta_{ik} y_j(t)\right) \qquad i, j, k = 1, 2, \ldots, n \qquad (2)$$

and then uses the errors $e_k(t)$ between the desired and actual outputs to compute the weight changes

$$\Delta w_{ij}(t) = \eta \sum_{k=1}^{n} e_k(t)\pi_{ij}^k(t) \qquad i, j = 1, 2, \ldots, n \qquad (3)$$

For large networks, the computation performed in each iteration of the RTRL algorithm is dominated by the sum of products in Equation (2). Hence, the number of basic operations performed in a single iteration (the problem size) is approximately n^4. If the time taken to perform a single multiplication and addition operation together is t_c, then the serial execution time is approximately

$$T_S \approx t_c n^4 \qquad (4)$$

3. Hypercubes and Real-Time Recurrent Learning

In this paper, we restrict our attention to hypercube-connected multicomputers that employ store-and-forward routing and single-port communication [5]. The time to deliver an m-word message between two processors that are l connections apart is $t_s + t_w ml$, where t_s is the startup time, and t_w is the per-word transfer time (the inverse of the bandwidth). On a p-processor hypercube, a one-to-all broadcast of an m-word message can be performed in time $(t_s + t_w m) \log p$, and an all-to-all broadcast in time $t_s \log p + t_w mp$ [5].

A Parallel Formulation Based on Neuron Partitioning

Probably the simplest way of parallelising the RTRL algorithm is to partition the neurons uniformly among the p processors so that each processor receives n/p neurons. The processors are also assigned the incoming weights and derivatives associated with the neurons that reside in them. Specifically, weights w_{i*} and derivatives π_{i*}^* are assigned to the same processor as neuron i. Each processor computes the activations, derivatives, and weight changes for its partition of neurons at each time step. To compute new activations using Equation (1), each processor needs the activations of all neurons. Thus, an all-to-all broadcast, in which each processor sends its n/p activations to all other processors, must be performed. To compute new derivatives using Equation (2), each processor needs the weights, $f'(u)$ values, and activations, of all neurons. Hence, three more all-to-all broadcasts are needed, one with messages of size n^2/p, and two with messages of size n/p. To compute the weight changes using Equation (3), each processor needs the error values of all neurons. So, one final all-to-all broadcast with messages of size n/p is required. When p is large, each processor spends approximately $t_c n^4/p$ time in computation. So, ignoring lower-order terms, the parallel execution time for a single iteration of this algorithm is

$$T_P \approx t_c \frac{n^4}{p} + 5t_s \log p + t_w n^2 \qquad (5)$$

A Parallel Formulation Based on Weight Partitioning

The second parallel formulation uses a well-known embedding of a $\sqrt{p} \times \sqrt{p}$ grid of processors in a $p = 2^{2k}$ processor hypercube [6]. The processors in each row and column of the grid form a $2^k = \sqrt{p}$ processor hypercube. Also, the communication subnetworks corresponding to the different rows and columns are disjoint. The $n \times n$ weight matrix is partitioned over the $\sqrt{p} \times \sqrt{p}$ grid such that each processor receives a $n/\sqrt{p} \times n/\sqrt{p}$ block of the matrix (Figure 1(a)). The n neurons are distributed along the diagonal of the grid so that each processor receives $n/\sqrt{p}$ neurons. The processors are also assigned the derivatives associated with the weights that reside in them. Specifically, derivatives π_{ij}^* are assigned to the same processor as weight w_{ij}.

To compute new activation values, the activations are first aligned with the incoming weights of each neuron using columnwise one-to-all broadcasts (Figure 1(b)). Each row of processors then collectively computes the new activations for $n/\sqrt{p}$ neurons by performing the required multiplications, and summing up the result at the respective diagonal processors using rowwise single-node accumulations (Figure 1(c)). To compute new derivatives, each processor needs the weights and $f'(u)$ values of all neurons; each processor also needs the activations of neurons contained in the diagonal element of the same column. The weights are redistributed using an all-to-all broadcast with messages of size n^2/p. The $f'(u)$ values are redistributed using a two-step procedure: first, each diagonal processor broadcasts its $n/\sqrt{p}$ $f'(u)$ values to the other processors in the same column; then each processor broadcasts the $n/\sqrt{p}$ values received during the first step to all the other processors in the same row. The activations are redistributed using columnwise one-to-all broadcasts. To compute the weight changes, each processor needs the errors of all neurons. As these errors are distributed among the diagonal processors, the same two-step broadcast procedure that was used to distribute the $f'(u)$ values in the derivative computations, can be used here as well. When p is large, each processor spends approximately $t_c n^4/p$ time in computation. So, ignoring lower-order terms, the parallel execution time for a single iteration of this algorithm is

$$T_P \approx t_c \frac{n^4}{p} + \frac{9}{2} t_s \log p + t_w n^2 \qquad (6)$$

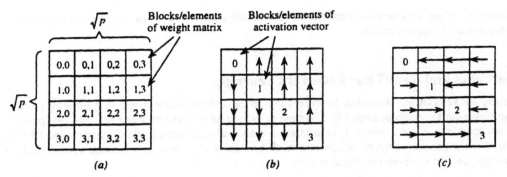

Figure 1. *Distribution and movement of data in the weight-partitioned formulation ($p = 16$).*

A Parallel Formulation Based on Derivative Partitioning

The third parallel formulation uses an embedding of a $q \times q \times q$ grid of processors in a $p = q^3 = 2^{3\lambda}$ processor hypercube [6]. The rows of processors that lie in each dimension of the grid form $2^\lambda = q$ processor hypercubes. The $n \times n \times n$ array of derivatives is partitioned over the $q \times q \times q$ grid such that each processor receives a $n/q \times n/q \times n/q$ block of derivatives (Figure 2(a)). The $n \times n$ weight matrix is partitioned over the topmost plane of processors so that each processor receives a block of size $n/q \times n/q$ (Figure 3(a)). The n neurons are partitioned among the q processors that lie on the diagonal of the topmost plane so that each processor receives n/q neurons (Figure 4(a)).

The new activation values are computed at each time step using the same procedure that was used in the weight-partitioned formulation; only this time, the computation takes place on the topmost plane of processors. Each processor computes new values for its partition of derivatives at each time step. In order to compute a new value for the derivative π_{ij}^k, it is necessary to have derivatives π_{ij}^*, weights $w_{k\bullet}$, activation value y_j, and value $f'(u_k)$. Hence, all processors require all of the derivatives in their respective vertical columns of processors. Each processor in plane $k = i$ requires all of the weights in the ith row of processors·in the topmost plane, and all of the $f'(u)$ values in the diagonal processor of the ith row in the topmost plane. Each processor in plane j requires all of the activation values in the diagonal processor of the jth column in the topmost plane.

The derivatives are redistributed using an all-to-all broadcast along the k axis with messages of size n^3/q^3 (Figures 2(a) and 2(b)). The redistribution of the weights is performed in three steps. First, each row of blocks is moved to a different plane such that the ith row of blocks occupies the same position in plane $k = i$ as it did initially in the topmost plane $k = 0$ (Figure 3(a)). Now each row of blocks is replicated across every row of processors in the kth plane using concurrent one-to-all broadcasts along the i axis (Figure 3(b)). At this point, the kth row of blocks is distributed across every row in the kth plane of processors. The final step involves performing an all-to-all broadcast along the j axis so that each processor in the kth plane ends up with the entire kth row of blocks (Figures 3(c) and 3(d)). The redistribution of the activations is accomplished using concurrent one-to-all broadcasts in the planes perpendicular to the j axis (Figures 4(a) and 4(b)). The redistribution of the $f'(u)$ values is accomplished in two stages. First, each block of vector elements is moved to a different plane such that the ith block occupies the same position in plane $k = i$ as it did initially in the topmost plane (Figure 5(a)). The second step involves performing concurrent one-to-all broadcast in the planes perpendicular to the k axis (Figures 5(b) and 5(c)).

In order to compute the weight changes, the error values are first redistributed using the same communication operation that was used to redistribute the $f'(u)$ values in the derivative computations. Each vertical column of processors then collectively computes the weight changes for n^2/q^2 weights by performing the required multiplications, and summing up the result at the respective topmost processors using single-node accumulations along the k axis. When p is large, each processor spends approximately $t_c \, n^4/p$ time in computation. So, ignoring lower-order terms, the parallel execution time for a single iteration of this algorithm is

$$T_P \approx t_c \frac{n^4}{p} + 4t_s \log p + t_w \left(\frac{n^3}{p^{2/3}} + \frac{n^2}{p^{1/3}} \right) \tag{7}$$

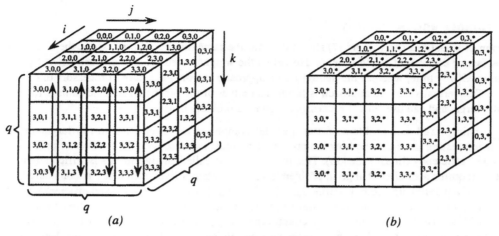

Figure 2. *Redistribution of the derivatives in the derivative-partitioned formulation (p = 64).*

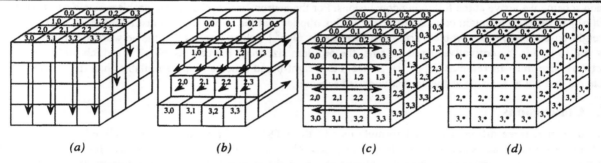

Figure 3. *Redistribution of the weights in the derivative-partitioned formulation (p = 64).*

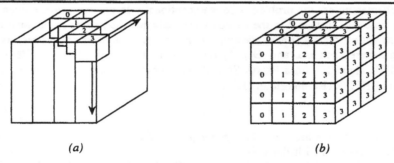

Figure 4. *Redistribution of the activation values in the derivative-partitioned formulation (p = 64).*

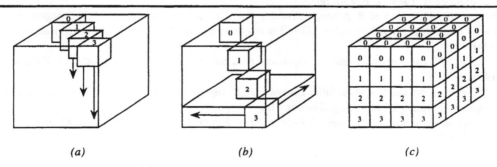

Figure 5. *Redistribution of the f′(u) values in the derivative-partitioned formulation (p = 64).*

4. Performance and Scalability

A comparison of Equations (5), (6) and (7) shows that, for the same number of processors, the neuron-based scheme is almost as fast as the weight-based scheme. However, the weight-based scheme can use $\Theta(n^2)$ processors to run the problem in $\Theta(n^2)$ time, whereas the neuron-based approach can only use $\Theta(n)$ processors to run the problem in $\Theta(n^3)$ time. The derivative-based approach is faster than either of the other two schemes unless the problem size is exceptionally large, and can use $\Theta(n^3)$ processors to run the problem in $\Theta(n)$ time.

As well as running fixed-size problems faster, parallel computers are often used to run larger problems. In this situation it is interesting to determine how the problem size must increase with the number of processors in order to maintain a fixed efficiency (linear speedup). This function of p is called an algorithm's isoefficiency function [5]. An algorithm that requires a smaller change in problem size to maintain a fixed efficiency is considered more scalable. The efficiency of a parallel algorithm is defined as $E = T_S/pT_P$. So, to maintain a fixed efficiency we must increase the problem size in such a way that the serial execution time T_S increases in proportion to the processor-time product pT_P. Note also, that the degree of concurrency imposes a lower bound on the isoefficiency function because, if it is exceeded, some of the processors will be idle and the efficiency will drop. Balancing the various terms of the processor-time product against the serial execution time and considering the degree of concurrency of each scheme we arrive at the following conclusions. For the neuron-based scheme, the problem size must increase as $\Theta(p^4)$ in order to maintain constant efficiency. This implies that the network size must increase as $\Theta(p)$. For the weight-based scheme, the problem size must increase as $\Theta(p^2)$ (which implies that the network size must increase as $\Theta(\sqrt{p})$); for the derivative-based scheme, the problem size must increase as $\Theta(p^{4/3})$ (which implies that the network size must increase as $\Theta(p^{1/3})$). Hence, the weight-based scheme is more scalable than the neuron-based scheme, but not as scalable as the derivative-based scheme.

5. Conclusions

In this paper, three different parallel formulations of the RTRL algorithm have been presented: a neuron-based scheme, a weight-based scheme, and a derivative-based scheme. Theoretical results show that, for the same number of processors, the neuron-based scheme is almost as fast as the weight-based scheme. However, the weight-based scheme can use more processors to run the same-sized problem faster. The derivative-based scheme is faster than either of the other schemes unless the problem size is exceptionally large, and can use even more processors to reduce the execution time still further. For the neuron-based scheme, the network size must increase as $\Theta(p)$ in order to maintain constant efficiency (linear speedup) with increasing numbers of processors. This is reduced to $\Theta(\sqrt{p})$ for the weight-based scheme, and $\Theta(p^{1/3})$ for the derivative-based scheme. We are in the process of implementing the RTRL algorithm on a Parsys SN9500 multicomputer and have plans to implement a parallel formulation of a hybrid BPTT/RTRL algorithm [1].

References

1. Chauvin, Y. and D.E. Rumelhart, ed. *Backpropagation: Theory, Architectures, and Applications*. 1995, Lawrence Erlbaum Associates: Hillsdale, NJ.
2. Williams, R.J. and D. Zipser, *A Learning Algorithm for Continually Running Fully Recurrent Neural Networks*. Neural Computation, 1989. 1: p. 270-280.
3. Kumar, V., S. Shekhar, and M.B. Amin, *A Scalable Parallel Formulation of the Backpropagation Algorithm for Hypercubes and Related Architectures*. IEEE Transactions on Parallel and Distributed Systems, 1994. 5(10): p. 1073-1090.
4. Zhang, X., et al., *The backpropagation algorithm on grid and hypercube architectures*. Parallel Computing, 1990. 14: p. 317-327.
5. Kumar, V., et al., *Introduction to Parallel Computing: Design and Analysis of Algorithms*. 1994, Redwood City, CA: Benjamin/Cummings Publishing Company Inc.
6. Saad, Y. and M.H. Schultz, *Topological Properties of Hypercubes*. IEEE Transactions on Computers, 1988. 37(7): p. 867-872.

Derivation of a Convex Hull Energy Function

J. Willey[1], M. Zaghloul[2], H. Szu[3], R. Walinchus[4]

Abstract

This paper presents the derivation of a convex hull energy function. Minimization of the energy function reduces probability of error in feedforward neural networks (NNs).

1 Background

In an earlier paper the authors showed that convex topology is a useful conceptual tool to predict and understand the performance of feedforward NNs [1]. The output coding of each neuron in each layer determines the constraints on the class-specific convex hulls in the afferent sampled space. Learning is accomplished by maximizing the separation of the convex hulls. Cauchy simulated annealing was employed to minimize an energy function incorporating the topological constraints. This paper derives a variant of the convex hull energy function presented in the earlier work. The derivation presented here will prove that the energy function has the following properties: one, $E < 0$ when the convex hulls are disjoint; and two, $E = 0$ when the hulls are non-disjoint.

2 Introduction

The following notation will be used throughout the discussion below:

$E^2 \equiv$ the Euclidean space of dimension 2
$A \equiv \{a_1, a_2\}$ the set of two points in E^2
$\overline{a_1 b_1} \equiv$ the line segment connecting a_1 to b_1
$\triangle a_1 b_1 a_2 \equiv$ the closed triangle a_1, b_1, a_2
$d(a_1, a_2) \equiv$ a measure of the distance between a_1 and a_2, units of length
$d(\triangle a_1 b_1 a_2) \equiv d(a_1, b_1) + d(b_1, a_2) + d(a_2, a_1)$, a measure of the boundary of $\triangle a_1 b_1 a_2$, units of length

[1]Code 5344, NRL, Washington, DC 20375
[2]EECS Dept, George Washington University, Washington, DC 20052
[3]Code B44, NSWCDD, 10901 New Hampshire Ave, Silver Spring, Md 20903
[4]PMA2133, Naval Air Systems Command, Arlington, VA 22243

$C\{A\} \equiv$ the convex hull [2] of A

$S_{\{A\}} \equiv$ a measure of the boundary of $C\{A\} = 2\,d(a_1, a_2)$

Before beginning the derivation, consider why an energy function representing convex hull separability is of interest. The probability of error of a feedforward NN is a function of topological constraints at each layer-space of the NN. The output layer is coded by class. For zero error, each neuron with a distinct class output coding must sample a space in which class-specific convex hulls must be separated. The authors' earlier paper showed that if the hulls in the afferent space are not separable the network will have finite error. For two classes A and B, the nth neuron, whose output coding is distinct, will have error proportional to:

$$P_n(E) \propto P(A) \int_{C\{A\} \cap C\{B\}} p_y(y \mid A)dy + P(B) \int_{C\{A\} \cap C\{B\}} p_y(y \mid B)dy \quad (1)$$

where $P(A)$ is the probability of class A, $p_y(y \mid A)$ is the conditional probability density function of class A, and $C\{A\}$ is measured in the afferent space of the neuron. Hence, an energy function that measures class-specific convex hull separation may be exploited to minimize the probability of error.

3   Derivation of a Convex Hull Energy Function

Consider E^2, containing two classes of sample points, A and B, with two points per class. To show that:

$$E = S_{\{A \cup B\}} - \left[\sum_{i=1}^{2} S_{\{A \cup b_i\}} - S_{\{A\}} \right] \quad (2)$$

has the property of $E = 0$ if the hulls are non-disjoint, and $E < 0$ if the hulls are disjoint, the proof examines six cases of jointedness between $C\{A\}$, $C\{B\}$, and $C\{A \cup B\}$. All other combinations are specializations of these six cases.

Case 1.   Let the hulls be disjoint, $C\{A\} \cap C\{B\} = \emptyset$, and none of A or B are interior to $C\{A \cup B\}$, see figure 1. Prove that $E < 0$.

Proof.   From inspection of figure 1 and the triangle inequality, one has:

$$2\,d(a_1, a_2) < d(\triangle\, a_1 c a_2)$$

$$2\,d(b_1, b_2) < d(\triangle\, b_1 c b_2)$$

or

$$2\,[d(a_1, a_2) + d(b_1, b_2)] < d(\triangle\, a_1 c a_2) + d(\triangle\, b_1 c b_2) \quad (3)$$

adding $d(\triangle\, a_1 c a_2) + d(\triangle\, b_1 c b_2)$ to both sides of (3) and simplifying one has:

$$d(\triangle\, a_1 c a_2) + d(\triangle\, b_1 c b_2) < 2\left[d(a_1,c) + d(a_2,c) + d(b_1,c) + d(b_2,c)\right]$$

or

$$d(a_1,a_2) + d(b_1,b_2) < d(a_1,b_2) + d(a_2,b_1)$$

hence:

$$d(a_1,a_2) + d(b_1,b_2) - d(a_1,b_2) - d(a_2,b_1) < 0 \qquad (4)$$

Adding the quantity $d(a_1,b_1) - d(a_1,b_1) + d(a_2,b_2) - d(a_2,b_2) + 2\left[d(a_1,b_1) - d(a_1,b_1)\right] = 0$ to (4) and rearranging terms one has:

$$
\begin{aligned}
E \;=\;\; & d(a_1,a_2) + d(a_1,b_1) + d(b_1,b_2) + d(a_2,b_2) - \\
& \left[d(\triangle\, a_1 b_1 a_2) + d(\triangle\, a_1 b_2 a_2) - 2\,d(a_1,a_2)\right] < 0
\end{aligned}
\qquad (5)
$$

but:

$$S_{\{A\cup B\}} = d(a_1,a_2) + d(a_1,b_1) + d(b_1,b_2) + d(a_2,b_2)$$

$$\sum_{i=1}^{2} S_{\{A\cup b_i\}} = d(\triangle\, a_1 b_1 a_2) + d(\triangle\, a_1 b_2 a_2)$$

hence (5) becomes:

$$E = S_{\{A\cup B\}} - \left[\sum_{i=1}^{2} S_{\{A\cup b_i\}} - S_{\{A\}}\right] < 0 \qquad (6)$$

Q.E.D.

Remark. By inspection:

$$\sum_{i=1}^{2} S_{\{A\cup b_i\}} - S_{\{A\}} = \sum_{i=1}^{2} S_{\{B\cup a_i\}} - S_{\{B\}} \qquad (7)$$

thus (6) is symmetric with respect to the labels A and B.

Case 2. Let the hulls be disjoint, $C\{A\}\cap C\{B\} = \emptyset$, and let one of the points from A or B be interior to $C\{A\cup B\}$, see figure 2. Prove that $E < 0$.

Proof. From inspection of figure 2 and the triangle inequality, one has:

$$2\,d(a_1,a_2) < d(\triangle\, a_1 b_1 a_2)$$

adding $d(\triangle\, a_1 b_2 a_2)$ to both sides and simplifying:

$$d(\triangle\, a_1 b_2 a_2) - \left[d(\triangle\, a_1 b_1 a_2) + d(\triangle\, a_1 b_2 a_2) - 2\,d(a_1,a_2)\right] < 0 \qquad (8)$$

but:

$$S_{\{A \cup B\}} = d(\triangle\, a_1 b_2 a_2)$$

$$\sum_{i=1}^{2} S_{\{A \cup b_i\}} = d(\triangle\, a_1 b_1 a_2) + d(\triangle\, a_2 b_2 a_2)$$

hence (8) becomes:

$$E = S_{\{A \cup B\}} - \left[\sum_{i=1}^{2} S_{\{A \cup b_i\}} - S_{\{A\}} \right] < 0 \qquad (9)$$

Q.E.D.

Case 3. Let the hulls be non-disjoint, $C\{A\} \cap C\{B\} = \alpha$, where $\alpha \in \{a_1, a_2, b_1, b_2\}$, see figure 3. Prove that $E = 0$.

Proof. From inspection of figure 3:

$$d(\triangle\, a_1 b_1 a_2) = 2\, d(a_1, a_2) = S_{\{A \cup b_1\}} = S_{\{A\}}$$

$$S_{\{A \cup B\}} = S_{\{A \cup b_2\}}$$

hence:

$$S_{\{A \cup B\}} - S_{\{A \cup b_2\}} - S_{\{A \cup b_1\}} + S_{\{A\}} = 0$$

or:

$$E = S_{\{A \cup B\}} - \left[\sum_{i=1}^{2} S_{\{A \cup b_i\}} - S_{\{A\}} \right] = 0 \qquad (10)$$

Q.E.D.

Case 4. Let the hulls be non-disjoint at a single point, $C\{A\} \cap C\{B\} = \alpha$, where $\alpha \notin \{a_1, a_2, b_1, b_2\}$, see figure 4. Prove that $E = 0$.

Proof. From inspection of figure 4 one has:

$$S_{\{A \cup B\}} = d(\triangle\, a_1 b_2 a_2) - d(a_1, a_2) + d(\triangle\, a_1 a_2 b_1) - d(a_1, a_2)$$

or

$$S_{\{A \cup B\}} - [d(\triangle\, a_1 b_2 a_2) + d(\triangle\, a_1 a_2 b_1) - 2\, d(a_1, a_2)] = 0 \qquad (11)$$

but

$$\sum_{i=1}^{2} S_{\{A \cup b_i\}} = d(\triangle\, a_1 b_2 a_2) + d(\triangle\, a_1 a_2 b_1)$$

hence (11) becomes:

$$E = S_{\{A \cup B\}} - \left[\sum_{i=1}^{2} S_{\{A \cup b_i\}} - S_{\{A\}} \right] = 0 \qquad (12)$$

Case 5. Let the hulls share a common line segment $C\{A\} \cap C\{B\} = \overline{a_j b_k}$, see figure 5. Prove that $E = 0$.

Proof. If $\overline{a_j b_k}$ is the common line segment then:

$$S_{\{A \cup B\}} = 2\, d(a_m, b_n)$$

where

$$m = \left\{ \begin{array}{ll} 2 & j = 1 \\ 1 & j = 2 \end{array} \right. \qquad n = \left\{ \begin{array}{ll} 2 & k = 1 \\ 1 & k = 2 \end{array} \right.$$

then:

$$2d(a_m, b_n) = 2d(a_1, a_2) + 2d(b_1, b_2) - 2d(a_j, b_k)$$

rearranging and simplifying:

$$2d(a_m, b_n) - [2d(a_1, a_2) + 2d(b_1, b_2) - 2d(a_j, b_k)] = 0$$

$$2d(a_m, b_n) - [2d(a_1, a_2) + 2d(a_m, b_n) - 2d(a_1, a_2)] = 0 \qquad (13)$$

but

$$\sum_{i=1}^{2} S_{\{A \cup b_i\}} = 2d(a_1, a_2) + 2d(a_m, b_n)$$

hence (13) becomes:

$$E = S_{\{A \cup B\}} - \left[\sum_{i=1}^{2} S_{\{A \cup b_i\}} - S_{\{A\}} \right] = 0 \qquad (14)$$

Q.E.D.

Case 6. Let the hull of one sample set lie on the boundary of the second set $C\{A\} \cap C\{B\} = C\{B\}$ see figure 6. Prove that $E = 0$.

Proof. If $C\{A\} \cap C\{B\} = C\{B\}$ then, by inspection,

$$S_{\{A \cup B\}} = S_{\{A \cup b_1\}} = S_{\{A \cup b_2\}} = S_{\{A\}}$$

hence:

$$E = S_{\{A \cup B\}} - \left[\sum_{i=1}^{2} S_{\{A \cup b_i\}} - S_{\{A\}} \right] = 0 \qquad (15)$$

Q.E.D.

Remark. By inspection (7) holds for cases 2-6, thus (9), (10), (12), (14), and (15) are all symmetric with respect to the labels A and B.

4 Minima in the Energy Function

To minimize the energy function independent of the selection of class labels, consider:

$$E = S_{\{A \cup B\}} - \left[\sum_{i=1}^{2} S_{\{A \cup b_i\}} - S_{\{A\}} \right] = S_{\{B \cup A\}} - \left[\sum_{i=1}^{2} S_{\{B \cup a_i\}} - S_{\{B\}} \right] \quad (16)$$

By inspection, minimization of $S_{\{A\}}$ and $S_{\{B\}}$ will lower E. In the limit, the intraclass samples occupy infinitesimal volumes, $S_{\{A\}} \to 0$ and $S_{\{B\}} \to 0$, whence:

$$E \cong S_{\{A \cup B\}} - \left[\sum_{i=1}^{2} S_{\{A \cup b_i\}} \right] \quad (17)$$

$S_{\{A\}} \to 0$ and $S_{\{B\}} \to 0$ imply:

$$\sum_{i=1}^{2} S_{\{A \cup b_i\}} \cong 2\, S_{\{A \cup B\}} \quad (18)$$

thus (17) becomes:

$$E \cong -\frac{1}{2} \left[\sum_{i=1}^{2} S_{\{A \cup b_i\}} \right] \quad (19)$$

which is minimized by maximizing the distances between interclass samples. Hence a necessary condition for the minima of E is a distribution of class-specific convex hulls that follow the *mini-max* rule.

5 Conclusion

The energy function given by (2) captures the essence of separability between two class-specific convex hulls for two samples per class in E^2. The energy function has the property $E < 0$ when the convex hulls are disjoint, and $E = 0$ when the hulls are non-disjoint. The energy function is symmetric with respect to class labels. An examination of the minima of (2) showed that a necessary condition for the minima of E is a distribution of convex hulls that follows the *mini-max* rule. The generalization of an efficient energy function in E^n [3-6] remains a research opportunity.

6 Acknowledgement

This research grew out of a problem related to automatic target recognition supported in part by one of the authors; Dr. R. Walinchus. His co-authors gratefully acknowledge his encouragement.

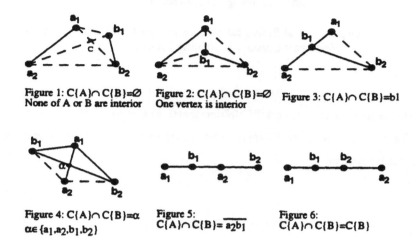

Figure 1: C{A}∩C{B}=∅
None of A or B are interior

Figure 2: C{A}∩C{B}=∅
One vertex is interior

Figure 3: C{A}∩C{B}=b1

Figure 4: C{A}∩C{B}=α
α∈ {a₁,a₂,b₁,b₂}

Figure 5:
C{A}∩C{B}= $\overline{a_2b_1}$

Figure 6:
C{A}∩C{B}=C{B}

7 References

1. J. Willey, H. Szu, and M. Zaghloul. "Generalization and learning by convex topology". *Proceedings of the IJCNN'92*. Vol II, pp 395-401, Beijing, China, Nov 3-6, 1992.

2. J. van Tiel. *Convex analysis, an introductory text.* John Wiley & Sons, New York, 1984.

3. F. P. Freparata, and M. I. Shamos. *Computational geometry, an introduction.* Springer-Verlag, New York, 1985.

4. N. K. Sancheti, and S. S. Keerthi. "Computation of certain measures of proximity between convex polytopes: a complexity viewpoint." *Proceedings of the 1992 IEEE International Conference on Robotics and Automation* (Cat. No. 92CH3140-1), Vol III, pp 2508-13, May 12-14, 1992.

5. B. Chazelle. "An optimal algorithm for intersecting three-dimensional convex polyhedra". *30th Annual Symposium on Foundations of Computer Science* (Cat. No. 89CH2808-4), pp 586-91. IEEE Comput. Soc. Press, Oct 30-Nov 1, 1989.

6. Kallay, M. "Convex hull algorithms in higher dimensions," *unpublished manuscript,* Dept of Mathematics, University of Oklahoma, Norman, Oklahoma, 1981.

Fractal Cellular Neural Network for Associative Memory

Junsheng Wang, Qiang Gan, and Yu Wei

Department of Biological Science and Medical Engineering,
Southeast University, Nanjing 210096, P. R. China

Abstract: Fractal cellular neural network(FCNN) presented in this paper can retrieve stored patterns with noisy inputs. The performance of the FCNN is better than the fractal neural network(FNN) proposed by Y. Baram for associative memory.

1. Introduction

Fractal neural network(FNN) for associative memory was proposed by Y. Baram in 1989[1]. The behavior of FNN is better than that of a fully connected network of the Hopfield type. The FNN consists of small subnetworks interconnected in a layered hierarchy. Information is stored in the form of subpatterns and retrieved in the form of their permutations. Cellular neural network(CNN) for associative memory was proposed by D. Liu et al. in 1993[2]. In this paper, we present a fractal cellular neural network(FCNN) and apply it to associative memory.

A CNN can be defined by the following equations:

$$\frac{dx_{ij}}{dt} = -x_{ij} + \sum_{kl \in Nr(ij)} A(ij; kl) * f(x_{kl}) + I \tag{1}$$

where $i = 0, 1, ..., N-1; j = 0, 1, ..., M-1$. $N*M$ is the number of neurons in the CNN, A and I are called cloning templates,

$$f(x_{ij}) = \frac{1}{2}(|x_{ij}+1| - |x_{ij}-1|) \tag{2}$$

and Nr(ij) is a r-neighborhood of neuron (ij), defined by

$$Nr(ij) = \{kl: \max(|k-i|, |l-j|) \le r, \quad r \text{ is an integer}\} \tag{3}$$

2. FCNN for Associative Memory

The network structure of FCNN is similar to that of FNN described by Y. Baram except for the connection form of neurons. Neurons are fully connected in each subnetwork of FNN, but connected by the neighborhood rule of CNN in each layer of FCNN. Fig.1(a) shows a network consisting of four layers of subnetworks. Neurons in the first, the second, the third and the forth layers of subnetworks are connected by r-neighborhood, 2r-neighborhood, 4r-neighborhood and 8r-neighborhood respectively, as shown in Fig.1(b), (c), (d) and (e) respectively. Any neuron can belong to one layer or at most two layers.

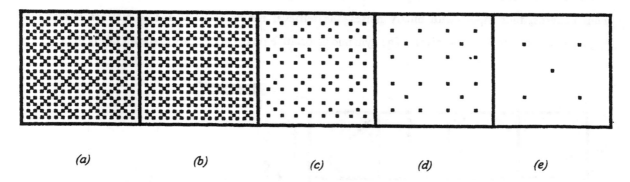

(a)   (b)   (c)   (d)   (e)

Fig.1 The structure of FCNN: (a) the whole network; (b) the first layer; (c) the second layer; (d) the third layer; (e) the forth layer.

The FCNN can withstand extensive damage because of the high degree of self-similarity. Moreover, damaged neurons or subnetworks can be repaired or recreated locally without recreating or rewiring the whole network, which stands in contrast to CNN.

In FCNN, information is stored in the form of subpatterns in each layer of subnetworks. According to the design procedure given in [2], the cloning templates in each layer can be obtained respectively. The cloning template in FCNN is the summation of those in each layer. It is clear that the neighborhood in FCNN is not defined by (3). It has a special neighborhood structure.

A FCNN can be described by

$$\frac{dx_{ij}}{dt} = -x_{ij} + \sum_{s=p}^{p+S_{ij}} \sum_{kl \in N_{r'}(ij)} A(ij; kl) * f(x_{kl}) + I \tag{4}$$

where, if the neuron (ij) belongs to a layer only, p denotes the number of the layer where the neuron (ij) is located. And if the neuron (ij) belongs to two layers, p denotes the number of the lower layer of the two layers.

$$S_{ij} = \begin{cases} 0, & \text{if the neuron (ij) is in the first or the highest layer only} \\ 1, & \text{otherwise} \end{cases} \tag{5}$$

and

$$Nr'(ij) = \left\{ kl: \max(|k-i|,|l-j|) \leq r', \quad r' = r * 2^{s-1}, \text{ neurons (ij) and (kl) belong to the s-th layer} \right\}$$

3. Simulation Experiments and Discussions

For the convenience of comparing with FNN, we choose the same patterns and inputs as those in [1]. Four patterns, four inputs with binary noises, the retrieval results of FNN and FCNN are shown in Fig.2(a), (b), (c) and (d) respectively. The dynamic associative process of FCNN is shown in Fig.3.

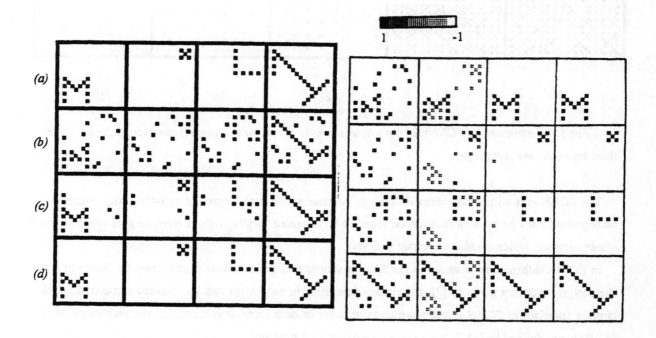

Fig.2 The retrieval results of FNN and of FCNN response to the inputs with binary noises, (a) four patterns, (b) noisy inputs, (c) results of FNN, (d) results of FCNN.

Fig.3 The dynamic associative process of in FCNN.

In another experiment, ten patterns(printed characters A-J), and two inputs(characters A and J) are used, the associative results of FNN and FCNN are obtained, as shown in Fig.4(a), (b), (c) and (d) respectively.

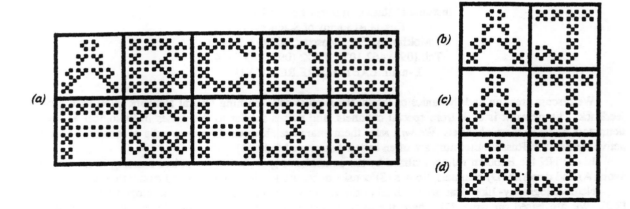

Fig.4 The associative results of FNN and FCNN in response to inputs(A and J), (a) patterns(A-J), (b) inputs(A and J), (c) results of FNN, (d) results of FCNN.

From the above results, it can be seen that the behavior of FCNN for associative memory is better than that of FNN.

REFERENCES

[1] Y. Baram, IEEE Trans. on Systems. Man, and Cybernetics, Vol.19, No.5, 1989, pp.1133-1141.

[2] D. Liu. and A. N. Michel, IEEE Trans. on Circuits and Systems, Vol.40, No2, 1993, pp.119-121.

TIME- PULSE NEURAL NETWORK OF THE AUTOWAVE TYPE.

Yu.I. Balkarey, A.S. Cohen, M.I. Elinson, M.G. Evtikhov, Yu.N.Orlov.

Institute of Radio Engineering and Electronics,
Russia Academy of Sciences,
11 Mokhovaya Str., Moscow, 103907, Russia
Tel: (095) 462 1031; FAX: (095) 203 8414
E-mail: LAB191@IRE.RC.AC.RU

We discuss creation and dynamics of digital time- pulse self- learning Neural Network (NN) with global feedback. The network is built from special channels. and pulses similar to the pulses in biological axons or neuristors move in these channels. We will refer them autowave channels, because media of locally connected active elements in Russian literature are often called Autowave Media [1].

In our NN the Hebbian rule is realized by the coincidence gate during the pulses meeting in the crossed axon (A) and dendrite (D) channels. Somas (S) consist of counters, where the temporal summation is provided.

Neuroholography- like ideas are realized in the network. Such ideas have been developed for a long time [2,3]. We are based on work [3] where the analogy between such a holography in many layer media of autowave channels and optical holography is discussed in detail. Time- pulse correlations during the meeting of different layers' pulses play a role of phase correlations in optics. Not only the position of pulsed neuron but the frequency of its spikes are very important for output information analysis.

In numerical experiments we demonstrate the stationary synaptic matrix forming and associative properties of the network.

All circuits of the proposed NN were designed on the base of digital technology. The digital system has many useful properties. It has a simple homogeneous structure, which is fully compatible with modern microelectronic technology, and can be constructed from the standard elements (waiting generators, triggers, counters, etc.). It is possible to vary the inhibitory and excitatory processes in the network. There are new parameters- pulse velocities in axon and dendrite channels, pulse counting regimes, etc.- which are important for network dynamics. Depending on technology the number of neurons can vary from hundreds to thousands.

ARCHITECTURE OF THE NEURAL NETWORK

As a prototype we use the architecture of analog Kohonen NN [4]. The realization of such a network is rather difficult due to complication of synaptic circuits.

Network functioning is based on interaction between pulses which move along the D and A channels with finite velocities. Meetings of these pulses in the certain moments and certain places are the main physical mechanism which realizes the Hebbian rule. Synaptic weights can be binary (0,1) or integer. So the time- pulse correlations are important in our network.

The network architecture is shown in Fig.1. The autowave channels are marked by the solid lines, electric connections (where the pulse velocity is supposed infinite) are marked by the thin lines.

Information I feeds periodically the system of autowave channels IC and is transformed into the system of pulses. Every IC channel is connected with corresponding group of the main dendrite DA channels (multiplication of the input) which are used for somas excitation. The pulse velocity in DA channels is V_{DA}.

The important point is the existence of channels DI with the pulse velocity V_{DI}. DI channel is similar to the DA channel, but DI does not connected with input elements and transmits the inhibitory influence on soma. So DA and DI channels act on soma in different ways, and we can vary excitation and inhibition in broad interval.

Outputs of neurons OUT are connected with autowave channels A (V_A is the pulse velocity in A channels) which realize the feedback. These channels interact with DA channels and memory circuits M.

The autowave channels are realized on the base of the well- known waited generators. All elements are based on "AND-NO" gates.

In fact, the whole NN matrix is built from cells CM (Fig.2), and every cell has elements of channels of all types.

Let discuss the process of memorizing during the pulse meeting in channels DA and A. This event is fixed by logical AND- gate "&1". Output of "&1" turns the memory element M on. Output of M feeds AND-gate "&2". So the binary connection between DA and A is created.

For the memory cells the RS flip-flops is used.

Interaction with the memory M is realized by the following.

In the cell shown in Fig.2,a the pulse of A channel feeds "&2", and the output of "&2" feeds the

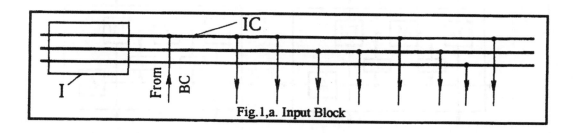

Fig.1,a. Input Block

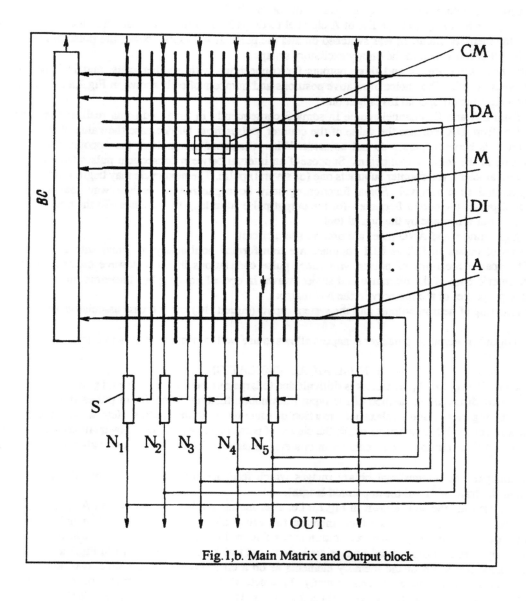

Fig.1,b. Main Matrix and Output block

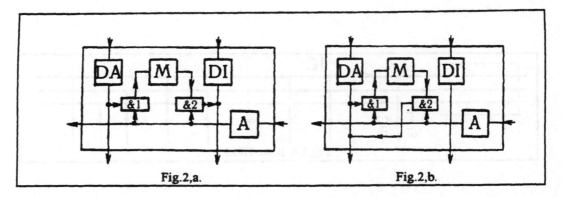

Fig.2,a. Fig.2,b.

inhibitorychannel DI. Hence if the memory circuit M was switched on and the pulse in A channel come, the pulse in DI arises. Therefore this cell is equivalent to the binary inhibitory synapce.

In the cell shown in Fig.2,b the pulse of A channel feeds "&2", and the output of "&2" feeds the channel DA. Hence if the memory circuit M was switched on and the pulse in A channel come, the pulse in DA arises. Therefore this cell is equivalent to the binary excitatory synapce.

All cells have three inputs and three outputs for connections with another cells, and NN matrix can contain both types of cells. The choice of relative positions and numbers of cells shown in Fig.2,a and 2,b is the problem which requires the special investigation.

Pulses from DA and DI channels come in soma S consequently in time and soma realizes the temporal counting. Pulses from DA increase the value of the counter, pulses from DI decrease the value of the counter. Of course, intervals between pulses do not coincide. When the soma accumulates the appointed quantity of pulses, activation in the soma output begins. Suppose if an interval between consequent pulses from DA larger then the time parameter t, the counter subtracts one (or several) pulse. The next cycle may begin immediately or after the appointed time interval. Soma functioning may be organized in such a way that at the fast accumulation of pulses the output frequency (or the output pulse train length) increases. So the neuron become quasi- analogous but it is made by the digital tools.

Waiting generators and AND gates are used in soma circuit.

The flows of pulses in DA and DI channels are transformed nonlinearly in somas into the flow in A channels. The spatial meetings of pulses with time- pulse correlations in the autowave channels form the analog of the interference of the reference and subject waves in optical holography. Therefore one can suppose the associative properties of the memory in the NN matrix.

The connecting of neuron outputs and the system inputs (circuit BC) can increase associative properties of NN [7].

Digital principle and integer synapces allows to use well known elements and circuits.

NUMERICAL SIMULATION

The choice of the optimal parameters is difficult due to large number of elements and parameters: types of cells CM and their distribution; method of the input information feeding; velocities of pulses in the channels; soma thresholds; regimes of soma relaxation; reaction of soma on inhibiting pulses. Here we demonstrate the simplest examples of the NN associative work; the choice of parameters was grounded by qualitative reasons.

As a time unit the minimal pulse delay τ in channel element is used, all other intervals are measured in the τ units.

1. We analyze one dimensional binary images which feed the channels DA (every "1" in the image transforms into the train of "1" of the appointed length).

Firstly we use only the cells shown in Fig.2,b i.e. after interaction between a pulse in A channel and the memory element M, the pulse arises which increase the value of the soma counter. Then only orthogonal images can be used and their associative restoration is possible by arbitrary (even one "1") image fragment.

2. For analysis of non-orthogonal images we have to use two kind of cells shown in Fig.2,a and 2,b. For simplicity we place two kinds of the memory elements as on a chess board. For example, two nonorthogonal images are written into the memory consequently. Parameters: delays in the elements of A, DA, and DI channels are τ, 3τ, and 2τ respectively; soma threshold is 4 pulses; soma relaxation time is 200τ; images feed the DA channels every 97τ. The stationary state is reached after $\sim 1000\ \tau$.

Number of neuron	1	2	3	4	5	6	7	8	9	10	11	12	13	14	15	16	17	18	19	20	21	22	23	24
Image 1	1	1	0	0	0	0	1	0	0	1	0	1	0	1	0	1	0	1	1	0	0	1	0	1
Image 2	1	0	0	1	1	1	0	1	0	0	0	1	1	.0.	0	0	1	1	0	0	0	1	0	1
Fragment of Image 1	1	1	0	0	0	0	1	0	0	1	0	1	0	1	0	0	0	0	0	1	0	0	0	0
Fragment of Image 2	1	0	1	1	1	1	0	1	0	0	0	1	0	0	0	0	0	0	0	0	0	0	0	0

Due to existence of inhibitory pulses we can restore nonorthogonal images by their fragments. Of course, these fragments have to be considerably larger then one element. For example the images 1 and 2 can be restored by arbitrary fragments of six units, and also by distorted fragments.

3. We also analyzed two dimensional images. The network of 64 neurons and images 8x8 were used. Every image is multiplied by the input block as discussed above and feeds DA channels. An input image line produced pulse trains in every 8th DA channel (1st line fed 1, 9, 17, etc., 2nd line fed 2, 10, 18, etc.). After stationary synaptic matrix forming only a few number of somas corresponding the certain image continue the work. We can call them the image code. This code can be restored by the image fragment and even by the distorted fragments.

Three nonorthogonal images

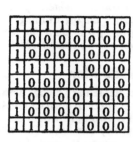

Image 1   Image 2   Image 3

are written into the memory consequently. Parameters: delays in the elements of A, DA, and DI channels are τ, 2τ, and τ respectively; soma threshold is 4 pulses; soma relaxation time is 65τ; an image feed the DA channels every 70τ. The stationary state is reached after $\sim 1000\ \tau$.

The code of the image 1 is 5, 12, 24, 29, 41, 51, 61; the code of the image 2 is 3, 22, 41, 43, 49, 58; the code of the image 3 is 1, 9, 12, 24, 49, 52, 56, 63.

Distorted Image 1 produces the same code as the initial image 1.

Varying the relative numbers of excitatory and inhibitory cells (Fig.2,a and Fig.2,b) it is possible to reduce or increase the code size. For detailed image processing it is also possible to take into consideration the frequencies of the code neurons pulsing.

Distorted Image 1

Thus the computer simulation demonstrates the stable stationary synaptic matrix forming and the associative properties of the memory in the time- pulse system with binary synapses.

CONCLUSION

We proposed and investigated numerically the new digital time- pulse neural network with global feedback. The basic elements of the network are one dimensional unidirected autowave channels.

The finite velocity of pulse propagation along the channels allows us to use the meetings of pulses in the crossed channels for synaptic matrix forming in accordance with Hebbian rule. The correlation between the excitatory and inhibitory properties of the system can be controlled.

The self- learning and associative properties of the memory are demonstrated.

This work was supported by the Russian Fund for Fundamental Researches (Grant 94-01-01538).

REFERENCES

1. V.A.Vasilev, Yu.M.Romanovskii, D.S.Chernavskii, V.G.Yakhno. Autowave Processes in Kinetic Systems. Berlin: VEB Deutsher Verlag. 1986.
2. P.R. Westlake. The Possibilities of Neural Holographic Processes within the Brain. Kybernetik, vol. 7, no. 4, pp. 129- 153, 1970.
3. Yu.I.Balkarey, M.G.Evtikhov, M.I.Elinson. Autowave Media and Neural Networks. Proceedings SPIE, vol. 1621, pp. 238- 249, 1991.
4. T.Cohonen. Self- Organization and Associative Memory. Springer, 1984.
5. A.A.Frolov. Structure and Functions of Learning Neural Networks. In: Neurocomputer as the Base of Computer Intelligence (A.A.Frolov, G.I.Shulgina, Eds.). Moscow, Nauka Publ., pp. 92- 110, 1993.

SOME STATISTICAL RESULTS FOR WINNER-TAKE-ALL NETWORKS WITH SPARSE RANDOM INNERVATION AND COACTIVITY-BASED LEARNING

Patrick Shoemaker

U.S. Naval Command, Control & Ocean Surveillance Center,
Research, Development, Test & Evaluation Division (551)
San Diego, CA 92152-6365
USA

Abstract

Some basic statistical features of the winner-take-all network with sparse random innervation are examined, and the effects of a simple coactivity-based learning rule discussed. The results are applicable to a range of neural network models employing sparse random connectivity, coactivity-based learning, and winner-take-all networks as part of their architectures. Results suggest constraints on network size and other parameters if a network is to participate in a clustering operation, as in the Granger, Lynch, and Ambros-Ingerson (GLA) model of early olfactory processing [1-5]. It is shown how learning can result in "pattern capture," and two mechanisms of capture are identified: capture by precedence, in which a pattern is captured from one cell by another by virtue of precedence in the order of pattern presentation during training, and capture by overtake, in which input to the capturing cell for the pattern to be captured grows faster than that for the original winner, by virtue of the growth of synaptic weights from input fibers also active on other patterns which elicit wins from the capturing cell.

1. Introduction

An elementary neural network which has been considered as a computational building block for more sophisticated networks in abstract and biological models [1-8], as well as in neuromorphic engineering [9,10], is the winner-take-all network, in which only one (or possibly a few) of the most strongly stimulated neurons in a group become active at any one time. The winner-take all characteristic is usually moderated by some global inhibitory feedback, often presumed to result from lateral inhibition in biological models. Several authors have dealt with the case in which the excitatory input to a winner-take-all network is from a relatively large input fiber tract that forms sparse random synapses onto cells in the network [1-5,7,8]. Of particular interest for the present work is a model of early olfactory processing due to Granger, Lynch, and Ambros-Ingerson (GLA), which deals with the interacting structures of the olfactory bulb and piriform cortex in small mammals such as rodents and lagomorphs [1-5]. Among its emergent computational properties is the ability to perform hierarchical clustering of input vectors, whose components represent activities of various classes of olfactory receptor cells. In this model, the olfactory bulb (which receives and processes signals from the receptors) projects output axons to the piriform cortex, where excitatory synapses are formed in a sparse, random fashion. The piriform cells are arranged in winner-take-all networks of relatively modest size (less than 100 cells), and their (sparse) pattern of activity represents the system output. The model learns according to an unsupervised learning rule modeled after the neurobiological phenomenon of long-term potentiation (see, for example, [6]). When enabled, learning involves coarse weight increments of synapses between coactive bulb and piriform cells. Weights saturate after continued updating, and they do not decay. It is by this learning rule that the model acquires the ability to cluster its inputs: the patterns of winning cells in the piriform winner-take-all networks become very similar or identical for a set or cluster of mitral input patterns which are sufficiently similar. The sparse interconnections, coarse weights and a number of the model's other features make it amenable to direct analog implementation (whether in a neurobiological or artificial [10] substrate), an advantage not shared by many of the artificial neural networks which have been studied in recent years.

This paper is concerned with basic properties of the winner-take-all input/output relation that derive from the assumption of sparse random innervation. Dynamics of the neurons and the mechanisms of the winner-take-all process are not considered; both input and output neurons are treated as two-state devices (either "active" or "inactive") and it is assumed that a single winning excitatory cell -- that with the largest input -- is resolved by the winner-take-all network. It is also assumed that many winner-take-all networks are involved in processing of signals supplied by the input fibers, and therefore the input-output mapping for a generic network is examined, for arbitrary (but relatively sparse) patterns of input fiber activation, using statistics which arise from the assumed sparse random nature of synaptic contact. In addition, the effects of a simple coacitvity-based, incremental learning rule like that employed in the GLA olfactory model are considered. Learning can be seen to result in "pattern capture," i.e., after learning has occurred, an excitatory winner-take-all cell may win in response to a pattern that would not elicit a win from the same cell in the naive network. This process is dependent on the difference (i.e., Hamming distance) between the pattern in question and patterns to which the network has been exposed during learning, as well as other details of the learning experience. Pattern capture is the fundamental mechanism by which the GLA model learns to cluster input data. In addition to the GLA model, the results derived are applicable to a range of neural networks employing sparse random connectivity, coactivity-based learning, and winner-take-all networks as part of their architectures, and to problems in which similarity between input patterns is a metric with informational value.

2. Statistics of the Naive Winner-Take-All Network with Sparse Random Innervation

The assumption of sparse random synaptic contact allows certain aspects of the input-output relation of the winner-take-all (WTA) network to be analyzed using order statistics for the random variable(s) characterizing occurrence of the synapses. Although the relevant random variables are discrete, asymptotic distributions (which are typically

Gaussian) may be used to characterize WTA behavior as the dimensionality of the input to the network becomes large. For reasons which will become apparent from the analysis, WTA networks with a limited number of excitatory cells (small "samples") but with a large input fiber tract (large "population") are considered.

To begin with, suppose that there are N input fibers running through the region of dendritic arborization of the excitatory cells in a WTA network, and that the presence of a synapse between a particular axon and dendrite is a random event with first-order probability p, typically taken to be on the order of 0.1. Let q represent the fraction of the total number N of the input fibers that are active for a given pattern of activity on the input fibers; q will generally be regarded as relatively small and constant across different input patterns, due to normalization or other constraints on the total activity of the cells in the structure which supplies input to the WTA networks.

2.1. The distribution of active synapses on a dendrite

When a particular pattern of input activity is applied, the number of synapses from *active* fibers onto a general WTA dendrite is a random variable, which will be called I. Knowing the interconnection probability p, input activation q, and the specific constraints on connectivity in principle allows the computation of the probability distribution $\mathbf{f}$ of I: $\mathbf{f}(i) = P[I = i]$. By way of example, if the synapses are made randomly with probability p and with no other constraints (tacitly assumed in the remainder of the paper), this probability is given by a binomial distribution: $\mathbf{f}(i) = \binom{qN}{i} p^i (1-p)^{qN-i}$. In the GLA olfactory model, the total number of synapses onto a dendrite is specified

to be a fixed number pN, leading to a hypergeometric distribution for I : $\mathbf{f}(i) = \binom{qN}{i}\binom{N-qN}{pN-i} \Big/ \binom{N}{pN}$. Associated

with $\mathbf{f}$ is the cumulative distribution $\mathbf{F}(i) = P[I < i] = \sum_{k=0}^{i-1} \mathbf{f}(k)$ for i > 0.

Both the binomial and hypergeometric distributions above are asymptotically Gaussian with mean pqN as N increases without limit. Let the new random variable X=I/(qN) characterize the fraction of the active input fibers which synapse onto the general dendrite. The form of the asymptotic probability distribution for X is

$$f(x) = \left(2\pi\sigma_x^2\right)^{-1/2} \exp\left(-(x-p)^2 / \left[2\sigma_x^2\right]\right). \qquad \text{(EQ 1)}$$

If f derives from a binomial distribution, the variance is $\sigma_x^2 = p(1-p)/(qN)$. As is typical for an asymptotic distribution, the variance tends to zero as 1/N with increasing N (regardless of the underlying discrete distribution). Treating f as a density, the asymptotic cumulative distribution F(x) = P[X<x], and the asymptotic expectation of an (F-integrable) function of X, may be written in integral form.

2.2. The distribution of active synapses on the dendrite of a winning cell in the naive network

Consider next the responses of the cells in a generic WTA network of n cells to a particular pattern of input fiber activation. The fractions of active inputs contacting these cells are n random variables with identical asymptotic distribution f. Their largest order statistic, which we shall denote $X^{(n)}$, is by definition is the function of the n variables which takes the value of the largest among them. This statistic is of particular significance because, in a naive network in which all the weights are at equal initial values, $qNX^{(n)}$ is identically the number of active synapses on the winning cell. The probability $P[X^{(n)} < x]$ (i.e., the cumulative distribution of $X^{(n)}$) is simply the probability that all n out of n cells are contacted by a fraction smaller than x of the active inputs: $P\left[X^{(n)} < x\right] = P[X < x]^n \sim F(x)^n$. The asymptotic probability distribution for $X^{(n)}$ is the density $d/dx\,[F(x)^n] = nF(x)^{n-1}f(x)$. The difference between the mean μ of $X^{(n)}$ and the mean p of X goes as $1/\sqrt{N}$, and the variance ς^2 of $X^{(n)}$ goes as 1/N, so for illustration the normalized quantities $\gamma = (\mu - p)/\sigma_x$ and ς^2/σ_x^2 are displayed in Fig. 1 for interconnect probability p = 0.1 and for various values of WTA network size n:

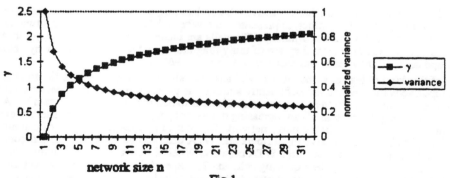

Fig.1
Parameters of the distribution of active synapses on winning cell in the naive network

2.3. Probability of a single cell winning on multiple patterns in the naive network

Consider now the probability that two different patterns of input fiber activation elicit the same winning cell in a naive winner-take-all network. Define overlap r as the number of input fibers active for both of two input patterns (i.e., 2(qN-r) is the Hamming distance between the two patterns, if each has qN active fibers), and let relative overlap ρ = r/(qN) represent the fraction of input fibers active for both patterns.

Let random variables X and Y represent the fraction of active input fibers contacting a cell for the first and second patterns under consideration, respectively. They have an asymptotic joint cumulative distribution function G (i.e., $P[X < x \cap Y < y] \sim G(x, y)$), which is an implicit function of the overlap fraction ρ. Now (again in the naive network with all synaptic weights at the same initial values), the probability that a particular cell with X=x and Y=y wins on both patterns is the probability $G(x,y)^{n-1}$ that the other n-1 cells in the patch have X and Y values smaller than x and y, respectively, and thus, accounting for all n combinations of one winner and n − 1 losers possible among the n cells in the network, the total probability that one of the cells wins on both patterns with X=x and Y=y is $nG(x, y)^{n-1}$. It is the (asymptotic) expected value of $nG(X,Y)^{n-1}$ that we seek:

$$P[\text{one cell wins on two patterns}] \sim n \int_0^1 \int_0^1 G(x, y)^{n-1} \, \partial^2 G(x, y) \, / \, (\partial x \partial y) \, dx dy \ . \qquad (EQ\ 2)$$

By reverting to discrete random variables, the density $\partial^2 / \partial x \partial y \, [G(x, y)]$ can ultimately be derived as a conditional probability $P[X = x \cap Y = y] = P[Y = y | X = x] P[X = x]$:

$$\partial^2 G(x, y) / \partial x \partial y = (2\pi \sigma_x \sigma_y)^{-1} \exp\left(-(y - [\rho x + (1 - \rho) p])^2 / [2\sigma_y^2] \right) \exp\left(-(x - p)^2 / [2\sigma_x^2] \right), \qquad (EQ\ 3)$$

where the variance $\sigma_y^2 = (1 - \rho) [\rho x (1 - x) + p (1 - p)] / (qN)$.

Numerical integration with N large may be used to evaluate G(x,y) and ultimately the asymptotic expression for P[one cell wins on two patterns] in EQ(2). Computed values of this probability as a function of overlap fraction ρ are shown in Fig. 2, with network size n as a parameter. As before, interconnect probability p = 0.1. These curves show that, unless a WTA network is rather modest in size, the degree of overlap required to elicit multiple wins from a single cell is very high. This has implication for the process of pattern capture by overtake described below..

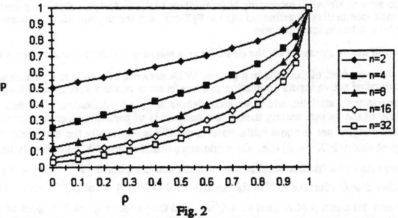

Fig. 2
Probability of a single cell in the naive network winning on two patterns with overlap ρ, for several WTA sizes

3. Learning and Pattern Capture

Now consider a WTA network in which coactivity-based learning takes place. Assume that a series of input patterns (which may or may not all be distinct) is presented to a generic WTA network one at a time and the weights of synapses between active input fibers and winning WTA cells are incremented at each presentation. Synaptic weights are normalized so that in the naive state they are of unity magnitude, and specified to grow by constant finite increment Δ at each update, until they reach saturation at some value $1+\Delta_{max}$.

As a result of this kind of learning, the GLA model has been shown to acquire the ability to cluster its input data: for patterns of input activation which are sufficiently similar, the piriform output codes become highly overlapping, though they are not necessarily so in the naive network. If this is to occur, it is clear that certain WTA cells must "capture" (i.e., begin to win on presentation of) an increasing number of patterns in an input cluster as learning progresses, at the loss of other cells which won in the naive network. In order to analyze the process of capture, recall that only the weights of synapses between coactive input fibers and WTA cells can be incremented, and consider a cell that is to capture a pattern from a second cell within a WTA network. When learning is initiated, it must be supposed that: 1) Some *other* patterns elicit wins from the capturing cell, and 2) Some of the synapses whose weights are incremented when the capturing cell wins, must also be active on the pattern to be captured as well. It is the growth of these weights which ultimately allows the capturing cell to win on the captured pattern.

3.1. Capture by precedence

Suppose that in the naive network, a cell C_1 wins on presentation of an input pattern P_1 (with average μ active synapses) and that a second cell C_2 wins in response to m other patterns which have average relative overlap ρ with P_1. The expected fraction of active fibers contacting C_2 in response to P_1 (referring to EQ. 3) is $\rho\mu + (1-\rho)p$. Of these synapses, $\rho\mu$ is the fraction (on average) also active for one of the other patterns. If the m patterns are presented before P_1 when learning is initiated, then the expected input to C_2 in response to P_1 becomes $\rho\mu + (1-\rho)p + m\rho\mu\Delta$ after updating. (In this and subsequent references, inputs to piriform cells are assumed normalized by qN.) Therefore, in the "average" case, capture of P_1 by C_2 takes place after presentation of the m patterns if $\rho\mu + (1-\rho)p + m\rho\mu\Delta > \mu$, or if

$$\rho > (\mu - p) / [(\mu - p) + m\mu\Delta] . \qquad \text{(EQ 4)}$$

However, as noted above, $(\mu - p)$ goes as $N^{-1/2}$, so for any $m > 0$ this condition is met by arbitrarily small ρ in the asymptotic limit. That is to say, a cell which wins on even a single pattern, if its weights are the first ones incremented, will tend to capture any other pattern with non-zero relative overlap if the number of input fibers N is sufficiently large!

We define *capture by precedence* to mean capture of patterns by virtue of precedence in the order in which input patterns occur during learning. It is not possible to preclude capture by precedence and it may in fact serve a useful purpose (i.e., any novel experience will make *some* impression in such a system when learning is enabled), but clearly it must be limited if information about relations *between* input patterns is of primary importance. The right-hand side of EQ(4), which we call ρ_c, defines in an average sense a range of patterns subject to capture by precedence in terms of relative overlap with patterns eliciting wins in the naive state.

From the definitions of ρ_c and γ, some algebraic manipulation yields $\gamma[(1-\rho_c)/\rho_c - m\Delta] = \rho\sigma_x m\Delta$. The right-hand side of this expression is non-negative, as is γ, from which we conclude that ρ_c can be no larger than $1/(1+m\Delta)$. Considering capture range for training on presentation of a single pattern (i.e., $m = 1$) and utilizing the variance σ_x^2 obtained in the case of random independent synapses, we obtain $\rho_c = [1 + \Delta[\sqrt{pqN/(1-p)}/\gamma + 1]]^{-1}$. By way of example, we evaluate this expression for parameter values p=0.1, q=0.2, and Δ=0.1 (typical of those used in the GLA model), and for the case of N = 10,000 and network size n = 16. These figures yield ρ_c=0.51; in other words, in the "average" network, any pattern overlapping the training pattern by more than 51% tends to be subject to capture by precedence in a single update. Although a detailed statistical analysis of capture by precedence is beyond the scope of this paper, these results suggest that, for fiber tracts of realistic size, Δ, p, q, or some combination thereof ought to be considerably smaller than those values assumed.

3.1. Capture by overtake

Consider now the case when pattern P_1 is *not* captured by precedence. Assume that during learning P_1 is presented to the network in repeated "epochs," and that for each such presentation, m other patterns which elicit wins from C_2 are also presented. If C_2 is to capture P_1, then clearly the growth rate of the input to C_2 for P_1 (average $m\rho\mu\Delta$ per epoch) must exceed the growth rate of the input to C_1 for P_1 (average $\mu\Delta$ per epoch) during learning. We refer to capture by this mechanism as *capture by overtake*. Neglecting for the moment any saturation of the weights, this condition is met in the average case if $\rho > 1/m$.

However, the process of overtake is ultimately limited by weight saturation. Let μD_1 represent the expected change in the input to C_1 for P_1 and let $\rho\mu D_2$ represent the expected change in the input to C_2 for P_1 due to training. If epochs are indexed by a (discrete) variable t, then we may write $D_1(t) = t\Delta$ if $t\Delta<\Delta_{max}$ and $D_1(t) = \Delta_{max}$ after saturation. The quantity $D_2(t)$ can be shown to take the form $D_2(t) = \binom{m}{k} p_o^{k-1} (1-p_o)^{m-k} \Delta_k(t)$, where $\Delta_k(t) = kt\Delta$ if $kt\Delta < \Delta_{max}$ and $\Delta_k(t) = \Delta_{max}$ otherwise, and where p_o is the probability that a synapse is active for any pair of the patterns eliciting an initial win from C_2 (i.e., the relative overlap among them divided by μ). Given these definitions, we have $(\mu + \mu D_1)$ for the expected input to C_1 for P_1 and $(\rho\mu + (1-\rho)p + \rho\mu D_2)$ for the expected input to C_2 for P_1, so capture will occur in the "average" case if

$$\rho > \min_t [(\mu - p + \mu D_1(t)) / (\mu - p + \mu D_2(t))] \qquad \text{(EQ 5)}$$

If $\Delta_{max}/(m\Delta)$ is an integer, the minimum in EQ(5) can be shown to occur after $t = \Delta_{max}/(m\Delta)$ updates (i.e., when weights common to all m patterns have just reached saturation).

By way of example, in Fig. 3 we plot ρm for ρ satisfying EQ(5) with equality, against the size of the input fiber tract N, for a particular WTA network. The size of the network is n=16, m=5 distinct patterns are assumed to elicit initial wins from the capturing cell in the naive state, and weight saturation is assumed to occur after 10 updates with saturated weights larger than naive weights by a factor of 2.4. In this case, minimum ρ is reached after two updates. It can be seen that ρm approaches the minimum value of unity only for fiber tracts of very large size N.

Once a pattern has been captured by overtake, weights on the capturing cell which are active for the pattern will grow with further learning and contribute to expansion of the capture range of the cell; analysis of this secondary process, however, is beyond the scope of this paper.

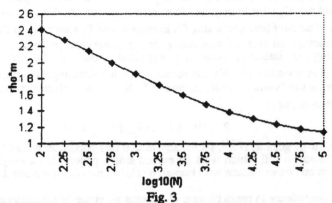

Fig. 3
Product of relative overlap and number of winning patterns of capturing cell vs. input tract size (particular case)

4. Discussion and Conclusions

In this paper, some basic statistical features of the winner-take-all network with sparse random innervation were examined. The results are of particular relevance for the Granger, Lynch, and Ambros-Ingerson (GLA) model of early olfactory processing [1-5], but are in fact applicable to a range of neural network models employing sparse random connectivity, coactivity-based learning, and winner-take-all networks as part of their architectures.

The distributions of active synapses onto dendrites of typical and winning cells were discussed, and the probability of two patterns eliciting the same winning cell in the naive network were derived. In addition, the effects of a simple coactivity-based learning rule were examined and the process of pattern capture due to learning was introduced. Two mechanisms of capture were identified: capture by precedence, in which a pattern is captured from one cell by another by virtue of precedence in the order of pattern presentation during learning, and capture by overtake, in which input to the capturing cell for the pattern to be captured grows faster than that for the original winner, by virtue of the growth of synaptic weights on input fibers also active on other patterns which elicit wins from the capturing cell. Capture by precedence must be limited (by limiting connectivity, activity in input patterns, and/or weight increment size) if the network is to develop a functionality based on relations between input patterns (as is the case if it is to cluster data, for example). In order to initiate capture by overtake, we note that a "nucleus" of similar patterns (or frequent reappearance of patterns when learning is enabled) must be present in the data from which a network learns. By examining the probability that two patterns will elicit the same winning cell as a function of overlap between the patterns, we conclude that very high overlap is required in such a nucleus unless the WTA network is modest in size; we speculate that this must be the case if the network is to perform clustering.

Acknowledgments

The author thanks R. Granger, C. Hutchens, R. Shah, and I. Lagnado for their assistance. This work was supported by the U.S. Office of Naval Research.

References

1. J. Ambros-Ingerson, R. Granger, and G. Lynch, "Simulation of paleocortex performs hierarchical clustering," *Science* vol. 247, pp. 1344-1348, 1990.
2. J. Ambros-Ingerson, *Computational Properties and Behavioral Expression of Cortical-Peripheral Interactions Suggested by a Model of the Olfactory Bulb and Cortex*, Ph.D. Dissertation, University of California, Irvine, 1990.
3. R. Granger, J.A. Ambros-Ingerson, P. Anton, and G. Lynch, "Unsupervised perceptual learning: a paleocortical model," Ch. 5 in *Connectionist Modeling and Brain Function*, S. Hanson and C. Olsen, Eds., MIT Press, Cambridge, MA, 1990.
4. R. Granger, J.A. Ambros-Ingerson, and G. Lynch, "Derivation of encoding characteristics of layer II cerebral cortex," *Journal of Cognitive Neuroscience* vol. 1, pp. 61-87, 1989.
5. G. Lynch and R. Granger, R., "Simulation and analysis of a simple cortical network," *Learning and Motivation* vol. 23, pp. 205-241, 1989.
6. G. Lynch, *Synapses, Circuits, and the Beginnings of Memory*, MIT Press, Cambridge, MA, 1986.
7. B. Graham and D. Willshaw, "Capacity and information efficiency of a brain-like associative net," proceedings, Neural Information Processing Systems 7, Morgan Kaufmann, San Francisco, CA, 1994.
8. J. Buckingham, *Delicate Nets, Faint Recollections: A Study of Partially Connected Associative Network Memories*, Ph.D. dissertation, University of Edinburgh, 1991.
9. J. Lazzaro, S. Rychebusch, M.A. Mahowald, and C.A. Mead, "Winner-Take-All Networks of O(N) Complexity," California Institue of Technology Technical Report Caltech-CS-TR-21-88, 1989
10. P.A. Shoemaker, C.G. Hutchens, and S. Patil, "A heirarchical clustering network based on a model of olfactory processing," *Analog Integrated Circuits and Signal Processing* vol. 2, pp. 297-311, 1992.

Novel Learning in Self-Architecting Artificial Neural Networks *

Frank Lu
Department of Physics, American University
4400 Massachusetts Avenue, Washington, DC 20006
Telephone: (202)625-6010, e-mail: flu@american.edu
Joseph T. DeWitte, Jr.
Department of Electrical and Computer Engineering, George Washington University
10631 Glen Hannah Drive, Laurel, MD 20723
Telephone/Fax: (301)490-0611, e-mail: dewitte@seas.gwu.edu
Harold Szu, Ph.D.
Naval Surface Warfare Center, Dahlgren Division, Code B44
10901 New Hampshire Avenue, Silver Spring, MD 20903
Telephone: (301)394-3097, Fax: (301)394-3923, e-mail: hszu@ulysses.nswc.navy.mil

July 5, 1995

Abstract

In this paper, we investigate the behavior of a self-architecting neural network with a new learning rule. It is an outgrowth of work by Stassinopoulos, Alstrøm, and Bak [4, 5] with two significant modifications to their Adaptive Performance Network (APN) model: we have articulated an L^1 energy function and a non-unity energy threshold in the weight update equation; we also perform normalization on the instar instead of the outstar. To test this novel learning prescription for self-architecting networks, we apply this new model to a form of the Exclusive-OR (XOR) problem. The model discovers a solution architecture on its own, showing much the same self-organizing behavior of APNs. This modification indicates that the basic structure of an APN is quite tolerant of changes to the learning rule. That is, APNs may be quite robust, and may be an important paradigm for the different types of neural networks found in biological systems.

1   Introduction

At last year's conference, WCNN '94, Dr. Per Bak of Brookhaven National Laboratory gave a plenary talk on the subject of self-organizing neural networks. In the proceedings for the conference, the there appeared an accompanying paper by Stassinopoulos, Bak, and Alstrøm entitled "Self-organization in a simple brain model" [4]. This paper outlined a new model for a self-organizing artificial neural network, called an *Adaptive Performance Network* (APN). This new model was developed out of some previous work in the study of sandpile dynamics [3, 1, 2]. Sandpile behavior is known in the physics community as *self-criticality*, and is characterized by a $1/f$ power spectrum in measures of phase transition size and duration. The authors of the WCNN '94 paper developed a neural network model based on the self-criticality idea. They included some very interesting simulations that showed the self-organizing behavior of this new model by examining two major experimental cases as follows.

First, they considered a 256-neuron net organized into 16 layers with each neuron receiving weighted inputs from the three neurons in the previous row. We can describe this situation simply by using the terms coined by Grossberg, Kohonen, and others: *instar* refers to the set of connections coming into a neuron,

---

*The authors wish to acknowledge the helpful discussions and encouragement from Dimitris Stassinopoulos, Per Bak, and Preben Alstrøm

while *outstar* refers to the connections emanating from a neuron. Therefore, Stassinopoulos *et. al.* used an instar of size 3 for their simulations. A random set of 16 neurons was chosen for one input pattern; another set of 16 neurons for another input. Two randomly selected neurons in the bottom row were selected for one pattern; another two neurons in the bottom row for the other pattern.

The second case consisted of 256 *randomly-connected* neurons. An instar of three was used, meaning that the network was again sparsely connected. As for the layered case, two sets of 16 neurons were used for inputs and two sets of two neurons for outputs—all randomly chosen.

In all cases, the neurons were of the binary *on-off* type. If a neuron was in the firing state, it put out a unit-level signal, which got multiplied by a weight before becoming the input to another neuron. If the neuron was in the off state, it provided no signal to its outstar set.

For both the layered and random experiments, the following schedule was followed. One input pattern was presented for 2000 iterations, during which time the network weights were allowed to change. The first input pattern was removed from its 16-neuron set, and the next pattern was presented to its 16-tuple for the next 2000 iterations with more weight updates taking place. This prescription was then repeated over and over.

For both the random and layered nets, the same qualitative behavior was observed. After a period of searching around for a solution as the inputs were presented and switched again and again, the network suddenly found a *solution* architecture. That is, the APN discovered, on its own, a set of weights that allow the correct outputs to be quickly generated from the given input patterns. This fast switching typically occurs in tens of iterations after a switch in the input pattern.

As observed in [4], one of the particular advantages of the APN model is that there is no distinction between training and recall modes. The rules by which the net operates are always in effect. After a period of self-organization, however, the APN will show the *appearence* of switching to recall mode. The authors showed, by ablation of some of the nodes in the net or by the addition of a new pattern, that the network can be induced to revert to an *apparent* training condition. Once it self-organizes to a new solution, the net's output behavior will once again look like a simple recall operation.

The authors of the present paper have been interested in self-architecting neural networks for several years [6, 7, 8]. For example, [8] describes a neural net chip that was built which could actually grow connections between neurons, according to the so-called *Peter, Paul, and Mary* principle. Thus, the structure and behavior of the APNs reported in [4] was very intriguing to us. We have been investigating how such nets could be used to solve the Exclusive-OR (XOR) problem. During the course of this research, we found that the original APN model could be modified in some fairly significant ways without altering the basic features of its self-organizing dynamics. That is, even with our modifications to the learning equations, the resulting network still exhibits a random-like searching period, followed by a rapid transition to a solution architecture, that is characteristic of APNs.

2   Results

In our simulation work, we made two modifications to the APN equations, and applied the new model to a variant of the Exclusive-OR (XOR) problem.

The equations for updating parameters in our modified APN are relatively simple and are given as follows:

$$v_i' = \text{step}(\sum_{j=1}^{N_{in}} W_{ij} v_j - \Theta) \tag{1}$$

$$\Theta' = \Theta + \epsilon \, \text{sgn}(n_f - N_{f,out}) \tag{2}$$

$$E = \frac{1}{N_o} \sum_{i=1}^{N_o} v_{out,i} \oplus d_i = \, <\underline{v}_{out} - \underline{d}>^1 \;\; (E \in L^1) \tag{3}$$

$$W_{ij}' = W_{ij} + [\eta \, \text{sgn}(E - E_0) W_{ij} (1 - W_{ij}) + \bar{n}] \, v_i' v_j \tag{4}$$

$$W'_{ij} \quad \rightarrow \quad W'_{ij} \Big/ \sum_{j=1}^{N_{in}} W'_{ij} v'_j \, . \tag{5}$$

Our modifications to the APN model given in [4] are contained in equations (4) and (5) as explained below.

Equation (1) explains how to determine the new on-off firing state for a neuron. The quantities v_i and v'_i represents the output of neuron i at the beginning and end of an iteration, respectively. All of the weighted inputs from a neuron's instar ($N_{in} = 3$) are summed together and compared against a global threshold. Equation (2) indicates how to update this threshold. If more output neurons are firing than should be, the network is too active. This condition is counteracted by increasing the threshold a small amount ϵ. For our experiments, $\epsilon = 0.025$. If too few neurons are firing, the network is too sluggish, so the threshold is decreased so more will fire in the next iteration. The quantity $N_{f,out}$ controls how many of the output neurons should fire. As shown in Figure 1, only one of the four output neurons should fire for an input pattern, so $N_{f,out} = 1$ in our simulations. The quantity E in equation (3) can be interpreted as an error energy of a sort. It is the L^1-norm of the difference between the desired output pattern vector and the actual one produced by the net. In the original APN, the L^1 error energy is used in a very *harsh* way. If the energy is not exactly zero, then all the weights are punished (weakened). Only if the network produces a *perfect* match to the desired output pattern are the weights rewarded (strengthened).

Equations (4), and (5) are our departures from the APN network in [4] and [5]. The original punish-reward weight update equation has been generalized to the form shown in equation (4) by the introduction of the signum function and the use of a error energy *threshold*, E_0. If $E_0 = 1$, the weight update equation is identical to that in an unmodified APN. For our simulations, we relaxed this behavior, letting $E_0 = 0.9$. The rationale for this is that the network should be given some time to search for an adequate solution near one that *initially* is not perfect, rather than forcing it to give up so quickly. The Hebbian bilinear term can be recognized at the far right of the equation, but the large bracketed multiplicative factor turns the standard Hebbian into what may be termed a *statistically bipolar Hebbian*. The punish-reward rule embodied in the signum function accounts for the bipolarity. The noise term $\bar{n}$ introduces a small random quality to the Hebbian and serves to provide the network with new solution hypotheses. It is similar to the mutation function in genetic algorithms and the statistical search schedules followed in simulated annealing. In our simulations, we used uniform pseudo-random numbers in the range [-0.1,0.1] for $\bar{n}$.

The values used for the remaining parameters are as follows. The weight update strength was $\eta = 0.0.18$. A one in the input pattern translated to a real value of 1.5 for the input intensity, while a zero mapped to 0.0. The initial global theshold value was set at 0.8.

Equation (5) performs *instar normalization*. This is a departure from the original APN design which used *outstar normalization*. This difference has a definite interpretation in biological modeling. Neurons in the brain, for example, can be viewed simplistically as having an input side and an output side. The input to a neuron is a dendritic tree formed by synaptic connections coming from other neurons. The synapses in this dendritic tree are in proximity to the given neuron relative to the distance its *output* signal travels. In the human brain, for example, tens of thousands of dendrites typically impinge on a given neuron. Instar normalization implies that the neuron is tuned to its linear operating range of the input sum. Although real neurons exhibit finite dynamic range, and therefore, non-linear behavior if the total input from the dendritic tree is large, it has been shown experimentally, by K. Pribram for example, that neurons spend most of their time operating in their linear range. Our use of instar normalization, mimics the response of biological neurons to their dendritic tree input.

When a given neuron fires, its output side is activated and a pulsed signal is sent out through the axon to the neuron's outstar. This signal travels quite some distance relative to the cell's distance to its input dendritic tree. This long communication distance is thought to be the evolutionary reason for pulsed coding of the axonal signal. The physical reason is that the cell can generate only so much energy in the form of voltages and currents, which results in a recovery period for the cell while it recharges for the next output. This sequence of firings and recoveries results in a pulsed signal observed in axons. The constraint on neuronal firing energy is thus the rationale for the outstar normalization used in the original APN model.

In simulating the modified APN, the equations are done in the order given above. This can be easily remembered via the following memory device: FiTE-WiN, which stands for *F*iring state computation, *T*hreshold update, *E*nergy computation, *W*eight update, and *i*nstar *N*ormalization.

The modified APN model just described was used to solve the XOR problem as shown in Figure 1. A sparsely-connected 4x4 layered network was chosen as the initial architecture. There were four input patterns that were successively applied to the inputs of the top layer of neurons. An input pattern was applied for many iterations until the energy of the network, also known as the *performance*, crossed the E_0 threshold. Then the input was switched to the next pattern. This process was repeated over and over. The right hand side shows the architecture that was finally reached. It was deduced from the final weights, which all converge to extreme values on the unit interval due to the quadratic term $W_{ij}(1 - W_{ij})$ in equation (4). Figure 2 illustrates the initial random weight set and the final converged set.

Figures 3 through 6 depict aspects of the network's behavior. All figures show the abrupt transition from learning to recall at around iteration number 5,700. This is the same type of behavior seen in the original unmodified APN networks using $E_0 = 1$ and outstar normalization. The threshold shows an interesting abrupt change in value around iteration 10,000. We do not yet have an explanation for this. It must be noted that these plots do not show individual quantities at every iteration. In the case of the performance, it was averaged over every 100 iterations to reduce the number of data points that needed to be plotted. Similarly, the parameters in the other figures are simply sampled every 100 iterations.

3   Conclusions and Future Work

What is surprising is that even though the punish-reward scheme is softened and normalization is done over instars rather than outstars, the network still converges to a solution in much the same way as the unmodified APN. This may indicate that the APN architecture is quite robust. APN networks might serve as a rather general model for all sorts of neural network configurations found in biological systems. In the use of a *statistically bipolar* Hebbian, APNs take the first step toward models that use non-linear learning dynamics. We believe that this type of dynamics is needed to understand the nature of intelligence.

Figure 7 shows a key direction for future research. Traditional energy functions are functions of weights and time, from which gradient-descent methods are used to derive weight update equations. We believe the next important direction for research will be in the development of energy functions that incorporate architecture. In this way, it may be possible to create new neurons and weights that were not in any *initial* architecture. This might allow, for example, for a more brainlike optimization behavior. In the XOR problem at hand, for example, it might allow the evolution from a good 3-neuron solution (input buffer neurons don't count as computational elements) to the optimal 2-neuron solution as depicted in the upper part of the figure. This would involve the *death* of a neuron and the *birth* of two new connections.

Another area we are investigating is the memory capacity of APN networks. This subject has been studied by Amari and McEliece, among others, for other neural network models, such as the Hopfield network. Researchers at the Center for Adaptive Systems at Boston University have similarly analyzed Adaptive Resonance Theory network capacity. In a capacity analysis of APN structures, we may discover the degree of truth in the old canard that humans only use a small percentage of their brains.

Since the APN model seems to capture some of the brain's self-organizing behavior whether the dendritic tree instar normalization or axon outstar normalization is used, it is natural to think of combining the two. Perhaps such a dual model will exhibit additional behavior that can be identified with known characteristics of biological brains. The relatively simple set of equations that govern the APN cannot be expected to mimic many of the more complicated functions of biological nets, to explain consciousness for example, but APNs might provide a methodology for the current holy grail in engineering: more *intelligent* machines.

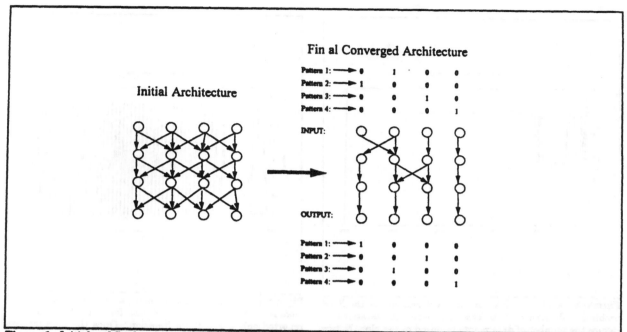

Figure 1. Initial and final architectures for the modified Adaptive Performance Network (APN). The initial architecture was a sparsely-connected 4x4 layered network with an instar size of 3. The final architecture is inferred by removing weights with values of zero.

Initial Random Weights

Weights	Neighbor 1:	Neighbor 2:	Neighbor 3:
Neuron 5:	0.0054051	0.110553	0.494024
Neuron 6:	0.264733	0.0321558	0.439595
Neuron 7:	0.462559	0.412305	0.434629
Neuron 8:	0.297008	0.353781	0.339894
Neuron 9:	0.438185	0.134922	0.0812308
Neuron 10:	0.0331128	0.095233	0.343598
Neuron 11:	0.484904	0.408795	0.127837
Neuron 12:	0.315455	0.287225	0.380103
Neuron 13:	0.239847	0.308819	0.422358
Neuron 14:	0.48438	0.180058	0.0909804
Neuron 15:	0.473501	0.0401185	0.397229
Neuron 16:	0.129855	0.358974	0.0132145

Final Converged Weights

Weights	Neighbor 1:	Neighbor 2:	Neighbor 3:
Neuron 5:	0	0	1
Neuron 6:	1	0	0
Neuron 7:	0	1	0
Neuron 8:	0	1	0
Neuron 9:	0	1	0
Neuron 10:	0	0	1
Neuron 11:	1	0	0
Neuron 12:	0	1	0
Neuron 13:	0	1	0
Neuron 14:	0	1	0
Neuron 15:	0	1	0
Neuron 16:	0	1	0

Figure 2. Initial and final modified APN weights. The initial weights were uniform pseudo-random numbers between 0 and 1/2. The final weights are driven to extreme values on the unit interval by the quadratic term in the weight update equation: $W_{ij}(1-W_{ij})$.

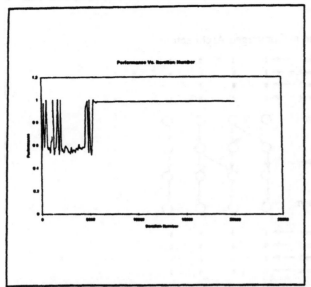

Figure 3. Modified APN network performance for the XOR problem. Performance is averaged over 100 iterations to reduce the number of data points required in the plot. Notice the self-organized switch from learning to recall around iteration 5,700.

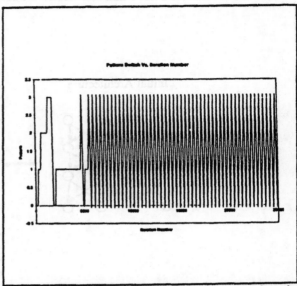

Figure 4. Switching of the input pattern presented to the modified APN. Switching of the four input patterns is reported only every 100th iteration. Once the learning has been completed, however, the network is able to report the correct output within ten iterations after an input pattern switch.

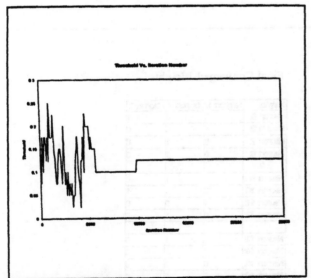

Figure 5. Threshold evolution. The threshold value is reported every 100 iterations. Notice the switch around 5,700 iterations from learning mode to recall mode. The network figured out how to do this on its own—no change in the training algorithm was needed to induce this behavior. The interesting jump around 10,000 iterations has yet to be explained.

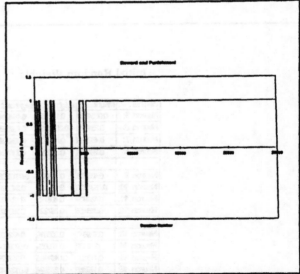

Figure 6. Reward-or-punishment evolution. The global reward or punishment to the weights is reported every 100 iterations. Again, there is an abrupt self-organized switch in behavior around 5,700 iterations.

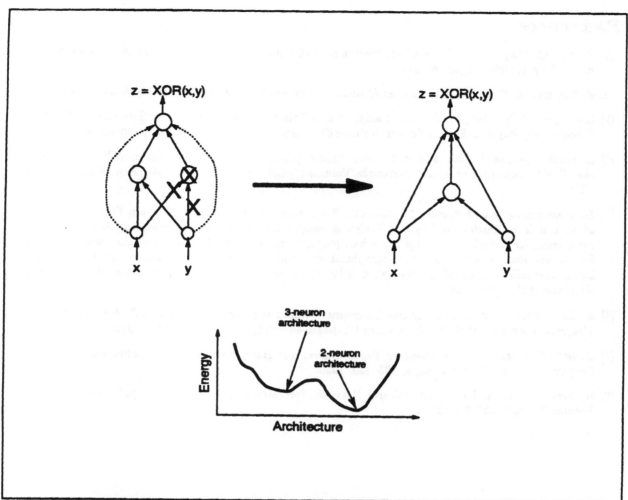

Figure 7. A proposed key direction for future research. Traditional energy functions are functions of weights and time, from which gradient-descent methods are used to derive weight update equations. We believe the next important direction for research will be in the development of energy functions that incorporate architecture. In this way, it may be possible to create new neurons and weights that were not in any *initial* architecture. This might allow for a more brainlike optimization behavior. It might, for example, allow the evolution from a good 3-neuron solution (input buffer neurons don't count as computational elements) shown on the left to the optimal 2-neuron solution on the right. This would involve the *death* of a neuron and the *birth* of two new connections.

References

[1] P. Bak, C. Tang, and K. Wiesenfeld, "Self-organized criticality", *Physical Review A*, Volume 38, Number 1, July 1, 1988, pages 364-374.

[2] P. Bak and K. Chen, "Self-Organized Criticality", *Scientific American*, pages 46-53, January 1991.

[3] S.-C. Lee, N. Y. Liang, and W.-J. Tzeng, "Exact Solution of a Deterministic Sandpile Model in One Dimension", *Physical Review Letters*, Volume 67, Number 12, pages 1479-1481, September 16, 1991.

[4] D. Stassinopoulos, P. Bak, and P. Alstrøm, "Self-organization in a simple brain model", *Proceedings of the World Conference on Neural Networks*, Volume I, pages 4-26, June 5-9, 1994, San Diego, California, USA.

[5] D. Stassinopoulos and P. Bak, "Democratic Reinforcement: A Principle for Brain Function", preprint of an article submitted to *Physical Review* in early 1995. In addition to providing some new results comparing APN performance against a backpropagation network, the version of this paper submitted for publication corrects a minor typographical regarding the weight normalization rule used in [4]. An instar normalization equation was stated in [4], but in fact outstar normalization was the basis for the simulations that were run.

[6] H. Szu, "Hairy Neuron Convergence Theorems Without the Precision of Timing", *International Joint Conference on Neural Networks*, Volume III, pages 469-476, Washington, D.C., 1990.

[7] H. Szu, "Neural Networks Based on Peano Curves and Hairy Neurons", *Telematics and Informatics*, Pergamon Press, Volume 7, pages 403-430, 1990.

[8] H. Szu, J. Kim, I. Kim, "Live Neural Network Formations on Electronic Chips", *Neurocomputing*, Volume 6, pages 551-564, 1994.

Fixed Point Versus Bifurcation Coupling among Cubic Neurons

Charles C. Hsu, Harold Szu*
Department of Electrical Engineering and Computer Science,
The George Washington University, Washington, DC. 20052
*NSWCDD, Code B44, Silver Spring MD 20903

Abstract

A continuous N-shaped function is proposed as a transfer function in the Artificial Neuron Network. A cubic polynomial function is used to implement the continuous N-shaped function, and the peak value (λ)of the cubic function is interpreted as the knob to control the chaotic behavior of neurons. Bifurcation coupling of collective neurons is demonstrated through the simulations of two chaotic neurons. The characteristic of the bifurcation coupling can be applied to change the fuzzy membership function. Application of the continuous N-shaped function is included.

Introduction

The relationship of fuzzy membership function and chaos was studied in [1]. The research of the collective chaotic neurons is attractive since the logistic function and the Piece-wise linear (PWL) N-shaped function of a single chaotic neuron were stated in [2,3,4]. In this paper, we have a close look at the chaotic behavior of the collective neurons. We propose a cubic polynomial function to implement a continuous N-shaped function. The modified cubic N-shaped function is controlled by λ which is dependent on the peak of the cubic polynomial function. The bifurcation spectrum of the cubic N-shaped is given. In addition, the collective chaotic neurons with different continuous cubic N-shaped functions (different peak values) are considered. The bifurcation coupling of these chaotic neurons are simulated. The characteristic of the coupling bifurcation can be used to change fuzzy membership functions which was study in [1]. Application of this continuous cubic N-shaped function which is able to be applied in de-noise problem is included.

Model and Simulations

The continuous cubic N-shaped function is expressed in equation (1), where l is the dependent on the peak of the cubic N-shaped function. There are three intersection points with the x which are 0, 0.5, 1. The continuous N-shaped cubic functions with different peak values, λ, are plotted in Fig.1 The bifurcation spectrum of the cubic N-shaped function in space of λ is displayed in Fig.2. It is very interesting to notice that there exists a discontinuous in the cubic N-shaped bifurcation, and the bifurcation spectrum is very similar to one of the logistic Feigunbaum function [5].

$$f(x)=10*\lambda*x*(x-0.5)*(x-1.0)+0.5 \tag{1}$$

The collective chaotic neurons with the cubic N-shaped function is considered. The model description is shown in the following:

$$u_i = \sum_{i=1}^{n} w_{ij}v_j \tag{2}$$

$$v_i = f(u_i) \tag{3}$$

where function f is a cubic N-shaped function expressed in equation(1), u_i is the input of the i-th neuron, v_i is the output of the i-th neuron, w_{ij} is the weights between neuron i and neuron j.

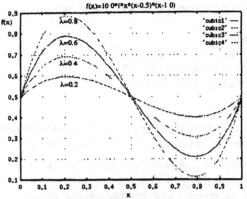

Fig.1   The continuous N-shaped cubic functions with different peak values, λ.

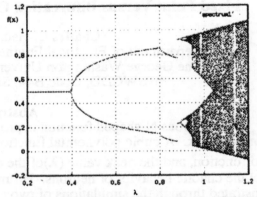

Fig.2   The bifurcation spectrum of the cubic N-shaped function in space of λ

For simplicity, we choose 2 chaotic neurons by using Hopfield connection which is shown in Fig.3. The knob λ values of the cubic N-shaped functions in three neurons are different. In neuron 1, the knob is λ and the knob is λ+0.2 for neuron 2. The weights are fixed and dependent on the initial conditions. The self weights , w_{11} and w_{22} are zero. Since the weights are fixed and dependent on initial conditions of u_i, the chaotic behavior of the model is very sensitive to u_i . The chaotic behavior of four different initial conditions are simulated and shown in Fig.4, Fig.5, Fig.6, and Fig.7. From Figure 2, we can observe that the single neuron with the cubic N-shaped function is chaotic if λ is greater than 0.92. When the neurons are connected as in Fig.3, neuron 1 should be chaotic if λ > 0.92, and neurons 2 should be chaotic if λ > 0.72. However, the bifurcation coupling of this case is shown in Fig.4 in which both neurons are in chaotic when λ > 0.879. This is because the mutual effect drives both neuron into chaos in the same phase.

If the underlying fuzzy dynamics is bifurcation route toward to chaos, then we expand the chaotic data set efficiently on this set of nesting triangular membership functions(MF), regressing from a non-overlapping crisp MF becoming an overlapping fuzzy MF as discussed in [6]. We have shown that the analogy between the bifurcation route to chaos and the crisp route to fuzzy overlapping in [6]. Note that the result has taken into account of the standard FMF overlapping & complementing characteristics, but without the details of the ratio $\Delta T/\Delta t$ in [6]. This coupling bifurcation gives an approach to change $\Delta T/\Delta t$ of the membership function in Fuzzy Logic.

Since the weights are fixed by the initial conditions of u_i, the initial values of u_i are very sensitive to the coupling bifurcation. Different simulations are displayed in Fig.5, Fig.6, and Fig.7. It is very interesting to plot the energy of the collective neurons in different chaotic behavior. The energy function is described in [7] shown the following:

$$E = \alpha \sum_{i,j} w_{ij} v_i v_j \qquad (4)$$

where E is the energy of the model, v_i is the output of the i-th neuron, w_{ij} is the weights between neuron i and neuron j, α is a scalar parameter. The energy landscape of the initial weights ($u_1 = 0.3$, $u_2 = 0.5$, and λ=1) and the chaotic weights weights ($u_1 = 0.3$, $u_2 = 0.3$, and λ=1) are shown in Fig.8.

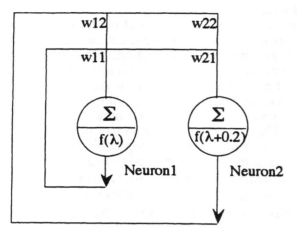

Fig.3 The structure of the collective chaotic neurons when the number of neurons is 2.

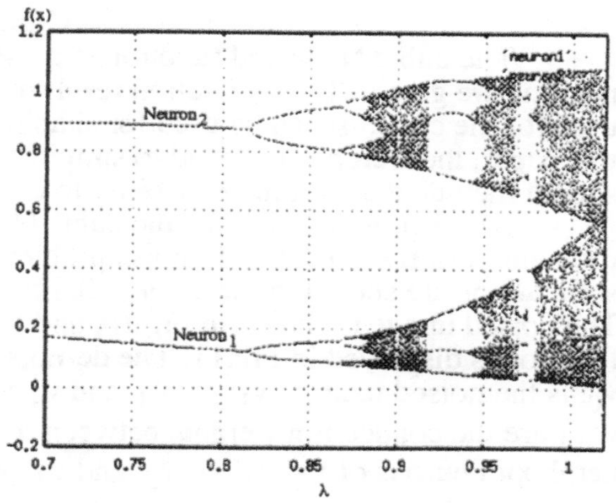

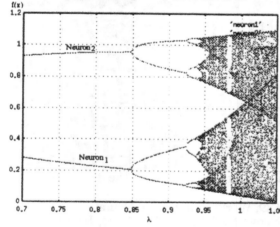

Fig.5 Chaotic bifurcation of two neurons in space of λ when $u_1 = 0.3$, $u_2 = 0.4$.

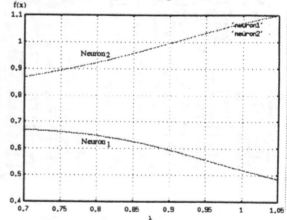

Fig.4 Chaotic bifurcation of two neurons in space of λ when $u_1 = 0.3$, $u_2 = 0.3$.

Fig.6 Chaotic bifurcation of two neurons in space of λ when $u_1 = 0.3$, $u_2 = 0.5$.

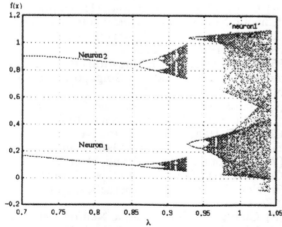

Fig.7 Chaotic bifurcation of two neurons in space of λ when $u_1 = 0.3$, $u_2 = 0.2$.

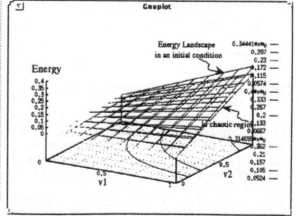

Fig.8 The energy landscape of the initial weights and the weights when the collective neurons are in chaotic region.

Conclusion

The cubic N-shaped function is presented and the simulations of the collective neurons are given. The simulation result reveals that the coupling bifurcation may be used for the crisp. It can be used for shaping fuzzy membership function. However, in this paper, the weights are fixed to simplify the analysis. The further advanced studies should include the learning capability to control chaotic behavior by changing w_{ij}.

Another application for the cubic N-shaped collective neurons is the de-noise problem. For instance, the de-noise problem is stated in [8], and the de-noise the simulations are shown in Fig.9, Fig.10, Fig.11. The original image is shown in Fig.9. The noised image is shown in Fig.10, and the de-noised image by using cubic N-shaped function is displayed in Fig.11. The de-noise image model is displayed in Fig.12, where v_0, is the noised neuron, v_1, v_2, v_3, and v_4 are its neighbor neurons. $w_{0,1}$, $w_{0,2}$, $w_{0,3}$, and $w_{0,4}$ are the connection weights between the noised neuron and its neighborhood. The neighbor neurons of v_0, v_1, v_2, v_3, and v_4, perform as a small collective chaotic neuron network and try to recover the noised neuron.

更欲黃白 上窮河日 一千入依 層里海山 樓目流盡	更欲黃白 上窮河日 一千入依 層里海山 樓目流盡	更欲黃白 上窮河日 一千入依 層里海山 樓目流盡
Fig.9 The original image.	Fig. 10 The noised image	Fig. 11 The de-noised image

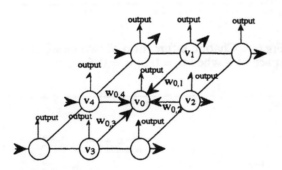

Fig.12 The de-noised image model.

Reference

[1] H. Szu, J. Garcia, L. Zadeh, C. Hsu, J. Dewitte, Jr., M. Zaghloul, "Multi-Resolution Analyses of Fuzzy Membership Functions by Means of Chaotic Neural Networks" pp 675-681, WCNN, San Diego, June, 1994

[2] Charles C. Hsu, Mona E. Zaghloul, Harold H. Szu, "CMOS Circuit Implementation to Control Chaotic Neurons", Proceeding pp. 684-689, World Congress on Neural Networks(WCNN), San Diego, June 1994

[3] Charles Hsu, M. Zaghloul, Harold Szu, "CMOS Current Mode Circuit to Control Neurons", Submitted to Journal of Circuits, Systems, and Computers, IEEE

[4] Charles Hsu, M. Zaghloul, Harold Szu, "Chaotic Neuron Models and Their Electronic Circuit Implementation", Accepted to Neural Network, IEEE Transaction

[5] Awrejcewicz, J. "Bifurcation and chaos in simple dynamical systems, Singapore, Teaneck, N.J., World Scientific, 1989

[6] Harold Szu, Charles Hsu, M. Zaghloul, "Chaotic Neural Network Architecture", Chapter 7, Handbook of Neural Network and Fuzzy Logic, McGraw-Hill, Printing

[7] J. J. Hopfield, D. W. Tank, "Neural Computation of Decision in Optimization Problems", Biological Cybernetics, 53 pp141-152, 1985

[8] Charles C. Hsu, "Chaotic Neuron Network Model and VLSI Implamentation", Doctor's Dissertation, The George Washington University, Washington, D.C., May, 1995

Optical Character Recognition using Haar Wavelets

Kim Scheff, Naval Research Laboratory, Washington, DC. 20375,
Lik Wong, SAIC, McLean, VA,
Harold Szu, NSWC Dahlgren Division, Code B44, White Oak, MD 20903

Abstract The Optical Character Recognition (OCR) work of Szu and Scheff[1] has been revisited with the addition of the use of a Wavelet Transform (WT) as a feature extraction preprocessing algorithm prior to the Gram-Schmidt Orthogonalization (GSO) technique described in [1]. The results for this initial set of data shows promise for the application of this algorithm to other data sets. In a few cases, the current approach did not work well where the input exemplars have only one pixel difference, and when the usual image raster scan line-by-line in the horizontal direction give a sparse column vector w.r.t. the vertical stroke of OCR. A segmentation technique for the USPS zip code data set is described along with 2-D Haar transform on the segmented data.

Keywords- neural networks, wavelets, Haar transforms, Optical Character Recognition, OCR, projection tomography, Gram-Schmidt Orthogonalization.

1. Introduction.

Optical Character Recognition (OCR) has a long history (cf. review [2]) and plays a central role in automatic pattern recognition. To overcome the overtraining problem associated with using the neural networks technology, OCR was performed using the Gram-Schmidt feature extraction method in 1990 [1] to cluster intra-class samples about the mean while maximizing inter-class separation. This approach was re-examined in this paper in lieu of the projection technique in tomography in order to retain as much information as possible while providing the necessary separation for fault tolerance. In addition, this technique constructs directly the interconnection matrices using the results of the Gram-Schmidt process (feature vectors) and hetro- and auto- associative memory matrices, rather than a slow and local-minimum-difficulty learning rule such as used in Back-Error Propagation.

The other major contribution of this approach is it's use of the parallel orthogonality theorem of a fixed point of cycle 2 proved by Szu and Tan[3]. This theorem states that if

$$\{[AM][AM]f_i\} = f_i$$

where [AM] is an associative memory made up of orthogonal vectors then f_i is orthogonal to all vectors used to make up [AM]. Recall that

$$[AM] = \sum_{c=1}^{M} |f_c><f_c| \text{ - diagonal terms;} \qquad \text{and} \qquad <f_c|f_{c'}> = \delta_{cc'} ,$$

where f_c is the feature vector of the c-th class, $\delta_{cc'}$ is the Kronecker Delta function, $|><|$ is an outer product notation, $<|>$ is an inner product notation and {} indicate a thresholded output. The theorem states that if and only if

$$[AM]f = -f, \quad \text{and} \quad [AM](-f) = f, \qquad \text{then} \quad <f|f_c> = \delta_{f,f_c}.$$

Thus, as the number of classes, M, increases; the numerical effort increases linearly rather than combinatorialy. In addition, the thresholded outputs are not the typical binary outputs, but ±1 or bipolar. For these reasons, this algorithm can be readily implemented in either optical or electronic hardware.

2   Hetero & Auto Associative Memory Neural Networks

The network consists of two layers. The first is a feed forward single layer hetro-associative memory [Fig. 1] with an interconnection matrix, FE, given by

$$[FE] = \frac{1}{BS} \sum_{c=1}^{M} \sum_{s=1}^{S} | f_c > < e_{cs} |, \quad FE_{ii} = 0,$$

where B is the number of bits, S is the number of samples per class and e_{cs} is s-th sample from the c-th class. The second layer [AM] is constructed by

$$[AM] = \frac{1}{B} \sum_{c=1}^{M} | f_c > < f_c |, \quad AM_{ii} = 0.$$

3   Haar Wavelets.

The data was preprocessed using a 1-D Haar wavelet. A good description of the Haar wavelet is given by Meyer [2]. The Haar wavelet has the bipolar value 1 over the interval [0, 1/2), -1 over the interval (1/2, 1] and zero elsewhere. The interval is then translated and dilated to form the family of wavelets used to preprocess the data. When Haar tfm is made periodical, it resembles Wash tfm. In our case the data set consists of 4 classes each containing 5 samples of 4x4 raster scanned letters.

The wavelet family formed in this case consisted of 16 orthogonal wavelets with 8 of interval length of two pixels, 4 of length 4 pixels, 2 of length 8, 1 of length 16 and 1 of length 32 (i.e. consist of all 1's, and is the DC term). The wavelets were implemented as a16x16 matrix, [HW] such that $[HW][HW]^{-1} = [I]$. The sample vectors now contain spatial frequency information and become the data which is implemented in the aforementioned network. Note that [HW], [AM] and [FE] are the same size and the same matrix multiplication routine can be used on all three processes simplifying hardware implementations.

4   Implementation.

After human supervisor classifies the input patterns and Haar wavelets are applied, the initial feature vectors are the thresholded average of the samples of that class. These initial feature vectors are as a rule not mutually orthogonal. The orthogonalization is performed by toggling individual pixels in each of the feature vectors and reapplying the Gram-Schmidt orthogonalization procedure. The pixels which are toggled are those which have a variance within a class greater than a predetermined threshold while pixels with variances less than the threshold are not toggled. The feature vector combination which is closest to mutually orthogonal then becomes the set of feature vectors.

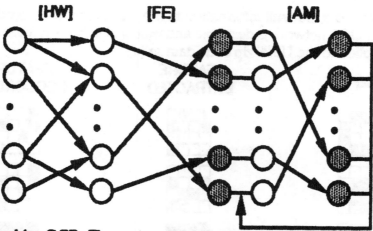

Figure 1. Network used for OCR. The raster scanned pixel data is preprocessed and input into the feature extraction layer of the neural network. The outputs of the feature extraction is fed into the associative memory.

5. Generalization to 2-D.

Generalizing to 8x8 characters makes 2-D implementations of this technique practical. The amount of variation the 4x4 data is not enough to make 2-D study worthwhile. The USPS zip code data set consists of 2500, 300 dpi, 256 gray level scanned images of handwritten zip codes. This zip codes have the attributes expected in handwritten data, including different letter heights, slants, connected letters and so forth. One of the major tasks is to separate and segment the data into 8x8 pixel images. A characteristic of the data is that some of the handwritten zip codes were written at a slant.

This makes separation of the individual characters difficult. One approach is to (binary) threshold each pixel a scanned image and sum the columns of the resulting matrix. If separation occurs between two characters, at least one column sum should be zero. If the zip code is written at a slant, this will not occur until a thresholding is done as such a high level that the signature is unrecognizable even by the author.

If the thresholding is done by summing is done by passing a slanted line through the image and adding the pixels on the line, nulls occur when the slant angle is close to the angle of the written text. This approach[4] is analogous to tomography and segmentation of text can be automated. The resulting segmented characters are mapped to an 8x8, bipolar pixel space for input to the processor.

$$65473$$

Example of USPS handwritten zip code after binary thresholding.

6. Summary.

The Haar transformed data shows similar if not better results using the same data set as [1]. The failures of this approach are understandable and occurred when single pixel (1 of 16) difference occurred between samples from different classes. The 1-D approach is interesting for comparison to earlier work, but still information in the y-direction is ignored. The 2-D generalization of this OCR network is desirable and practical in both software and hardware and is currently being applied to the USPS zip code data set[4].

SAMPLE	FEATURE EXTRACTED	FEATURE RECOGNIZED

Sample data using Haar wavelets for preprocessing. Note differences between feature extracted and feature recognized.

References:
1. Szu, H, and Scheff, K, "Gram-Schmidt Orthogonalization Neural Networks for Optical Character Recognition", *Journal of Neural Network Computing* Winter 1990, pp. 5-13; also in IJCNN-90 Proceedings, Washington DC 1990.
2. Meyer, Y., *Wavelets, Algorithms and Applications*, SAIM, Philadelphia, 1993, ISBN 0-89871-309-9.
3. Szu, H, and Tan, J, " Can Associative Memory Recognize Characters?", *U.S. Postal Service Advanced Technology Conference*, Wash., DC, May 3-5 1988, pp. 1003-1007.
4. Scheff, K, Ph. D. Thesis, Clark University, 1995.

Projection Features Using the
Discrete & Continuous Wavelet Transform

Joe Garcia and Harold Szu
Naval Surface Warfare Center, Dahlgren Division
NSWCDD Code B44
10901 New Hampshire Ave.
Silver Spring, MD 20903-5640

Abstract A projection transform maps boundaries into points. We define a projection wavelet transform that uses the continuous and discrete wavelet transforms and allows boundaries over multiple scales to be represented. This type of transform can generate space-scale features and can serve as a preprocessor for a neural network.

I. Introduction

Research into biological vision systems seems to indicate that the brains of people and animals decompose images into constituent features. The recent wavelet approaches developed in the last decade may embody this aspect of biological systems. Biological vision systems are good at detecting outlines & boundaries of shapes[1,2]. If an outline is broken up into segments, these segments could be considered the basic features or primitives of a shape. These feature would have the following properties: orientation, scale and position. The orientation is the direction the line segment is oriented betweem 0-180 deg. Scale pertains to the "sharpness" of a boundary section. This is more property of interior boundaries, e. g., the boundary between the wing and fuselage of a blended wing style aircraft appears gentle at close range but sharper at longer range. An outside edge, e.g., the edge between the wing and background, appears sharp at any range. The last property, position, is more difficult to quantify. This is because an edge defines to different levels of resolution. The transverse position resolution, i. e., along the direction perpendicular to the edge, is precise while the lengthwise position resolution is imprecise. This is because moving across a boundary it is obvious where the boundary begins but moving along the boundary it is much less obvious where one edge segment ends and another begins. After all, the change of a boundary segment is realized from a discernable change in orientation, but along the boundary this is changing gradually. Because of this directional disparity of resolution Cartestian coordinates are a poor choice to represent the position of a line segment.

Projection transforms such as the Hough[3] transform have been developed for computer vision. The Hough transform maps a line of a particular orientation into a point. Here the position resolution along the length of the line is completely lost. A partial Hough transform would map a line segment into a point but would maintain some lengthwise position resolution on the order of the segment's length. Scale plays a role in determining the segment length. A sharp boundary requires a small length to determine a line segment while a blurry boundary requires a relatively long length to define a segment. The Continuous Wavelet Transform[4] (CWT) is ideally suited to measure the scale of the boundary in the transverse direction. It also maintains position resolution for all scales. A variation of the Discrete Wavelet Transform[5,6] (DWT) is suited to representing the position resolution along the length of a segment. The DWT position resolution decreases with scale. A projection transform that extracts line segment features over all scales can be implemented by a DWT in the lengthwise direction and a CWT in the transverse direction for all rotations of an image in the range of 0-180 deg.

II. Projection Transform Features

A projection is a mathematical operation that maps a boundary into a point. One well known projection transform is the Hough transform

$$\lambda(\phi, x') = \int_{-\infty}^{\infty} \mu(x', y') dy',$$

$$\begin{pmatrix} x' \\ y' \end{pmatrix} = \begin{pmatrix} x\cos\phi + y\sin\phi \\ -x\sin\phi + y\cos\phi \end{pmatrix} \begin{pmatrix} x \\ y \end{pmatrix},$$

where $\mu(x,y)$ is the input image, ϕ is the orientation and x' is the transverse direction position of the line. The above transform is a global transform. This means some information is distributed over the entire transform making it effectively lost. In the case of the Hough transform it is the positional resolution along the segment lengthwise or y' direction. Let us define a lengthwise direction preserving transform

$$\lambda(\phi, x', Y') = \int_{-\infty}^{\infty} \mu(x', y') f(Y'-y') dy',$$

where f is some kernel such as a gaussian or square weighting function. To detect edges along the x' direction for all scales we apply the wavelet transform to λ

$$\Lambda(\phi, a, X', Y') = \int_{-\infty}^{\infty} \lambda(\phi, x', Y') \psi(a, X'-x') dx'$$

$$= \int_{-\infty}^{\infty} \int_{-\infty}^{\infty} \mu(x', y') f(a, Y'-y) dy' \psi(a, X'-x') dx'.$$

It is necessary to redefine f as a function of a because the integration radius of f to resolve a particular direction will be dependent on a. The above uses a continuous function f along the segment direction. A projection transform must compress along the direction of a segment. The above must also be related to a discrete image that would be used in some type of digital system. We define the wavelet projection transform (WPT) by redefining Λ for a discrete image

$$\Lambda(\phi, a(Y'), X', Y') = \sum_{x=-\infty}^{\infty} ref\ DWT_{y'} [\ \mu(x', y')] \psi[a(Y'), X'-x'],$$

where *ref* DWT$_{y'}$ is the low pass or reference output for all scales of the DWT in the y' direction. It is a function of x' and Y'. In the DWT, the scale is a function of the position Y' in the transform domain. Thus a must be a function of Y' because the X' direction scale must correspond to the Y' direction scale. There is uncertainty of position along the length of a line segment, i.e., in the y' direction. Because this uncertainty increases with scale, the DWT is ideal to represent this. On the other hand, there is certainty of position in the transverse direction. The CWT along this direction preserves this.

III. Processing

Fig. 1 A) represents a test image containing edges at three different scales; Fig. 1 B) is an F-18 fighter; Fig. 1 C) is the WPT of the test image; while Fig. 1 D) is the WPT of the F-18 image. Both WPTs are over three spatial scales (3-5 levels down) with the lowest resolution on the top and the highest on the bottom. For each scale the horizontal direction represents the transverse segment length position while the vertical direction represents the orientation between 0-180 deg. Notice that each edge in Fig. 1 A) has a corresponding peak scale in Fig. 1. C).

IV. Discussion and Conclusion

The above WPT processing can simplify the representation of complex image features. Features are basically categorized by their orientation, scale and position. The wavelet basis permits efficient representation of the positional uncertainty of the boundary segments. This type of preprocessing should improve the image recognition performance of neural networks. Previous work on classifying time series signals has demonstrated improved neural network performance when combined with a wavelet preprocessor[7].

V. References

1.   S. W. Kuffler, J. G. Nicholls & A. R. Martin, From Neuron to Brain, 2nd ed., Sinauer Associates Inc., Sunderland MA, 1984.

2.   D. Marr, Vision, Freeman, San Francisco, 1982.

3.   Ballard, D. H. and C. M. Brown, Computer Vision, Prentice-Hall, Englewood Cliffs, NJ, 1982.

4.   Y. Sheng, D. Roberge, H. Szu, & T. Lu, "Optical wavelet matched filters for shift-invarinat pattern recognition," Opt Lett., Vol. 18, No. 4, pp. 299-302, Feb 15, 1993.

5.   M. Vetterli and C. Herley, "Wavelet and Filter Banks: Theory and Design," IEEE Trans. Sig. Proc., Vol. 40, No. 9, pp. 2207-2232, Sept. 1992.

6.   M. Antonini et al, "Image Coding Using Wavelet Transform," IEEE Trans. Image Proc., Vol. 1, No. 2, pp. 205-220, Apr 1992.

7.   H. Szu, X-Y Yang and B. Telfer, "Neural network for scale-invariant data classification," Phys. Rev. E, Vol. 48, No. 2., pp. 1497-1501, Aug 1993.

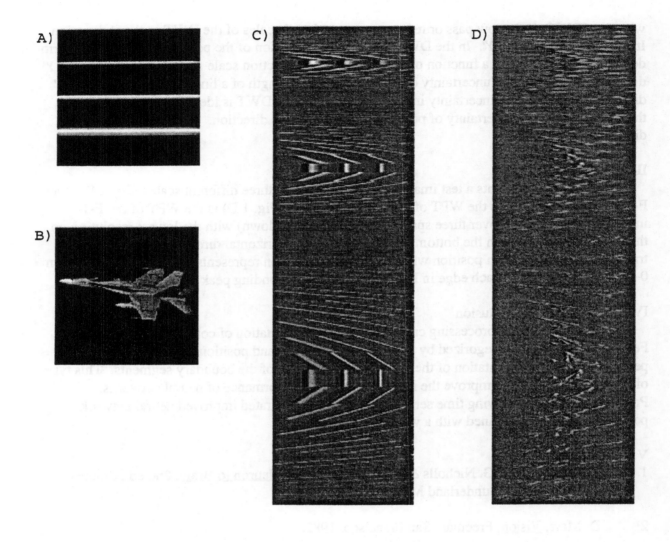

Fig. 1 A) test image with edge segments of different scales at two orientations; B) F-18 fighter; C) WPT of the test image; D) WPT of the F-18.

Genetically Connected Artificial Neural Networks

Todd R. Stratton[*]
USAF, Air Force Institute of Technology
Department of Electrical Engineering and Computer Science
The George Washington University
Washington D.C., 20037

1. Introduction

Applications of the artificial neural network (ANN) vary from discipline to discipline, but the rate at which an ANN converges (training time), and the error level (SSE or MSE) that the network trains to are important to all interested parties. Since John Holland formalized the basic theory of the genetic algorithm (GA) in 1975, a flexible new search technique has become available for researchers interested in using a genetically analogous process to help increase the efficiency of solving problems that defy traditional approaches.

The general structure of the human cerebral cortex is that of a many layered biological neural network (Fischbach 92). The number of neurons in the brain has been estimated at 100 billion, with the number of interconnections between neurons ranging from 10,000 - 80,000 depending on the type of neuron (Fischbach 92). But the specialized networks of the brain (visual cortex , speech processing areas, motor cortex etc.) are not fully connected with all the other areas, rather, they presumably pass their "conclusions" on to be processed with other signals in the brain (Schatz 92). By consolidating a specific function to a particular BNN, that one network can become very well trained for it's dedicated function.

Assuming there is no way for a genetic encoding to completely map the individual connections of a human brain, nature has arrived at a method of mapping different BBN's to one another in terms of connective architecture that is very successful. From these ideas the research project of using a GA to determine a more optimal connection strategy than a straightforward one-to-one connection scheme, between stand-alone ANN's, emerged. Simple, preliminary simulations indicate statistically significant support for the hypothesis.

2. Analysis

Methods of combining ANN's and GA's have generally seen the use of a GA to assist some aspect of an ANN's operation (Schaffer, et al. 92). Typically, GA's are used to evolve a topology (Hintz and Spofford, 90), to pre-process the training set in some way, or to use a GA as the learning function of a network. The approach presented here is implemented as a combination of evolving a topology of connections and modifying the training set.

Determining how to map a problem into the chromosomes that are used to represent the search space can be one of the more difficult aspects of using a GA. However, the only time the GA needs domain knowledge of the problem it is trying to solve is during the evaluation of each population member (Buckles 92). Typically, for ANN's, the fitness measure used is some value of error that the network converges to, or possibly, an error value for some test set (Schaffer et al 92). The fitness measure used here was based on a combination of training epochs and the sum of squared errors (SSE) of the network being evaluated.

In order to test the hypothesis, a group of five ANN's were configured to model the integration of four sensors with a single output network (the "motor" network). The concept is analogous to integrating the signals of our eyes and ears in order to move our head in the direction of a startling sound. For example, if a sound is heard underneath us, there may be no visual cues as to what the source was, but the ear's result is to tell us to effectively "look down." The sensor networks consisted of two "eyes" and two "ears." There is a left and right eye and a left and right ear. The goal was to, through the use of a GA, determine how well non-intuitive methods of connection between the sensor network outputs and inputs to the motor network

---

[*] E-mail address: stratton@hp3-745.gsfc.nasa.gov

perform as opposed to a one-to-one connection scheme. Figure 1 depicts graphically the differences between the two general methods.

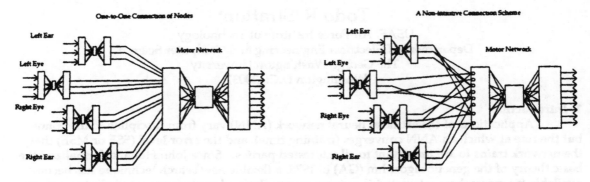

Figure 1. One-to-one vs. a non-intuitive connection scheme. Note that the numbers of inputs and outputs are not representative of the actual simulations.

It is important to note that the problem used here is a very simple one, and could be learned by a single backpropagation network with little problem. However, the proof of concept is more important at this stage because it is the possibility of designing a large system with this connection scheme that may help ANN's find more useful applications. Additionally, this problem was designed so that some useful correlation between which and how each node was connected to each other could be surmised from the results.

In order to implement the GA, the problem being optimized must be represented in terms of a string of characters. In this case, a binary alphabet {0,1} was chosen. By using a binary alphabet, the connection between nodes can be described as either present (1) or absent (0). For each output node of the sensor networks, 1..n bits will be set aside for the connections that node has. For a motor network input layer with 16 nodes, n=16. Since each sensor output node can be connected to more than one node of the motor input layer, 2^n connections are possible for each node from the sensor networks. For the sensor/motor network problem, each chromosome in the GA is 256 bits long. The first 16 bits are the connections for sensor output node 1, the next 16 bits are for sensor output node 2, etc. This method of representation allows all possible connections between the individual nodes of the sensor outputs and the motor inputs.

Another challenge of using GA's is that a proper fitness function must be developed to evaluate each member of the population in a meaningful way. For this case, each connection scheme derived by the GA needs to be applied to a ANN, which will provide a final error level after a specified amount of training time. In order to simulate actual connections between the networks, a number of steps had to be taken. To take advantage of existing software that is available (Arthur Cocoran's LibGA genetic algorithm routines written in C and the University of Stuttgart's Neural Network Simulator), a process was developed that allowed new training sets, to be created. Code was developed that allows a chromosome to be parsed one bit at a time, while at the same time keeping track of the sensor output and motor input node a particular bit refers to. When a (1) is encountered in the chromosome, the output activation from the source node is added to the input activation of the destination (motor network) node. When the whole chromosome is parsed, the new patterns that have been generated are made into a training set, and used in training an untrained motor network. This has the affect of changing the connection architecture. The training error level at a given epoch is reported to the GA as the fitness for that phenotype.

Additionally, the option of passing the summed inputs for the motor network through the sigmoid function is provided. This allows either passing of data bounded from 0..1 or data that is simply greater than or equal to 0.

3. Simulations

There are a number of interesting tests that can be run on these networks. The primary concern was to show that the GA provides either lower training time, lower training error or both. Populations of size 10 were chosen to facilitate project time constraints. Although 10 is a very small population size, there is some evidence (Goldberg 89) that small populations sizes can provide very good results, especially if the most fit members from one run of a simulation are combined with randomly initialized members in a new pool. The introduction of "new" solution possibilities often result in an even more optimal genotype.

All chromosomes were 256 bits in length. Initial training of the sensor networks was done with 52 patterns, and they were trained to a SSE of 0.2 for the whole network. A new training set was created from the sensor network results which consisted of 46 patterns. This was the base pattern that represented a one-to-one connection of sensor output nodes and motor input nodes.

A motor network with randomly initialized connection weights was created and saved so that all tests in a GA simulation were trained on the same initial network. Tests on a pool of randomly initialized members and on a pool of half random and half heuristic members were run. Heuristic members were generated based on simple rules such as: connect every other sensor output node with every other motor input node, connect any 4 sensor output nodes to any 1 motor input node, where each motor input node has no more than 4 inputs. These were included in the hopes of introducing a less "dense" bit pattern that often results from a 50/50 probability of initializing a single bit of the chromosome. These two tests were run with the summed inputs of the motor net first being passed through a thresholded sigmoid function, then the test with a pool of random members was tested without being passed through the sigmoid function. All training was done with backpropagation with a momentum term and networks were allowed to learn for 2000 epochs. The momentum constant, α, was set at 0.5.

Other proposed tests include simulations where the number of output nodes in the sensor nets is greater than the number of nodes for the motor network inputs, and vice versa. Also, different types of transformation functions, other than the normal sigmoid should be experimented with. Additionally, larger populations should be examined.

4. Results

On a pool of randomly initialized members, results indicate that the GA will consistently evolve a connection scheme that allows the network to train to an error level less than that of the one-to-one connection. In one case the control (one-to-one) connection trained to a SSE of 1.15. This was the best any control connection did on the networks, with values typically ranging from 1.2 to 2.5. In one run of the GA, a random pool resulted in an initial average population fitness of 2.673. By the fifth generation a member with an SSE of 0.8850 and four other members with SSE's of 0.988, 0.9735, 0.937, 0.889 had been found. The GA converged to a fitness of 0.885 after 6 generations. Convergence to the minimum error was typically smooth, with no sharp peaks or valleys present in the error levels of the network being trained.

The same test without a sigmoid conversion of the summed outputs of the sensor nets resulted in a slightly better result. Although initial population fitness averaged an SSE of 3.901, by the tenth generation the GA converged to a fitness of 0.8410. The second most fit individual had an SSE of 0.9791. Convergence of the non-sigmoid test was very erratic during training. Many peaks and valleys would typically be found in just a few epochs, however the error eventually converged.

Tests on the half-random pool provided statistically significant results. The GA converged by the eleventh generation to a minimum fitness of 0.726. Other members with finesses below 0.8 were 0.734, 0.756, 0.744, 0.738 and 0.761. Figure 2 depicts the most fit connection scheme found for the networks.

The most fit member of the population was taken to be compared against the one-to-one connection scheme in an average case scenario. A set of ten motor networks with different randomly initialized weights was created to find the average performance of these schemes.

Both schemes were trained on these 10 motor networks. The average performance of the one-to-one connection was an SSE of 1.869. The average performance of the GA connection scheme was 1.279. A t-test on the data reports a confidence of 98% that the means are significantly different (α at .5 level).

5. Discussion

Initial test results indicate that using a GA as an optimizing search for finding a better connection scheme than a standard one-to-one connection scheme has merit. All tests run resulted in the GA evolving a better network connection scheme than one-to-one or random schemes. These results apply to training up to and including 2000 epochs. Different initial weights affected the outcomes of the ultimate network training error more often than originally anticipated. It is often the set of initial weights that make a difference in how long a network takes to converge. On the average, the standard deviation of error for GA solutions appeared to be less than the standard deviation for one-to-one schemes.

More complete simulations would allow for detailed analysis of the action the GA is performing on this problem. It is hoped that the GA is doing a sort of feature amplification or feature clarification. Possibly by recognizing parts of patterns that contribute to training success, the GA is using nodes activated by those patterns more often. Additionally, the GA may be ignoring nodes that contribute little to the final result of the motor network.

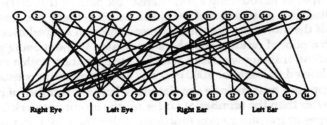

Figure 6. Most fit solution to connection problem.

It is hoped that using a method like the one proposed here may allow the simultaneous processing of a number of different aspects to some stimulus with groups of connected ANN's. This is analogous to how the brain's visual pathways work. Different areas of the visual cortex are sensitive to movement, color, edges, etc., and processing of these aspects of vision happen concurrently (Schatz 92).

References

Buckles, Bill P, and Petry, Frederick E. <u>An Overview of Genetic Algorithms and their Applications</u> Genetic Algorithms, IEEE, 1992.

Fischbach, Gerald D., "Mind and Brain", Scientific American, Sept. 92, pp. 48-57.

Goldberg, David E., "Sizing Populations for Serial and Parallel Genetic Algorithms," Proc. 3rd Int'l Conf. on Genetic Algorithms, 1989 pp 70-79.

Hintz K J, Spofford J J, "A Genetic Algorithm as the Learning Procedure for Neural Networks," Proc. 5th IEEE Int'l Symp. on Intelligent Control, 1990, pp. 479-84, vol. 1.

Koza, John R., <u>Genetic Programming - On the Programming of Computers by Means of Natural Selection</u> MIT Press, 1992

Schaffer, J. David, Darrel Whitely, and Larry Eshelman, "Combinations of Genetic Algorithms and Neural Networks: A survey of the State of the Art," IEEE Workshop on combinations of Genetic Algorithms and Neural Networks, pp 1-37, 1992.

Schatz, Carla J. "The Developing Brain" Scientific American, Sept 92, pp 61-67.

A Scalable Hybrid Neural Accelerator

Bassem A. Alhalabi and Magdy A. Bayoumi

The Center for Advanced Computer Studies
The University of Southwestern Louisiana Lafayette, Louisiana 70504

Abstract:

In this research, we developed a new complete system-level chip-set open architecture for feed-forward model with full connectivity and back-propagation learning. The system is based on two distinct chips, SynChip and NeuChip which may be cascaded to form networks matching any given application. The projected performance is 10,240 MCPS/MCUPS per SynChip and linearly grows thereafter. We devised a new embedded/distributed addressing technique which made the system self-contained. It also enhanced the system scalability as it allows multiple-chip enabling. Each SynChip has 32x32=1024 analog synapses, SynMod, and a local host-independent refreshing mechanism. Each NeuChip has 32 analog neuron, NeuMod, with special parallel learning hardware. The SynMod and NeuMod modules are designed with all-analog technology which enabled us to incorporate on-chip dynamic learning and maintain high degree of scalability, the two main characteristics which could not be found together in other systems. Furthermore, interfacing to the outside world is made universal as to accommodate virtually any digital or analog host systems via direct I/O ports. Each NeuChip supports 32-analog and 128-digital direct I/O lines which can be clustered into any word-length format to further enhance the system scalability. Also, the system may operate in continuous, step-discrete, or burst-discrete modes. Other features such as fault-tolerant capabilities, selective chip auditing, and a stand-by mode are provided.

I. Preliminaries

Artificial neural networks have demonstrated a great potential for tackling nonlinear applications such as acoustics, linguistics, vision, control, optimization, security, financial, medical, industrial, and consumer products due to the high degree of connectivity and parallelism. In particular, analog neural systems offer small components and consequently relatively higher parallelism. However, only few proposals are found in the literature which address complete systems especially with on-chip learning. They all lack either scalability, direct neural I/O ports, on-chip dynamic learning, fault-tolerance capabilities, data conversion, full parallelism or any combination of the above.

I.1. Analog Synaptic Storage

Synaptic weight storage has been the most challenging design issue in analog neural network paradigm especially if on-chip learning is required. The analog weight value (stored on a capacitor for example) must be made adjustable through some switching techniques (transistors) associated with the capacitor. This transistor association breeds an unpleasant leakage which inevitably shortens the life of the weight storage, and wherefore, refreshing mechanisms are evolved. Of course the best storage to solve this problem is the digital static RAM which does not require refreshing hardware. But if analog functional units are to be used for their superiority, then all digital weights must be converted to analog. This conversion in return necessitates that each synapse must be equipped with a DAC and/or ADC. This trade off between digital storage with DAC/ADC and analog storage with refreshing brought up several schemes and techniques for weight storage and update handling.

Some authors like [2..Bose91] used analog storage for the synaptic weights so that they eliminated the need for weight conversion from digital to analog and vice versa. Moreover, because they did not support on-chip learning, they used external RAM to permanently store all the weights and sequentially reload (refresh) them to the analog capacitors through two on-chip DACs. This approach not only makes learning impossible to incorporate on chip, but it also makes dynamic learning extremely slow to implement as a host procedure. The difficulties arise from the need to modify the statically stored weights in accordance to dynamically generated weight updates.

Another interesting scheme of synaptic storage handling is found in [8..Spie92], where authors used digital storage and not only without refreshing but also without the addition of DACs. They used a 6–bit digital weight as an on/off multiplying switching pattern and a current split/recombine mechanism. This approach, however, makes learning too inefficient to incorporate on chip due to the large size of hardware that would be required to generate and impose the weight updates.

In comparison to the preceding schemes, we used all analog components. (See Table.1 for more detailed comparisons.) In our proposal, we used capacitors to store weights as voltages and developed a new analog technique to refresh them on chip. Also, the graded update signals are generated in analog and added to the weights via simple local analog adders. This localization of weight update makes the burden size of the learning procedure on the digital host minimal and independent of the overall network size, the advantage that permits an arbitrarily large size of neural networks. In contrast, external or internal digital storage creates a significant data transfer bandwidth bottleneck during weight updates especially with large size networks.

I.2. On-Chip Learning

Hardware support for an on-chip learning greatly overtaxes the silicon area of the neural system and substantially affects the formation of the architecture. Therefore, based on their particular applications, many early authors found it more efficient to leave the learning procedure to the host and spare the entire chip area for massively integrated neural processors [8..Spie92] [2..Bose91]. However, the submicron integration technology plus the vast amount of activities to improve analog techniques and tools, have been greatly facilitating the realization of on-chip learning. On-chip learning is essential in applications where learning new patterns is frequently needed and it must be dynamically performed. Due to the regularity of its data flow patterns and the widespread of its applications, we focussed on backpropagation.

One of the interesting learning schemes is found in [7..Shim92]. Although the authors used analog functional blocks to perform all weight multiplication and product summation, they implemented the weight update procedure using digital components. Because the weight was stored in a digital register, its graded updates had to be digitally computed and imposed which required an additional ADC and a digital adder for each synapse. This would have significantly increased the silicon area, and therefore, their optimal solution was to time-share one learning control circuit for every 64 synapses. The update procedure (10 steps) is implemented by firmware and sequentially applied to synapses within each group of 64 synapses.

In contrast to the above proposal and some others (See Table.1 for more detailed comparisons), we used all analog components for the learning algorithm. The graded update signal after its generation within each synapse body, is recognized in analog as a small voltage signal and added to the weight (which is also stored as a voltage) by a voltage adder. The learning control, however, is still digital but very insignificant in area and the whole update procedure is one step.

I.3. Why the New Architecture

The challenging design issue of analog storage and refreshing especially if on-chip learning is required have inspired the evolution of several schemes and techniques. The local RAM/DAC pair for every synapse is very appropriate if on-chip learning is not required. This provides stable weights without refreshing. If on-chip learning is required, however, the solution of adding an ADC to every synapse is too expensive. Yet an alternative way is to time-share the learning control which makes learning too slow. Therefore, to acquire a relatively large and fully parallel network with a reasonable increase in hardware cost, we concluded that all-analog weight storage and update procedure must be used. This was the basis of the architecture we developed. The advantage of this

Table 1:

Comparisons of Design Properties of Various Analog ANN

| Papers & Auothers | Weights | | Learning | | |
	Storage Mechanisim	Refreshing Method	Methodology	Control (Speed)	Weights Updating
Our Proposal	- Ang Capacitor	- Microscopic with ind clock - Special HW in Synapse Module - Sense 32 Synapses @1C. Compare to 16-level refrence Correct to the upper bound Repeat 32 time for whole chip	- On-Chip HW - BP - Batch or Pattern	- HW (Fast)	- 1-Step Analog Procedure $\delta_i[l] = f'(h_i[l]) \sigma_i[l]$ $\sigma_i[l] = \sum_j \delta_j[l+1] w_{ji}[l+1]$
T. Shima JSSC 92 [7..Shim92]	- 8-b register & 8-b DAC	- Not applicable	- On-Chip HW & FW - BP & Hebbian - Batch only	- HW 1 to 64 (Slow)	- 10-Step Digital Procedure $\Delta w_{ij} = \delta_j \times ()$, on-chip Quantized by 1-b ADC Inc/Dec 8-b momentum counter ($\sum \Delta w_{ij}$) update 8-b wieght using the counter One counter for 64 syn [9 S @10C]
B. Boser JSSC 91 [2..Bose91]	- Ang Capacitor and ext RAM	- Ext control with ind clock - 2 DACs on chip (6-b) connected to ext weight RAM	- Host Algoritm	- Host	- Not supported Host sequential procedure
J. V. Spiegel JSSC 92 [8..Spie92]	- 6-b shift register	- Not applicable	- Host Algoritm	- Host	- Not supported Host sequential procedure
M. Holler IJCNN 89 [3..Holl89]	- Diff Volt EEPROM cells	- Not applicable	- Host Algoritm	- Host	- Not supported Host sequential procedure
S. Satyanarayana JSSC 92 [6..Saty92]	- Ang Capacitor	- Same as updating	- Host Algoritm - Gradient-Based Learning		- Digital data from host - 8 DACs off chip - 8 wieght update at a time

new full-analog learning is two folds. First, it does not have time-shared digital components, the characteristic which explores the true natural parallelism of neural networks. Second, it is relaxed from the sequential nature of digital procedures, the advantage which emphasizes on the spontaneity of analog components behavior. These two pluses add to the overall speed of our system.

System scalability and expandability is a very important design measure and it must be carefully incorporated. It is achievable through chip-set basis and modular design strategy. We observed the lack of scalability in most of the previous work and that was one of our main enhancement goals. Topological programmability, however, is not as important because full connectivity is provenly sufficient and economical in analog paradigm. Therefore, we did not account for programmable topology.

Embedded and distributed address decoding technique (versus the conventional one) eliminates all external address decoding hardware making the overall system more self-contained and easier to build and manage. Moreover, it enhances the system scalability as it randomly allows simultaneous chip enabling. This technique is a very unique feature of our system and have not been previously reported.

Finally, building a fast neural system that is capable of real-time computations would not be as meaningful as if it is equipped with direct I/O ports capable of importing and exporting data both in real time. There has been a major lack in such direct I/O ports especially those which simultaneously support both analog and digital formats. Our projected architecture favorably accounted for analog/digital direct I/O ports.

II. A Scalable Modular Neural Architecture

The proposed full analog architecture is based on two distinct chips, SynChip and NeuChip, whose block diagrams and their interconnection relationships are illustrated in Fig.4. This 2–Chip Set architecture is originally proposed by [1..Alhalabi94]. The NeuChip consists of 32 analog neuron modules (NeuMod) and a digital control block (NeuLogic). The SynChip consists of an array of 32x32 analog synapse modules (SynMod), a digital control block (SynLogic), a voltage reference of 16 levels, and 32 refreshing blocks (RefMod). These two chips may be cascaded on a regular grid to build a neural network of any arbitrary input, output, and/or layer sizes.

The SynChip has two sets of analog lines (dotted lines): 32 horizontal analog lines (HAL1–i–32) and 32 vertical analog lines (VAL1–j–32). The HALs are all physical analog wires which run horizontally across each SynChip from left to right and from one SynChip to another till they mate directly to the left side of the NeuChip within the same layer. Same thing for the VALs except that they run vertically to mate directly to the right side of NeuChip of the previous layer. Both HALs and VALs are bidirectional analog lines which either collect current signals from SynMods and inject them into the NeuMods, or take voltage signals form NeuMods and distribute them to SynMods. The direction and kind of analog signals are dependent on the mode of operation as will be discussed later.

The NeuMod blocks generate/collect the HAL signals from the left side and the VAL signals from the right side to mate with the SynChips as explained earlier. However, these HALs and VALs do not pass through the NeuMods as they do in the SynMods case, instead, they are either initiated or terminated. For an insight on this difference, see Fig.1.

The solid hexagons labeled SS1-8 (synapse switches) in the SynMod (Fig.1) are all passive analog switches each of which is controlled by a dedicated digital control signal (not shown in the figure for clarity) from the Switches Control block. These digital control signals are level-sensitive (high=on and low=off). The triangular block labeled Buff is a voltage buffer which helps the weight capacitor Cw retains its voltage level against charge sharing with other functional units. The η block represents the learning factor which is a constant generated at the SynChip level and distributed to all SynMods in the SynChip. Capacitor Ca is utilized to temporarily store the last activation value when the mode of operation is switched to learning. Switch SS4 and the RefVolt horizontal line are utilized by the refreshing mechanism to refresh the synaptic weights as will be explored later. Finally, SS1 is provided to load/unload the weight value to/from capacitor Cw. For complete detailed description of this architecture refer to [1..Alhalabi94].

III. Neural Operations and Data Flow

After system initialization, the configuration procedure is executed to configure all the chips in the system as to comply with one given mode and/or neural operation. Subsequent executions may be invoked as needed for different neural operations. All configuration information is stored in the CONFIG registers inside the NeuChip and SynChip. Decoding the CONFIG bits is primarily done inside the NeuLogic/SynLogic blocks (Fig.4) and finally within Switches Control block (Fig.1). The final settings of all switches for all possible neural operations determine the state of the ANN system. Now we will discuss the data flow and some neural operations.

The VALj line (Fig.1) carries the activation value $a_j[l-1]$ as a voltage level from the previous layer and passes it vertically to all SynMods$_{(1j-32j)}$ in all SynChips within the same layer. This activation value and the weight value w_{ij}, stored in capacitor Cw, are respectively presented by SS7 and SS2 to the voltage multiplier $a_j w_{ij}$. The multiplier acts as a current source and its output whose value is proportional to the inputs voltage levels is passed to the HALi line via switch SS6. The HALi line horizontally collects all current contributions $\{a_j[l-1]w_{ij}[l]\}$ from all SynMods$_{(32-i1)}$ of all SynChips within the same layer and present the accumulated current to the corresponding NeuMod which is a current-summing OpAmp. Thus, in the recall mode, SS2, SS6, and SS7 are on and the data flows into the SynChips as voltages via the VAL lines and flows out as currents via the HAL lines.

In the neuron module, NeuMod (Fig.1), the summation block $h_i = \Sigma_j a_j w_{ij}$ is a current-summing OpAmp which adds up all currents $\{a_j[l-1]w_{ij}[l]\}$ accumulated on the HALi line. The sum is adjusted by the nonlinear function block $f(h_i)$ to compute the activation value $a_i[1]$ for the next layer. This activation value is presented as a voltage level on the VALi line via switch NS8 (Fig.1). Therefore, in a normal recall mode, only NS1 and NS8 are turned on. However, if there is a desire to monitor the activation values of any layer [l] by the host, switch NS6 may be turned on and the analog value $a_i[1]$ is digitized by the ADC block and its 4-bit representation is read off the 4-bit data lines D(4i-4)-(4i-1). Note that the data bus of the host is 128-bit wide allowing the host to read all of the 32 4-bit activation values from the 32 NeuMods in one NeuChip in one bus cycle.

In the learning mode, SS5 and SS8 are on instead of SS6 and SS7 as to allow data to flow backward. Error signals $\delta_i[l]$ (Fig.1), coming from the NeuChips of the same layer, flow into the SynChips as voltages via the HAL lines, get manipulated, and flow out as currents $\{\delta_i[l]w_{ij}[l]\}$ via the VAL lines. These currents which are the product outputs of the individual $\delta_i w_{ij}$ voltage multipliers accumulate vertically on the VAL lines and finally get added up in the NeuChips of the previous layer. The third voltage multiplier in the SynMod calculates the weight update value $\Delta w_{ij} = a_j \delta_i \eta$. The product output is added (by the Adder Block) to the original value of the weight which is temporarily stored in Co. The new weight value is finally stored in Cw via switch SS3.

At the VALi line, a set of currents $\{\delta_j[l+1]w_{ji}[l+1]\}$ accumulate and pass to the summation block $\sigma_i = \Sigma_j \delta_j w_{ji}$ via NS12. The output sum passes NS11 to the multiplier $\delta_i = f'(h_i)\sigma_j$ to generate the error $\delta_i[l]$ which is outputted at HALi via NS2. Note that the multiplier obtains the value $f'(h_i)$ from the $f'(h_i)$ block whose input value h_i was temporarily stored in capacitor Ch during the recall phase. Switch NS3 turns off in the learning phase to retain the Ch voltage level.

IV. Simulations and Analysis

In this section, we discuss the simulation of the NeuChip and SynChip. We wrote a simulator based on a network of 2 layers arranged as 32x32x32. This network requires 3 NeuChips and 2 SynChips as illustrated in Figure 2. The simulation has been carried out on the MasPar due to its massive computational power. We used the MP-1 with 2K processors which are capable of performing arithmetic and logical operations simultaneously. The mapping method we developed for the recall and training algorithms acquires synapse-level parallelism. It maximizes parallelism by unfolding the ANN computation to its smallest computational primitives and processes these primitives in parallel. An average run for the simulator (10 patterns and 500 iterations) would take only 2 minutes. Hardware description of MP-1 the may be obtained from the MasPar hardware manuals [4..MasPar].

IV.1. The Simulator

The simulator is written in the MasPar Application Language (MPL) which is a parallel version of the standard C language. A good tutorial reference for the MasPar programming is [5..Parallab]. The simulator reads the training set (patterns and targets) from a data file and the simulation and network parameters from the parameters file. The simulator takes 32 x 4-bit digital inputs (the size of one chip) and generates an output of the same size. In the following sections we will examine several experiments for different data sets and parameters settings.

We used two set of simulation data with different input and output sizes. The first training set is obtained from the button faces of the 12-botton telephone keypad (0–9, *, and #). These twelve buttons are created as 9x11 bit-map images and inputted to the simulator as 99–bit vector patterns. The target outputs are the corresponding English name for each button (ONE, TWO, etc...). The simulator reads the inputs in 4-bit clusters regardless of the actual data size and generates the outputs in the same fashion. The leading bits in the patterns and targets are filled with zeros. The second set of data is made up from normal English strings. We used one string as input and another with a meaningful relation to the first as a target. (e.g. "It is a Nice Day" ⇔ "Go Vacation".)

IV.2. Simulation Experiments and Results

Refreshing Rate

Based on a typical value of $1\mu V/1\mu S$ for the voltage leakage across the synaptic capacitors, it is estimated that the refreshing procedure must be invoked at least every 20 mS in order to keep the weights within 98% accuracy.

Refreshing While Learning, RWL, Technique

In this experiment, we tried the new technique of invoking the weight refreshing procedure while the system is being trained. For this experiment, we used the telephone button faces. We ran the simulator for different values for the refreshing resolution (in particular, we used 4, 5, and 6 bits). For every resolution value, we ran the simulator for different values for the RWL frequency. In other words, every number of iterations, we invoke one refresh (refresh_while_learn parameter). Every run of all above combinations produced an output which is the number of iterations the simulator had to perform in order to train the system. All results of the above experiments were plotted in Figure 3. We observed that when we refresh the weights every number of iterations (90 for this data set), the network learns regardless of the number of refreshing bits (about 400 iterations). However, performing refreshing at higher resolution such as 5-bit (or 6-bit) would make the network learn with less RWL frequency, 20 (or 50) iterations. This experiment indicates that RWL with a proper rate would not affect the learning process in terms of the required number of iterations.

Fault Tolerant Learning

The target of this experiment is to verify that RWL makes the weights more robust. For this experiments, we used the English string matching set of data. We conducted several experiments and found out that RWL makes the trained network recall patterns for longer times before the weights have to be refreshed. This proves that the weights are more tolerant for leakage or degradation during the recall operation.

Other experiments also indicated that if we train the network without RWL, then, during recall, it becomes necessary to refresh at higher resolutions such as 5 or 6 bits. When we used 4-bit refreshing, we experienced some unmatching outputs.

Input/Output Clustering

From the above experiments, we experimentally proved that inputs and outputs can be clustered in any size. In the telephone keypad experiments, we used 99-bit input and clustered them into groups of 4-bit. With the English strings data, we used 8-bit ASCII representation for the English characters and also clustered them in 4-bit pieces. And in both cases, the outputs were read as 2-Hex ASCII characters.

V. Conclusions

We have discussed various techniques and methodologies for the development and construction of analog and hybrid neural networks. Detailed comparison between several architectures established in the last few years was depicted in Table.1. We found out that analog neural networks are more emulative to the brain than digital counterparts due to their superior spatio-temporal processing power.

Based on all previous work deficiencies and the foreseen enhancements, we developed a neural architecture based on two distinct chips: SynChip and NeuChip as shown in Figure 4. These two chips may be cascaded in a regular-grid fashion to build a neural network for any given application of any arbitrary input, output, and layer sizes.

We adopted analog technology in designing the synapse and neuron modules, SynMod and NeuMod, due to its superiority; it is higher in speed and smaller in size in contrast to digital counterparts. The entire neural computations within the modules are performed in analog. These analog operations provide a natural implementation of neural models as it loosely emulates the information flow of biological systems. Digital circuitries, however, are employed to facilitate the interface and communication with conventional digital host computers.

We experimentally proved that our architecture is functionally correct. We also concluded that in order to get consistent results during recall operations, the RWL concept should be used during learning. It enhances the network fault tolerance and makes refreshing less frequently needed.

Bibliography

[1] B. A. Alhalabi and M. A. Bayoumi. A hybrid chip set for artificial neural networks. *Proceedings of World Congress on Neural Networks*, vol.II:pp.624–630, San Diego, CA., June, 1994.

[2] B. E. Boser and E. Sackinger. An analog neural network processor with programmable topology. *IEEE Journal of Solid-State Circuits*, vol.26(no.12):pp.2017–2025, December 1991.

[3] M. Holler and S. Tam. An electrically trainable artificial neural network (etann) with 10240 "floating gate" synapses. *International Joint Conference on Neural Networks*, vol.II:pp.191–196, June 1989.

[4] MasPar. *MP-1 System Hardware Manuals*.

[5] R. Pickering and J. Cook. Parallel processing: A self-study introduction. Technical Report #pl-jc-93.0, Parallab Dept., University of Bergen, Bergen, Norway, 1993.

[6] S. Satyanarayana and Y. P. Tsividis. A reconfigurable vlsi neural network. *IEEE Journal of Solid-State Circuits*, vol.27(no.1):pp.67–81, January 1992.

[7] T. Shima and T. Kimura. Neuro chips with on-chip back-propagation and/or hebbian learning. *IEEE Journal of Solid-State Circuits*, vol.27(no.12):pp.1868–1876, December 1992.

[8] J. V. Spiegel and P. Mueller. An analog neural computer with modular architecture for real-time dynamic computations. *IEEE Journal of Solid-State Circuits*, vol.27(no.1):pp.82–92, January 1992.

Digital Host

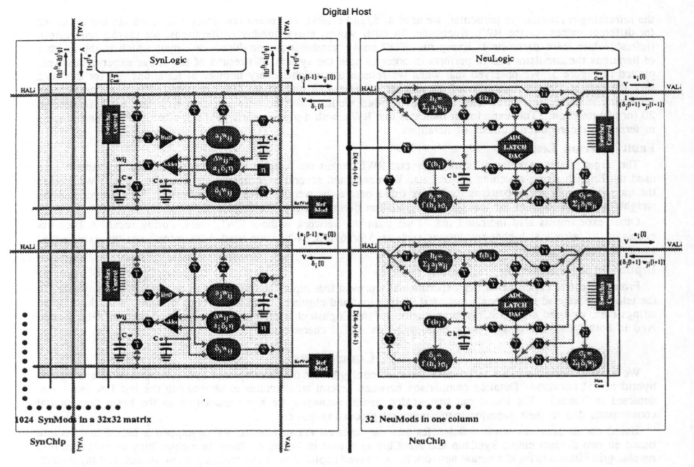

Figure 1:
A Detailed Close-up of a NeuChip and a SynChip to Show the Interconnection Between the SynMod and NeuMod Modules and Their Internal Structure.

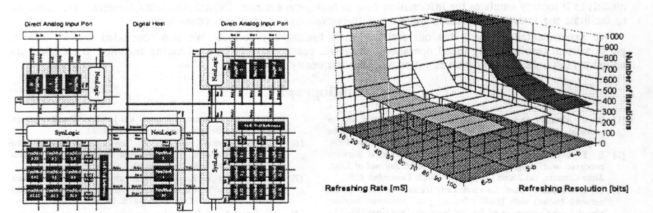

Figure 2:
A 2-layer Perceptron for Simulation.

Figure 3:
Number of Iterations Versus Refreshing Rate and Number of Refreshing Bits.

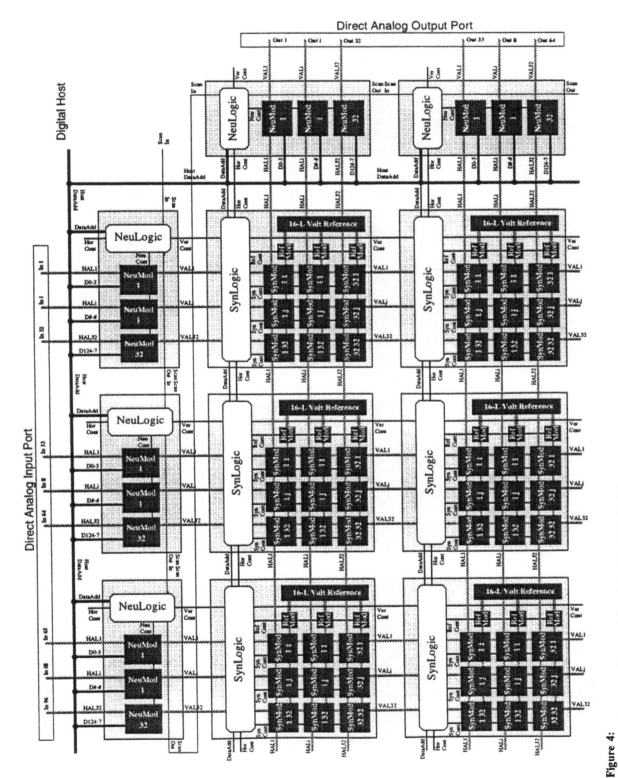

Figure 4:
A One-Layer Perceptron Constructed from 6 SynChips & 5 NeuChips.

Novel Results Session

Function Approximation

Novel Results on Stochastic Modelling Hints for Neural Network Prediction

Radu Drossu   Zoran Obradović[1]

School of Electrical Engineering and Computer Science
Washington State University, Pullman, Washington, 99164-2752

Abstract

In a companion study [2], the appropriateness of the stochastic *hint* for selecting an appropriate neural network (NN) architecture for time series prediction problems is analyzed. This study explores further the validity of the original hint, as well as the appropriateness of additional hints in the context of more complex prediction problems. Experiments performed on both the entertainment video traffic series, previously used, as well as on an artificially generated nonlinear time series on the verge of chaotic behavior (Mackey-Glass series) indicate that the initial knowledge obtained through stochastic analysis provides a reasonably good hint for the selection of an appropriate NN architecture. Although not necessarily the optimal, such a rapidly designed NN architecture performed comparable or better than more elaborately designed NN's obtained through expensive trial and error procedures.

1 Introduction

Time series prediction problems typically deal with either predicting a characteristic process parameter for the next time step (prediction horizon one), or with predicting a parameter several steps ahead (prediction horizon larger than one). The first objective of this study is to explore the validity of the stochastic hint proposed in [2] regarding an appropriate NN architecture for noise corrupted data, as well as for a more complex time series (Mackey-Glass series). An additional objective is to investigate the relevance of a stochastic hint regarding an appropriate sampling rate for a given prediction horizon.

The goal of this study is not to obtain "the optimal" NN architecture for a given problem, but to provide rapidly (through a fast stochastic modelling) an architecture with close to optimal performance. Since the hint is obtained from a linear model, for more complex problems the NN might be over-dimensioned (similar performance might be obtained using a smaller machine and less training data). However, the exhaustive trial and error procedure involved for determining such an optimal machine could be costlier than the stochastic hint-based alternative.

2 ARMA Hints for Neural Networks

The hint explored throughout the experiments is whether the order of the most appropriate stochastic model provides an indication of the appropriate number of NN inputs: feedforward NN with p or $p+1$ external inputs for an AR(p) process or recurrent NN with p or $p+1$ external and q context inputs for an ARMA(p,q) process. The choice of p or $p+1$ external inputs from the hint depends on whether the stochastic pre-processing step is done without or with discrete differentiation respectively. Since the stochastic modelling of the data sets considered in the experiments indicated AR(p) models as the most appropriate, all the analyzed NN architectures were of feedforward type.

For prediction horizons larger than one, different sampling rates can be employed, which makes the trial and error NN architecture selection even more impractical. Consequently, an additional hint regarding the most appropriate data sampling rate is also addressed in the study.

3 Experimental Results

For prediction with horizon one on entertainment video data un-corrupted by noise, the performance of the hint-based NN was not consistently better than that of the corresponding stochastic model [2]. Additional

[1] Research sponsored in part by the NSF research grant NSF-IRI-9308523.

experiments using the same data led to slightly better results for the stochastic model as compared to the NN model. As the computationally more powerful NN model is expected to yield better performance for problems of increased complexity [4], in this study the following problems were considered: (1) influence of increased prediction horizon; (2) influence of noise corruption; (3) influence of increased complexity of the data set.

The first data set used in the experiments consisted of a real life, compressed, entertainment video traffic data used in an ATM (Asynchronous Transfer Mode) network, in which each sample represents the size of a corresponding compressed video frame [1]. The difficulty associated with this data set is the *non-stationarity* (data distribution changes over time), as well as the existence of "outliers" (values very different from neighboring ones). The data set consisted of 2000 samples, of which the first 1000 were used for parameter estimation and NN training and the last 1000 for model validation and NN testing.

The second data set is artificially generated and is obtained by a delay differential equation (also known as Mackey-Glass series):

$$\frac{dx(t)}{dt} = \frac{Ax(t - \tau)}{1 + x^{10}(t - \tau)} - Bx(t)$$

Experiments were performed for $A = 0.2$, $B = 0.1$, $\tau = 17$, case in which the system exhibits chaotic behavior. The difficulty associated with this data set is the high *nonlinearity*. The data set consisted of 3000 samples out of which various experiments used either the first 1000 or the first 2000 values for parameter estimation (training), and the following 1000 for model validation (testing).

The influence of increased prediction horizon and noise corruption was analysed in the context of the entertainment video traffic data set, whereas the influence of increased data complexity was analyzed in the context of the Mackey-Glass series. A data pre-processing step was employed for both stochastic and NN modelling that encompassed a logarithmic smoothing and a first order differentiation in the case of the stochastic models, and just a linear scaling in the case of the NN models. These transformations were performed in all experiments if not specified otherwise. Reported NN results were obtained using a learning rate $\eta = 0.01$, a momentum term $\alpha = 0.7$, training for 6000-40000 training epochs and averaged over 10 runs with different initial random weights, if not specified otherwise.

3.1   Influence of Increased Prediction Horizon

Experiments for a prediction horizon 10 analyse whether an appropriate sampling rate based on the stochastic modelling hint is adequate. In addition, similar to the prediction horizon one hint, it is explored whether an appropriate AR(p) model indicates the use of a feedforward NN with $p + 1$ external inputs (the additional input accounts for the first order differentiation in the stochastic pre-processing). To predict the process, $\hat{x}$, at time step $t + 10$ using k process values up to time t, sampling rates 1, 2, 5 and 10 (divisors of the prediction horizon) are considered.

For horizon h larger than one, the prediction can be done either in a *direct* or in an *incremental* fashion. In the direct approach, the NN is trained to predict directly the h-th step ahead without predicting any of the intermediate $1, \ldots, h - 1$ steps. In the incremental approach, the NN predicts all the intermediate values up to h steps ahead by using the previously predicted values as inputs for predicting the next value. Since the incremental approach lead to an undesirable accumulation of error for our data set, the presented results are obtained by using the direct approach.

Sampling	Model	- μ	MSE	r^2
1	AR(5)	-1.635	534.640	0.667
1	NN 6-6-1	-191.596	623.589	0.556
2	AR(4)	4.042	544.573	0.442
2	NN 5-5-1	-177.545	557.727	0.406
5	AR(5)	1.759	928.670	0.131
5	NN 6-6-1	24.472	880.784	0.222
10	AR(4)	31.118	855.588	0.361
10	NN 5-5-1	10.223	1004.144	0.333

Table 1: Different Sampling Rates for Horizon 10

Model	μ	MSE	r^2
AR(5)	-1.635	534.640	0.667
NN 3-3-1	-272.557	691.800	0.446
NN 4-4-1	-192.799	625.247	0.552
NN 5-5-1	-232.390	664.002	0.498
NN 6-6-1	-191.596	623.589	0.556
NN 7-7-1	-201.559	636.116	0.540

Table 2: Sampling Rate 1 for Horizon 10

The most appropriate AR models obtained for different sampling rates, as well as the corresponding NN models are presented in Table 1. The stochastic models indicate a sampling rate 1 as the most appropriate. The NN results confirm the hint drawn from the stochastic analysis, according to which a sampling rate 1 is the most appropriate. Except for the case of the 5-5-1 NN applied for sampling rate 10, all the NN's employed the bias removal post-processing described in [2]. The parameters μ (mean), MSE (root mean squared error) and r^2 (coefficient of determination) are also defined in [2].

Table 2 summarizes the results obtained for the best stochastic model, as well as for different representative NN's for a sampling rate 1. The NN's employed a similar bias removal post-processing as in the case of prediction horizon one. The table indicates that the NN having 6 inputs yielded the best prediction, this being consistent with the hint provided by the stochastic modelling (allowing again an additional external input as compared to the most appropriate AR(5) model to account for the first order differentiation). NN architectures much larger than the ones indicated were also experimented with, but their performance was poor (the coefficient of determination, r^2 was 0.160 for a 20-20-1 architecture and -0.025 for a 30-30-1 architecture respectively).

The conclusions that could be drawn from these experiments are: (1) the data sampling rate indicated by the stochastic models seems to be appropriate also for the NN models; (2) the hint provided by the stochastic analysis regarding the number of external inputs is effective also for larger horizons; (3) the performance of the AR models is still better, this indicating that the complexity of the data sets might still be too low.

3.2 Influence of Noise Corruption

Another practical problem is constituted by the prediction in a noisy environment. For such an experiment, an additive Gaussian noise is introduced to the entertainment video traffic data and predictions with horizon one are performed. The first experiment used un-corrupted (noise-free) data for parameter estimation and data with 50% noise for model validation. The noise level is computed as a ratio of the standard deviation of the additive noise and the standard deviation of the un-corrupted data. NN results employed the previously discussed bias removal post-processing.

The results for the most appropriate stochastic model, as well as for some of the representative NN models are presented in Table 3. It can be observed that the stochastic model is outperformed by the corresponding 6-6-1 NN. Table 3 also includes experimental results for an 80% noise level in the model validation data. Again, the NN outperforms the corresponding stochastic model, but this time more significantly. For comparison purposes Table 3 includes also the results obtained for a random walk (RWALK) predictor on 50% and 80% noise corrupted data. A random walk predictor is a trivial predictor, in which the next predicted value is identical to the last observed process value. The very low values for the coefficient of determination obtained for the random walk predictor as compared to both stochastic and NN models show clearly that both models are capable of extracting useful information even in the conditions of such a high noise level.

The conclusions drawn from this experiment are: (1) the NN corresponding to the most appropriate stochastic model has a better performance than the other tested NN's; (2) in this problem the performance of the NN is better than that of the corresponding stochastic model.

Noise Level	Model	r^2
50%	AR(5)	0.359
50%	NN 3-3-1	0.382
50%	NN 4-4-1	0.413
50%	NN 5-5-1	0.421
50%	NN 6-6-1	0.430
50%	NN 7-7-1	0.427
50%	NN 8-8-1	0.429
50%	RWALK	0.0655
80%	AR(5)	0.095
80%	NN 6-6-1	0.232
80%	RWALK	-0.293

Table 3: Performance on Noisy Data

Model	Training Set Size	r^2
AR(24)	1000	0.751
NN 25-25-1	1000	0.914
NN 25-25-1	2000	0.925
AR(29) *	1000	0.767
NN 29-29-1	1000	0.917
NN 29-29-1	2000	0.929
NN 4-10-10-1	1000	0.912
NN 4-10-10-1	2000	0.936

Table 4: Performance on Mackey-Glass Data ("*" stands for no differentiation)

3.3 Influence of Increased Complexity of Data Set

The final experiment uses a well known benchmark problem, the Mackey-Glass time series. In accordance to previously published results [3], a sampling rate six is used for predicting six steps ahead.

The pre-processing step for the stochastic model included either both logarithmic smoothing and first order differentiation (yielding a most appropriate AR model of order 24) or just the logarithmic smoothing (leading to a most appropriate AR model of order 29). Experiments without first order differentiation were performed in this case since the data was apparently "stationary".

In contrast to the previous experiments, the NN results were obtained as an average over three runs with different initial random weights, since training was computationally too expensive for ten runs.

In addition to NN learning performed on the training set used for stochastic modelling (1000 examples), additional experiments were performed using a twice larger training set (2000 examples). The motivation for these additional experiments was the concern that the original 1000 training examples might not be enough to fit the parameters (weights) of the NN's corresponding to the AR(24) and AR(29) stochastic models. Instead of comparing the stochastic hint-based NN's to the NN's of somewhat different architectures obtained through a trial and error process as previously, here the results are compared versus an earlier reported "optimal" NN topology with 4 inputs and two hidden layers of 10 units each [3].

The conclusions drawn from this experiment are: (1) a differentiation pre-processing step in the stochastic modelling for this time series is not needed; (2) the performance of the NN's is much better as compared to the most appropriate stochastic model; (3) the stochastic hint-based NN's performed similar to the "optimal" NN architecture, further supporting the hint-based design approach; (4) although the hint-based NN might appear to be highly over-dimensioned as compared to "the optimal" network, training and prediction in an actual hardware implementation would be faster for the hint-based architecture since it contains a single layer of hidden units as compared to two such layers in the "optimal" architecture.

4 Final Remarks and Further Research

Although NN's are computationally more powerful models than the linear stochastic models, there are important real life problems in which a simple stochastic model can outperform NN's (see Section 3.1). Anyhow, there are many problems in which the computational power of NN's is beneficial (see Sections 3.2, 3.3). Consequently, when predicting time series, both methodologies should be considered before deciding upon the most appropriate prediction model.

Experiments suggested that a NN architecture selected according to the hint provided by the stochastic analysis performs comparable or better than NN architectures determined through a trial and error procedure. It is important to emphasise that the goal of the proposed hint-based approach is not to find "the optimal" NN architecture for a given problem but to provide rapidly (after a fast stochastic analysis) a NN architecture with close to optimal performance. Further research is needed to explore the validity of these hints to other time series prediction problems as well as to extend the study from AR to ARMA modelling hints (that would indicate the choice of a recurrent NN).

References

[1] R. Drossu, T. V. Lakshman, Z. Obradović and C. Raghavendra, "Single and Multiple Frame Video Traffic Prediction Using Neural Network Models," *Proc. IEEE Networks 94*, Madras, India, 1994.

[2] R. Drossu and Z. Obradovic, "Stochastic Modelling Hints for Neural Network Prediction," *Proc. World Congress on Neural Networks*, Washington, D.C, 1995.

[3] A. Lapedes and R. Farber, "Nonlinear Signal Processing Using Neural Networks: Prediction and System Modelling," *Technical Report*, LA-UR87-2662, Los Alamos National Laboratory, Los Alamos, New Mexico, 1987

[4] Z. Tang et al., "Time Series Forecasting Using Neural Networks vs. Box-Jenkins Methodology," *Artificial Neural Networks: Forecasting Time Series*, V. R. Vemuri and R. D. Rogers eds., IEEE Computer Society Press, 1994, pp. 20-27.

Function Learning with Stochastic Spike Train Input: Weight Compensation by Learning Rate Adjustment

Y Guan   T G Clarkson
Department of Electronic and Electrical Engineering

X Meng   J G Taylor
Department of Mathematics

King's College London, Strand, London WC2R 2LS, UK

A learning rate adjustment rule is presented for real-valued function approximation using a pRAM neural network. The learning rate in stochastic reinforcement training is adjusted by an input spike invariance related non-linear function which eases the memory saturation problem caused by the uneven distribution of addressing probabilities. The algorithm integrates a series of single output spike to approximate function values and updates memory contents on spike signal basis, so it is hardware realisable.

INTRODUCTION

Reinforcement learning requires less external information to guide the learning process of a neural network and is a good compromise between computational complexity and learning speed. It is an appropriate choice when a hardware implementation is possible so that the learning speed is less of a problem than with software simulation packages widely used on conventional serial computers. The probabilistic RAM (pRAM)([1]-[3]) is a stochastic and maximally non-linear device. One advantage of its hardware design is the capability of fast on-chip learning under the reinforcement learning rule, which can be easily manipulated with pRAM output spike trains.

An N-input pRAM (or N-pRAM) has 2^N memory locations, indexed by the binary address vector $\underline{u}$, containing probabilities $\alpha_{\underline{u}}$: if the pRAM is addressed by the binary vector $\underline{u}$ then $\alpha_{\underline{u}}$ is the probability that the binary output a will be equal to 1. The firing probability of the pRAM to input vector $\underline{i}$ is:

$$\text{Prob}(a=1 \mid i) = \sum_{\underline{u}} \alpha_{\underline{u}} \prod_{j=1}^{N} [u_j i_j + (1 - u_j)(1 - i_j)] \tag{1}$$

The variable $\alpha_{\underline{u}}$ may be represented by a binary spike train of length R. Accessing location $\underline{u}$ R times results in a stream of output bits a(r), r = 1...R; $\hat{\alpha}_{\underline{u}}$, a stochastic approximation to $\alpha_{\underline{u}}$, is then given by

$$\hat{\alpha}_{\underline{u}}(R) = \frac{1}{R} \sum_{r=1}^{R} a(r)$$

The memory update rule is

$$\Delta \alpha_{\underline{u}} = \rho[(a-\alpha_{\underline{u}})r + \lambda(\bar{a} - \alpha_{\underline{u}})p] \times \delta_{\underline{u},!} \tag{2}$$

where the learning rate is ρ and the decay rate is λ, r is the reward and p the penalty signals with r = 1 - p.

In neuronal terms working with real-valued inputs corresponds to using mean firing frequencies: a real input vector $\underline{x}$ may be approximated by the time-average of R successive binary input patterns $\underline{i} \in \{0,1\}^N$:

$$x_j = \frac{1}{R} \sum_{r=1}^{R} i_j(r) \tag{3}$$

Then the output y has potential contributions from all 2^N memory locations

$$y = \sum_{\underline{u}} \alpha_{\underline{u}} \prod_{j=1}^{N} [u_j i_j + (1 - u_j)(1 - i_j)] = \sum_{\underline{u}} \alpha_{\underline{u}} X_{\underline{u}} \tag{4}$$

where $X_{\underline{u}}$ is the probability that $\underline{u}$ is addressed. The output y is approximated by the random variable $\hat{y}$, which is computed in an R-step sampling process such that

$$\hat{y}(R) = \frac{1}{R} A_{\underline{u}} \tag{5}$$

where $A_{\underline{u}}$ is the total number of 1's emitted by location $\underline{u}$ when accessed

$$A_{\underline{u}} = \sum_{s=1}^{S_{\underline{u}}} a_{\underline{u}}(s), \quad a_{\underline{u}} \in \{0, 1\} \tag{6}$$

and S_u is the access count for location $\underline{u}$ ($\sum_u S_u = R$, $X_u = S_u/R$).

Algorithms for binary output learning tasks have been developed and successful applications in pattern classification have been proved (eg.[3] and [4]). Since general learning requires real-valued input and output signals, our interest in learning here is focused on continuous functions. A natural extension of the previous binary input pattern classification methods is to approximate the real input vector $\underline{x} \in [0,1]^N$ and output variable $y \in [0,1]^N$ by eqs. (3) and (5) respectively. However this direct approximation for $\underline{x}$ may cause memory contents to be improperly saturated at some locations (contents are driven to their limiting binary values), which is due to the maximum addressing probability to those locations. For example, a 2-input pRAM has four memory locations: α_{00}, α_{01}, α_{10} and α_{11}. If we connect a single input variable x to the pRAM in a way as shown in Figure 1a and let x take a continuous value in $[0,1]$, an extreme case of sampling, the addressing probability of each location of the pRAM will be:

$$X_{00} = \int_0^1 (1-x)^2 dx = \frac{1}{3} \qquad X_{01} = \int_0^1 (1-x)x\,dx = \frac{1}{6}$$

$$X_{10} = \int_0^1 x(1-x)dx = \frac{1}{6} \qquad X_{11} = \int_0^1 x^2 dx = \frac{1}{3}$$

As a result, α_{00} and α_{11} will have heavier "burdens" and often saturate more quickly than α_{01} and α_{10}.

In order to avoid the memory saturation, paper [5] suggested to use a transformation on the input as shown in Figure 1b. The transformation used in [5] is to tabulate the input interval which ensures the equal addressing probabilities from the input to every memory location.

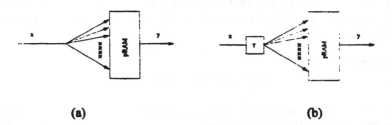

$$(a) \qquad\qquad\qquad\qquad (b)$$

Figure 1. (a) Direct connections of x to the input of a pRAM; (b) Connections of input x to the input of pRAM after transformation T.

Given input data lying between the tabulated values, and the associated function values, the learning process is required to find the function values for the tabulated values, so that the function values for all independent inputs can be achieved by normal interpolation. This is called "reverse" interpolation. In the algorithm, the input interval $[0,1]$ is divided into 2^N-1 tabulars, for an N-input pRAM. The tabulated values are the set C:{ 0, $1/(2^N-1), 2/(2^N-1),..., (2^N-2)/(2^N-1)$, 1}, which corresponds to the pRAM binary address set D:{ (00...0), (00...1),..., (11...0), (11...1)}. With this mapping, addressing probability X_u for each memory location $\underline{u}$ will be the same, as x takes values in $[0,1]$ and this addressing will not cause a saturation problem since each memory location will have the same addressing probability when x changes in $[0,1]$. Details of the algorithm were described in [5] with demonstration examples.

Training rates adjustment algorithm

The reverse interpolation algorithm works well for small sized tasks where the number of input variables is small, because the limitation on the number of input lines of a pRAM node. If the number of the input variables is large, training with the direct connection of input variables to the pRAM net is a better choice, but we need to find a way to solve the weight saturation problems caused by the uneven distribution of addressing probabilities of memory locations.

It is noted that the saturation of weights always takes place in those locations which are at or close to 0...00 or 1...11 (in Hamming distance) if the direct connection of the input variables to the network is applied (Figure 1a). The variance of input spikes, given length of R, is

$$\sigma^2(x) = x(1-x)/R \tag{7}$$

The saturation actually occurs at the locations which has small variance. If the normalised input variable x is close to the value of 0.0 or 1.0, it keeps addressing the memory locations 0...00 or 1...11 (or nearby locations) during the whole length of updating cycle R, and certainly these memory contents will easily be saturated. On the other hand, the input variables with larger variance (e.g. input x is 0.5) have almost even addressing probabilities to every memory location, and it is unlikely to make any memory content saturated. In the updating cycle of the same length R, the modification amount for any saturated memory content is smaller compared with that made by the input spike with larger variance. As a result, the training always favours the input variables with small variance and the input with larger variance is difficult to get the accurate output value.

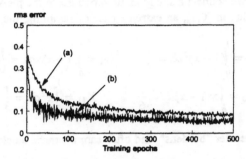

Figure 2. (a) The rms error for training without $\rho(\sigma^2(x))$ adjustment;
(b) The rms error for training with $\rho(\sigma^2(x))$ adjustment.

It is understood, from the above analysis, that the effect of variance of input spikes on weight updating should be considered during training. It is suggested in this paper that the training rate ρ in eq.(2) is adjusted according to the variance of input spike trains (eq.(7)). As a result, training will be fair to all input variables and the weight saturation problem can be solved.

For training rate adjustment, we let

$$\rho(x) = c[4x(1-x)]^k \rho_0$$

where x is the input, c ($0<c<1$) is the fine tuning parameter, and $k = 1, 2, ...$ The coefficient 4 is a normalisation scalar. It can be seen that ρ is a function of input variance $\sigma^2(x)$. The adjustment function takes the shape that is similar to Gaussian distribution function with mean value of 0.5. It ensures that a larger learning rate is assigned for an input which has larger variance in its spike train representation. Therefore the updating amount is larger for those locations at or around 0...00 and 1...11, which have smaller addressing probabilities when the variance of input spikes is larger. The memory contents at those locations therefore will not be easily saturated since the updating amount for large variance input spikes is compensated by a large learning rate and it can compete fairly in quantity with small variance input spikes.

The parameters c and k are chosen depending on the learning tasks. A larger k means a sharply decreased compensation for the training rate as the variance of input spikes decreases.

A training example is given in this paper in which a pRAM neural net is trained to approximate the function $\sin(x)$. The network contains eight 8-input-pRAMs in the first layer and one 8-input-pRAM in the output layer. R is 100 in this case. Initial value ρ_0 is 0.1 and λ is 0.005. Figure 2a shows the rms error of the training task without $\rho(\sigma^2(x))$ adjustment in which training stabilises after about 400 epochs and rms error is about 0.08. The training result with $\rho(\sigma^2(x))$ adjustment is shown in figure 2b. The $\rho(\sigma^2(x))$ adjustment algorithm has been demonstrated to be successful: fast convergence (stabilises after 200 epochs) and small rms error (about 0.05). Here c is chosen to be 0.5 and k is 4.

If a sigmoidal squashing function is added between the input and output layers, the learning accuracy can be further improved. Figure 3 illustrates the simulation results for the above learning task but with the squashing function added. Without $\rho(\sigma^2(x))$ adjustment, the training stabilises after about 300 epochs and rms error is 0.05; while with $\rho(\sigma^2(x))$ adjustment the training stabilises after about 100 epochs and rms error is reduced to 0.02-0.03. The cost of adding the squashing function is that the training takes L times longer for an L layer pRAM net since in each layer it needs to integrate the output L times before the output is sent to the squashing function.

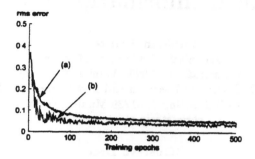

Figure 3. The rms error for training with sigmoidal squashing function added between input and output layers: (a) without $\rho(\sigma^2(x))$ adjustment and (b) with $\rho(\sigma^2(x))$ adjustment.

Discussions

A function approximation method with reinforcement learning has been discussed in the paper in which the learning rate ρ is adjusted according to the variance of the input spikes. While in [6] a stochastic reinforcement learning algorithm is suggested for non-RAM based neural nets and in [7] an algorithm manipulating the integration length R depending on the output error, the $\rho(\sigma^2(x))$ adjustment method in this paper considers only the values of input variables, rather than any feedback values such as output error. The effect of uneven addressing probability distribution of input spikes to memory locations is compensated so that the weight saturation in some particular locations can be solved. The method has been demonstrated to be successful in both learning speed and accuracy. The compensation can also be realised by adjusting the length of the updating cycle R. A larger R is assigned if the input spikes has large variance which enables more updating for the memories addressed by these input variables; a smaller R is assigned otherwise. It is equivalent to the $\rho(\sigma^2(x))$ adjustment algorithm and similar results have been obtained. The development of this algorithm aims at finding real world applications such as solving control problems.

References

[1]   T G Clarkson, C K Ng, D Gorse and J G Taylor, "Learning probabilistic RAM nets using VLSI structures", *IEEE Transaction on Computers*, 41(12), 1552-1561 (1992).

[2]   T G Clarkson, Y Guan, D Gorse and J G Taylor, "Generalisation in probabilistic RAM nets", *IEEE Transactions on Neural Networks*, Vol.4, No.2, March, 1993, pp.360-364.

[3]   Y Guan, T G Clarkson, J G Taylor and D Gorse, "Noisy reinforcement training for pRAM nets", *Neural Networks*, Vol.7, No.3, 1994, pp.523-538.

[4]   Y Guan, T G Clarkson, J G Taylor and D Gorse, "A noisy training method for digit recognition using pRAM neural networks", Proc. IEEE International Joint Conference on Neural Networks, Beijing, China, Nov. 1992, pp.I/673-678.

[5]   Y Guan, T G Clarkson, J G Taylor and D Gorse, "A stochastic reverse interpolation algorithm for real-valued function learning for robot control", Proc. IEE Third International Conference on Artificial Neural Networks, Brighton, UK, May 1993.

[6]   V Gullapalli, "A stochastic reinforcement learning algorithm for learning real-valued functions", *Neural Networks*, 3, 671-692, 1990.

[7]   D Gorse, J G Taylor and T G Clarkson, "A pulse-based reinforcement algorithm for learning continuous functions," In: WCNN'94, San Diego, 1994.

Neural Learning of Chaotic Symbolic Sequences: A Dynamical Information Loss Analysis

Christian Schittenkopf
Technische Universität München
Arcisstraße 21, 80290 Munich, Germany
Siemens AG, Corporate Research and Development, ZFE T SN 41
Otto-Hahn-Ring 6, 81739 Munich, Germany
chris@train.zfe.siemens.de

Gustavo Deco
Siemens AG, Corporate Research and Development, ZFE T SN 41
Otto-Hahn-Ring 6, 81739 Munich, Germany
Gustavo.Deco@zfe.siemens.de

Abstract

We introduce a new entropy measure for the study of the statistical correlation between the whole past (infinite memory) of a time series and its state p steps ahead into the future. We call this measure *source-p-step mutual information*, which can be seen as an extension of the concept of Kolmogorov-Sinai (KS) entropy in chaos and of Shannon's source entropy in alphabet sequences. Calculations show that the loss of information for the logistic map and the Belousov-Zhabotinski map (BZ map) can only be analyzed if the word length is greater than one. We train neural networks on these maps. The trained networks define nonlinear, recurrent maps which preserve and loose information in a way similar to the original maps.

1 Introduction

In recent years there has been great interest in information theoretic based descriptions of chaotic time series (Eckmann & Ruelle, 1985, Matsumoto & Tsuda, 1987, 1988, Shaw, 1981). Most publications concentrate on calculating important quantities of chaotic systems like entropy, entropy rate and mutual information which we review in section 2. We introduce a quantity which we call *source-p-step mutual information* that measures the statistical correlation between the *whole* past of a time series and its state p steps ahead into the future. This generalized mutual information extends the concepts of source entropy (Shannon, 1948) and KS entropy in the sense that the conditional entropy between the whole past (instead of the last state) and the state p steps ahead is included. In fact, when we look only one step into the future our definition is related with the KS entropy. Section 3 contains our computer experiments with the BZ map and the logistic map. We train neural networks on these two maps and generate symbolic sequences by using the trained networks as nonlinear, recurrent maps. For both maps we compare the decay of mutual information with increasing look ahead and find that the networks have captured the dynamics of the underlying systems very well.

2 Theory

Let us define a time series $\{x_k\}, k = 1, 2, \cdots$ and a partition β of the attractor A which is a set of disjoint boxes B_i (not necessarily of equal size), i. e.

$$\beta = \{B_i\}_{i=1}^N, \bigcup_{i=1}^N B_i = A \text{ and } B_i \cap B_j = \emptyset, i \neq j. \tag{1}$$

By interpreting each box B_i as a state i we transform the original, real-valued time series $\{x_k\}, k = 1, 2, \cdots$ into a sequence $\{i_t\}, t = 1, 2, \cdots$ of N different symbols and thereby define a symbolic dynamics. Let $p_{(1)}^{i,\beta}$ denote the probability (for a certain partition β) of observing symbol i. Then the entropy of the symbolic sequence is defined as (Shannon, 1948)

$$H^\beta = H^\beta_{(1)} = -\sum_i p^{i,\beta}_{(1)} \log p^{i,\beta}_{(1)}. \tag{2}$$

Taking the logarithm to the basis 2 we measure the uncertainty in units of bits. This definition can be extended to sequences (blocks, words) of length n by

$$H^\beta_{(n)} = -\sum_i p^{i,\beta}_{(n)} \log p^{i,\beta}_{(n)} \tag{3}$$

where $p^{i,\beta}_{(n)}$ is the probability to find a block of kind i if a block of length n is randomly chosen from the sequence (There are at most N^n different blocks.). The quantity $H^\beta_{(n)}$ is called the block entropy which is the average information needed to distinguish blocks of length n. Similarly we define $H_{(n,p)}$ as the entropy of the set of patterns which are the concatenation of n subsequent symbols and the symbol p steps ahead. Hence $H_{(n,1)} = H_{(n+1)}$. Shannon also introduced the source entropy

$$h^\beta = \lim_{n\to\infty} H^\beta_{(n)}/n = \lim_{n\to\infty} (H^\beta_{(n+1)} - H^\beta_{(n)}) \tag{4}$$

which is a characteristic quantity. For periodic time series $h^\beta = 0$, for stochastic processes $h^\beta = \infty$ and for chaotic systems $0 < h^\beta < \infty$ (Leven et al., 1994). In the literature h^β is also referred to as entropy rate (Cover & Thomas, 1991).

$$h = \sup_\beta h^\beta \tag{5}$$

is called the Kolmogorov-Sinai (KS) entropy or metric entropy (Fraser, 1989) of the underlying dynamical system from which we measured the time series $\{x_k\}, k = 1, 2, \cdots$. Each partition for which the supremum (5) is reached, is called a *generating* partition. In the remainder of this paper we only deal with generating partitions and hence we skip the index β. For one-dimensional maps h equals the largest Lyapunov exponent λ_{max}. If we make predictions a finite and non-zero value of h expresses that these predictions are meaningful only for a certain number of steps into the future because some amount of information is lost at each step.

Now we introduce a new measure for the loss of information which is consistent with the definition of the KS entropy. The *source-p-step mutual information* $I_{(p)}$ is defined as

$$I_{(p)} = \lim_{n\to\infty} I_{(n,p)} \ , \ I_{(n,p)} = H_{(1)} + H_{(n)} - H_{(n,p)} \tag{6}$$

where $I_{(n,p)}$ is the mutual information between a word of n subsequent symbols and the symbol p steps ahead. It is easily seen that $\forall n \forall p : 0 \leq I_{(n,p)} \leq H_{(1)}$. For chaotic time series we expect $I_{(n,p)} > I_{(n,p+1)}$ which expresses the loss of information. For the special case $p = 1$ we get

$$I_{(1)} = H_{(1)} - \lim_{n\to\infty} (H_{(n,1)} - H_{(n)}) = H_{(1)} - \lim_{n\to\infty} (H_{(n+1)} - H_{(n)}) = H_{(1)} - h \tag{7}$$

and therefore

$$h = H_{(1)} - I_{(1)}. \tag{8}$$

This means that the amount of information we loose in predicting the next symbol equals h. As a result the source-p-step mutual information $I_{(p)}$ is an extension of the concept of KS entropy to p steps and measures the statistical correlation between the whole past and the symbol p steps into the future.

3 Experiments

In order to simplify the analysis we discuss 1-D maps and use an elementary partition which is obtained as follows: Suppose we have a one-dimensional map $x_{n+1} = f(x_n)$ which maps an interval $[a; b]$ onto itself. Let $f(x)$ have a maximum at $\hat{x}$, $a < \hat{x} < b$, where $f(\hat{x}) = b$. Starting with an appropriate x_0 we get a binary sequence if we write 0 whenever $x_{n+1} \leq \hat{x}$ and 1 whenever $x_{n+1} > \hat{x}$ (Györgyi & Szépfalusy, 1985). Hence the partition of the interval $[a; b]$ consists of two elements, $[a; \hat{x}]$ and $(\hat{x}; b]$.

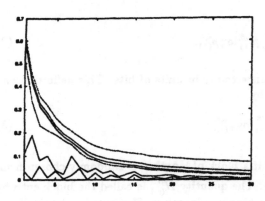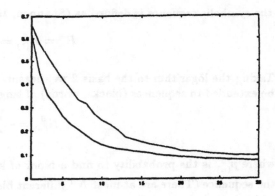

Figure 1: (Left) The mutual information $I_{(n,p)}$, $1 \le p \le 30$, of the symbolic sequence of the original BZ map: the values for n are 1,2,5,10,15 and 20 from bottom to top. (Right) $I_{(20,p)}$, $1 \le p \le 30$, for the symbolic sequences of the original BZ map and the BZ map learned by the neural network.

3.1 The BZ map

The BZ map is directly related to a chemical reaction (Herzel & Pompe, 1987):

$$f(x) = \begin{cases} (-(1/8 - x)^{1/3} + A)\exp(-x) + B & : \quad a \le x < 1/8 \\ ((x - 1/8)^{1/3} + A)\exp(-x) + B & : \quad 1/8 \le x < 3/10 \\ C(10x\exp(-10x/3))^{19} + B & : \quad 3/10 \le x \le b \end{cases} \tag{9}$$

with

$$A = 0.50607357, B = 0.023288528, C = 0.121205692, a = 0.023289577, b = 0.812569626, \hat{x} = 3/10.$$

According to these parameters we calculated a sequence of 50000 symbols the mutual information $I_{(n,p)}$ of which is shown in figure 1 (left). As one can clearly see the decay of information with increasing look ahead p is only visible for $n \ge 5$. The two curves at the bottom of figure 1 ($n = 1$ and $n = 2$) do not reveal the dynamics of the BZ map adequately.

We also trained a feedforward network with one input neuron, five nonlinear, hidden neurons and one nonlinear output neuron for several thousand cycles on the original, real-valued BZ map. Then we produced a sequence of 50000 binary symbols with the network in the following way: Let $NN(x)$ denote the output of the network for a given input x. If we take $NN(x)$ as the new input we get the output $NN(NN(x))$. By repeating this iteration scheme, i. e. $x_{n+1} = NN(x_n)$, we get a time series produced by the network which can be transformed into a binary sequence as described above. This sequence was clearly distinguishable from the original one because the error for the BZ map grows with about $\exp(0.3) \approx 1.35$. In contrast to that the curves of $I_{(n,p)}$ of both symbolic sequences shown in figure 1 (right) are similar. Therefore our network has captured the real dynamics of the BZ map.

3.2 The logistic map

We did experiments with the logistic map for $r = 3.9$:

$$f(x) = 3.9x(1 - x) \quad \text{with } a = 0.0950625, b = 0.975, \hat{x} = 0.5. \tag{10}$$

We trained a network with one input neuron, three nonlinear, hidden neurons and one linear output neuron on $f(x)$. Then we generated a sequence of 30000 binary symbols by iterating eq.(10) and another sequence of the same length by using the trained neural network. The details are described above. Figure 2 (left) shows the quantity $I_{(n,p)}$ for $1 \le p \le 10$ and $n = 1, 2, 5, 10, 12$ from bottom to top. Note that $I_{(n,p)}$ is monotonically decreasing only for $n \ge 5$. For $n \to \infty$ all curves tend towards zero which means that after a finite number of steps into the future the information about the present state is practically lost. Figure 2 (right) is a plot of $I_{(12,p)}$, $1 \le p \le 10$ for both symbolic sequences. The amount of information one has about a future state decays in a similar way for both sequences. This observation indicates that the network has captured the dynamics of $f(x)$.

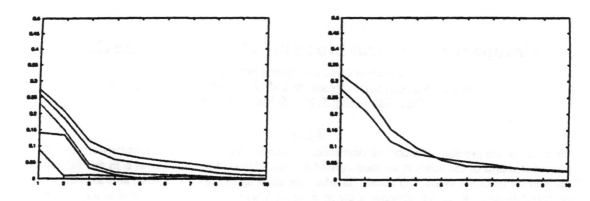

Figure 2: (Left) The mutual information $I_{(n,p)}$, $1 \leq p \leq 10$, of the symbolic sequence of the original logistic map: the values for n are 1,2,5,10 and 12 from bottom to top. (Right) $I_{(12,p)}$, $1 \leq p \leq 10$, for the symbolic sequences of the original logistic map and the logistic map learned by the neural network.

4   Summary

The source-p-step mutual information $I_{(p)}$ was introduced as a useful extension of the concept of KS entropy. Our calculations for two standard chaotic maps showed that the decay of the mutual information $I_{(n,p)}$ with increasing look ahead p is only visible for $n \geq 5$. We trained neural networks on each map and found that concerning the information loss the networks had really learned the underlying dynamics.

Literature

T. A. Cover & J. A. Thomas. (1991) *Elements of Information Theory*, Wiley.

J. P. Eckmann & D. Ruelle. (1985) Ergodic Theory of Chaos and Strange Attractors. *Rev. Mod. Phys.* **57**, 617.

A. M. Fraser. (1989) Information and Entropy in Strange Attractors. *IEEE Trans. Inf. Theory* **35**, 245.

G. Györgyi & P. Szépfalusy. (1985) Calculation of the Entropy in Chaotic Systems. *Phys. Rev. A* **31**, 3477.

H. P. Herzel & B. Pompe. (1987) Effects of Noise on a Nonuniform Map. *Phys. Lett. A* **122**, 121.

R. W. Leven, B. P. Koch & B. Pompe. (1994) *Chaos in dissipativen Systemen*, Akademie Verlag.

K. Matsumoto & I. Tsuda. (1987) Extended Information in One-dimensional Maps. *Physica 26D*, 347.

K. Matsumoto & I. Tsuda. (1988) Calculation of Information Flow Rate from Mutual Information. *J. Phys. A* **21**, 1405.

C. E. Shannon. (1948) A Mathematical Theory of Communication. *Bell Sys. Tech. J.* **27**, 379.

R. Shaw. (1981) Strange Attractors, Chaotic Behaviour and Information Flow. *Z. Naturf.* **36a**, 80.

Unsupervised Neural Modeling of Chaotic Time Series

Gustavo Deco and Bernd Schürmann

Siemens AG, Corporate Research and Development, ZFE T SN 4

Otto-Hahn-Ring 6, 81739 Munich, Germany

Abstract

We focus on the problem of modeling time series by learning statistical correlations between the past and present elements of the series in an unsupervised fashion. This kind of correlations is in general and especially in the chaotic domain, non-linear. Therefore, the learning algorithm should be able to extract statistical correlations between the elements of the time signal. This problem can be viewed as a special case of factorial learning. Factorial learning may be formulated as an unsupervised redundancy reduction between the output components of a transformation that conserves the transmitted information. An information-theoretic based architecture and learning paradigm that implement this formulation are introduced.

I. Introduction

Modeling time series by learning from experiments can be viewed as the extraction of statistical correlations between the past and future values of the time series signals. In particular, in the case of chaotic series, due to their short-term predictability, a thorough study of statistical correlations between components of the embedding vector yields the only way to distinguish between a purely random process and a chaotic deterministic series, eventually corrupted by colored or white noise. In fact, most of the relevant dynamic invariants that characterize such series are measures of these correlations between past values and the future evolution of the time series. Neural network modelings were implemented using supervised learning paradigms and feedforward [1-2] or recurrent architectures [3]. However the problem of extracting statistical correlations in a sensorial environment is the subject of unsupervised learning. In fact, Barlow[4] proposed the principle of redundancy reduction as the goal of unsupervised learning. The brain performs statistical decorrelation of the input environment in order to extract statistically independent relevant information. The goal of redundancy reduction is to factorize the input probability distribution without loosing information. The aim of the present work is to formulate an architecture and a learning paradigm for the unsupervised extraction of statistical correlations between the past and future elements of a time signal in order to model the behavior of the dynamical system. We employ a single layer architecture that attempts to extract correlations considering only the past relative to each element of an embedding vector. The architecture is always reversible, conserves the volume and therefore the transmitted information. In general the environment is non-Gaussian distributed and non-linearly correlated. The learning rule decorrelates statistically the elements of the output by minimization of an upper bound of the mutual information between the components of the output using Gibbs second theorem. In the case of chaotic modeling the method yields an information-theoretic based theory for the determination of the embedding dimension which is a topical problem in modern chaos research[5].

II. Dynamical Modeling

For modeling a chaotic system from the observation of measures realized on the chaotic attractor we review briefly the Takens-Method[6] called *phase-space reconstruction*, and results in a d-dimensional "embedding space" in which the dynamics of the multidimensional attractor is captured. Let us assume a time series of a single measured variable of a multidimensional dynamical system. It has been shown that in nonlinear deterministic chaotic systems it is possible to determine the dynamical invariants and the geometric structure of the many-variable dynamic system that produces the single measurement from the observation of a single dynamical variable. Given is a chaotic system $\vec{y}(t+1) = \vec{g}[\vec{y}(t)]$. Let us define an observable measurement $x(t) = f[\vec{y}(t)]$. The Takens-Theorem assures that for an embedding $\vec{\xi}(t) = [x(t), x(t-\tau), \ldots, x(t-d\tau)]$ a map $\vec{\xi}(t+1) = \vec{F}[\vec{\xi}(t)]$ exists which has the same dynamical characteristics as the original system $\vec{y}(t)$ if $d = 2D + 1$ where D is the dimension of the strange attractor. The theorem implies that all the coordinate-independent properties of $\vec{g}( )$ and $\vec{F}( )$ will be identical. The proper choice of d and τ is an important topic of investigation [5]. The goal of unsupervised neural network modeling is to learn the map given by $\vec{F}( )$, by learning the statistical correlations between the time successive elements (future from the past) of the embedding vector by observing the different training embedding patterns.

III. Unsupervised Extraction of Statistical Correlations

In this section we present the architecture and the learning paradigm that perform an unsupervised extraction of correlations in the input given by the embedding vector of a time series, by reducing the redundancy between the extracted features and conserving the information. Let us define an input vector $\vec{x}$ of dimension d distributed according to the probability distribution $P(\vec{x})$, which is not factorial, i.e. the components of $\vec{x}$ are correlated. The goal of Barlow's unsupervised learning rule is to find a transformation

$$\vec{y} = \vec{F}(\vec{x}) \tag{1}$$

such that the components of the d-dimensional output vector $\vec{y}$ are statistically decorrelated, i.e.

$$P(\vec{y}) = \prod_{i}^{d} P(y_i), \tag{2}$$

and the information is transmitted without loss. The transformation $\vec{F}$ will be performed by a neural network. The constraint of perfect transmission of information for deterministic neural networks is equivalent to the condition of invertibility of the network. The transmitted entropy H satisfies

$$H(\underline{y}) \leq H(\underline{x}) + \int P(\underline{x}) \ln\left(det\left(\frac{\partial \vec{F}}{\partial \vec{x}}\right)\right) d\underline{x} \tag{3}$$

where equality holds only if $\vec{F}$ is bijective, i.e. reversible. Conservation of information and bijectivity is assured if the neural transformation conserves the volume, which mathematically can be expressed by the fact that the Jacobian of the neural transformation should have determinant unity. We formulate an architecture that conserves always the volume, independent of the values of its weights, so that

$$H(\vec{y}) = H(\vec{x}). \tag{4}$$

The architecture employed in this paper is shown in Figure 1.

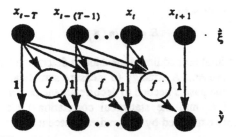

FIG. 1. Volume-conserving neural architectures.

The dimensions of input and output layer are the same and equal to d. The analytical definition of the transformation defined by this architecture can be written as

$$y_i = x_i + f_i(x_0, ..., x_j, \vec{\omega}_i), \qquad with \; j < i \tag{5}$$

where $\vec{\omega}_i$ represents a set of parameters of the function f_i. Note that independent of the functions f_i, the network is always volume-conserving. In particular, f_i can be calculated by another neural network, by a sigmoid neuron, by polynomials (higher order neurons), etc. Due to the asymmetric dependence on the input variables and the direct connections with weights equal to 1 between corresponding components of input and output neurons, the Jacobian matrix of the transformation defined in eq. (5) is an upper triangular matrix with diagonal elements all equal to 1, yielding a determinant equal to 1. In this paper we will use higher order networks. The functions f_i are assumed to be polynomial. The outputs are given by the following update equations:

$$y_i = x_i + \sum_{j=0}^{i-1} \omega_{ij} x_j + \sum_{j,k=0}^{i-1} \omega_{ijk} x_k x_j + ... \qquad . \tag{6}$$

The triangular structure of this network not only assures conservation of entropy in the transmission from the inputs to the outputs but also a transformation that attempts to decorrelate a component from only the past components which is the kind of correlation that we need in time series modeling.

IV. Minimization of mutual information

Let us now concentrate on the second aspect of factorial learning, namely the decorrelation of the output components. Here the problem is to find an invertible transformation that satisfies eq. (2). The major problem is that the distribution of the output signal is not necessarily Gaussian. We now present a technique to achieve this goal by minimization of the mutual information between the components of the output. The mutual information between the output components is defined as

$$MH = \sum_{i=1}^{d} H(x_1, ..., x_{i-1}; x_i) = \sum_{j} H(y_j) - H(y). \tag{7}$$

Due to the fact that MH is a measure of the amount of information between the components of the outputs, it is also a measure of statistical correlations between the components of the outputs. In fact, statistical independence as expressed in eq. (2) then is equivalent to

$$MH = \sum_{j} H(y_j) - H(y) = 0 \tag{8}$$

This means that in order to minimize the redundancy at the output we minimize the mutual information between the different components of the output vector. Due to the fact that the herein defined structure of the neural network conserves the entropy, i.e. $H(y) = H(\hat{x}) = constant$, the minimization of MH reduces to the minimization of $\sum H(y_j)$. The second theorem of Gibbs assures that the entropy of a distribution has an upper bound given by the entropy of a Gaussian distribution with the same variance as the original one. Using this theorem we can reduce the problem of statistical decorrelation to the problem of minimizing the upper bound of the entropies $\sum H(y_j)$, i.e. the sum of the output variances (which is the entropy of a sum of Gaussian distributions). If the variance of each component is denote by $\aleph_j$, then

$$minimization(MH) \equiv minimization(Tr(ln(diag(\aleph_j)))). \tag{9}$$

In other words, the cost function is defined as

$$E = \sum_{j} ln(\aleph_j) . \tag{10}$$

It is important to remark that the optimal embedding dimension is determined by the number of points in the past that are correlated statistically with the present. A strategy to measure statistical correlations is by trying to decorrelate statistically and then seeing how far the past is needed to decorrelate the present, or in other words how many points in the past are necessary to model (i.e. find the statistical correlations) the present. The learning rule for both decorrelation techniques can be easily expressed by the gradient descent method.

V. Results and Simulations
The first experiment concerns the chaotic time series generated by the logistic map. In this case the noisy logistic map was used to generate the input

$$x_2 = 4x_1(1 - x_1) + \upsilon \tag{11}$$

where υ introduces 1% Gaussian noise. It is important to remark that the noise is not white but colored, due to its inclusion in the iterative mapping. In this case a one-layer polynomial network of second order trained with the cumulant expansion techniques was used. The learning constant was $\eta = 0.01$, and 10000 iterations of training were performed. Figure 2.a and 2.b plot the input and output space of this experiment after training is finished, respectively. As is clear from Figure 2.b, the strongly correlated input (past and present of the chaotic time series, i.e. embedding vector with delay equal to two) is decorrelated. All the information was allocated practically in one of the coordinates of the output, leaving the second merely for the representation of the noise. Analyzing the weights of the trained network, the polynomial r.h.s of eq. (11) is recovered. This means that the deterministic part that generates the chaotic time series was modeled, even in the presence of colored noise which was decorrelated and allocated in the second coordinate of the output. The second example uses the Henon-map. In this case the exact embedding is known and given by

$$x_{n+1} = 1 - 1.4x_n^2 + 0.3x_{n-1} \tag{12}$$

which means that the required delay for modeling of the variable x is exactly 2 points in the past.

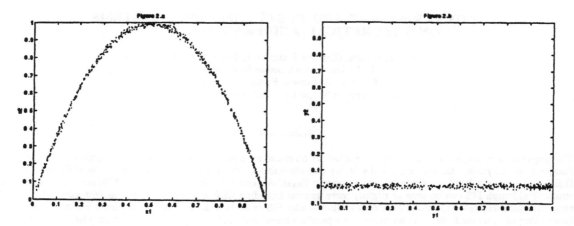

FIG. 2: Input and output space distribution after training for the logistic map. (a) input space; (b) output space of the network.

We take on purpose a six-dimensional embedding vector. We use a single polynomial neural network of order 2 which was trained with there described techniques. Figure 3 shows the evolution in time after training of each output component. We note that after component 3 the output is constant meaning that the network has figured out how to decorrelate this output using the past. Hence two points in the past are sufficient to model the map. In fact, the polynomial generated by the trained network corresponding to output 3 is the r.h.s of eq. (12). The polynomials corresponding to outputs 4,5 and 6 are also identical to the r.h.s of eq. (12), i.e. the terms and inputs too far in the past were automatically pruned by the learning algorithm.

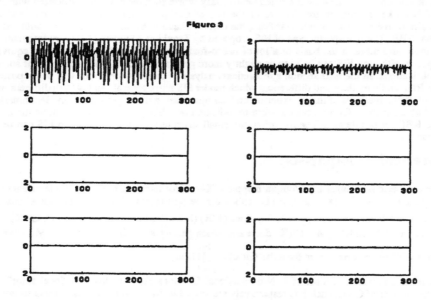

FIG. 3. Outputs of a 6-input and 6-output neural network for the Henon map.

In summary, we believe that the methods developed offer a novel instrument for analyzing real world data of complex nonlinear processes.

References:

[1]   M. Casdagli, *Physica D* 35, 335 (1989).
[2]   A. Albano, A. Passamante, T. Hediger and M. E. Farell, *Physica D* 58, 1 (1992).
[3]   G. Deco and B. Schürmann, IEICE, Trans. Fund. of Elec., Comm. and Comp. Science, E77-A, 1840-45 (1994).
[4]   H. Barlow, National Physical Laboratory Symposium N. 10, London (1959).
[5]   K. Pawelzik and H.G. Schuster, *Phys. Rev. A* 43, 1808 (1991).
[6]   K. Takens, Dynamical Systems and Turbulence, Warwick, 1980, ed. D.A. Rand, and L.S. Young, Lecture Notes in Mathematics 898, New York: Springer-Verlag, 366-381 (1980).

COMPARING RBF AND FUZZY INFERENCE SYSTEMS
ON THEORETICAL AND PRACTICAL BASIS

Hugues Bersini, Gianluca Bontempi and Christine Decaestecker
IRIDIA - Université Libre de Bruxelles - CP 194/6
50 Av. F. Roosevelt, Brussels 1050, Belgium
bersini@ulb.ac.be gbonte@ulb.ac.be cdecaes@ulb.ac.be

Abstract

This paper aims at helping to clarify the current confusion raised by a lot of works comparing or merging neural net with fuzzy inference systems. On the theoretical side, we first show that a specific family of neural nets: Radial-Basis Functions (RBF) and a specific family of fuzzy inference systems: Tagaki-Sugeno fuzzy inference systems (FIS) are nearly equivalent structure although FIS can be seen as slightly more general including RBF as a result of some architectural options and simplifications. However the small differences which render FIS more general can lead to a different interpretation of the functioning of these methods. In order to resolve a problem more easily RBF projects the problem data into a new abstract space whereas FIS roughly try to decompose such a problem and thus to allow for a lot of local operations, smoothly combined in some overlapping regions. On the practical side, experimental comparisons will be presented on Benchmark problems of classification and identification. Current results seem to indicate that while it is worth maintaining the more simple and less parametrized RBF for problems of classification, the small structural additions leading to FIS can be of interest for function identification.

1. Introduction

Today the debate is vivid between the adepts of fuzzy logic (restricted here to the users of Fuzzy Inference Systems (FIS)) and neural nets on the respective qualities of each method when applied on the same type of applications: classification, function identification and adaptive control. The confusion pervading such a debate has not been alleviated by the explosive development of a new field labeled neuro-fuzzy where features typically associated with the architecture and functions of NN like multilayer architecture or the use of backpropagation have been imported into the fuzzy community. The aim of the paper is to help clarifying the current situation by showing (together with works of Jang [6] and others [8]) that RBF [7] and a special type of FIS proposed by Tagaki and Sugeno [10] (very frequently met as Fuzzy Controllers and more and more at the basis of a lot of neuro-fuzzy developments) are almost two equivalent forms of input/output mapping, although FIS can be seen as slightly more general including RBF as a result of some architectural options and simplifications. In the next section a theoretical analysis of these two methods will be proposed first to show how FIS embrace RBF and why the small differences which render FIS more general can lead to a different interpretation of the functioning of these methods. Finally experimental comparisons will be presented on Benchmark problems of classification and identification. Current results seem to indicate that while it is worth maintaining the more simple and less parametrized RBF for problems of classification, the small structural additions leading to FIS can be of interest for function identification.

2. A Theoretical Comparison

We suppose a generic multilayer input/output mapping: $X \rightarrow Y$ for handling problems of classification and function identification of dimension N: $X = (x_1, .., x_N)$ (in the following we will suppose for clarity the output space Y to be one-dimensional). The hidden layer is composed of K functions $Gl(X)$ (l=1..K) with "bounded support", $Gl(X_c^l) = 1$ for X_c^l the center of the lth support, $0 \leq Gl(X) \leq 1$ and $Gl(X)$ decreases when getting away from the center. Moreover we make the further choice that $Gl(X)$ be factorizable on the axis: $Gl(X) = \prod_{i=1}^{N} Gl(xi)$.

The next layer is composed of a set of K N-dimensional functions $Fl(X)$ (called the "local actor") thus the same number of F as the number of G and each F is respectively associated to one G which serves to mark its zone of influence. The last layer computes the final output Y by a certain global combination of the G-F functions. Fuzzy Inference Systems are obained when the $Gl(xi)$ (called "membership functions" in the fuzzy community) are taken to be triangles, trapezoids or Gaussians function centered in X_c^l (here for the comparison we will restrict to Gaussians: $Gl(xi) = \exp-(\frac{xi - x_{ci}^l}{d})^2$) and the final combination is the weighted average, in which the influence of each "local actor" Fl is weighted by the value of its associated Gaussian:

$$Y = \frac{\sum_{l=1}^{K} Gl(X)Fl(X)}{\sum_{l=1}^{K} Gl(X)}$$

In terms of fuzzy logic each couple Gl-Fl is the expression of a lth rule such as:

IF x_1 is A_1^l and x_2 is A_2^l and ... x_n is A_n^l THEN $Y = F(X)$

where the A_i^l are the linguistic labels of the variable i (small, average, big...) associated to rule l. It is this possible writing of FIS in terms of linguistic production rules (readability being originally a key property of FIS) that requires the functions G to be factorizable provided the logical connective AND be numerically transposed into a product. Relaxing this readability would allow to enlarge the set of acceptable G (including ellipsoid not parallel to the axis). Classically in FIS either F is a constant α^l or F is a linear sum: $Fl(X) = \sum_{i=1}^{N} \alpha_i^l x_i + \alpha_{n+1}^l$

It is easy to see (with others before us [6] [8] in the fuzzy community) that by taking the combination to be the weighted sum and no longer the weighted average and by restricting each function F to be a constant, the outcome is a perfect equivalence between RBF and FIS. Now these two small structural additions which characterize FIS can have surprising implications on the respective interpretation of how the two methods work. In RBF (with constant F and weighted sum combination) the first layer (like for classical MLP) treats the input data so as to project them into a new space in which the final operation, whatever task it is: identification or classification, can be accomplished in the simplest linear way (this is the basic message of Cover's theorem underlying RBF classifiers). The advantages are manifold: use of fast clustering algorithms for locating the Gaussians, acceleration of any form of gradient-based algorithm due to the locality of the Gaussians (learning in some place does not unlearn in some others), use of one shot algorithm for linear optimization of the second layer, proofs of convergence and proofs of stability for adaptive control, reduced sensitivity to the order of presentation, etc... Although the first layer acts in the problem input space, the second linear layer now acts in an abstract space without clear correspondence with the problem space.

With FIS the story is different. The Gaussians mark the zone of the input space where the local actors F (the output of the fuzzy rules) will perform their simple function (we suppose in the following to keep the F linear although they can have whatever shape). So the Gaussians naturally entail a problem decomposition and each F will face the problem in a restricted zone of the input space: a local classifier or a local approximator. In contrast with RBF the second linear layer always act in the problem space but in a restricted part of it: F can be seen as a local perceptron or a local linear approximator, whose zone of influence is marked by its associated Gaussian and a smooth transition is guaranteed between the effects of different F acting in distinct but overlapping zones. The difference between RBF and FIS in function identification is very sharp: FIS locally approximate a function in a linear way and a smooth interpolation between two linear approximators is based on the respective overlap of a precise input with the intersecting "fuzzy" partitions. In RBF what make the local approximation are clearly the Gaussians and not the constant weights.

3. A Practical comparison

RBF and FIS have been experimentally compared on 2 Benchmark problems of classifications, first on *Geometrical Data*: it is a two-classes problem defined in a two-dimensional space. The classes are delimited by two circles entailed in a square and instances are uniformly distributed over the whole surface of the square. Then on *Wave Forms* data: the problem is composed of 3 classes, each of them being a linear combination of three distinct wave forms. Each instance is composed by a vector or 21 continuous values. These data are thus distributed over a large multidimensional space and are known as a difficult problem when noise is present (in this last case, the Bayes rule gives a classification error rate of 14 %). Then they have been compared on the task of identifying a two dimensional function taken in [9] and given by: $y=4\sin(\pi x_1) + 2\cos(\pi x_2)$

For the classification tasks, the optimization procedure we followed is identical to the one given in [4]. Indeed this paper is the extension of an experimental work presented in [4] comparing several forms of RBF for classification applications. An initialization strategy is used to determine the number and location of the Gaussians centers and the widths. It is linked to the detection of clusters in the pattern space which define groups of similar patterns. It is an unsupervised task interfering with a discriminating task and related to the classification task. The initialization strategy operates in two phases, first unsupervided localization of centers in each class and then supervised elimination of non-representative centers. Then since both RBF and FIS are linear at the output level, this layer is optimised by using a pseudoinverse method. We further tried to optimize all parameters by a gradient method but we did not notice any improvement. This might indicate that optimizing RBF and FIS by the decomposed two steps approach (clustering + pseudoinverse), a faster (above all for high-dimensional problems) and more robust approach, is the best learning procedure to adopt for problems of supervised classification. It is worth to mention that the most satisfactory results obtained in this preceding experimental work [4] was by using the weighted average instead of the weighted sum. One difference between RBF and FIS was then already eliminated in favour of the FIS (if we admit that FIS use the weighted average from the beginning). The remaining comparison was then to test the possible benefits gained by transforming the second layer from constant to linear functions.

We then compare the best form of RBF (the global output is the weighted average) with FIS. Notice that FIS need at the output level and by Gaussian as many linear functions as classes in the problem (2 for Geometrical Data and 3 for Wave form data).

With Geometrical Data the use of FIS allows a slight improvement. The results (the average of percentage of correct classifications on 10 runs) were:

For the non-noisy problem: RBF (with weighted average) obtained 96.3 on the training set and 95.4 ± O.88 (the standard deviation on 10 runs) in accuracy. FIS obtained 98 on the training set and 96.4 ± 0.4 in accuracy. For the noisy problem (an overlapping between the classes): RBF obtained 87.2 on the training set and 85.2 ± 1 in accuracy. FIS obtained 88.4 on the training set and 85.5±0.97 in accuracy. Notice that FIS use much more parameters than RBF due to the introduction of the linear functions. There is an addition of 4K parameters (K being the number of Gaussians, the dimension of the input space is 2 and there are 2 classes). To be really fair the two structures to compare should be encoded with almost the same number of parameters.

This is what we nearly did with the waves form data but the results we obtained were now in favour of RBF. Since the input space has 21 dimensions and since the number of parameters becomes now very sensitive to the number of Gaussians (22x3xK for FIS and Kx3 for RBF), we used 20 Gaussians for RBF and 3 for FIS (one by class). We treated only the noisy problem (adding Gaussian noise) where RBF (with weighted average) obtained 87.5 on the training set and 84.9±0.50 in accuracy. FIS obtained 91.0 on the training set but 80.8 ± 1.41 in accuracy. So FIS was better to represent the data set but victim of overfitting. This is intuitively understandable and turns to be a recurrent experimental observation. Since FIS aim at locally fitting the problem at its best and since its number of parameters grows very rapidly with the input space dimension, it is more inclined to overfitting weaknesses. This overfitting tendency being more and more effective as the number of dimension increases.

On the function identification problem and in order to reinforce the significance of the comparison, we decided to compare RBF in their original form: weighted sum and constant output, with FIS in their "fuzziest" form: use of triangular G instead of Gaussians, weighted average and linear output (one linear function by partition - the product of two triangles). As initialization procedure we used an unsupervised K-means on all the input data. A pseudoinverse method was used for optimizing the linear part. An important difference with the classification Benchmark previously described was the use of a gradient method for tuning the parameters of the G functions composing the first layer (two parameters: base and center for each G whatever Gaussian or triangular). After several testing, the optimization method we decided to use was the Davidon-Fletcher-Powell (DFP) method which appeared much more robust than the simple gradient-method. In contrast with classification tasks, the addition of a gradient-based optimization procedure (above all for tuning the centers, these RBF are called "Generalized RBF" in [5]) when using RBF as function identifiers has been recommended by different authors [5] [11]. Then the final optimization procedure become the repeated succession of the pseudoinverse at the second layer and DFP at the first one. In order to make a fair comparison between RBF and FIS with respect to the number of parameters, always higher for FIS, we gradually increased for each method the number of G so as to discover for both the minimal and optimal structure.

When using a gradient tuning of the parameters, the use of triangle instead of Gaussians for the G functions, and despite their non-derivability at one point (which does not seem to pose practical difficulties), allows a considerable acceleration in computer time.

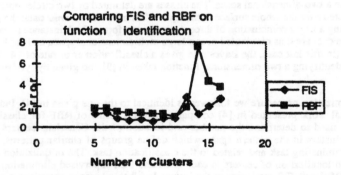

Fig.1: Experimental Results on a 2-dimensional function identification task

The learning was done by a cross-validation procedure over 200 samples. The results were averaged on 10 runs. As the graph indicates, the lowest average quadratic error (Err=0.546) was obtained with an FIS containing 10 clusters (so 40 + 30=70 parameters) to be compared with the best RBF (Err=0.903) containing 12 clusters (so 48+12=60 parameters). So here again FIS consumes slightly more parameters than RBF but this drawback has less impact when the dimension of the problem is kept low and mainly this can lead to reasonably improve the performance.

4. Conclusions

This paper aims at helping to clarify the current confusion raised by a lot of works comparing or merging neural net with fuzzy controllers. We have first shown that a specific family of neural nets: Radial-Basis Functions (RBF) and a specific family of fuzzy inference systems: Tagaki-Sugeno fuzzy inference systems (FIS) (both being more and more used in the two communities) are nearly equivalent structure. Thus despite their different origins and when being used for the same applications: classification, function identification and adaptive control, these two methodologies have clearly converged. The advantages gained by meging them (the neuro-fuzzy methods) is not clear anymore. The difference is even harder to perceive than RBF is known to work better when used in their normalized form i.e. using the weighted average which is the classical combination operator of FIS. Both methods share a lot of advantages: "local functioning", "rapid learning", "use of two steps optimization procedure", and by just tuning the linear output level: "proofs of convergence and stability". They also show common drawbacks, the most critic being the curse of dimensionality, the associated problems of overfitting and thus the risk of degraded performance in generalization for high-dimensional problems.

We have shown that by using as output layer a set of linear functions (one possible shape of the F functions) rather than a set of constants, the way both methods are working can be interpret differently. In order to resolve a problem more easily RBF projects the problem data into a new abstract space whereas FIS roughly try to decompose such a problem and thus to allow for a lot of local operations. FIS by principle need a lot more parameters and this need increases rapidly with the dimension of the problems. So on the whole we can suspect (and this was clearly confirmed by our experimental results on classification problems) that the use of adaptive FIS should be reserved to low dimensional problem. Since RBF in general have a same curse of dimensionality problem and are claimed to be preferable to MLP mainly for small problems, this could be still more likely for FIS.

For supervised classification tasks, various observations were made. The two-step optimisation procedure (clustering followed by pseudoinverse) works finely as compared with a global gradient method. Indeed it makes a lot of sense to locate the Gaussians where the clusters of each class are. The final classification is half-done in that way. Normalized RBF seem to work better and with much less parameters than FIS. FIS, with as many perceptrons as the number of classes multiplied by the number of Gaussians, is rapidly victim of overfitting. Then decomposing a task of classification into a lot of sub-classification acting locally as intrinsically proposed by FIS classifier does not seem to be a very promising road.

For identification tasks, the story is different. First a global gradient method for tuning the G functions (in addition to the initial clustering) coupled with a pseudoinverse method for the output part seem to be an interesting procedure. It can be intuitively understood since the initial position of the clusters is much less meaningful than in the classification case. Clustering is just a rapid way to locate the data of the problem and there is no reason that their resulting precise position be optimal with respect to the identification task which is done subsequently at a higher level by the linear local actors. For low dimensional problems at least FIS could work better than RBF. Triangles instead of Gaussians might be a nice alternative when computer time required for learning is low (like for adaptive control). It is well known that in the absence of prior knowledge on a set of points to interpolate to new ones, a low order interpolation is the recommended way. Therefore the local type of smooth interpolation inherent to FIS can be a better road than RBF to approximate low-dimensional complicated and rugged functions

References

[1]   Bersini H. & Gorrini V., 1993, FUNNY (FUzzY or Neural Net) Methods for Adaptive Process Control In *Proceedings of the first European Congress on Fuzzy and Intelligent Technologies*, pp. 55-61.

[2]   Bersini H. & Gorrini V., 1994, An Empirical Analysis of one type of Direct Adaptive Fuzzy Control. To appear in *Fuzzy Logic and Intelligent Systems*. Li and Gupta (Eds) Kluwer Academic Publisher.

[3]   Bersini H., Nordvik, J-P. & Bonarini, A., 1993, A Simple Direct Adaptive Fuzzy Controller Derived from its Neural Equivalent. In *Proceedings of the Second IEEE International Conference on Fuzzy Systems*, pp. 345- 350.

[4]   Decaestecker C. and M. saerens (1995). Comparison of Different RBF networks for Pattern Classification. Submitted to this same conference.

[5]   Haykin S. (1994). Neural Networks, a comprehensive foundation. Macmillan College Publishing Company, Inc.

[6]   Jang R. J.S. & Sun C.-T., 1993, "Functional equivalence between radial basis function networks and fuzzy inference systems". *IEEE Transactions on Neural Networks*, 4 (1), pp. 156-159.

[7]   Moody J. & Darken, C.J. (1989). Fast learning in networks of locally tuned processing units. *Neural Computation*, 1, 281-294.

[8]   Nie, J. and D.A. Linkens (1993). Learning Control Using Fuzzified Self-Organizing Radial Basis Function Network - IEEE Transactions on Fuzzy Systems, Vol.1, No4.

[9]   Nomura H., Hayashi I. & Wakami N., 1992, "A learning method of fuzzy inference rules by descent method". In *Proceedings of the First IEEE International Conference on Fuzzy Systems*, pp. 203-210.

[10]   Tagaki, T. and M. Sugeno 1985: Fuzzy identification of systems and its application to modelling and control. *IEEE Trans. Syst. Man Cybern.*, vol SMC-15, no. 1, pp 116-132.

[11]   Wettschereck D. & Dietterich T. (1992). Improving the performance on the radial basis function networks by learning center locations. In J.E. Moody, S.J. Hanson & R.P. Lippman (Eds.), *Advances in Neural Information Processing Systems 4*. San Mateo, CA: Morgan Kaufmann, pp 1133-1140.

Generalization Capability of MLP-GBF and RBF Neural Networks

Brijesh K. Verma, *Member IEEE*
Warsaw University of Technology
Nowowiejska 15/19, Room. 225
00-665 Warsaw Poland
E-mail: Bverma@koral.ipe.pw.edu.pl

ABSTRACT-This paper presents the generalization capability of the Multi-Layer Perceptron with Gaussian Basis Functions (MLP-GBF) and the Radial Basis Function (RBF) neural networks. A new type of learning technique for MLP-GBF is proposed, which is similar to learning technique used in RBF neural networks. The both networks are implemented and generalization capabilities of these networks are compared and the results are presented.

I. INTRODUCTION

Radial Basis Function (RBF) [1,2] and Multi-Layer Perceptron (MLP) [2,3] neural networks have been used in many real world problems. A number of theoretical as well as practical results on RBF and MLP networks have been obtained. It has been shown that RBF networks have the universal approximation ability and they are faster in convergence than MLPs with iterative learning algorithms. However, there are some training methods for MLPs [3], which are also faster in convergence.

Generalization capability of the MLP trained by Error BackPropagation (EBP) [5] algorithm is usually higher than the RBF networks [2,3] but there are number of other problems [2,3] with EBP which have discussed over the past years since the pioneering works of Rumelhart [5]. We adopted the best features of the RBF and the MLPs networks and proposed a network which is simple for hardware implementation and also faster like RBF neural networks.

The remainder of this paper is divided into three sections. The structure of MLP-GBF and RBF networks and learning techniques are presented in the next section. Comparative results and generalization abilities are provided and discussed in Section III, and finally the paper is summarized in the concluding section.

II. NETWORKS AND LEARNING TECHNIQUES

The RBF/MLP-GBF network structure with n inputs and m outputs is shown in Figure 1. The RBF/MLP-GBF network implement the mapping function as follows:

$$o_k = f(\underline{x}) = \lambda_0 + \sum_{i=1}^{M} w_k \phi(\| \underline{x} - \underline{v}_i \|) \quad \text{for RBF networks} \tag{1}$$

$$o_k = f(\underline{x}) = \lambda_0 + \sum_{i=1}^{M} w_k \phi(\| \underline{x} * \underline{v}_i \|) \quad \text{for MLP-GBF networks} \tag{2}$$

where $w_k (i=1,...,M)$ are the parameters of the networks. The vectors $\underline{v}_i (i=1,...,M)$ are the function centers/hidden units, λ_0 is the bias and ϕ is a Gaussian basis function, which is defined below.

$$\phi(r) = \exp(-\frac{r^2}{2\sigma^2}) \tag{3}$$

where σ is the parameter controlling the width of the basis function, and can be fixed or varied for each center.

We considered multilayer perceptrons with single hidden layer and M hidden units. In MLP's case, v's are the weights of the hidden layer and w's are the weights of the output layer. We used linear function for output layer, because we wanted to use MLP similar to RBF networks, but if somebody wants to use nonlinear activation function at the output layer then we refer to [3].

The system of linear equations for output layer of the RBF/MLP-GBF networks can be expressed as follows:

$$\underline{o}_k = X\underline{w}_k \tag{4}$$

where

$$X = \begin{bmatrix} 1 & \Phi(\underline{x}_1 - \underline{v}_1) & . & \Phi(\underline{x}_1 - \underline{v}_M) \\ 1 & \Phi(\underline{x}_2 - \underline{v}_1) & . & \Phi(\underline{x}_2 - \underline{v}_M) \\ . & . & . & . \\ 1 & \Phi(\underline{x}_p - \underline{v}_1) & . & \Phi(\underline{x}_p - \underline{v}_M) \end{bmatrix} \qquad \textit{for RBF networks} \qquad (5)$$

$$X = \begin{bmatrix} 1 & \Phi(\underline{x}_1 * \underline{v}_1) & . & \Phi(\underline{x}_1 * \underline{v}_M) \\ 1 & \Phi(\underline{x}_2 * \underline{v}_1) & . & \Phi(\underline{x}_2 * \underline{v}_M) \\ . & . & . & . \\ 1 & \Phi(\underline{x}_p * \underline{v}_1) & . & \Phi(\underline{x}_p * \underline{v}_M) \end{bmatrix} \qquad \textit{for MLP-GBF networks} \qquad (6)$$

$\underline{w} = [w_1, \ldots, w_M]^T$, and $o = [o_1, \ldots, o_N]^T$

In real world applications, N (number of training pairs) is usually greater than M (number of centers/hidden units). Therefore, we need to solve an overdetermined system of equations. In this study, Modified Gram-Schmidt (MGS) algorithm [3] is used to estimates the weights of the output layer.

Training Algorithm for MLP-GBF/RBF Networks.

Step 1. Set the hidden units/fuction centers (less than the number of training pairs).
Step 2. Set the weights (v) of the hidden layer (random selected from training pairs).
Step 3. Calculate outputs of the hidden layer (use equation 1 or 2).
Step 4. Define a linear system of equations for output layer as in Equation (4).
Step 5. Calculate weights (w) of the output layer using MGS algorithm.
Step 6. Goto Step 4 and repeat m times (for each neuron in the output layer).

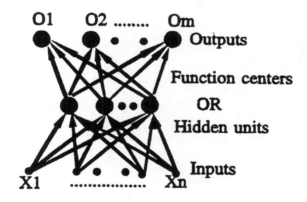

Figure 1. A MLP-GBF/RBF neural network

III. EXPERIMENTAL RESULTS

The both MLP-GBF and RBF networks have been implemented in C++ on an Apollo HP-UX 715/50 workstation. A number of experiments to show the generalization capabilities of the both networks have been provided but because of the limited paper length (max 4 pages), only three of them are presented below.

Experiment 1. Generalization in one variable function approximation problem.

In this experiment, we used one variable function as follows:
f(x) = 0.2 + 0.8*(x + 0.7*sin(2*3.14x))
We assumed $0 < x < 1$. The training data points were taken at the intervals of 0.05; thus, we had 21 data points as follows:
{(0,f(0)),(0.05,f(0.05)) ,...., (1,f(1))}

We used 101 evaluation points, taken at the intervals of 0,01. The evaluation data were used to verify the generalization power of the both networks. The actual outputs, estimated outputs and associated error for 101 evaluation points are shown in Figures 2 and 3. The results show that the generalization (interpolative power) is very good in both cases and the networks approximated the above function correctly.

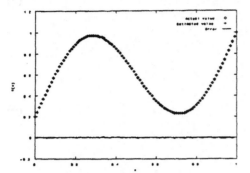

Figure 2. Generalization using MLP-GBF
network with 16 hidden units.

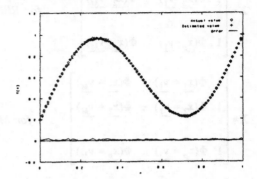

Figure 3. Generalization using RBF network
with 16 function centers.

Experiment 2. Generalization in two variables function approximation problem.

In this experiment, we used two variables function as follows:
$f(x,y) = (x^2 - y^2) * \sin(0.5 * x)$

The original function is shown in Figure 4. We used training data set with 50 points ($-1 < x < 1$ and $-1 < y < 1$). The both networks were trained using various (12, 16, 24, 36) hidden units/function centers. The results with 24 function centers/hidden units are presented in Figures 5 and 6. The results show that the generalization power of the both networks is very similar and they achieved good approximation.

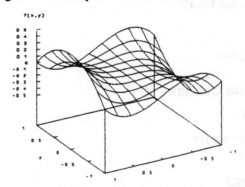

Figure 4. The original function.

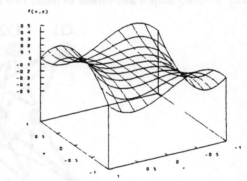

Figure 5. MLP-GBF network's
approximation.

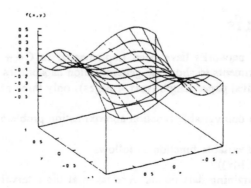

Figure 6. RBF network's approximation.

Experiment 3. Generalization in English character recognition problem.

The generalization capability of the MLP-GBF and the RBF networks has been tested on printed English characters. Training set was consisted of 26 English characters. Each character was encoded in as 8*8 pixel matrix. To show the generalization capabilities of the networks, three test sets were created with 10%, 20% and 30% distortion of each character. The networks had 64 inputs and 26 outputs with various function centers/hidden units. The results are presented in Table 1. As shown in Table 1, the MLP-GBF needed less neurons to get similar recognition accuracy as well as generalization power. In some cases RBF networks were better in generalization but overall, MLP-GBF network showed better performance.

Table 1. Comparative results for printed character recognition problem.

# of function centers (RBF) or hidden units (MLP-GBF)	RBF neural networks				MLP-GBF neural networks			
	Performance on training set [%]	Performance (generalization) on test set [%]			Performance on training set [%]	Performance (generalization) on test set [%]		
		10%*	20%*	30%*		10%*	20%*	30%*
12	56.00	56.00	52.00	36.00	88.00	88.00	76.00	36.00
16	88.00	88.00	84.00	60.00	96.00	96.00	80.00	56.00
20	96.00	96.00	96.00	64.00	100.0	100.0	96.00	52.00
26	100.0	100.0	100.0	80.00	100.0	100.0	100.0	76.00

* n% i.e., n % bits were random selected and converted into the opposite values.

IV. CONCLUSIONS

We have presented the Multi-Layer Perceptron with Gaussian Basis Function (MLP-GBF) and the Radial Basis Function (RBF) neural networks and the generalization capabilities of both networks have been compared. The comparative results are provided and discussed. The experimental results show that MLP-GBF and RBF networks have promising generalization power and MLP-GBF networks needed less neurons (hidden units/function centers) in hidden layer to reach at the same recognition and generalization accuracy. The MLP-GBF networks have other benefits such as easier hardware implementation and shorter response time because instead of Euclidean distance (as in RBF networks), they use simple dot product calculation. Although, MLP-GBF and RBF networks show similar generalization capability in real world problems, the MLP-GBF network is an attractive alternative to RBF networks.

REFERENCES

[1]. J. Moody, and C. Darken, "Fast learning in networks of locally-tuned processing units," Neural Computation 1, pp. 281-294, 1989.
[2]. J. Hertz, A. Krogh, and R. Palmer, "Introduction to the theory of neural computation," Addison-Wesley Publishing Company, USA, 1991.
[3]. B.K. Verma, "New training methods for multilayer prceptrons," PhD Dissertation, Warsaw Univ. of Technology, Warsaw, March 1995.
[4]. Y.H. Cheng, and C.S. Lin, "A Learning algorithm for radial basis function networks: with the capability of adding and prunning neurons," Proceedings of ICNN '94, pp. 797-801, Orlando, USA, 1994.
[5]. D.E. Rumelhart, C.E. Hinton, and R.J Williams, "Learning international representations by error propagation," In parallel distributed processing: Explorations in the microstructures of cognition, Cambridge: MIT press, 1986.
[6]. M.W. Mak, W.G. Allen, and G.G. Sexton, "Speaker identification using multilayer perceptrons and radial basis function networks," Neurocomputing, vol. 6, no. 1, pp. 97-117, 1994.
[7]. B.K. Verma, "Handwritten hindi character recognition using RBF and MLP neural networks," submitted to the IEEE Trans. on PAMI, 1995.

Error-Driven Placement of Neural Resources to Learn Trajectories *

N. H.-R. Goerke,   R. Eckmiller
Department of Computer Science VI - Neuroinformatik -
University of Bonn,
Römerstr. 164, D-53117 Bonn, F. R. Germany
Tel.:++49–228–550–247   FAX: ++49–228–550–425
e–mail: goerke@nero.uni-bonn.de

Introduction

In this paper two error-driven schemes of placing the resources (neurons) within the input space of a specialized neural network for trajectory learning are presented. Both heuristics for neural resource placement by adaptation of neural activity regions **Parcel Merging/Splitting** and **Sliding Parcels** including some simulation results are discussed.

The network and the corresponding learning scheme for trajectory storage has already been published in (Goerke et al. 1993, 1994).

The network is generating smooth trajectories by integrating sequences of piecewise constant accelerations $S'' = (x''(t), y''(t))$, stored as synaptic weights $\mathbf{W}^{(x)}, \mathbf{W}^{(y)}$ between P-Layer neurons and neural integrators, via velocities $S' = (x'(t), y'(t))$, into sequences of spatial positions $S = (x(t), y(t))$. Only one P-Layer neuron is active at a time, as defined by the parcel boundaries denoted "switch on", "switch off" thresholds. A desired trajectory $\hat{S}$ is appoximated by the network generated trajectory S consisting of a smooth sequence of parabolas.

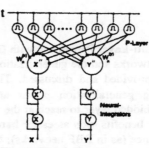

Fig. 1 The network:
2-dimensional case

For a given parceling situation that divides the input space T into N intervals of duration D_i, the weights $\mathbf{W}$ are learned according to the cumulative δ-rule after each epoch (one trajectory presentation):

$$_{new}w_n^{(x)} = _{old} w_n^{(x)} + \eta \cdot \delta_n^{(x)} \; ; \; \delta_n^{(x)} = \frac{1}{D_n} \sum_{t=0}^{t=end} (\gamma \Delta x_t'' + \beta \Delta x_t' + \alpha \Delta x_t) \cdot out_n(t)$$

where $\delta_n^{(x)}$ denotes the linear combination of the differences between desired and estimated acceleration, $\Delta x_t''$, velocity $\Delta x_t'$, and spatial position Δx_t cumulated for parcel n. The average position error $E_a := < \hat{S} - S >$ and the local position error $E_p(n)$ within parcel n are calculated as time-averaged Euclidian distances between ideal and generated position.

---

*Supported by the Federal Ministry for Education, Science, Research and Technology (BMBF)

Resource Placing: Adaptive Parceling

Both proposed parceling schemes follow the general policy of *placing the resources where they seem to be needed*. A generic assumption is that the local position error $E_p(n)$ can be reduced by locating more resources (neurons) in the temporal region with the largest error. Given a fixed number of neurons the On-, Off-thresholds of the P-Layer neurons are subsequently rearranged according to the local errors $\mathbf{E}_p$ generated by the network.

Parcel Merging/Splitting

Those two adjacent parcels i and j activating approximately the same acceleration vector are merged (*Parcel Merging*, Fig. 2) forming the new, larger parcel i with a new weight vector W_i calculated as median of the two former vectors.

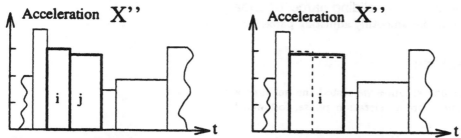

Fig. 2: Two adjacent parcels i,j are merged, to form a larger parcel i.

The former parcel j is subsequently placed in a position where more resources are needed (large arrow in Fig. 3). This allows parcel h with the largest error $E_p(h) \cdot D_h$ to be split in half, thus forming two new parcels h and j (*Parcel Splitting* Fig. 3).

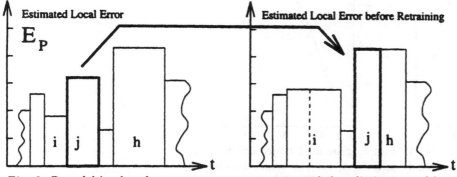

Fig. 3: Parcel j is placed were more resources are needed: splitting parcel h.

Sliding Parcels

If parcel i corresponds to a smaller local error $E_p(i)$ than neighbouring parcel j, its duration $\mathbf{D}_i$ will be increased by $R = \kappa \cdot D_j$ at the expense of an identical decrease of $\mathbf{D}_j$; κ is reduced during the progress of learning. Extension of this procedure to all neighbours and to all N parcels yields parcel movements (*Sliding Parcels*, Fig. 4) according to the error generated by the network.

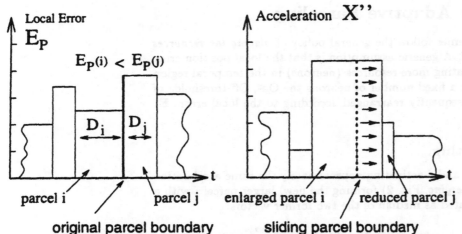

Fig. 4: The sliding parcels method for smoothly adjusting parcel boundaries.

Simulation and Results

To evaluate the proposed parceling schemes we tested the network with a trajectory consisting of two parts: one short acceleration phase, followed by a parabola (teacher in Fig. 5. and Fig. 6).

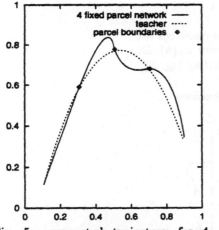
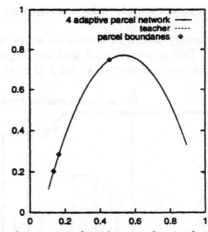

Fig. 5: generated trajectory for 4 uniform fixed parcels vs. original trajectory (teacher, dotted line). Parcel boundaries are marked.

Fig. 6: generated trajectory for 4 adaptive parcels vs. original trajectory (teacher as in Fig. 5). Parcel boundaries are marked.

The learning curve (Fig. 7) demonstrates the evolution of the average error E_a for several parceling steps. Up to learning step 1100 a *Merging/Splitting* procedure is performed every 200 steps, from step 1200 to 2000 every 200 steps the *Sliding parcels* method was applied. Due to the global effect of rearranging the local parcel boundaries and a fixed learning rate η, the average error may rise or oscillate. Reducing the learning rate after each parceling step for a while prevented in some cases error osscillations.

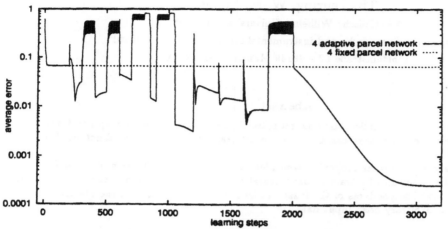

Fig. 7: Average error plotted against learning steps for a network with 4 neurons: fixed uniform parcel size vs. adaptive parcels. Abrupt changes in the average error are caused by adaptive parceling, whereas the smooth parts of the learning curve indicate *normal* weight learning. Broad black areas are caused by oscillations of the average error.

Discussion and Conclusion

Based on the idea of gathering the resources where the local error is large, two methods for adaptive parceling were presented (*Merging/Splitting* and *Sliding Parcels*). Both policies adapt to the individual structure of the trajectory, thus significantly improving the storage accuracy compared to learning with fixed uniform parcel sizes. A combination of both policies typically results in a smaller final error E_a and shows faster convergence.

The proposed general policy of locally concentrating resources including the two presented methods of adaptive parceling applies also for RBF- function approximator networks, although the results have solely been presented for the case of learning trajectories with a specialized function approximator.

References

Goerke, N. H.-R., Müllender, C. M., and Eckmiller, R., (1993), Trajectory storage network with recurrency, In: Proc. World Congress on Neural Networks, WCNN'93, Portland, Vol. III, 285-288.

Goerke, N. H.-R., Held, J., and Eckmiller, R. ,(1994), Error-Driven Adaptive Parceling for Efficient Trajectory Storage, In: Proc. Int. Conference on Artificial Neural Networks, ICANN'94, Sorrento, Marinaro, M. and Morasso, G. (eds.) Springer-Verlag 1994, pp. 1275-1278.

Learning Quality of Fuzzy Neural Networks

Th. Feuring, W.-M. Lippe *
Westfälische Wilhelms-Universität Münster
Institut für Numerische und instrumentelle Mathematik/Informatik
Einsteinstraße 62 – 48149 Münster – Germany

Abstract

Fully fuzzified neural networks called fuzzy neural networks can be trained with crisp and fuzzy data. In [3, 4] we have shown these networks can approximate arbitrary fuzzy continuous functions based on the extension principle.

These functions have some further properties which lead to a criterion for choosing a training set and yield a definition of the goodness of a trained fuzzy neural network. By defuzzifying the fuzzy network we get a crisp neural net. The goodness of the fuzzy net leads to the description of the maximum error of the crisp network for arbitrary crisp input data.

1 Introduction

It is a great problem of neural networks that the maximum output error of a trained neural net cannot be estimated – it can be measured for the training and the test set. There is no way to describe the error on other input patterns. To overcome this problem a characteristic training and test set is needed. But there are no criterions for finding such a characteristic set.

In this paper we investigate fuzzy neural networks, because fuzzy numbers can describe a continuous part of the "reality". These networks can be trained with fuzzy and crisp data and they produce fuzzy or crisp outputs. To minimize the computational expense we develop a fuzzy neural network where the input signals and the weights are from a special class of fuzzy numbers. In [3, 4] we have shown that these networks can approximate a special class of fuzzy continuous functions which can be characterized by another property. This property can be used to develop a criterion for "a good" choice of training data. Also the error of the fuzzy network can be estimated for arbitrary input patterns of the relevant input space. By defuzzifying the trained fuzzy neural network we get a crisp neural network and we can estimate the maximum error of the network for arbitrary crisp input data. With this method we can describe the goodness of a trained neural network. To put it another way: we can formulate a process for training a neural network which does not exceed a given maximum error.

2 Fuzzy Neural Networks

Fuzzy neural networks are fully fuzzified feedforward multilayer networks. An example (by M. GUPTA) for this can be seen in [5]. The network we investigate is similarly constructed. It consists of one input-layer, one output-layer and at least one hidden-layer. The activation and the output function of a formal neuron in a fuzzy neural network must be computed on fuzzy numbers because all weights of the network are fuzzy numbers. This network can be trained with crisp and fuzzy numbers and it computes crisp or fuzzy numbers as output data. So these networks naturally generalize crisp neural networks. In order to minimize the computational expense, we use *triangular* fuzzy numbers $\bar{a} = (a_m, a_l, a_r)_{trian}$ where a_m denotes the modal value and the non-negative real values a_l and a_r represent the left and the right fuzziness, respectively. The set of all triangular fuzzy numbers on $\mathbb{R}$ is called $\widehat{FZ}$. Triangular fuzzy numbers are fuzzy numbers in LR representation where the reference functions L and R are linear (see [2]).

Throughout this paper fuzzy numbers and functions will be denoted by letters with tildes on top of them. The operations we use in our fuzzy neural network are fuzzified by means of the extension principle.

---

[1] e-mail: feuring@math.uni-muenster.de, lippe@math.uni-muenster.de

The result of fuzzy adding numbers from $\widehat{FZ}$ is a triangular fuzzy number again. When we consider the fuzzy multiplication some problems concerning the computational expense arise. The result of a fuzzy multiplication based on the extension principle is a fuzzy number in L'R'-representation but it is difficult to compute the new functions L' and R' because they do not have to be linear. We approximate this fuzzy multiplication by linear reference functions so it computes a triangular fuzzy number again.

In classical backpropagation nets the activation function of a formal neuron is the sigmoid function $s_c(x) = (1 + exp(-cx))^{-1}$ for $c > 0$. With the same kind of approximation as above we obtain the equation for the extended sigmoid function. Obviously our fuzzy neural network maps triangular fuzzy numbers to triangular fuzzy numbers. But what functions can be modeled by this network? To get an answer we first want to take a look at fuzzy functions and their representations.

3   Properties of Monotonic Fuzzy Functions

The extension principle provides a general method for extending crisp mathematical concepts to fuzzy set theory. The operations in our fuzzy neural network are extended by the extension principle. So if we define fuzzy functions we have to take the extension principle into account. The following definition is inherently connected with the extension principle.

Definition 1 Let $\tilde{F}$ be a function with $\tilde{F} : \widehat{FZ}^n \to \widehat{FZ}^m$ with $\tilde{F} = (\tilde{f}_1, \ldots, \tilde{f}_m)^T$ and $\tilde{f}_j : \widehat{FZ}^n \to \widehat{FZ}$ for $1 \le j \le m$. We call $\tilde{F}$ monotonic, if for all $\tilde{\mathbf{a}} = (\tilde{a}_1, \ldots, \tilde{a}_n)^T$ and $\tilde{\mathbf{b}} = (\tilde{b}_1, \ldots, \tilde{b}_n)^T \in \widehat{FZ}^n$ with $\tilde{a}_i \subset \tilde{b}_i$ for all $1 \le i \le n$ holds: $\tilde{f}_j(\tilde{\mathbf{a}}) \subset \tilde{f}_j(\tilde{\mathbf{b}})$ for all $1 \le j \le m$.

It can be proved that the class of monotonic continuous fuzzy functions is identical with the class of continuous function extented by the extension principle (see [3]). Because of this we define fuzzy functions as follows:

Definition 2 A fuzzy continuous function[1] $\tilde{F}$ with $\tilde{F} : \widehat{FZ}^n \to \widehat{FZ}^m$ and $\tilde{F} = (\tilde{f}_1, \ldots, \tilde{f}_m)^T$ for $\tilde{f}_i : \widehat{FZ}^n \to \widehat{FZ}$ $(1 \le i \le m)$ is called a fuzzy function if $\tilde{F}(\tilde{x})$ is monotonic.

The set of all fuzzified continuous real functions meeting this definition is denoted by $\mathcal{F}_{ext}(\widehat{FZ}^n; n, m)$. It is easy to see that fuzzy neural networks are monotonic. But can any monotonic continuous fuzzy function be approximated by a fuzzy neural network? We answered this question in [3, 4] where we have shown that all fuzzy continuous functions $\tilde{F} \in \mathcal{F}_{ext}$ with $\tilde{F} \in \widehat{FZ}^n \to \widehat{FZ}^m$ can be approximated by our fuzzy neural networks.

We now study monotonic functions. The following lemma describes an important property of continuous fuzzy functions.

Lemma 3 Let $\tilde{a} \in \widehat{FZ}$ a triangular fuzzy number and $\tilde{f} : \widehat{FZ} \to FZ$ a fuzzy continuous function. Let $\tilde{a} \in \widehat{FZ}$ be a triangular fuzzy number and $\tilde{f}(\tilde{a}) = \tilde{b} \in FZ$. If $\mu_{\tilde{a}}(x_0) = 1$ then $\mu_{\tilde{f}(\tilde{a})}(y_0) = \mu_{\tilde{b}}(y_0) = 1$ for $f(x_0) = y_0$.

So modal values are mapped on modal values by fuzzy continuous functions based on the extension principle. We now give another characterisation of monotonic fuzzy functions. The following definition generalizes definition 1:

Definition 4 Let $\tilde{F} : \widehat{FZ}^n \to \widehat{FZ}^m$ be a fuzzy continuous function with $\tilde{F} = (\tilde{f}_1, \ldots, \tilde{f}_m)$ and $\tilde{f}_j : \widehat{FZ}^n \to \widehat{FZ}$ for $1 \le j \le m$. $\tilde{F}$ is called overlapping if the following inclusions hold: for arbitrary fuzzy vectors $\tilde{\mathbf{a}} = (\tilde{a}_1, \ldots, \tilde{a}_n), \tilde{\mathbf{b}} = (\tilde{b}_1, \ldots, \tilde{b}_n) \in \widehat{FZ}^n$

$$\text{supp}(\tilde{a}_i) \subset \text{supp}(\tilde{b}_i) \text{ for all } 1 \le i \le n \implies \text{supp}(\tilde{f}_j(\tilde{\mathbf{a}})) \subset \text{supp}(\tilde{f}_j(\tilde{\mathbf{b}})) \text{ for all } 1 \le j \le m .$$

In this definition $\text{supp}(\tilde{a}) := [a_m - a_l, a_m + a_r]$ describes the support of the fuzzy number $\tilde{a}$. An example for an overlapping function is given in figure 1. Obviously every monotonic fuzzy function is overlapping. But vice versa every overlapping fuzzy function is also monotonic.

Theorem 5 The class of overlapping fuzzy continuous functions is identical with the class of monotonic fuzzy continuous functions.

A proof for this theorem is given in [3].

---

[1] For the rest of this article it is sufficient to know, that a continuous fuzzy function has got analogous properties with properties of continuous crisp functions.

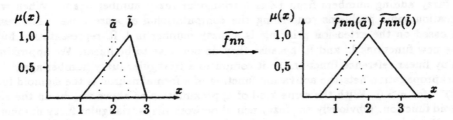

Figure 1: Example for the behaviour of an overlapping function.

4   Choosing the Training Set

The support of a fuzzy number is an interval in $\mathbb{R}$. The support of a fuzzy vector $\tilde{x} \in \widehat{FZ}^n$ is a simply connected set in $\mathbb{R}^n$. Because the relevant input space $U \subset \mathbb{R}^n$ of a fuzzy neural network is assumed to be compact, U can be covered by a finite number of open sets. This yields the following definition:

Definition 6 Complete Covering: *Let $U \subset \mathbb{R}^n$ be a compact set. A set K of fuzzy vectors*

$$K = \left\{ \tilde{x}^{(i)} \mid \tilde{x}^{(i)} = (\tilde{x}_1^{(i)}, \ldots, \tilde{x}_n^{(i)}) \in \widehat{FZ} \ \ for \ 1 \leq i \leq n \right\}$$

is called a complete covering of U, if for all $z = (z_1, \ldots, z_n) \in U$ there exist a fuzzy vector $\tilde{x}^{(j)} \in K$ such that

$$\mu_{\tilde{x}^{(j)}}(z_i) \neq 0 \quad for \ all \ 1 \leq i \leq n$$

holds.

Because U is assumed to be compact we can find a finite complete covering of U. This consideration leads us to the following:

Training Set Criterion: *The training set for a fuzzy neural network has to be a set of fuzzy vectors which completely cover the input space in order to yield satisfying results.*

This is the same idea which is used in constructing fuzzy controllers, where the input space is split up into linguistic terms for a good choice of linguistic rules.

5   Output Behaviour of the Fuzzy Neural Network

In this section we want to study the output behaviour of a trained fuzzy neural network. Therefore we assume the training set to be a finite complete covering. Let $((\tilde{x}_1^{(i)}, \ldots, \tilde{x}_n^{(i)}), \tilde{y}^{(i)})$ be such a training set for $1 \leq i \leq k$. To simplify the following considerations we assume the output dimension to be one. We also presuppose that a fuzzy learning algorithm can guarantee perfect learning of the training set. These assumption seems to be very hard, but we can weaken this.

Let $\tilde{u} = (\tilde{u}_1, \ldots, \tilde{u}_n) \in \widehat{FZ}^n$ be an arbitrary fuzzy vector of the covered input space. There are two possible situations. $\tilde{u}$ can be covered by only one or more than one training pattern. These situations will be studied now.

Case 1: There exists an index $j \in \{1, \ldots, k\}$ such that $\tilde{x}^{(j)}$ covers $\tilde{u}$. This means $\mathrm{supp}(\tilde{u}) \subset \mathrm{supp}(\tilde{x}^{(j)})$. Let $\widetilde{fnn}(\tilde{u}) \in \widehat{FZ}$ the output of the fuzzy neural network according to the input $\tilde{u}$. Because of theorem 5 and the monotony of fuzzy neural networks we get

$$\mathrm{supp}\left(\widetilde{fnn}(\tilde{u})\right) \subset \mathrm{supp}\left(\widetilde{fnn}(\tilde{x}^{(j)})\right) = \mathrm{supp}(\tilde{y}^{(j)}) \, .$$

This situation is shown in figure 1.

Case 2: Let $I \subset \{1, \ldots, k\}$ be a set of indexes such that $\mathrm{supp}(\tilde{u}) \subset \bigcup_{i \in I} \mathrm{supp}(\tilde{\mathbf{x}}^{(i)})$. Because fuzzy neural nets are overlapping and $\widetilde{fnn}$ is a fuzzy continuous function we get in this case

$$\mathrm{supp}\left(\widetilde{fnn}(\tilde{u})\right) \subset \bigcup_{i \in I} \mathrm{supp}\left(\widetilde{fnn}(\tilde{\mathbf{x}}^{(i)})\right) = \bigcup_{i=I} \mathrm{supp}(\tilde{y}^{(i)}) \ .$$

See figure 2 for an example.

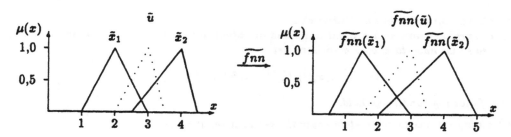

Figure 2: A test pattern covers two training patterns.

These two cases estimate the output of the fuzzy neural network topwards. Similary we can assess the output downwards. These observations shall be summarized in the following remark:

Note 7 *Let $((\tilde{x}_1^{(i)}, \ldots, \tilde{x}_n^{(i)}), \tilde{y}^{(i)})$ be a training set for $1 \le i \le k$ which has been perfectly learned by a fuzzy neural network. If $\tilde{u} \in \widehat{FZ}$ is a fuzzy vector of the input space then there exist two sets of indexes I, I' such that*

$$\bigcup_{i \in I'} \mathrm{supp}(\tilde{\mathbf{x}}^{(i)}) \subset \mathrm{supp}(\tilde{u}) \subset \bigcup_{j \in I} \mathrm{supp}(\tilde{\mathbf{x}}^{(j)})$$

holds. Because of theorem 5 and the monotony of fuzzy neural networks we can conclude

$$\bigcup_{i \in I'} \mathrm{supp}(\tilde{y}^{(i)}) \subset \mathrm{supp}\left(\widetilde{fnn}(\tilde{u})\right) \subset \bigcup_{j \in I} \mathrm{supp}(\tilde{y}^{(j)}) \ .$$

If a fuzzy neural network is trained perfectly by a set of fuzzy vectors which cover the relevant input space of the network (definition 6) the error of the network for arbitrary input patterns can be read from the training set.

We now transfer the results to crisp neural networks. For this we have to defuzzify the fuzzy neural network. The defuzzification process can easily be described by setting the fuzziness to zero (the modal values are computed independently from the fuzziness-values). So the crisp neural net only works on the modal values of the fuzzy neural network. Because this network was trained with fuzzy data before defuzzification we can make some statements about the output behaviour of the crisp neural network.

Definition 8 *The FL-goodness of learning gives the maximum error of a trained neural network for arbitrary input patterns.*

If we look at a feedforward network which is trained by the popular backpropagation algorithm we do not know anything about the FL-goodness of learning. This is an inherent problem of crisp neural networks.
If we study defuzzified fuzzy neural networks we can indicate the FL-goodness of learning. Let u be a crisp input vector. Then there exists at least one fuzzy training vector $\tilde{\mathbf{x}}^{(j)}$ such that $\mu_{\tilde{x}^{(j)}}(u_i) \neq 0$ for all $1 \le i \le n$. Moreover

$$u_i \in \left[(x_i^{(j)})_m - (x_i^{(j)})_l, (x_i^{(j)})_m\right] \quad \text{or} \quad u_i \in \left](x_i^{(j)})_m, (x_i^{(j)})_m + (x_i^{(j)})_r\right] \quad \forall \, 1 \le i \le n$$

holds where $\tilde{x}_i^{(j)} = ((x_i^{(j)})_m, (x_i^{(j)})_l, (x_i^{(j)})_r)_{trian}$. With $\mathrm{supp}(\widetilde{fnn}(u)) \subset \mathrm{supp}(\widetilde{fnn}(\tilde{\mathbf{x}}^{(j)})) = \mathrm{supp}(\tilde{y}^{(j)})$ we get

$$\left(\widetilde{fnn}(u)\right)_m \in \left[(y^{(j)})_m - (y^{(j)})_l, (y^{(j)})_m\right] \quad \text{or} \quad \left(\widetilde{fnn}(u)\right)_m \in \left](y^{(j)})_m, (y^{(j)})_m + (y^{(j)})_r\right] \ .$$

To conclude these observations we give the following theorem.

Theorem 9 FL-Goodness-of-Learning-Theorem:
Let $((\tilde{x}_1^{(i)}, \ldots, \tilde{x}_n^{(i)}), \tilde{y}^{(i)})$ $(1 \leq i \leq k)$ *be the training set of a fuzzy neural network which completely covers the input space. The FL-goodness of learning of the trained and defuzzified fuzzy neural network is given by*

$$FL\text{-}goodness \leq \max_{j \in \{1, \ldots, k\}} \left((y^{(j)})_l, (y^{(j)})_r \right).$$

With this we have found a method to get a trained neural network with a FL-goodness of learning less than a given $\varepsilon > 0$.

Goodness-Criterion for Neural Networks:
To develop a neural network with n input units and m output units where the maximum error of the outputs does not exceed ε, we have to choose a training set

$$\left((\tilde{x}_1^{(j)}, \ldots, \tilde{x}_n^{(j)}), (\tilde{y}_1^{(j)}, \ldots, \tilde{y}_m^{(j)}) \right) \ for \ 1 \leq j \leq k$$

such that the following conditions hold:

- *The training set has to completely cover the relevant input space.*

- *The maximum left and right fuzziness of the output $\tilde{y}^{(j)}$ does not exceed ε:*

$$(y_i^{(j)})_l \leq \varepsilon \quad and \quad (y_i^{(j)})_r \leq \varepsilon \quad \forall \, 1 \leq i \leq m, \ 1 \leq j \leq k.$$

In [6, 7] we have presented learning algorithms for our fuzzy neural networks. Even if these algorithms cannot guarantee perfect learning of a given fuzzy training set we find the theoretical observations of the FL-goodness of learning confirmed.

6 Conclusions

We have presented a fuzzy neural network. Theoretical examinations of the capacity of fuzzy neural networks lead to a class of monotonic fuzzy continuous functions which is very interesting in the theory of fuzzy neural networks. Because monotonic functions are overlapping and the relevant input space can be covered by fuzzy training vectors we can investigate criterions for a good choice of the training set. By defuzzifying this neural network we get informations about the maximum output error of the network for arbitrary crisp input data. This leads to the definition of the FL-goodness of learning. So the fuzzification of neural networks and the defuzzification of the trained networks gives us more information about the network behaviour than we can get without fuzziness.

References

[1] J. BUCKLEY; Y. HAYASHI: *Can fuzzy neural nets approximate continuous fuzzy functions?* Fuzzy Sets and Systems 61, pp. 43-52, 1994.

[2] D. DUBOIS, H. PRADE: *Fuzzy Sets and Systems: Theory an Applications.* Academic Press, New York, 1980.

[3] TH. FEURING: *Fuzzy-Neuronale Netze: Von kooperativen über hybride zu fusionierten vage-konnektionistischen Systemen.* Ph.D. Thesis, Westf. Wilhelms-Universität Münster, Germany, 1995.

[4] TH. FEURING, W.-M. LIPPE *Fuzzy Neural Networks are Universal Approximators* accepted for IFSA World Congress '95, Sao Paulo, Brasil.

[5] M. GUPTA, D. RAO: *On the principles of fuzzy neural networks.* Fuzzy Sets and Systems 61, pp. 1-18, 1994.

[6] W.-M. LIPPE, TH. FEURING, TH. BÜSCHER: *A fully fuzzified neural network based on the backpropagation algorithm.* Technical Report WWU Münster I−10/1995.

[7] W.-M. LIPPE, TH. FEURING, L. MISCHKE: *Supervised learning in fuzzy neural networks.* Technical Report WWU Münster I−12/1995.

Integral Representations for Construction of Approximating Networks

M. B. Zaremba and E. Porada

Département d'informatique
Université du Québec
Hull, Québec J8X 3X7, Canada

Abstract: The issue of building neural networks capable of approximating arbitrary continuous target functions is addressed in this paper. An approach based on integral representation of the desired function is presented. It is shown that the the continuous component of an integral representation can be generated by means of linear differential equations. The method allows the user to construct the network architecture by applying qualitative geometrical analysis of the space of input states.

1. Introduction

Function approximation capabilities of connectionist networks have been studied by several authors [2,3]. It has been proved among else that the networks can approximate an arbitrary continuous target function uniformly on compact domains in Euclidean space. The mathematical analysis has essentially been based on the Kolmogorov theorem known as the negative solution of the 13th problem of Hilbert. Theoretical complexity involved does not allow us to design a constructive method of learning from the mathematical demonstrations. A more promising approach is to to find exact integral representation of a desired function (with the use of a continuum of processing units [4]) and then approximate the integral by finite subsets of the continuum. The condition of constructiveness requires specific integral representations of the target function; an explicit integral has to be found that will allow for uniform convergence of its discrete approximations. This paper contributes to the development of such explicit regular integrals representing a target function. The learning method has been oriented especially for the use in measurement systems [1,5]. In such systems, a neural processor extracts a measurand (the current value of a physical parameter) from a sensor distributed signal. The input to the processor can be looked upon as a vector running through a one-parameter manifold in an Euclidian space. Thus, the problem arises of uniformly approximating, with a given precision, a target function defined on a one-dimensional manifold.

2. Integral Representation of the Target Function

Let us first define the architecture of the network. Vector $x \in R^N$ constitutes the input to the connectionist network under consideration. The first layer of connections between N input units and n hidden units combines the input signals into the hidden signals that are fed to the layer of hidden units. Thus, the input to a hidden unit has the form of $H = \phi(x \cdot m - \beta)$, where ϕ is the transfer function of the hidden unit, β denotes its bias coefficient, and m is the N-vector of connection weights between the input units and the hidden unit. We assume a transfer function of the form $\phi(x) = 0$ if $x < 0$ and $\phi(x) = x$ if $x > 0$. The bias of a hidden unit can be expressed as $\beta = b \cdot m$, where b is a fixed N-vector. Consequently, the hidden signal can be written as the following function of x:

$$H_{m,\beta}(x) = (x - b) \cdot m \quad \text{if } (x - b) \cdot m > 0 \qquad (1)$$

$H_{m,\beta}(x) = 0$ otherwise. The second layer of connections combines the hidden signals into a numerical output signal, generated by the output unit.

$$F_{out}(x) = \sum_{j=1}^{n} H_j(x)\mu_j \qquad (2)$$

where n is the number of hidden units and μ_j denotes the weight of the connection between hidden unit j and the output unit. The problem of function approximation by connectionist networks consists in constructing a hidden layer and defining weights μ_j such that $F_{out}(x)$ approximates a target function $f(x)$ uniformly in the domain X with a desired precision. Assuming a continuum of hidden units, we consider the integral output function:

$$I_{out}(x) = \int_C H_k(x)d_\mu(k) \qquad (3)$$

where C is the continuum, $H_k(x)$ represents the hidden signal produced by hidden unit k, and μ denotes a weight distribution in C. The integral representation can be defined indirectly by means of Fourier transform. Our method aims at directly constructed finite measures and explicit integrals. In this paper we report results concerning the case where X is a one-dimesional compact manifold in R^N.

Let us consider implications of the representation theorems when it comes to the function approximation capabilities of the connectionist networks. A crucial requirement for the constructive universal approximator is an explicit form of the measure μ. Such a form can be used in constructive procedures for finding discrete approximations of the exact integral representation; we can approximate a Riemann integral by the discrete Riemann sums. For a given $x \in X$, we get finite linear combinations of appropriately selected hidden signals which represent the output function at point x as closely as required. By the uniform continuity of the integral output function, $F_{out}(x)$ approximates the integrals $I_{out}(x)$ uniformly in any given compact domain $X \subset R^N$.

3.   Geometrical Method for Integral Representations

In this section, we outline the integral representation theorem for the case where X is a regular in R^N, i.e., a parametric differentiable curve without loops:

$$x = x(s) \in R^N, \quad x(s_a) \neq x(s_b) \text{ for } s_a \neq s_b, \quad dx/ds \neq 0 \quad \text{for } s \in [s_0, s_1] \qquad (4)$$

We consider an arbitrary target function f defined on X. We express the target function by means of the variable s and assume that $f(s)$ is a smooth function. Now we construct an integral representation of the target function, assuming that the parametric curve $x(s)$ satisfies the convex separability condition. The definition of the separability involves partitioning of the curve into the two following complementary arcs:

$$A_\sigma = \{x(s): s \leq \sigma\}; \qquad B_\sigma = X \setminus A_\sigma = \{x(s): s > \sigma\} \qquad (5)$$

The curve meets the convex separability condition if

$$\text{conv}(A_\sigma) \cap B_\sigma = 0, \qquad s_0 \leq s \leq s_1 \qquad (6)$$

where $\text{conv}(A)$ denotes the convex hull of a set $A \subset R^N$. Notice that a planar spiral curve or a helice in R^3 satisfy the condition. In the case of piecewise regularity, the method described below is applied for each regular arc of the geometrical curve. The general method involves extensive geometrical procedures which we will not go into detail in this paper.

For a given $\sigma \in [s_0, s_1]$, let g_σ be a vectors othogonal to the hyperplane tangent to conv(As) at point $x(s)$; the length and the sense of g_σ is determined by the condition

$$dx/ds|_\sigma \cdot g_\sigma = 1 \tag{7}$$

The tangent hyperplanes are not uniquely defined, so the vector function $\sigma \rightarrow g_\sigma$, called generic function, can be constructed in different manners. For planar curves fulfilling the convex separability condition, the initial value s g_{s0} has to be co-linear with the derivative dx/ds at $s = s_0$. We use the σ units for the integral representation of our target function $f(s)$, so $K = [s_0, s_1]$. In this way, the generic function is a continuous function defined on a compact topological space.

Now we determine the weight distribution $\mu(\sigma)$. According to (1), we have for all s

i) $H_\sigma(x(s)) = (x(s) - x(\sigma)) \cdot g_\sigma$ if $s - \sigma < \sigma < s$

ii) $H_\sigma(x(s)) = 0$ if $\sigma \geq s$ (8)

The construction of weight distribution on K is accomplished by locally extending both the distribution μ and the domain where the output function exactly represents the target function. Thus, we extend $\mu(s)$ and the exact representation on segment $[a, a+\delta]$, assuming that weights $\mu(\sigma)$ are already defined in $[s_0, a]$ and $f(s) = F(s)$ for $s \leq a$, where $F(s)$ is the current output function. Under condition ii) in (8), hidden units $\sigma > a$ do not modify the output function at points $s < a$, so, for the purpose of the extension, it is sufficient to find $\mu(\sigma)$, $a \leq \sigma < a+\delta$ such that:

$$\mu(a)H_\sigma(x(s)) + \int_a^{a+\delta} H_\sigma(x(s))d\mu(\sigma) = f(s)-F(s), \quad a \leq s < a+\delta \tag{9}$$

The continuous component will represent the function

$$f^*(s) = f(s) - F(s) - \mu(a)H_\sigma(x(s)), \quad f^*(a) = df^*/ds|_a = 0 \tag{10}$$

Now, the problem is to find continuous distribution $\mu(\sigma)$, $a < \sigma < a + \delta$, such that

$$\int_a^{a+\delta} H_\sigma(x(s))d\mu(\sigma) = f^*(s), \quad a < s < a + \delta \tag{11}$$

The following theorem gives a solution.

Theorem. *Consider the solution $v(\sigma)$ of the linear differential equation*

$$dv/d\sigma + [g_\sigma \times d^2x/d\sigma^2]\, v(\sigma) = (d^2 f^*/d\sigma^2)\, g_\sigma \tag{12}$$

with the initial condition $v(a) = 0$. The derivative $dv/d\sigma$ is co-linear with g_σ, i.e. $dv/d\sigma = \mu(\sigma)g_\sigma$, where the the function $\mu(\sigma)$ fulfills (11).

Proof: Since $[g_\sigma \times d^2x/d\sigma^2]\, v(\sigma) = ((d^2x/d\sigma^2)\, v(\sigma))\, g_\sigma$, we have $dv/d\sigma = \mu(\sigma)g_\sigma$ where $\mu(\sigma) = d^2 f^*/d\sigma^2 - (d^2x/d\sigma^2)\, v(\sigma)$. Thus

$$d^2 f^*/d\sigma^2 = \mu(\sigma) + (d^2x/d\sigma^2)\, v(\sigma) = d/d\sigma((dx/d\sigma)\, v(\sigma))$$

The last equation can be checked by direct computation, using (7). Consequently, $dx/ds_\square \cdot v(\sigma) = df^*/d\sigma$

since the two members coincide at $\sigma = a$ and have equal derivatives. The left-hand member, in turn, is a derivative of the expression

$$I(s) = \int_a^s [x(s) - x(\tau)] \cdot d\nu/d\tau$$

In fact:

$$dI/ds = d/ds(x(s) \cdot \int_a^s d\nu(\tau) - \int_a^s x(\tau) \cdot d\nu(\tau)) = (dx/ds) \cdot [\nu(s) - \nu(a)] = (dx/ds) \cdot \nu(s)$$

having taken into consideration the initial conditions. Thus $I(s) = f^*(s)$, because $I(a) = f^*(a) = 0$. On the other hand,

$$I(s) = \int_a^s [x(s) - x(\sigma)] \cdot g_\sigma \mu(\sigma) \, d\sigma = \int_a^s H_a(x(s)) \, d\mu(\sigma) = \int_a^{a+\delta} H_a(x(s)) \, d\sigma$$

because of (8). The theorem is proved. ∎

This theorem shows that the continuous component of an integral representation can be generated by means of linear differential equations. This is particularly important in neural network practice: various well established methods of the approximative solutions can be applied as learning methods. Moreover, the regularity of exact solutions ensures good convergence of discrete representations to the integral representation, allowing for construction of optimal connectionist networks approximating a given target function with a desired precision.

4. Conclusions

The method of integral representation proposed in this paper makes it possible to construct a neural network for a particular function approximation task. The construction method works efficiently even if the number of hidden processors is fairly limited. This capability is of importance in a number of applications. The constructive learning method based on geometrical analysis of the input space and subsequent integral representations is currently a subject of research in opto-electronic measurement systems, where the target function is obtained by a calibration process. The neural network is able to handle complex patterns generated by distributed sensor signals.

References

[1] W. J. Bock, E. Porada, and M. B. Zaremba, "Neural processing-type fiber-optic strain sensor", IEEE Trans. Instrum. and Measurement, Vol. 41, No. 6, 1992, pp. 1062-1066.
[2] K.-I. Funahasi, "On the approximate realization of continuous mappings by neural networks", Neural Networks, Vol. 2, 1989, pp. 183-192.
[3] K. Hornik, M. Stinchcombe, and H. White, "Multilayer feedforward networks are universal approximators", Neural Networks, Vol. 2, 1989, pp. 359-366.
[4] B. Irie and S. Miyake, "Capabilities of three-layered perceptrons", IEEE Second International Conference on Neural Networks, San Diego, 1988, pp. I:641-648.
[5] M. B. Zaremba, W. J. Bock, and E. Porada, "The recognition and measurement of optically detected physical variables using interactional neural networks", Proceedings Int. Conf. "Neural Networks", San Diego, Vol. 2, 1991. pp. 77-85.

The Nonlinearity Measures of MultiLayer Perceptron

Tong Fan, Bingzheng Xu, and Yonghong Jiang

Institute of Electrical Engineering & Automation
South China University of Technology
Guangzhou, 510641, P. R. China
Phone: 086+20-711-3540, Fax: 086+20-551-6862

Abstract—In this paper, some measures are proposed initially to assess the nonlinearity of MultiLayer Perceptron (MLP). By these measures, we can reveal the relationship of the nonlinearity of training data to that of MLP, and the potential of the hidden layers. Furthermore, our research reveals that the inner representation of MLP is closely related to the nonlinearity of the function learnt by MLP.

I. Introduction

As the hidden layer was introduced, the MLP has obtained some strong capabilities and became a powerful tool to solve some complicated problems. However, there exist some theoretical problems for applications. A number of attempts have focused on these issues. Regarding the aspect of approximating ability, G. Cybenko [1] investigated the situation of a three layer perceptron. Its extension has been applied by K. Hornik and M. Stinchcombe[2] demonstrating that one hidden layered MLP is capable of approximating any Borel measurable function, provided sufficient hidden units are available. Under certain conditions, K. Hornik [3] showed that an MLP with a single hidden layer is capable of arbitrary accurate approximation of a function as well as its derivative. The other important issue of MLP research is how to construct an MLP with an appropriate scale for learning parsimony. K. G. Mehrotra, C. K. Mohan, and S. Ranka[4], considered how large the training data set and the scale need be if the network is to be selected for certain problem.

In this paper, our purpose is to investigate the potential of MLP from a different angle by employing differential geometry[5] as a powerful analytic and descriptive technique. In research of neural networks, S. Amari initially developed the theory of information geometry—the variant of differential geometry. Such studies [6] [7] are to elucidate the capabilities and limitations of a family of neural networks with a given architecture. The methods of information geometry are discussed by S. Amari [8]. Here, by using differential geometry, our task is to provide the definitions of the nonlinearity of MLP, which enable us to make a strict analysis of nonlinear characteristics of MLP and the relationship of the network topology to its nonlinearity. In our research, it is quite interesting that extensive connections between MLP and nonlinear regression (NR) were uncovered. Hence, a review of our study from the view of statistics is made in Section III. In section IV, we discuss the calculation of these measures following the work of D. M. Bates and D. G. Watts[9].

II. Definitions of Measure of Nonlinearity

Given an MLP with a single hidden layer, the number of neurons is denoted by n_1, n_2, n_3 in input, hidden, and output layers respectively. The training sample data with the size of n_s is:

$$S = \{(x_1, y_1), (x_2, y_2), ..., (x_{n_s}, y_{n_s})\}.$$

Let n_w be the dimension of weight space through the point Out, i.e., $n_w = n_1 \times n_2 + n_2 \times n_3$. The output is denoted by Out. An MLP can be viewed as a function of its weight which are the parameters. The network maps the n_w-dimensional weight parameter space onto a surface in the

n_s-dimensional sample space. Each point W^0 in the weight space maps to a point $Out(w^0)$ on the solution locus. An arbitrary straight line in the weight space through W^0 can be expressed using the geometric parameter τ by,

$$W_h: \quad W(\tau) = W^0 + \tau h$$

where $h = (h_1, h_2, \ldots, h_{n_w})$ is any non-zero vector. This line generates a curve, "weight perturbation effect line", C_h on the solution locus π where

$$C_h: \quad O_h(\tau) = Out(W^0 + \tau h).$$

Let $\varepsilon = \tau h$. The tangent to curve C_h at $\tau = 0$ is

$$\overset{\bullet}{O}_h = \frac{dO_h}{d\tau}\Big|_{\tau=0} = \sum_i \frac{\partial O}{\partial w_i}\Big|_{w^0} \frac{dw_i}{d\tau}\Big|_{\tau=0} = \sum_i u_i h_i,$$

which can be written more compactly using the $n_s \times n_w$ matrix $U^{\bullet}$ whose ith column is u_i, as

$$\overset{\bullet}{O} = U^{\bullet} h.$$

The tangent vector to C_h is therefore a linear combination of the vector $\{u_i\}$ and all such linear combination is composed of the tangent plane at $Out(w^0)$.

We define the second partial derivative vectors $\{u_{ij}\}$ by

$$u_{ij} = \frac{\partial^2 O}{\partial w_i \partial w_j}\Big|_{w^0},$$

with elements $u_{tij} = \frac{\partial^2 O_t}{\partial w_i \partial w_j}, t = 1, \ldots, n_s$, and collect them into the $n_s \times n_w$ matrix of n_s vectors $U^{\bullet\bullet}$. $U^{\bullet\bullet}$ is an $n_w \times n_w \times n_s$ array, whose operation rules or bracket product, can be found in D. M. Bates and D. G. Watts[9] and C. L. Tsai[10]. From this notation, the acceleration of the perturbation line C_h, the second derivative of $O_h(\tau)$ at $\tau = 0$ can be expressed as:

$$\overset{\bullet\bullet}{O}_h = \frac{d^2 O_h}{d\tau^2}\Big|_{\tau=0} = \sum_j \partial(\sum_i u_i h_i)\Big|_{w^0} \frac{dw_j}{d\tau}\Big|_{\tau=0} = \sum_i \sum_j u_{ij} h_i h_j = h^T U^{\bullet\bullet} h.$$

The acceleration vector $\overset{\bullet\bullet}{O}_h$ can be decomposed in three components, $\overset{\bullet\bullet}{O}_h^N$ normal to the tangent plane, $\overset{\bullet\bullet}{O}_h^P$ parallel to $\overset{\bullet}{O}_h$, and $\overset{\bullet\bullet}{O}_h^G$ parallel to the tangent plane normal to $\overset{\bullet}{O}_h$, so

$$\overset{\bullet\bullet}{O}_h = \overset{\bullet\bullet}{O}_h^N + \overset{\bullet\bullet}{O}_h^P + \overset{\bullet\bullet}{O}_h^G,$$

where the tangential acceleration components can be combined into a total tangential acceleration $\overset{\bullet\bullet}{O}_h^T = \overset{\bullet\bullet}{O}_h^P + \overset{\bullet\bullet}{O}_h^G$.

On the basis of this decomposition, we can define two curvatures to measure the nonlinearity of MLP.

Definition 1. The intrinsic curvature of MLP in the direction of h is defined as

$$K_h^N = \left\| \overset{\bullet\bullet}{O}_h^N \right\| \Big/ \left\| \overset{\bullet}{O}_h \right\|^2,$$

which is an intrinsic property of the surface π.

Definition 2. The weight-effects curvature of MLP in the direction of h is defined as

$$K_h^T = \left\| \overset{\bullet\bullet}{O}_h^T \right\| \Big/ \left\| \overset{\bullet}{O}_h \right\|^2,$$

which is caused by the network weight parameterization.

In above definitions, every direction is considered. In practice, we usually just measure the maximum nonlinear effect. So we introduce two other measures.

Definition 3. The maximum intrinsic curvature of MLP is defined as

$$\Gamma^N = \max K_h^N.$$

Definition 4. The maximum weight effect curvature of MLP is defined as
$$\Gamma^T = \max K_h^T .$$
To evaluate the average effect of nonlinearity of MLP, we introduce the following definitions.

Definition 5. The mean square intrinsic curvature of MLP is defined as
$$(\gamma_{RMS}^N)^2 = \frac{1}{S} \int_{|h|=1} (\gamma_h^N)^2 ds,$$
where S is the surface area of the unit sphere, ds is the area element on this sphere.

Definition 6. The mean square weight-effect curvature of MLP is defined as
$$(\gamma_{RMS}^T)^2 = \frac{1}{S} \int_{|h|=1} (\gamma_h^T)^2 ds,$$
where S is the surface area of the unit sphere, ds is the area element on this sphere.

These given definitions of nonlinearity measures characterize the contribution of every neuron to the representation of nonlinearity, and enable us to make a complete and precise analysis of nonlinear learning capacity of MLP and its relationship to the network weight-distributed coding scheme. The distributed representation refers to the use of population activities of many units to represent features on computation. It has two characteristics. One is the ability of massively parallel computation. The other is that the representation of pattern learnt is collective, which means that, when some parts of neurons in the system are broken, the network is able to maintain its functions and performance gracefully. The latter is reflected in its fault tolerance. Such a population coding scheme is supported by the experiments of S. K. Kostyk and P. Grobstein[11]. The connection of nonlinearity measures to the fault tolerance was addressed in T. Fan, B. Xu and Y. Jiang[12].

III. A Review of MLP from the view of Statistics

At first, in order to make comparison, we describe the NR model briefly as follows:
$$y_i = f(x_i, \theta) + \varepsilon_i, i = 1, ..., N,$$
where (x_i, y_i), $i = 1, 2, ..., N$, are the observed data, y_i is the ith response, x_i is a vector of known variables, θ is a $p \times 1$ vector of unknown parameters to be estimated, the response function f is known, the scalar function that is twice continuously differentiable in θ, and the errors ε_i, $i = 1, 2, ..., N$, are independent and identically distributed variables with mean 0 and variance σ^2. More details can be found in D. A. Ratkowsky's work[13]. Moreover, from the differential geometry view, D. M. Bates and D. G. Watts[9] proposed two kinds of measures of intrinsic and parameter-effects curvature for assessing the adequacy of the linear approximation for NR. Obviously, between MLP and NR, there are some similar aspects, which are included in the following Table 1.

Table 1. The Similarities of MLP Model and NR Model

MLP Model	NR Model
connection weight W	model parameter θ
training sample data	sample data
trained weight	Least Square Error Estimate (LSE)
network architecture	response function f
nonlinearity measures	curvature measures

By this comparison, we can view MLP as a novel regressor — **neural regressor**. However, there are some key differences between the neural regressor and the NR model. Though both of them use an assumed model to capture the underlying relationship by modifying the value of parameters in the models, the MLP can modify its entire nonlinear behavior by way of its neuron-distributed coding. Hence, the MLP is able to learn nonlinear function relationships by the collective contribution of every neuron in the system with its relatively fixed network topology. But as to NR, it cannot adapt its model response function. Therefore, the MLP model enjoys a more powerful nonlinear learning capacity than an NR model. Further, the MLP is more flexible and robust than the NR model. The flexibility and robustness are expressed by its distributed weight representation. As to the two measures we proposed, which are very similar to those of NR, though the measures of nonlinearity can take on such tasks as assessing the adequacy of the linear approximation of BP algorithm, the more important purpose of our study is to measure the nonlinear learning capacity. The reason is that the nonlinearity of MLP can be represented by the distributed weight code, though BP algorithm exploits a linear approximation.

IV. The Calculation of the Nonlinearity Measures of MLP

The similarities between the MLP model and the NR model, especially, that between our definitions and the work of Professors D. M. Bates and D. G. Watts, is of benefit to our research in calculating these measures. Following the line of their work, in this section, we will exploit their ideas to calculate these quantities. We make a transformation of the weight parameter space, by which the nonlinearity measures can be re-expressed. In this way, the calculation of these quantities can be simplified.

First, we make the QR decomposition of V

$$U^{\bullet} = Q\tilde{R} = Q\begin{pmatrix} R \\ 0 \end{pmatrix} \begin{matrix} \}n_w \times n_w \\ \}(n_s - n_w) \times n_w \end{matrix} = \underset{n_s \times n_w}{Q} \times \underset{n_w \times n_w}{R},$$

where R is nondegenerate upper triangular. This decomposition is actually equivalent to transformation of the co-ordinates in the parameter space, that is :

$$\phi = R(W - W^{\bullet}), W = W^{\bullet} + L\phi, L = R^{-1}$$

The columns of Q is an orthogonal unit vectors under new co-ordinates in tangent plane. Since

$$O = Out(\phi) = Out(W^{\bullet} + L\phi),$$

we have

$$\frac{\partial O}{\partial \phi} = \frac{\partial O}{\partial w}\frac{\partial w}{\partial \phi} = U^{\bullet}L = Q.$$

Further, we can calculate the second derivative vectors u_{ij} as

$$\frac{\partial^2 O_t}{\partial \phi_a \partial \phi_b} = \sum_{i=1}^{n_w}\sum_{j=1}^{n_w} \frac{\partial^2 O_t}{\partial w_i \partial w_j}\frac{\partial w_i}{\partial \phi_a}\frac{\partial w_j}{\partial \phi_b}, \quad (a,b=1,...,n_w; t=1,...,n_s),$$

and the matrix of the second derivative vectors in the ϕ co-ordinates as

$$\frac{\partial^2 O}{\partial \phi^2} \hat{=} V = L^T U^{\bullet\bullet} L.$$

where V is an $n_s \times n_w \times n_w$ array.

Hence, under the transformation, $U^{\bullet}$, $U^{\bullet\bullet}$ and h were transformed into Q, V and d.

We pre-multiply V by the $n_s \times n_s$ matrix Q' to obtain

$$P = [Q'][V] = [N'][V][Q'][Q]$$

Let

$$P^T = [N'][V], \quad P^N = [Q'][Q].$$

Based on this decomposition, the calculation procedures are offered.

1. The calculation of K_h^N and K_h^T :

$$(K_h^N)^2 = \left\| d'P^N d \right\|^2 = \sum_{t=1}^{n_s - n_w} (d'P_t^N d)^2 ;$$

and

$$(K_h^T)^2 = \left\| d'P^T d \right\|^2 = \sum_{t=1}^{n_s-n_w} (d'P_t^T d)^2 .$$

where P_t^N and P_t^T is the tth face of P^N and P^T respectively.

2. The calculation of $(\gamma_{RMS}^N)^2$ and $(\gamma_{RMS}^T)^2$:

$$(\gamma_{RMS}^N)^2 = \frac{1}{S(n_w)} \sum_{t=1}^{n_s-n_w} \int_{|d|=1} (d'P_t^N d)^2 ds$$

$$= \frac{1}{n_w(n_w+2)} \left\{ 2 \sum_{i=1}^{n_w} \sum_{j=1}^{n_w} \left\| P^N{}_{ij} \right\|^2 + (\left\| tr[P^N] \right\|^2) \right\};$$

and

$$(\gamma_{RMS}^T)^2 = \frac{1}{S(n_w)} \sum_{t=1}^{n_s-n_w} \int_{|d|=1} (d'P_t^T d)^2 ds$$

$$= \frac{1}{n_w(n_w+2)} \left\{ 2 \sum_{i=1}^{n_w} \sum_{j=1}^{n_w} \left\| P_{ij}^T \right\|^2 + (\left\| tr[P^T] \right\|^2) \right\},$$

whose proof will be given in our full paper.

3. The calculation of Γ^N and Γ^T: In order calculate the maximum intrinsic curvature and maximum weight-effect curvature, we exploit the algorithm in [10]:

Step 1. Initializing the direction d_i: $d_i = (0,\ldots,0,1)$;

Step 2. Calculating $g_i = [(d_i' P^N d_i)'][P^N d_i]$ and $\tilde{g}_i = g_i / \|g_i\|$;

Step 3. If $\tilde{g}_i' d_i < 1 - \varepsilon$ then setting $d_{i+1} = (3\tilde{g}_i + d_i)/\|3\tilde{g}_i + d_i\|$ and returning to Step 2;
   otherwise, $\Gamma^N = \|d_i' P^N d_i\|$.

The convergence criterion ε in step 3 stipulates how close d_i and the gradient direction are. The maximum weight-effects Γ^T can be calculated by the same algorithm with P^N substituted for P^T in steps 2 and 3. Here the algotithm is based on the necessary condition of maximum. In order to assure our solutions are the globe maximum, we can exploit the same technique in [10].

V. Experiments

We have designed three series of experiments. One is considered the comparison of the nonlinearity measures to the sample data sets from the above different functions with the same network size. The second deals with the problem of how the network size affects the corresponding nonlinearity measures for every function. The third one makes a comparison between an MLP model and some NR models[13]. Our experiments consider the nonlinearity measures of MLP learning different functions:

1) The polynomial functions with different orders, including:

   a) Simple Interaction Function:
   $$g^{(1)}(x_1, x_2) = 10.391((x_1 - 0.4) \times (x_2 - 0.6) + 0.036);$$

   b) Radial Function:
   $$g^{(2)}(x_1, x_2^-) = 24.234(r^2(0.75 - r^2)), \quad r^2 = (x_1 - 0.5)^2 + (x - 0.5)^2;$$

   c) Harmonic Function
   $$g^{(3)}(x_1, x_2) = 42.659(0.1 + \tilde{x}_1(0.05 + \tilde{x}_1^4 - 10\tilde{x}_1^2 \tilde{x}_2^2 + 5\tilde{x}_2^4)),$$
   $$\tilde{x}_1 = x_1 - 0.5, \tilde{x}_2 = \tilde{x}_2 - 0.5;$$

2) The exponential and logarithmic functions;

3) Chaotic Functions;

4) Additive Function:

$$g^{(4)}(x_1, x_2) = 1.3356(1.5(1 - x_1) + e^{2x_1 - 1} \sin(3\pi(x_1 - 0.6)^2),$$
$$+ e^{3(x_2 - 0.5)} \sin(4\pi(x_2 - 0.9)^2));$$

5) Complicated Interaction Function:
$$g^{(5)}(x_1, x_2) = 1.9(1.35 + e^{x_1} \sin(13(x_1 - 0.6)^2) + e^{-x_2} \sin(7x_2)).$$

The results of experiments will be given in the.full paper.

Acknowledgment: This work is supported by National Natural Science Fund of China. Though the thought and development of the definitions of nonlinearity measures by the technique of differential geometry came from our research, the format and work of Professors D. M. Bates and D. G. Watts[9] has been of great benefit to us in preparation of this paper as well as the calculation of these measures. Therefore, the authors would like to express their sincere gratitude to them. Our special thanks are due to Ms Judith of The Foreign Languages Department at South China University of Technology, for her cordial help in polishing our English.

References

[1] G. Cybenko (1989), "Approximation by superposition of a sigmoidal function," *Math. Control Signals Systems*, Vol. 2, pp. 304-314.

[2] K. Hornik, M. Stinchcombe and N. White (1989), "Multilayer feedforward networks are universal approximation," *Neural Networks*, Vol. 2, pp. 359-366.

[3] K. Hornik (1991), "Approximation capacities of multilayer feedforward networks," *Neural Networks*, Vol. 4, pp. 251-257.

[4] K. G. Mehrotra, C. K. Mohan, and S. Ranka (1991), "Bounds on the number of samples needed for neural learning," *IEEE Trans. Neural Networks*, Vol. 2, No. 6, pp. 548-558.

[5] W. Klingenberg (1983), *A course in differential geometry*, in Vol. 51 of Graduate Texts in Mathematics, Springer-Verlag, New York.

[6] S. Amari (1990), "Dualistic Geometry of the Manifold of High-Order neurons," *Neural Networks*, Vol. 4, pp. 443-451.

[7] S. Amari, K. Kurata and H. Nagaoka (1992), "Information geometry of Boltzmann Machines," *IEEE Trans. Neural Networks*, Vol. 3, pp. 260-271.

[8] S. Amari (1990), "Mathematical Foundation of Neurocomputing," *Proc. IEEE*, Vol. 78, pp. 1443-1463.

[9] D. M. Bates and D. G. Watts (1980), "Relative curvature measures of nonlinearity (with discussion)," *J. Roy. Statist. Soc., Ser. B*, 42 1-25.

[10] C. L. Tsai (1983), *Contributions to design and analysis of nonlinear models*, Ph.D. Thesis, Univ. of Minnesota.

[11] S. K. Kostyk and P. Grobstein (1987), "Neuronal organization underlying visually elicited prey orienting in the frog-ii,".*Neuroscience*, vol. 21, pp. 57-82..

[12] T. Fan, B. Xu and Y. Jiang (1995), "Fault Tolerance Analysis of MLP under External Perturbation," submitted to *ICNN'95*, Perth, Australia.

[13] D. A. Ratkowsky (1983), *Nonlinear Regression Modeling*, Marcel Dekker, New York.